EPICUREA

Epicureanism has had a long and complex history. Established in Greece in the fourth century BC in response to the peculiar needs of a new age, it gained an immediate and widespread following throughout the Mediterranean world, and in Roman times competed on equal terms with Stoicism for the allegiance of the citizens of the empire. It was singled out by the early Church as a dangerous enemy of the faith, and the philosophy of the Garden became the target of a bitter campaign of denunciation and distortion; it was a one-dimensional Epicurus – the champion of earthly delights – who kept the name of the School alive throughout the Middle Ages. Coinciding with a renewed interest in the antique world, an Epicureanism truer to its classical parent re-emerged to add an important dimension to Renaissance philosophical debate, and in the sixteenth and seventeenth centuries Epicurean theory contributed significantly to the growth of the new science.

The Epicurean Tradition is the first systematic and comprehensive study of the survival of Epicurean ideas from the ancient to the modern periods. It is useful background to more particular studies of 'epicurean' motifs in literature and art, and will interest students and specialists in the fields of classics, philosophy, religion, and the history of science.

Head of Epicurus in Pentelic marble.

THE
EPICUREAN TRADITION

HOWARD JONES

London and New York

First published 1989 in hardback by Routledge

First published in paperback 1992
by Routledge
11 New Fetter Lane, London EC4P 4EE

Simultaneously published in the USA and Canada
by Routledge
a division of Routledge, Chapman and Hall Inc.
29 West 35th Street, New York, NY 10001

British Library Cataloguing in Publication Data
Jones, Howard
      The epicurean tradition.
      I. Title
      187

Library of Congress Cataloging in Publication Data
Jones, Howard
      The Epicurean tradition/Howard Jones.
           p.   cm.
      Includes bibliographical references and index.
      1. Epicurus–Influence.   I. Title.
B573.J57   1992
187–dc20   91–41878
      0–415–02069–7 (hbk)
      0–415–07554–8 (pbk)

CONTENTS

Preface   vii

1 MAN FOR A SEASON   1

2 SCHOOL IN THE GARDEN   22

3 THE INVASION OF ITALY   62

4 THE CHRISTIAN REACTION   94

5 MEDIEVAL INTERLUDE   117

6 THE HUMANIST DEBATE   142

7 FRENCH REVIVAL   166

8 EPICURUS BRITANNICUS   186

  Notes   214

  Bibliography   262

  Index   270

PREFACE

A *nachleben* is the very last thing Epicurus anticipated. That it should have been so little tranquil only doubles the irony.

A recurring charge against Epicurus was that he refused to acknowledge a scholarly debt to others. Let me acknowledge mine now by stating that without the many works cited in the notes and bibliography this book would not exist. Even so, the story is far from complete. I have concentrated for the most part on the impact of the Epicurean philosophy upon the development of intellectual and scientific ideas. Other aspects of the tradition – Epicurean influences on literature and art and on the development of social and political theory – remain to be examined. I shall be gratified if the present book serves as a useful starting point.

I am pleased to record my gratitude to a number of boards and institutions whose assistance has been indispensable: the Social Sciences and Humanities Research Council of Canada, which awarded me a Leave Fellowship in 1985–6; the Board of Governors of McMaster University, which granted me a Research Leave for the same period; the Arts Research Board of McMaster University, for financial assistance in support of visits to European libraries; the staffs of the British Library, the Bibliothèque Nationale, the Huntington Library, the Pontifical Institute of Medieval Studies at the University of Toronto, and, not least, the Mills Memorial Library of McMaster University; the Directors of the Metropolitan Museum of Art, for permission to use a photograph of the Head of Epicurus as a frontispiece. Finally, my sincere thanks are due to Mrs Christa Schlechta for transforming ugly handwritten pages into readable typescript.

For the deficiencies which this book contains, *authoris culpa est*.

1

MAN FOR A SEASON

In the case of Epicurus, who believed firmly that death is the end, it is not without irony that his own death marked but the beginning of a journey which would take him far in time and distance from his native Samos. We shall not make the journey with him step by step. Rather, we shall contrive to meet up with him at various stopping places along the way. The further we travel, however, the more we must be prepared for him to be wearing a different face. While the outline may be familiar, the features will sometimes be blurred, the lines indistinct. It is important, therefore, that we pause at the start to equip ourselves with a faithful portrait.

Epicurus is as much as any philosopher a product of his age, and the essentials of his thought, as well as the appeal of the life style which he advocated, can be understood only with reference to the political, social, and intellectual forces which distinguish the Hellenistic from the Classical era. If the Battle of Plataea in 479 BC and the Battle of Aegospotami in 404 can be singled out as events which mark important turning-points in the history of fifth-century Greece, the Battle of Chaeronea in 338 can be assigned a corresponding role for the fourth century. Here the combined forces of Athens, Boeotia, Achaea, Corinth, Megara, Euboea, Acarnania, and Leucas succumbed to the superior strength of Philip II of Macedon, and a chapter in Greek history came to an end. Through this victory, together with the terms of the League of Corinth, which were ratified in the following year, Philip realized his aim of bringing the Greek states under his control, putting an end to their interstate warring, and securing a united partner for his campaign against Persia. If the Greek states could now enjoy stability, the price they paid was freedom. Yet it would be a mistake to regard the happenings of 338–337 as more than the culmination of events which were long in the making. Since the end of the Peloponnesian War the Greek states had been preparing their own downfall. The early decades of the fourth century witnessed a degree of internecine struggle which wasted material resources and sapped emotional energy to the point where the belated resistance against Macedon was but the last futile throes of a people which had rendered itself incapable of more than token effort.

But to point out that the Greek states were to a large extent the victims of their own failure to live in harmony is to tell only a part of the story. This political disunion itself was only the most visible symptom of a deep-rooted illness, a psychological *malaise* whose origins may be traced back to the period of the Peloponnesian War itself. It is noteworthy that in his account of the plague which ravaged the city of Athens during the first years of the war the historian Thucydides dwells with equal focus upon the physical symptoms of the disease and upon its psychological effects. While there were those who were prepared to risk their own lives in ministering to relatives and friends who were afflicted, there were more who abandoned all religious and moral conventions: 'neither fear of the gods nor respect for human sanctions had any restraining effect; in the one case men decided that it made no difference whether one worshipped or not, since death came to all regardless; in the other, no one expected to live long enough to be brought to trial and be made to pay the penalty for his wrongdoings'.[1] But in so far as the plague served to reveal the baser elements in human nature it is only a microcosm of the war itself. For in a number of places in his *History* Thucydides allows events themselves and the deliberations which attended them to disclose a new morality governing the actions of politicians and people alike, a morality born of the pressures of war and complemented by a novelty of speech and argument which is both child and parent of the changing ethical climate. The revolutions which broke out at Corcyra and other cities serve him as illustrations of a 'general deterioration of character throughout the Greek world' as 'human nature, given to crime even when law prevails, rejoiced to show its true self – dominated by passion, a violator of justice, and an enemy to anything better than itself'.[2] Similarly, the Athenian debate of 425 over the fate of the Mytilenaeans, in which 'self-interest' and 'advantage' are set against decency and a regard for justice as the only proper bases for action, makes it clear that we are in a world of situation ethics, where decisions are to be taken not with reference to absolute moral norms but in accordance with the convenience of the moment.[3]

There is much here, of course, of Thucydides the rationalist. As a product of the fifth-century enlightenment he stresses the human factor in the determination of events, and finds it easy to see a correlation between the worsening condition of contemporary society and a degeneration of human character which is both its cause and its effect.[4] To this extent, therefore, we must allow for a distorted picture. However, we have only to consider certain of Thucydides' contemporaries to see that it is not altogether out of focus. For example, we do not need to turn the comic dramatist into an ardent reformer to admit that Aristophanes perceived no less than Thucydides, and perhaps with greater concern, the emergence of an ethical nihilism which threatened to undermine the very foundations of Greek society. It is a confrontation between old and new values, which is presented nowhere more directly than in the *agon* scene in the *Clouds* where Right Argument and Wrong Argument battle for the allegiance of the prospective client Pheidippides. Here, at the middle point of the play, a marvellous display of verbal juggling earns Wrong Argument a temporary victory. It is only after the ruinous consequences of this new teaching have been revealed that the verdict is reversed, and in the *kommos* which brings the play to a close the Thinking Shop is burned down and its proprietors, Socrates and Chaerephon, are driven off.

Aristophanes' concerns are clear. In exposing Socrates and Chaerephon as charlatans, comical to be sure, but dangerous in their manipulation of truth and in their general disregard for traditional values, he was taking aim at the growing influence in Athenian life of the Sophistic movement. He was realist enough to recognize the powerful appeal which Sophistic ideas and techniques exercised upon a generation of young Athenians who were at once disillusioned through war and rebellious enough in spirit to embrace anything which possessed the double attraction of heterodoxy and novelty. But the subversion of old standards which the new education threatened was something which he was bound to resist.

What of Socrates? That Aristophanes cast him in the role of arch-Sophist is understandable from a dramatic point of view. There was nobody at Athens more unorthodox, and as material for parody

3

and caricature he could not be passed over. Yet the fact is that Aristophanes' portrayal is an ironic distortion. For, unless it can be shown that Plato's portrait of Socrates is from first to last an artful fabrication, it must be recognized that Socrates was no less an opponent of the Sophists than was Aristophanes himself, and for the same reasons. Of this the *Gorgias* alone offers sufficient illustration. Even if we allow that Plato's representation of Gorgias, Polus, Callicles, and Socrates is a dramatization, none the less we may take the basic disagreement between Socrates and the rest to be an accurate enough reflection of the gulf which separated the historical Socrates from the Sophists of his generation. And what is at issue is the refusal on the part of the professional teachers of rhetoric to accept what Socrates regarded as a primary responsibility, namely, that of instructing their pupils in the proper use of the techniques of persuasion. In Socrates' view the Sophists were dealers in a spurious art on a level with cookery. As the one caters to the pleasure of the palate while neglecting the well-being of the body as a whole, so the other flatters the ears and minds of the hearers but offers nothing of substance for moral direction or improvement.[5]

We have taken into account only three representatives of late fifth-century society, but the impression they leave is one which a fuller review of the sources would little alter. The closing decades of the fifth century witnessed a genuine crisis in public and private morality, a crisis born of two seemingly disparate parents: on the one side, a bold confidence in the sufficiency of human resource that could allow Protagoras to proclaim man 'the measure of all things'; on the other, a despair, intensified by the reality of war, at the gulf between man's promise and the visible fruits of human effort. It is against this background that we must view the events of the first half of the fourth century. The Peloponnesian War had been in a real sense the tragedy of Athens. Sophocles in the *Antigone* had sounded the warning note – 'Wonders are many, and none more wonderful than man . . . all-skilful man, all-inventive, all-resourceful . . . possessing skill beyond hope which brings him sometimes to evil, sometimes to good.'[6] Like the tragic hero the city had fallen victim to its own greatness, and those who survived the collapse could not but feel that they had seen the best of their times. For the spirit which characterizes the decades following the war is one of despondency, manifesting itself in an absence of true purpose. It is true that we witness a quite bewildering succession of alliances between various

4

states, each pushing for place, and this suggests that there was energy still. However, the motivating factor was no longer the kind of civic pride which supported political and military action during the previous century, but more often than not the manoeuvring of party factions seeking means of gaining or consolidating internal power. When finally Macedon presented the Greek states with a challenge to their survival, the will to resist lay deeply buried. For a reading of Demosthenes' *Olynthiacs* and *Philippics* confirms that the Athenian orator's greatest obstacle was not his political opponents, or Philip himself, but the apathy of his fellow citizens.

Up to this point we have spoken in general terms of the demoralizing, not to say paralysing, effects of the Peloponnesian War as they are manifested in the attitude and behaviour of whole states during the first half of the fourth century. Far from recovering the vitality and sense of purpose which they had possessed in abundance, the Greek states fell into a lethargy, awakened periodically by changing rivalries which were consequential only to the extent that they worked towards the eventual loss of Greek freedom. We need pursue the matter on this level no further. After Chaeronea and the League of Corinth the Greek states, while they retained a nominal autonomy, were without the opportunity for independent action. They settled into their role as partners in Alexander's campaigns, and a different chapter in Greek history begins to be written.

It is important, however, now that we have taken a broad look at the major political changes which occurred during the fourth century and considered the effects of these changes upon whole states, to examine their impact upon the lives of individuals during the period. For there is no doubting that it was profound. If we limit our attention to the citizens of Athens and go back to the close of the Peloponnesian War, we must recognize that those who survived that long struggle, and for most it had occupied the majority of their years, undoubtedly experienced those symptoms which are common to defeated peoples, but more intensely than most. For the Athenians had suffered a reversal of fortune as extreme as any in history. During the fifth century the Athenian citizen could look to his city with no ordinary pride. When, at the beginnning of the war, the Athenian leader Pericles, in an admittedly chauvinistic display, pronounced Athens 'the school of Hellas', he was making a claim whose truth all Greeks, Athenians and non-Athenians alike, recognized. The building programme on the Acropolis had transformed

5

the city into the architectural show-piece of the Greek world; the sculptural work of Phidias and his school represented the finest of its kind; the annual dramatic festivals presented the highest achievement of the tragic and comic art; the political and judicial system offered every citizen the opportunity to indulge his interest and exercise his talents in the everyday business of government and law; the city's position at the head of a powerful confederacy guaranteed its citizens security and prestige; the city's thriving commercial interests added the material benefits of trade with all parts of the Mediterranean world. In short, in terms of providing the citizens with security of person, material prosperity, intellectual and aesthetic stimulation, and the opportunity for personal fulfilment, fifth-century Athens had reached a stage of development that could be matched by no other state in the Greek world. It is against this that we must measure the fall of Athens at the close of the century. In a not wholly symbolic way the Athenians had been prepared. In his description of the plague Thucydides remarks that the citizens were presented daily with the sight of prosperous persons suddenly losing all they possessed. What had happened to some had now happened to all. The reversal was not so sudden, but it was no less final.

This does not mean that the military collapse of Athens brought life to a standstill or that the outward pattern of Athenian society was not recognizably the same. In fact, although she was never to regain fully her former prosperity, Athens recovered remarkably quickly from the material consequences of the war. Following a brief period during which the city was administered by the Thirty Tyrants, political institutions were restored, and in the wider sphere the city began to regain some of her former influence. It is none the less true that in fundamental ways the life of the Athenian citizen was considerably altered. During the first part of the fourth century he found himself living in a new city, new in the sense that the role it played in Greek affairs was so little decisive that commitment to civic and political activity could no longer compete with the more immediate claims of private life. After the conquests of Alexander he found himself living in a new world, a cosmopolitan universe of which Greece formed only a part. To the sense of disillusionment which alienated him from the affairs of his own city had been added a more general feeling of insignificance which served to intensify the impulse to turn away from the outer world and seek security and self-identity within the narrower sphere of private relationships.

It is a change which is reflected in the literature and the art of the period.[7] Already with the late plays of Euripides classical tragedy had been transformed into melodrama, the interest centring no longer around general moral and religious issues of concern to the audience at large, but around personal relationships between characters.[8] We know too little of the development of tragedy during the fourth century to be categorical, but it is generally agreed that the Euripidean trend was sustained; that the fourth-century tragedians, while they followed their classical counterparts in taking their plots for the most part from the stock of traditional myths, in selection and treatment displayed a pronounced interest in theatricality and effect rather than enduring substance. In short, the playwright was intent less upon confronting the audience with serious spiritual issues than upon creating an exciting world of intrigue and romance into which it could escape.

In comedy the change is even more marked. The distinction between Old, Middle, and New Comedy is itself a Hellenistic one, and, while we are not yet in a position to determine the place of Middle Comedy in the development of the genre, the contrast between Old and New Comedy is strikingly illustrative of our theme.[9] Old Comedy, as it is represented by Aristophanes, is essentially civic. As the festival which provides the occasion is a public event, so the issues which the poet addresses are for the most part societal issues which engage the attention of the theatre-goers not as individuals but as fellow members of the *polis*. The elements of parody, satire, personal invective, and topical allusion presuppose a shared experience of the varied pattern of contemporary Athenian society. This is not to say that the poet of Old Comedy is totally tied to the world of civic life. There is no dramatist more ready than Aristophanes to indulge in flights of fancy and to transport the audience into a realm of comic fantasy. Yet even here, as in the *Birds*, we are not totally removed from reality. Cloud-cuckoo-land cannot exist without the backdrop of Athens. And we can say as much of Old Comedy itself. With New Comedy the case is different. If Old Comedy is civic, New Comedy is domestic.[10] The setting may be urban, but it can be any Greek community. For the materials from which the writer of New Comedy constructs his plays are not the affairs of the city at large but incidents from family life. We meet husbands and wives, sons, mistresses and lovers, nurses, slaves, relatives, and neighbours. But it is not the humdrum of middle-class

7

living that we are invited to share. The world in which these characters move is one of intrigue and adventure, untimely errors and timely discoveries, a world of shipwrecks and pirates, foundlings and fortune seekers; above all, a world of coincidence and surprise, where events are largely out of human control, orchestrated instead by the goddess Tyche. As Onesimus in Menander's *The Arbitrants* soliloquizes, 'the affairs of men are shaky – every one!'[11] It occasions no surprise, of course, that in New Comedy little is what it seems. The improbable and incongruous are tried ingredients of the comic tradition. It may be worth remarking, however, that this world of confusion and insecurity, even if it is enough removed from actual domestic life to produce the desired comic effect, is none the less itself a reflection of the real world in which the Hellenistic audience found itself. It is ironic, though perhaps psychologically consistent, that the Greeks of the period should seek temporary relief from a world which they found unpredictable and bewildering in a make-believe world where unpredictability and bewilderment are dominant factors.

We have looked at tragedy and comedy as reflective of a general tendency on the part of Greeks of the fourth and third centuries to abandon affairs of civic and national importance in favour of the more immediate concerns of private life. For the dramatist, as for the audience, personal relationships and human nature itself assume an importance unmatched in other periods. 'O, Menander and Life, which of you copied the other?' is a fair comment.[12] The situations which they unfold may be unlikely enough, but Menander's plays serve as a mirror reflecting every facet of contemporary life and revealing every feature of the human temperament. The playwrights, however, were not the only writers to explore the complexities of human personality and behaviour. Writing shortly before Menander, the Peripatetic Theophrastus composed a series of thirty sketches of human types. Whether this work, the *Characters*, was designed to supplement rhetorical or ethical theory with practical examples or to support the Aristotelian view of the continuity of human personality, it is an academic piece and betrays the philosopher's interest in abstract classification.[13] At the same time, individually the sketches are deftly drawn and are certainly not without that acuteness of observation and richness of detail which so enlivens the plays of Menander. As for other writers of the Hellenistic period we need look only at the *Argonautica* of Apollonius

Rhodius, at the epigrams of Callimachus, Asclepiades, Posidippus, Meleager, and other poets of the *Anthology*, and at the *Idylls* of Theocritus to see that the psychology of human emotion continued to be an absorbing interest.

There is one further feature of Hellenistic poetry which touches upon our theme. This is its esoteric flavour. In some works, such as the *Hymns* and the *Aetia* of Callimachus, this manifests itself in an abundance of recherché mythological and geographical references and in the use of highly technical language. In others it is the subject-matter itself. One of the most popular works in antiquity was the *Phaenomena* of Aratus of Soli, a treatment in hexameters of astronomy and meteorology. The mid-second-century Nicander of Colophon devoted his poetic talents to a treatment of antidotes for animal bites (*Theriaca*) and remedies for food poisoning (*Alexipharmaca*). Philostephanus of Cyrene, a pupil of Callimachus, followed his master's *On the Rivers of the World* with a poem entitled *On Curious Rivers*. A complete list of the didactic poetry of the period would be lengthy. In part such works as these reflect a general fascination with the exotic and faraway at a time when Alexander's conquests had opened up new and exciting regions of the world. In part, they coincide with a prevailing interest in the accumulation and popularization of every kind of scientific, medical, astronomical, botanical, geographical, and philological information. But, whatever the inspiration, it is important that we recognize that much of Hellenistic poetry is poetry written for a scholarly elite capable of appreciating its sophistication and wealth of recondite learning. Indeed, what Lesky says about Antimachus, the early fourth-century writer of epic poetry, has wider application:

> in Antimachus we recognise a poet who consciously combined the work of a scholar with that of the artist. This means that poetry now withdraws from the association which in classical times bound artist and community into a firm unity. Only for the educated is it possible to follow the learned poet on his laborious way and something like 'l'art pour l'art' announces itself.[14]

We have been suggesting that dissociation from the wider community and withdrawal into a more select and private world is a recognizable feature of post-classical Greek society. It is clear that the poet follows the pattern.

Because it shares many characteristics with poetry we may look to the art of the fourth and third centuries for further illustration of certain of the general trends which we have been intent upon delineating. To begin with a general observation, a significant difference between classical and post-classical art is the extent to which the latter is emancipated from a preoccupation with civic or national political and religious ideals. In this respect the artist is at one with the ordinary citizen. What most concerned the latter during the decades following the Peloponnesian War and most especially after the loss of Greek freedom was his own personal situation, his relationship with his family and with those individuals in whose company he lived his daily round. We have seen that it is this domestic world which is mirrored in New Comedy. It is not surprising, therefore, to find the artist following the poet in abandoning the role of projecting the values of the community at large in favour of exploring private worlds, at the same time turning away from the ideal to the accidental and particular. It is a change of direction of which the art of portraiture offers particularly telling illustration.[15] If we look, for example, at Silanion's *Head of the Boxer Satyrus* (*c.* 335 Athens, National Museum), it is clear that, while the proportional shaping of the head itself links the piece with its ideal classical prototypes, the degree to which the sculptor has striven to capture in the facial bruisings and disfigurations the effort and endurance which define the subject's individual character places it in a new era. Similarly with the bronze statue of Demosthenes by Polyeuktos erected in the Athenian agora in 280 BC (Roman marble copy, Copenhagen, Ny Carlsberg Glyptothek). To the extent that it is a portrait of an orator it is typological. There was considerable interest in executing portrait statues of leading representatives of the major professions. At the same time, in the tradition of the Lysippean Alexander portraits the sculptor has attempted to go beyond the ideal orator portrait by conveying in the posture and expression his own conception of Demosthenes' unique personality.[16]

This concern on the part of the portrait sculptor with capturing the distinctive character of the subject is not unrelated to contemporary study of *ethos*, enduring disposition, whether inherent or learned. No less influential in fourth- and third-century art, however, is a parallel interest in *pathos*, immediate emotional response to various aspects of the human situation. Two contrasting and well-known examples, both from sculpture, will suffice.[17] The first is an Attic grave stele found near the Ilissus (c. 330 BC, Athens, National Museum). Carved in deep relief it shows the deceased as a young man, powerfully built but slack in posture, almost slouching, the expression on the face one of composure, but composure born of resignation rather than confidence; to his right, the aged father, supporting himself on his staff; to the left, close to the young man's feet, a small boy, huddled over, head resting on knees; on the other side of the feet, a hunting dog, asleep. There is nothing vital in the whole composition. Death has left nothing but hopelessness and indifference. The second is the *Hermes with the Infant Dionysus* of Praxiteles (c. 340 BC, copy, Olympia, Archeological Museum). Hermes is escorting the infant Dionysus to the safe-keeping of the nymphs of Nyssa, and is shown here pausing to tease the future god of wine by dangling a bunch of grapes just beyond the infant's eager grasp. Each is as playful as the other, and the faint smile on Hermes' lips betrays a mixture of tenderness and humour. What the sculptor has captured is a precious moment of reciprocal emotional response, totally enclosed and self-absorbed.

We have stressed that, in the degree to which fourth- and third-century art strives to capture the essential features of human character and explores the whole range of emotional response, it is consistent with a more general concern with the private world of the individual. In this we have by no means exhausted the range of interests pursued by the painters and sculptors of the period. Indeed, it is a period in Greek art as productive as any of new developments, both in subject-matter and technique. It may be said, however, that preoccupation with personal experience is not its least distinctive characteristic.

For a final reflection of the tendency during the fourth and third centuries for matters of civic or national interest to give way to more strictly private and personal concerns we may look to religion. The close connection which existed between religion[18] and the state during the classical period calls for little commentary. At Athens religion provided the very basis of social organization, as common cult membership gave identity to family, phratry, and tribe. As a highly organized institution the worship of the city's gods through sacrifices and festivals regulated the tempo of the citizen's life. Nor was religion a matter of empty ritual. The city's deities were not only its protectors but the providers of all the material benefits and amenities which life in the city afforded. To do them honour was more than a matter of prudence, it was a genuine expression of gratitude. For there is no doubt that in the eyes of the fifth-century Athenian the gods were more than deserving. Not only had the city been delivered from the peril of foreign domination, it had come to enjoy unmatched prosperity and prestige. Religion was an expression of patriotic pride.

The last quarter of the fifth century, however, saw the emergence of an intellectual movement whose rationalist and individualist premisses were to provide civic worship with a serious challenge. We have mentioned already the degree to which the historian Thucydides stresses the human rather than the divine factor in the determination of events. It is an attitude of mind which his contemporary Hippocrates brings to the study of disease, which he regards not as a divinely sent affliction, but as a natural occurrence capable of natural explanation. It is also an attitude of mind shared by representatives of the Sophistic movement, and it is from this quarter that the most serious attack upon the state religion came, though not in a direct way. For what the Sophists challenged was not contemporary religious observance as such, but the very basis of religion itself. For Prodicus the gods and goddesses owe their identity to their adoption as symbols of the variety of things in nature which mankind has found useful for sustaining and enriching life. For Critias the gods are no more than fictional creatures invented to encourage individuals to behave in accordance with the rules of society even when their conduct is unobserved. What we have, in short, are variations on a theme, namely, the antithesis between nature (*physis*) and convention (*nomos*). The gods are products of the latter and have no more sanction than the other institutions which constitute the framework of human society. When we add to this the fact that the world of nature was at the same time being explained by certain of the natural philosophers without reference to divine intervention, it is clear that traditional religious beliefs no longer satisfied the intellectual demands of a progressive segment of Athenian society. To what extent a similar scepticism touched the popular mind is difficult to gauge, but Aristophanes' *Clouds* is evidence enough that the average Athenian citizen was not unfamiliar with the new currents of thought. Whatever the case, the banishment of Protagoras and the condemnation of Socrates confirm the fact that in the eyes of the authorities the new teaching posed a real danger to established civic religion.

If towards the close of the fifth century organized state religion shows signs of losing its hold, albeit for a philosophically motivated elite, the fourth century introduces new factors calculated to hasten the process and widen its range. The chief among them we have touched upon more than once. It is the dispiriting effect of Athens's collapse as a result of the Peloponnesian War. The Athenians had relied upon the civic gods to sustain the city's cause, and they had been cruelly disappointed. The city had fallen; the empire was lost. If citizens were tempted to conclude that the gods had lost their power or had abandoned their concern, it was an understandable loss of faith. Moreover, as civic issues came to command less attention than matters of private interest, especially after Chaeronea, we are not surprised to discern a corresponding turning away from the gods of the community towards gods more likely to answer to personal needs. It is a fact, for example, that the healing god Asclepius gains an increased following as the fourth century advances. And we may add the foreign cults of Sarapis, Isis, and Cybele. In a desperate effort to find meaning and direction in a bewildering and unpredictable environment man began to worship Chance, personified and elevated to the status of goddess, with temples, altars, and appropriate emblems. This does not mean that the fourth and third centuries saw the end of civic worship. The established deities continued to enjoy their proper honours and distinctions. The Olympians were too much a part of Greek tradition to be abandoned. It is clear, none the less, that it is a case of form without substance. True religious experience was being sought more and more in attendance upon other deities, whose worship offered some promise of satisfaction of personal needs. To this extent religion is a faithful mirror of the general pattern we have traced in other aspects of early Hellenistic society.

Up to this point we have touched upon characteristics of the fourth and third centuries which need to be taken into account for a proper appreciation of the setting in which the philosophy of Epicurus is born. Certain keynotes have been sounded which taken together form a ground base for its major themes. Before turning to the exposition of the main features of Epicureanism which will form the substance of the next chapter, it is important for two reasons to say

13

something of Epicurus himself. First, there is no ancient philosophical school which takes its colour and identity more markedly from the personality of its founder than the Epicurean. Second, from an early date opponents of the Epicurean philosophy employ vilification of its founder as an adjunct to philosophical refutation, and not infrequently as a substitute for it.

As far as the second point is concerned it is ironic that Epicurus' personal life should have allowed such latitude to his detractors, since we are better supplied with information about him than is the case with most ancient thinkers. This latter is due mainly to the third-century AD doxographer and biographer Diogenes Laertius. Book X of his *Lives of the Eminent Philosophers* (*De clarorum philosophorum vitis . . . libri decem*) is a life of Epicurus into which are inserted three doctrinal letters composed by Epicurus (*Letter to Herodotus, Letter to Pythocles, Letter to Menoeceus*) and a list of Epicurus' *Principal Doctrines* (Κύριαι δόξαι). Diogenes' *Life* is not free from difficulties, but when supplemented by and checked against other sources it offers valuable information.[19] However, the damage to Epicurus' reputation had been done before Diogenes' attempt to set the record straight, and accusations which were made early proved to have an exceedingly long life. Some of these accusations we shall consider in due course. First some details concerning Epicurus' life and career.

Epicurus was born on the island of Samos in 341 BC. He was an Athenian citizen of the deme of Gargettus. His father Neocles had been sent to Samos as a settler in 351 and supplemented the income from his holding by working as a schoolmaster. Of Epicurus' mother, Chaerestrata, once we discount the story that she contributed to the family's earnings by working as an itinerant exorcist, ridding the locality of hobgoblins (with the boy Epicurus' help), we know nothing. It is likely that Epicurus' early education was provided by his father, though he may have heard the teachings of the Platonist Pamphilus, as is stated by Ariston and mentioned in the Suida. A reference to his first having studied philosophy at the age of 14 may refer to a visit to Teos on the coast of Asia Minor to study under Nausiphanes, a pupil of Democritus. However, this is a point to which we must return, since it has been argued that the visit to Teos took place at a considerably later date. What is known is that at the age of 18 Epicurus went to Athens to complete a mandatory two years of military service in the ephebate, the poet Menander being among his fellow conscripts. Whether he found time to acquaint himself with the latest teachings of the resident philosophers is unclear. If the opportunity did present itself he could have heard Theophrastus at the Lyceum (Aristotle was then in exile in Calchis) and Xenocrates, Plato's second successor, in the Academy. In fact, Demetrius of Magnesia states that Epicurus did hear the latter.[20] It is worth remarking also that during the period of his stay at Athens Epicurus had the opportunity to witness what Macedonian domination meant in real terms for the future of Greek political life. Two politicians who had proposed revolt against Macedon after Alexander's death, Hyperides and Demosthenes, met their end in 322, the one through execution, the other by his own hand, providing a vivid lesson, if one were needed, that political involvement could exact a heavy price, and that given the circumstances it was energy misplaced. It was a lesson which was to have considerable influence upon Epicurus' philosophy of living.

In 322 the Athenian settlers were evicted from Samos by Perdiccas, Alexander's agent in Asia, and Epicurus' father took refuge in Colophon. Epicurus, his military service completed, joined him there in the following year. He was 20 years of age, and he was to spend the next fifteen years, a formative period in his life, first at Colophon, then at Mytilene on the island of Lesbos, and later at Lampsacus on the Hellespont. What he did at Colophon we can only surmise. It would be pleasant to think with Festugière that his years there were 'years of solitary reflexion and meditation'.[21] Yet, while it is more than likely that he did turn his attention to philosophy, he had a living to make, and it is not improbable that he did so by teaching. And, to return to an earlier point, it has been argued that it was during this period that he made the visit to Teos to study with Nausiphanes.[22] Whether it was at this time or earlier that Epicurus' contact with Nausiphanes took place, there can be no doubt that, despite his openly hostile attitude towards him,[23] he gained a thorough knowledge of the principles of the atomistic philosophy at Nausiphanes' school. It was in 311 that Epicurus went to Mytilene to teach philosophy. To the extent that he gained Hermarchus as one of his pupils it was not a wasted enterprise, but his stay was short. There are indications that he was forced to leave after a year, and his later tract *Against the Philosophers at Mytilene* would suggest that he encountered a good deal of professional opposition. From Mytilene he went to Lampsacus and was considerably more successful. Among his pupils there were two prominent citizens, Idomeneus and Leontius, as well as Metrodorus, his brother

Timocrates, Colotes, Pythocles, and Polyaenus. With all these he initiated the close and enduring friendships which were to give the first phase of Epicureanism its distinctive character.

But the centre of philosophic activity was Athens, not Asia Minor. If Epicurus was to be more than a provincial teacher it was almost imperative that he establish himself in the leading city of the Mediterranean world. For a time, however, the political situation stood in the way. The proxy governor of the city was the Peripatetic Demetrius of Phalerum, and it was the Lyceum which enjoyed Macedonian favour. It was in June 307 that the situation improved. Athens was 'liberated' by Demetrius Poliorcetes, son of Antigonus. At the same time, however, a law was passed which required official permission to be granted before a philosphical school could be established, and it was not until this law was repealed in the following year that Epicurus judged the time right.[24] He moved to Athens with his pupils, purchased a house, and established the School. At the exact mid-point in his life he became Head of the Garden. Apart from occasional visits to Asia Minor, Athens was to remain his permanent home.

It has been possible to sketch a reasonably complete outline of Epicurus' life and career in terms of dates and places. More difficult is the question of determining the extent to which the main lines of his philosophy had been worked out by the time he established himself at Athens. In fact, our information allows us to do no more than state what is obvious. The texts which we possess come from Epicurus' years at Athens. They represent what he chose to put forth as his mature contribution to philosophical enquiry, and we must assume that it was during this settled period, when the curriculum of the School was being developed, that his views took final shape. At the same time, unless his thinking underwent a radical change at the time he established the School in Athens, and we have no evidence to suggest that it did, we must place the first, if tentative, formulation of his philosophic principles in the period when he was active in Colophon, Mytilene, and Lampsacus. While we cannot hope to go beyond this, an examination of possible influences upon him during this earlier period will not be out of place, especially in view of Epicurus' claim that he owed nothing to any teacher, and his open hostility towards certain teachers in particular.

As we have indicated, Epicurus' earliest exposure to philosophic studies may have been between the ages of 14 and 18 at the school of the Platonist Pamphilus on Samos. The curriculum would have called for instruction in geometry and arithmetic, as well as dialectic and rhetoric. How the young Epicurus reacted to these studies we cannot know. His later attitude towards the Platonists, however, was decidedly negative. He is said to have referred to Plato ironically as the 'golden one', and to his followers as 'flatterers of Dionysus'.[25] In his injunction to his pupil Pythocles to avoid *paideia* he may well have had the Platonic curriculum in mind.[26] More specifically, Book 14 of his Περὶ φύσεως is a rejection of Plato's theory of the elements and confirms that Epicurus did not condemn the Platonic philosophy out of ignorance. We may say, then, that, whether his acquaintance with the tenets of the Academy resulted from his early schooling on Samos or from hearing Xenocrates at Athens in 323–322, it led to a total rejection of Platonic teaching.

Epicurus' opinion of the other leading school, the Lyceum, was equally unfavourable. We have mentioned that during his stay in Athens in 323–322 he missed hearing Aristotle, but could have attended the lectures of Theophrastus. Whether he did or not, his later remarks about Aristotle's successor were decidedly hostile. It may have been Theophrastus whom he had in mind when he condemned the 'popular' philosopher as a 'leader of the rabble',[27] and his distaste for Theophrastus' treatise on music is attested by Plutarch.[28] Moreover, that Theophrastus was not in favour in the Garden is clear from the fact that Epicurus' own book attacking him was followed by at least two composed by a female member of the School, the courtesan Leontion.[29] As for Aristotle himself, Cicero attests that Epicurus assailed him in the most insulting fashion,[30] and we learn from other sources that he referred to him as a 'profligate' who 'ate up his patrimony, then enlisted and peddled drugs'.[31] As is the case with Plato, however, Epicurus' derogatory remarks, as well as the formal attacks by other members of the Garden, in particular Epicurus' successor Hermarchus, do not remove the fact that Epicurus' thought owes a great deal to Peripatetic teaching.

When we come to Nausiphanes we are on slightly firmer ground to the extent that we can be sure that Epicurus studied under him, despite Epicurus' own claim that he owed him nothing. At the same time, our information concerning Nausiphanes is slim. We know that he embraced the atomistic philosophy of Democritus and took as the goal of life what he termed 'undisturbedness' (ἀκαταπληξία),

17

after Democritus' 'imperturbability' (ἀϑαμβίη). He was the author of a treatise on epistemology and method called *The Tripod*. The epitome preserved in Philodemus' *Rhetoric* (first century BC) indicates that in science as in rhetoric Nausiphanes laid stress upon the empirical approach, the progression from the more to the lesser known, and the claim that Epicurus' *Canon* owes something to Nausiphanes in this respect may well be justified.[32] Epicurus' abusive references to Nausiphanes may have been prompted by what he regarded as his slavish acceptance of Democritus' 'deterministic' atomism, and do not prevent us from agreeing with Rist that Nausiphanes was 'the master from whom he probably derived most'.[33]

This review of Epicurus' relationship with contemporary schools takes us only so far. The substance of his philosophy itself will reveal more fully the measure of his debt to others and the degree to which his thought was shaped by reaction to their positions. What we do learn, however, is something of Epicurus' personality and something of the atmosphere in which the rival schools vied with one another. The charge that Epicurus was savage in his treatment of his opponents is a persistent one, and there is evidence that it was not groundless. But we must place it in context. We have only to follow the skirmishes of Demosthenes and Aeschines to be aware that invective was as much a part of courtroom life as legal argument, and there is no reason to suppose that the lawyers had a monopoly. Much as we might be tempted to think of philosophy as an academic pastime, the fact is that in the Hellenistic period it was a competitive profession in which a place was reserved for personal abuse. The gaining of pupils and patrons was not simply a matter of prestige, it was a means of financial support. If Epicurus was adept at insult and personal attack we cannot but think that his opponents were equally adept at replying in kind. His ingratitude towards his teachers is unpardonable, and to attempt to excuse it would be to engage in special pleading. His independence of mind is to be acknowledged as a rare and valuable quality which enriched his contribution to philosophy. That it bred in him an intellectual disdain for those who furthered his own philosophical development is a regrettable and all too human failing.

If the atmosphere outside the Garden was stressful, the atmosphere within was that of a community of friends, and a different side of Epicurus' nature emerges. The property which Epicurus purchased consisted of a modest house in the Melite district between the city and the harbour, and a small garden situated outside the Dipylon Gate on the road leading to the Academy.[34] The garden was used for lectures and the house for accommodation. The organization of the School was hierarchical.[35] Epicurus was 'leader' (*hegemon*) and the only one to be awarded the title 'wise man'. An oath was taken acknowledging his authority.[36] Other members, who were called *philosophoi*, were either associate leaders (*kathegemones*), as were Metrodorus, Epicurus' deputy, and Polyaenus, assistant leaders (*kathegetes*), as was Hermarchus, Epicurus' first successor, or pupils (*kataskeuazomenoi*). These last were of all ages and assigned to associate and assistant leaders according to age and proficiency. We may add to the residents of the house, in addition to the slaves responsible for its domestic operation, others who were engaged in maintaining the publication activities of the School. One of the slaves manumitted in accordance with Epicurus' will was Mys, and it has been argued that he was responsible for co-ordinating the work of these scribes and copyists.[37] Finally, we may mention the presence in the School of women other than female slaves. These were of two classes, women of high social standing, such as Themista, the wife of Leontius, and hetaerae, such as Hedeia of Cyzicus, and Leontion, whom we have mentioned already as authoress of two pamphlets attacking Theophrastus. It was the presence of the hetaerae in particular which provided Epicurus' opponents with an excuse to paint the Garden as a veritable School for scandal. Night-long orgies were rumoured. Epicurus himself was charged with having slept with Polyaenus' mistress Hedeia, and with Leontion, mistress and, later, wife of Metrodorus. He was also said to have written in erotic terms to Themista and others, and Diotimus the Stoic produced fifty lewd letters purportedly in Epicurus' hand. In short, life in the Garden was depicted as a continuous round of sexual indulgence.[38]

Two points need to be made. First, it is important not to be confused over the position of hetaerae in Athenian society. As free-born and unmarried women, generally of foreign origin, they were not subject to the same social restrictions as married Athenian women, and, while it was common enough for them to attach themselves to citizens of means and position as mistresses or female companions, they were not infrequently women of intellectual talent and accomplishment, who enjoyed a distinctly higher social standing than prostitutes. We have noted, for example, that Leontion was the author of at least two philosophical pamphlets, and these written in a style which Cicero commends.[39] Accordingly, the membership of hetaerae in the Epicurean community does not in itself justify the interpretation placed upon it by clearly hostile witnesses. Second, Epicurus' views on sexual indulgence are clear enough. An examination of his theory of pleasure will form part of the following chapter. It is sufficient here to point out that as a criterion for the proper selection of pleasures Epicurus establishes a threefold classification of desires, those which are natural and necessary, those which are natural but unnecessary, and those which are neither natural nor necessary.[40] As a kinetic pleasure which does not contribute to a continued absence of pain sexual indulgence belongs in the second category. Indeed, Epicurus states plainly that 'sexual intercourse never did a man any good, and it is fortunate if it did him no harm'.[41] This does not mean that sex is to be absolutely avoided. Even if it is not strictly necessary in terms of being requisite for absence of bodily pain and anxiety of mind, sexual desire is still a natural impulse and Epicurus recognizes as much. Indeed, in the *Symposium* he discusses whether before dinner or after dinner is the preferred time for sexual pleasure.[42] Epicurus' strictures are cautionary. What is important is that the possible discomforts attendant upon sexual indulgence be acknowledged and that there be a proper balancing of positive and negative effects. It is clear, then, that the charges of sexual profligacy are not supported by a consideration of Epicurus' declared attitude.

At the same time it is fair to say that association between members of the Garden was certainly freer than was usual in other schools, and the emphasis which Epicurus placed upon friendship, not only as a topic for philosophic discussion but as a practical aspect of human relationships, left him open to misrepresentation. More will be said on the subject of friendship when we come to examine Epicurus' theory of pleasure. For the moment we shall limit ourselves to the general observation that a clear distinction was made between friendship (ἔρως) motivated by passion and friendship (φιλία) pursued and cultivated as a means of creating a secure and comfortable atmosphere conducive to the acquisition of true pleasure. It was such an atmosphere which Epicurus strove to promote in the Garden, and there is ample evidence that Epicurus' own nature was not the least contributive factor. Diogenes Laertius speaks of his 'benevolence to all', and Cicero, not always the most sympathetic observer, concedes that Epicurus promoted friendship 'not only in words, but much more by his life, his actions, and his character'.[43] But Epicurus is his own witness. For there are fragments of his letters which it is impossible to read without feeling the warmth of his tenderness and affection towards those around him.[44] Moreover, the affection was mutual. Within the School Epicurus was revered as leader. As we have noted, to him alone belonged the title 'wise man' and his authority was unchallenged. His birthday was celebrated almost as a mystic rite. But respect was matched by genuine devotion. In their expressions of both his followers were generous. Indeed, we may agree with his opponents that they were unduly so. What we cannot question is the depth of their sincerity. Epicurus was not simply the intellectual leader of a philosophical movement, he was the father of a family.

2

SCHOOL IN THE GARDEN

Empty are the words of the philosopher who does not heal the suffering of man.

Epicurus

It is not our intention to give a detailed and comprehensive account of the Epicurean philosophy.[1] Rather, we shall focus upon certain aspects of Epicurus' thought which at later periods exerted noticeable influence or provoked keen reaction. We acknowledge the danger of seeing the parts at the expense of the whole. Epicurus' thought does form a unity in which the interdependent relationship between epistemology, physics, and ethics is as clear as in any ancient philosophical system, and the connections will force themselves upon us. It is a fact, however, that to Epicurus himself his 'system' was not of real importance. Nor were certain of its parts, in and of themselves. His interest in the physical world, for example, was not that of the natural scientist, his concern with logic not that of the dialectician. He viewed these and other branches of knowledge as important only to the extent that they add to our understanding of ourselves and the world in which we live.[2] For Epicurus' goal was not to build an abstract philosophical structure. It was to provide his fellow man with a means of securing happiness in a dark and hostile world. What bars the way is ignorance. The closer man can come to an understanding of the fundamental conditions of human existence – the workings of the cosmos, the constitution and activities of the gods, the nature of the human soul, the inner world of thought and feelings – the better prepared he will be to attain that tranquillity of mind in which happiness consists. But Epicurus himself is the most eloquent exponent of his philosophic goal –

Let not the young man delay to study philosophy, nor the old man grow weary. For no one can be too early or too late in seeking the health of the soul. Whoever says that the time for philosophy has passed or has not yet come is like the man who says that the hour for happiness has not yet arrived or has already gone. Philosophy beckons the young man and the old man alike, the one that as he grows older he might stay young in benefits as he recalls the things that have been, the other that though age has come upon him he might yet be young because he fears not the things that are yet to be.[3]

In studying Epicurus' philosophy we are reasonably well placed in terms of firsthand evidence. It is true that Epicurus was one of the most prolific of ancient philosophical writers and we have lost far more of his work than has been preserved. None the less, although there are points where the lack of greater detail is especially regrettable, the writings which do survive, in particular the letters to Herodotus, Pythocles, and Menoeceus, together allow us to gain a fairly complete picture of the main aspects of his thought. The problem is more where to begin. What we are missing is Epicurus' philosophical diary to reveal to us the order of his development as a thinker. Are we to suppose, for example, that Epicurus' earliest interest in philosophy was spurred by a concern for human behaviour and that he expropriated the atomism of Leucippus and Democritus because it provided convenient support for his ethical views? We would be in good scholarly company, and Epicurus would be seen to have responded to what we have suggested was the problem of closest concern during the period, namely, how to find personal meaning in an increasingly alien world. Against this, however, must be set what we know of Epicurus' early philosophical training. If it is true that he studied under the Platonist Pamphilus, it is mathematics and dialectic to which he would have been exposed; with Nausiphanes of Teos, and here we are more certain of influence, it is the physical aspects of atomism that would have commanded his attention. This is not to suggest that Epicurus did not give early thought to ethical questions; it is to caution against a

23

too ready assumption that his attention to physics was in the nature of an afterthought resulting in the creation of what has been termed a 'patchwork' philosophy. We shall see, in fact, that the interconnection between Epicurus' ethics and physics is such that weaving is a more appropriate image than quilting.

If we cannot follow Epicurus' philosophy along the lines of its historical development, we may look to the system fully developed to suggest its own starting-point. At the head of his own general exposition of his physics Epicurus placed a brief but important discussion of logic, or, more properly, canonics, and Bailey has well demonstrated that it is is indeed Epicurus' epistemology which 'supplies the one central principle of his philosophy on which all the rest hangs'.[4] This principle, simply stated, requires that 'all our investigations proceed in accordance with our sensations'.[5] Experience is to be the touchstone of truth, and no less in ethics than in physics. Just as Epicurus insists that in the study of nature we are wholly dependent upon and constrained by the evidence provided by the senses, so in ethics he rests his theory of pleasure not upon any rational argumentation but upon a direct appeal to experience. In due course we shall examine the details and implications of the application of this principle in both these spheres. First, however, we must be clear about the principle itself. For what Epicurus means by experience, that is, by the role of sensation in the acquisition and confirmation of knowledge, is as problematical as it is fundamental.[6]

We may begin with Diogenes' summation of what he takes to be the essence of Epicurus' canonic: ἐν τοίνυν τῷ Κανόνι λέγων ἐστὶν ὁ Ἐπίκουρος κριτήρια τῆς ἀληθείας εἶναι τὰς αἰσθήσεις καὶ προλήψεις καὶ τὰ πάθη – 'so in *The Canon* Epicurus says that the criteria of truth are the sensations and general concepts and the feelings'.[7] At first glance, Diogenes' formulation would seem to contradict what we have taken to be the Epicurean position, namely, that sensations alone are the *iudicia rerum*. Further examination of Diogenes' terms, however, establishes that in fact the three seemingly distinct criteria are reducible to one, and that strict Epicurean doctrine is preserved.

We shall consider first what is meant by 'sensations' (αἰσθήσεις). For Epicurus sensation occurs when there is material contact between one of the sense-organs and an external object. Whereas in the case of touch and taste the physical nature of this contact is easy enough to appreciate, with the other senses contact is not so obviously direct, and some explanation is required. In the case of sight the sense-organ is touched not by the external object itself but by an image (εἴδωλον), or, more precisely, by a rapid succession of images, atomic in composition, emanating from the object and forming what Epicurus terms a 'sense-impression' (φαντασία). It is this sense-impression which the eye perceives at the moment of sensation. In some cases, when the object is close at hand, the sense-impression will be clear (ἐναργής); in others, when the object lies further away or when the perceiver is inattentive and merely a passive recipient, it will be less distinct. In order to render a sense-impression as clear as possible, and so of greater value in acquiring knowledge, it is necessary for the perceiver to focus keenly, a process which is applicable in the case of all the sense-organs and is termed by Epicurus 'attention of the senses' (ἐπιβολή τῶν αἰσθητηρίων). In the case of hearing and smell a similar stream of atoms of different shapes and sizes is emitted by the object, impinging upon the respective organ and causing there the disturbance of atoms which is sensation.

What we have described in outline is Epicurus' account of primary sensations. We can postpone for the moment the manner whereby simple sensations are used as the basis for the formation of judgments about the external world. At this point it is important to note only that the senses provide our only contact with that world and are the only means of acquiring knowledge of it. In *Principal Doctrines* 23 Epicurus warns that, if the evidence of the senses is resisted, then the only basis for judgment is abandoned.[8] Yet we must be clear as to the value of sensations, for it would be a mistake to claim that sensations necessarily give us knowledge of objects. Epicurus is explicit in stating that sensation *per se* is irrational (ἄλογος), that is, it makes no judgment.[9] It is simply an event, presenting objects not necessarily as they are but as they appear to the perceiver at the particular moment and in the particular circumstances. At another time and in other circumstances the same object may appear differently. It may be the case that the second sensation presents the object in truer fashion than the first. However, as a sensation, an event taking place, the first is no less 'true' than the second. For in this context 'truth' has, not propositional, but experiential value only, so that Epicurus is able to say that 'all sensations are true'.[10]

25

If individual sense-impressions constitute the full extent of our information about the external world, it is the case that this information, in and by itself, falls short of knowledge. Epicurus is explicit on this point.[11] Sense-impressions certainly represent objects, but with such a variable degree of exactness that no single sense-impression is of guaranteed value. If sense-impressions are to serve properly as foundations for judgments it is necessary that there be some way of determining which are reliable and which are not. We have already alluded to the importance of 'attention' in rendering sense-impressions as clear as possible, but clarity, while requisite, is not in itself sufficient guarantee that there is a true correspondence between impression and object. The procedure which Epicurus recommends, and this brings us to the second of Diogenes' terms, is the formation and application of general concepts or preconceptions (προλήψεις). In fact, Epicurus regards general concepts as essential to any kind of enquiry or deliberation.[12] What Epicurus means by a general concept is not without difficulty. Diogenes, as we have seen, speaks of προλήψεις almost as variants of αἰσθήσεις. That there is a real difference between the two, however, is clear from his more expansive treatment in 10.33:

> They [the Epicureans] speak of the general concept as an apprehension or correct opinion or thought or general notion stored away in the mind, that is, a remembrance of something which has frequently appeared from without: for example, 'such and such a thing is a man'.

The distinction between sense-impressions and general concepts, then, is that the former are the results of a purely physical experience, the contact between object and sense-organ, while the latter stem from a secondary source, namely, the abstractive operation of the mind. At the same time, if general concepts are different from sense-impressions in terms of efficient cause, as aggregates of particular sense-impressions they are materially dependent upon them, and it is this which allows Epicurus to classify the two together.

So much for the formation of general concepts. What role does Epicurus assign to them in the acquisition of knowledge? The answer lies in a distinction between general concepts and sense-impressions which we have not yet noted. Sensory experience supplies us with information concerning the external world. Indeed, it is our only source of information. But, as we have noted, this information is of limited value. Even the clearest and most distinct impressions fail to provide a reliable basis for propositions concerning the real nature of things. General concepts, on the other hand, are characterized by a clarity which amounts to self-evidence, and which gives them the compelling force which individual sense-impressions lack.[13] In short, what we have in general concepts are basic definitions which, because they carry with them their own guarantee, can serve as criteria to which we can refer particular sense-impressions, and which we can use to test the validity of propositions. Further, since general concepts give significance to the names we attach to things, they open the way for meaningful linguistic expression.[14]

We come now to the third of Diogenes' terms – feelings (πάθη). As we have noted, every sensation, that is, every contact between object and sense-organ, involves a disturbance of the atoms which constitute the sensory nerve-endings. According to Epicurus, this movement of atoms may affect the person agreeably or disagreeably, that is, may arouse feelings of pleasure or pain, and it is these two feelings which are meant by πάθη. As criteria, however, they play a different role from primary sensations and general concepts. Whereas these are guides to the truth, the feelings are criteria for action, determining our response to particular sensory experiences. Pleasure is appropriate to us, pain is foreign.[15] Hence, and we shall see that this is of particular importance in the context of Epicurean ethical theory, we are given natural grounds for choosing what to pursue and what to avoid.

Our consideration of Diogenes' testimony confirms the empirical basis of Epicurus' theory of knowledge. Of the three criteria which he recognizes, sensations, general concepts, and feelings, the second owe their origin entirely to the first, while the third are concomitants of sensations themselves. We must note, however, that while Epicurus insists that all our investigations must proceed in accordance with these criteria, he does not claim that they remove all possibility of error. We have remarked that sensations are 'true' only at the level of appearances, and we must add that general concepts are subject to improper application. In referring sense-impressions to general concepts we may be led to make false identifications. Similarly, wrong opinion may vitiate the comparisons we make between one general concept and another. Furthermore, there are areas of enquiry which are too remote for clear observation or which lie beyond the scope of sensory experience altogether, where we must proceed by analogy with perceived phenomena. Accordingly, Epicurus introduces certain secondary principles which must be observed.

In the case of objects which can be subjected to close observation (πρόδηλα), the procedure to be followed is simple enough. If our first observation is from a distance, the judgment we make must be provisional only and be regarded as awaiting confirmation (προσμένον ἐπιμαρτυρήθεσθαι).[16] The test is closer inspection. If the data provided by such inspection coincide with our earlier sensation, then our original judgment may be taken as confirmed. If, on the other hand, counter-evidence is forthcoming, then the original judgment must be regarded as false. To take an example to which both Diogenes Laertius and Sextus Empiricus allude, we may observe a tower from a distance and on the basis of its appearing to be round form a preliminary judgment that it is so. As we move closer, we observe that, in fact, the tower is square, and our first judgment is invalidated.[17] Now what we have in this instance is not a case of one sensation correcting another. Epicurus is explicit in saying that such correction is impossible: every sensation is 'true' in itself.[18] It is the case, rather, that false opinion had been added to sensation to produce an erroneous first judgment, and it is this judgment which has been overruled.

Of things which do not admit of close inspection (ἄδηλα), the first class consists of the heavenly bodies (μετέωρα). Here we cannot look for confirmation. What we must rely upon is absence of counter-evidence (οὐκ ἀντιμαρτύρησις), that is, conformity between the hypothesis and other perceived phenomena.[19] A consequence of this principle, which Epicurus is quite prepared to face, is that we may have to accept more than one explanation of the same phenomena. Indeed, Epicurus argues that, since in celestial matters we are dealing with probability only, the acceptance of multiple explanations is in no way unscientific. What would be illogical would be to accept one explanation and reject another when the second is no less in agreement with phenomena than the first.[20] The second class consists of things which cannot be perceived at all, such as atoms and void. Here too sense-evidence plays an essential role. In celestial matters it is the part of perceived phenomena to act as a check upon hypotheses regarding things less distinctly seen. With things lying completely beyond the range of the senses, sense-evidence provides the starting point for inference. For example, the fact that void exists, even though it is not seen, is established as follows: we observe movement taking place; but movement is impossible without void; therefore, void exists.[21]

This review of the main aspects of Epicurus' epistemology confirms its thoroughly empiricist basis. Our senses bring us into direct contact with the physical world and supply our only information about it. The impressions which constitute sensations provide the basis for general concepts, which in turn serve both as a check upon sensations themselves and as foundations for judgments. Confirmation of judgments involves further appeal to the senses. With objects which lie close at hand, it is a case of closer inspection; with phenomena more remote or wholly insensible, it is a case of framing hypotheses on the basis of what can be observed and of ensuring that such hypotheses are not at variance with sense data. We must next review the results of Epicurus' own application of these criteria to the investigation of nature.

We have noted Epicurus' reluctance to acknowledge the influence of previous thinkers, and this extends to the fifth-century atomists Leucippus and Democritus. He went so far as to say that the former never existed, and his remarks concerning the latter were decidedly unflattering.[22] None the less, it is the atomism of Leucippus and Democritus which supplies the foundation for Epicurus' physical doctrine. Why he should have denied the existence of Leucippus we cannot speculate. With respect to Democritus, it may be that he regarded him as strictly a natural philosopher. For to Epicurus natural philosophy cannot be justified as an end in itself. The study of nature is worth while only to the extent that an understanding of the workings of the universe contributes to a happy life. As such, Epicurus took it seriously. Indeed, as he tells his disciple Herodotus, he made it a constant preoccupation.[23] However, if Epicurus adopted fifth-century atomism he did not do so without certain modifications, and he provided his own argumentation for its basic principles. For this we may turn conveniently to the *Letter to Herodotus*, with supplementary reference to the sometimes fuller account given by Lucretius.

Epicurus' reliance upon experience is evidenced in the three basic principles which he takes as the starting-point in his discussion of the physical world – (1) that nothing is created out of nothing, (2) that nothing is destroyed into nothing, and (3) that the universe has always been and will always be as it is now.[24] If things were created out of nothing, then we would witness everything springing forth not from fixed seeds, but at random, something which would controvert our observation;[25] similarly, if things perished into nothingness, then the sum of matter would by now have been exhausted, something which is likewise contradicted by experience;[26] as a corollary, if there is no creation of new material, then it follows that the sum of matter in the universe is constant.[27] It is experience too which vouches for the two existents which Epicurus posits as the sole constituents of the universe, body and empty space. That the former exists is universally attested; as to the latter, the existence of bodies demands somewhere wherein they exist, and, since bodies are perceived to move, there must be empty space through which this movement takes place.[28]

Having established that the universe consists of body and void, Epicurus proceeds to distinguish between body in the form of the compound structures which we perceive (συγκρίσεις), and body in the form of the units of matter from which these compounds are formed. If principle 2 is to be observed, that is, if there is to be a limit set to dissolution, then the primary units into which compounds are resolved must themselves be stable and indivisible (ἀμετάβλητα, ἄτομα).[29] In addition, because the universe is unbounded, a point which Epicurus again establishes with reference to experience, there being nothing perceivable beyond the universe by which its boundaries can be determined,[30] these primary units must be infinite in number. Likewise, void must be boundless in extent. For, if there were a limited number of atoms in infinite void, they would be too scattered to experience the collisions necessary for effecting unions, and, conversely, if there were an unlimited number of atoms in finite space they would be too packed together to find their appropriate places.[31]

What, apart from indivisibility, are the properties which belong to atoms? Here, Epicurus draws a further distinction between perceptible compound bodies and the discrete units of matter of which they are composed. The qualities which pertain to the former are changeable to the degree that compounds themselves are subject to change, whether this be through an alteration in the arrangement of their component particles or through the addition or loss of particles. The only qualities which persist through change are size, shape, and weight, and it is these three primary properties alone which Epicurus assigns to the component particles themselves.[32]

As physical objects atoms must have size, but Epicurus is not definite as to the number of different sizes there might be. Some considerable variation in size is required to account for the different qualities of things and their different effects upon our senses. At the same time, experience dictates that it is a limited variation, otherwise there could exist atoms large enough to be seen.[33] Here Epicurus may be arguing against Democritus, for there is testimony that Democritus accepted the existence of very large atoms, though, as Rist has pointed out, he may have done no more than allow an infinite variation in size without believing that atoms large enough to be seen actually exist.[34] There remains the question whether or not there is a lower limit to the size of atoms. Epicurus answers in the affirmative. To admit that no lower limit exists would be to accept the infinite divisibility of matter, a concept which Epicurus rejects for two reasons. First, he insists that the process of infinite division will lead to eventual destruction; in short, infinite division would contradict the very identity of atoms as physical minima representing the permanent substratum of matter. Second, infinite divisibility entails an infinite number of parts, each of which must have some size; but the sum of an infinite number of extended parts, however small, must result in an object infinite in size.[35] Yet, this is not to say that atoms, while physically indivisible, are without parts. Indeed, it is the parts of atoms that determine their size, shape, and weight. However, these parts (*minimae partes*), which are limited in number, are both physically and conceptually inseparable from one another and have no existence independent of the atom itself.[36]

Size demands shape, and here Epicurus is more definite. The immense variety of things in nature requires that there be an incomprehensible (ἀπερίληπτον) number of atomic shapes. However, there cannot be an infinite (ἄπειρον) number, since there would come a point where further increase in the number of different shapes could no longer be effected by rearrangement of the minimal parts within the atom, but would require an increase in the number of minimal parts, a process which, if unlimited, would result in atoms large enough to be seen.[37] Moreover, experience suggests that there is a limit to the number of shapes. The qualities of things in nature, while they are so varied as to demand an incomprehensible number of shapes, are none the less bounded by extremes – there is a limit to beauty, ugliness, heat, cold – and such limits would not exist if the range of shapes were endless.[38] There are, however, an infinite number of atoms of each shape, something which is required, Lucretius mistakenly argues, if the total sum of atoms is to be infinite.[39]

The third property belonging to atoms is weight. Whether or not Democritus attributed weight to atoms is a matter of dispute. Even if he did, however, it is reasonably certain that he did not look to weight as a cause of atomic motion. Since he believed that atoms had existed *ab aeterno* and that there had never been a time when they were not incessantly moving, cause of motion was not a question.[40] For Epicurus, on the other hand, weight is an essential property of atoms and is the first cause of their movement.[41] We would speak more strictly, however, of weight as the cause of the primary movement of atoms, since there are secondary types of atomic motion where factors other than weight are responsible. What we mean by primary movement is the movement through the void of 'free' atoms, that is, atoms which have not yet become entangled in compounds, and the effect of weight is to cause these atoms to move downwards unless they are impeded through contact with other atoms or compounds.[42] It is contact with other atoms or with compounds which leads to one of the secondary types of atomic motion, which we shall consider in due course. First, however, we must examine what Epicurus means by 'downward' in infinite space. Whether or not Epicurus was responding to Plato's rejection of the notions 'up' and 'down' in infinite space, his detailed, if somewhat unclear, treatment of the question confirms that he recognized that his use of the term 'downward' required some explanation. He admits that we cannot speak of 'up' and 'down' with reference to absolute highest and lowest points. At the same time, he insists that we can do so with reference to a fixed point. Just as in everyday language we are accustomed to referring to movement from our head to our feet as movement 'downwards' and to the reverse as movement 'upwards', so by using ourselves as fixed points in the universe we may speak of atoms as moving in a 'downward' direction without doing violence to the concept of infinitely extended space.[43]

Epicurus speaks of 'free' atoms then as being impelled perpendicularly downwards through the void by their own weight. We must note, however, that this discussion is essentially on a theoretical plane, since his reference is to a condition which for the most part no longer obtains, a stage which is historically, or at least logically, prior to the point when atoms came into contact one with another to form the compound structures which constitute the visible world. But, if at this prior stage the 'free' atoms are imagined as falling perpendicularly downwards through the void, how was contact between them first brought about? Certainly, Epicurus was not free to adopt the position of Democritus. For the latter the explanation lay in the fact that the weight of the heavier atoms caused them to fall more rapidly and to collide with lighter atoms below them, thus bringing about a sequence of random bumpings and jostlings which resulted in atoms of different shapes combining one with another. Epicurus, however, held that all atoms move downwards through the void at uniform speed regardless of their weight, there being nothing to obstruct them, with the result that the possibility of heavier atoms overtaking lighter ones is precluded. Of Epicurus' response to the problem the *Letter to Herodotus* gives no indication, but there is ample later testimony that it took the form of the celebrated theory of the atomic 'swerve' (παρέγκλισις), according to which, to follow Lucretius' presentation, at an undetermined time and in undetermined places atoms veered slightly from their course, in this way setting the stage for the collisions requisite for the formation of compounds.[44]

The importance of this assumption of an arbitrary and unpredictable deviation from the laws of nature for Epicurus' psychology will concern us in due course. For the moment we note only that this second type of atomic motion serves to bring about the third, namely, that which results from the blows sustained by atoms as they clash with one another. Here we must note first that the collisions brought about by the 'swerve' may affect atoms in different ways. In the case of every atom which collides with another the blow (πληγή) which it receives causes it to be deflected from its course in a trajectory which is determined by the angle at which the two atoms meet. However, what happens to particular atoms after this deflection can vary. Some atoms will experience in their new trajectory no further immediate contact with other atoms. In these cases, when the directional impulse which they have received as a result of the blow diminishes, the effect of their weight supervenes and they begin gradually to resume their former path downwards

33

through the void. In the case of a larger number of atoms, however, a first collision is followed by others in succession, with the result that they are incessantly tossed and buffeted about, to employ Lucretius' celebrated image, like motes in a sunbeam.[45] In both cases, however, since we are still dealing with 'free' atoms travelling through the void, the blows have no effect upon the speed at which the atoms move.

This is the case also with those atoms, and these are the majority, which as a result of collisions become entangled with other atoms to form compounds. Before we examine the motion of atoms within compounds, however, a word is needed concerning the manner in which compounds are formed. As Epicurus explains it, the entanglement (περιπλοκή) of atoms results in the formation of an atomic webbing or shell (τὸ στεγάζον) which constitutes the peripheral surface of the compound (σύστημα). Within this outer shell, however, the constituent atoms are never at rest, but are engaged in an unceasing series of meetings and reboundings, so that there is kept up within every compound a continuous vibration (παλμός). Now within some compounds the degree of atomic interlocking or the nature of the enclosing shell may allow the constituent atoms to rebound to greater distances than is the case within other compounds, and it is this inner texture of the compound, considered in terms of these intervals (διαστήματα), or, in other words, in terms of the amount of void which the compound encloses, which determines its density or rarity.[46]

To return to the question of the speed of atomic motion within a compound, two points are of importance. First, since even within the confines of a compound structure the atoms are moving through void, they experience no retardation apart from the momentary checks (ἀντικοπαί) which result from collisions with other atoms in the compound, and so travel at the same uniform speed as 'free' atoms. The second point has to do with the relation between the motion of individual atoms within the compound and the motion of the compound itself. How, for example, do we account for the fact that certain compounds move at a faster rate than others? If a compound derives its speed from the velocity of its constituent atoms, then, since in all compounds atoms move at the same absolute speed, the speed of the compounds should be uniform. How is it, again, that certain compounds remain stationary even though their atoms are ceaselessly moving? Epicurus' answer to these

34

questions lies in the consideration that, while the motion of every compound is indeed the sum of the motions of its atoms, this sum will vary from compound to compound. The reason is that within a compound the atoms do not all move in the same direction. The motion of some atoms is in the same direction as that of the compound itself and these serve to accelerate its speed; others move in a contrary direction and serve to retard it. Thus the velocity of the whole body is determined by the aggregate speed of its atoms after the directional factors have been taken into account. To take the two extremes: if all the constituent atoms move in the same direction as the whole body, then the compound will move at 'atomic' speed; if the number of atoms moving in the same direction as the whole body is balanced by the number moving in the contrary direction, then the compound will be stationary.[47]

Up to this point we have been dealing with an atomic world which lies below the level of perception. We have discussed Epicurus' conception of atoms in terms of their three essential properties – size, shape, and weight. In the context of the last we have examined how atoms come into contact one with another, and the nature of atomic motion, both that of 'free' atoms and that of atoms which have entered into compounds. Consideration of compounds brings us closer to the observable world, and we must now examine Epicurus' view of how that world comes to possess the characteristics which present themselves to the senses.

We may begin by returning to the question of compounds. We have seen that one of the effects of the atomic swerve is to cause atoms to clash together and become entangled, forming compound structures which may take the form of clusters of atoms more or less closely interlaced one with another, or of 'free' particles enclosed within an encompassing atomic mesh. These compounds, which are still too small to be visible, combine with others to form the larger units of matter which are the objects of the phenomenal world. We must note, however, that it appears not to be a simple case of any compound or nucleus combining with any other. In accordance with the principle enunciated early in the *Letter to Herodotus* (38), namely, that not everything is created from everything, Epicurus seems to suppose that certain compounds are especially suited, by reason of their configurations or the motions which they perform, to combine with others to form objects of a particular kind. Certainly, he speaks in more than one place of 'seeds' (σπέρματα) of things in a way which suggests that he means not individual atoms, but groups of atoms,[48] and Lucretius' frequent use of 'seeds' (*semina*) in this sense confirms that the distinction was part of Epicurean teaching.[49]

We gain a fuller understanding of compounds, however, and the way in which they differ from the individual atoms of which they are composed once we examine them in terms of their qualities. As we have seen, atoms possess three properties only – size, shape, and weight. These are permanent and unchanging attributes. Compounds share these same properties, with the difference that in the case of compounds these properties may change or perish as the compounds themselves change or dissolve. That compounds possess additional properties, however, is evidenced by sense-experience. We taste objects because they possess savour, we smell objects because they possess odour, and experience tells us that objects are hot, or cold, or of a particular colour. But what does it mean to say that objects 'possess' taste, smell, heat, cold, colour, and so forth? Are we to suppose that these qualities have an existence in and of themselves, independently of bodies, in the manner of Platonic Forms?[50] Are we to accept the Stoic position that they are material and separable parts of bodies?[51] Are we to suppose with Democritus that they have no existence at all outside our own subjective experience?[52] Epicurus rejects all these views.

As to his own position, he gives only a general statement and we must look to Lucretius for an elaboration of the details. In brief, sensible qualities depend upon the size, shape, and arrangement of the atoms which make up an object.[53] Differences in taste, for example, are accounted for by differences in atomic shapes. Honey tastes sweet because it is made up of particles which are round and smooth; wormwood tastes bitter because its particles are hooked.[54] Similarly, harsh sounds or foul smells are properties of things which are composed of atoms rougher in texture than those which make up objects producing sounds or smells which are pleasing.[55] In the case of colour it is a question of both shape and arrangement. The arrangement of atoms determines an object's colour, but differences among the shapes of the atoms allow for variation in arrangement, which causes certain objects to assume different colours at different times.[56] Sensible qualities then are properties (συμβεβηκότα) of bodies in a way which makes qualities and bodies mutually dependent. Separate from bodies, qualities can have no existence. At the same time, it is the aggregate of its qualities which gives a body its permanent identity.[57]

36

In the foregoing review of the fundamentals of Epicurean physics we began with a discussion of the two basic realities, void and atoms, and proceeded to examine the manner in which the latter, the ultimate units of matter, combine to form the objects of the phenomenal world. We shall next consider certain aspects of this world, its origin, growth, and eventual dissolution, as preparation for an examination of what Epicurus has to say about the beginnings of human life and the development of civilization.

Epicurus makes a distinction between world (κόσμος) and universe (τὸ πᾶν). We have seen above that the universe is boundless in extent. Our world is but a 'circumscribed portion of sky' (περιοχή τις οὐρανοῦ) with a definite boundary within which are contained the earth itself as well as the heavenly bodies. Nor is our world unique. The infinite number of atoms in the universe have formed and will continue to form an infinite number of separate worlds, some like ours, some different, some taking their place in between existing worlds, some coming into being where previous worlds have passed away. For worlds are nothing more than vast atomic compounds, and like every compound each has a beginning and an end.[58] As to the manner in which worlds are formed, Epicurus deviates from his atomistic predecessors. Leucippus had held that in the beginning all atoms in the universe had been lumped together in a mass and that worlds had been formed as a result of atoms dropping away and being caught up in a whirl. Democritus had posited that atoms moved freely through the universe and that worlds had been created when pockets of atoms were gathered together in a vortex, which he equated with Necessity, and as a result of this whirling motion were forced into the appropriate formation. Epicurus rejected both these views. He regarded Leucippus' concept of an original *plenum* as mistaken and Democritus' Necessity as superfluous. In his view, all that is required for the formation of a world is the meeting together of a sufficient number of atoms of appropriate shape in an arrangement which allows for the requisite atomic motions.[59]

The terms which Epicurus employs for the three key phases in this formational process are προσθέσεις, διαρθρώσεις, and μεταστάσεις.[60] Their meaning we may best examine by referring to Lucretius' elaboration of this aspect of Epicurean cosmogony.[61] The initial gathering together of the material which would form our world was no more than a confused jumble of atoms of every kind, which clashed and rebounded but failed to sustain any permanent formations (*non omnia sic poterant coniuncta manere*). There then took place the first two stages in Epicurus' scheme – the separating out of atoms as like particles joined like (*paresque/ cum paribus iungi res*), and the articulation of the elements which would form the recognizable features of the world – the earth, the sea, and the heavenly bodies (*membraque dividere et magnas disponere partes*). The third stage saw the disposition of these elements in their respective locations: the heavy atoms of earth settled at the bottom in the centre, while the lighter and rounder atoms were squeezed upwards; of these, the lightest of all, particles of ether mixed with fire, rose highest and formed themselves into a mesh covering and enclosing the entire world (*levis ac diffusilis aether/ . . . omnia sic avido complexu cetera saepsit*); the next lightest took their place midway between this surrounding ether and the earth to form the sun, the moon, and the other heavenly bodies. There then followed a further distinction of the world's features: as the fiery and airy particles rose upwards, so the earth sank still further; at the same time it contracted in size and exuded a salt sweat which filled the hollows on its surface to form the seas (*succidit et salso suffudit gurgite fossus*); further contraction of the earth due to the blows of the wind and the rays of the sun kept up the process. Thus, by degrees, evolved the form of the world as we see it.

Before we proceed to review what Epicurus and Lucretius have to say concerning the primal condition of the earth and the development of human society, two further points need to be noted. First, just as our world had a beginning, so it will have an end. In this, it is no different from any other compound. Epicurus states clearly that all worlds will at some point be dissolved,[62] but it is again Lucretius who supplies the details.[63] His treatment takes the form of an analogy with the process of growth and decay in the human body. Throughout its life a body experiences a constant taking in and giving out of atoms. During its period of growth it receives a larger number of atoms than it gives off, and continues to do so until it reaches its peak. At this point there is an equal balance between particles gained and particles lost. Decline sets in when this balance is disturbed as the full-grown body, because of its bulk, begins to give off more particles than it is taking in. Decline continues as the body finds it increasingly difficult to distribute food to its various parts and the amount of nourishment it receives becomes less than it requires. Thus the body is finally brought to a state where it can no longer sustain the force of the blows which assail it from without. The world itself follows a similar pattern of growth and decay. From the beginning it takes in a constant supply of atoms from outside until it reaches the limit of its growing period.[64] Even those atoms which do not find their way in serve to preserve the world by battering against its shell and checking the outward flow of atoms.[65] But atoms do escape, even from the start, and by degrees the number of atoms escaping begins to exceed the number taken in, and the world loses substance. The atoms which are battering against it from without cease to preserve the world, serving now to undermine the interlacings of its shell until the whole structure crumbles.[66] We may add that in Lucretius' view there are manifold signs that the world is already in decline (*fracta est aetas effetaque tellus*), and he prays that his own generation will not see its end.[67]

The second point, which we shall discuss more fully when we come to examine Epicurean theology, is that in the origin and operation of the world nothing is owed to divine agency. In the *Letter to Herodotus* Epicurus prefaces his brief treatment of celestial phenomena with a warning against the belief in a divine being who 'controls and ordains' the motions of the heavenly bodies, and he assails the notion that these bodies are themselves divine.[68] It is in Lucretius, however, that we find a more comprehensive discussion. He touches upon the issue at various points throughout his poem, but it is towards the beginning of Book V, in a polemic which is directed primarily against Stoic views, that he refers most directly to Epicurus' arguments.[69] Addressing himself first to the idea that the heavenly bodies are divine, he repeats Epicurus' denial, but goes further: far from being divine, the heavenly bodies (as well as the earth, the sky, and the sea) are not even alive, since 'soul', the principle of life, can reside only in its appropriate place, namely, the human body.[70] He next contests the view that, though the world itself is not divine, the gods none the less dwell in its parts and control them. What makes this impossible, he argues, employing a principle similar to that above, is that for divine beings, whose nature is extremely fine, the world with its gross texture is an inappropriate abode. Finally, he adduces a series of arguments, which are close to those given to the Epicurean spokesman in Cicero's *De Natura Deorum*, to counter the popular notion that the gods created the world either for their own pleasure or for the benefit of man.[71] The life of the gods has always been one of tranquillity and

39

perfect enjoyment; only if they had been discontented with their existence would the gods have been induced to seek pleasure in the novelty of creating a world. As for their having created the world for man's advantage, what need did they have of his gratitude? What disadvantage would it have been for man not to have been created at all? Why, if man's needs were their concern, would the gods have created a world so deficient in resources, so hostile to humankind, and so demanding of human effort? Finally, how could the gods have created a world for which they had no pattern? Lucretius' arguments admittedly take us beyond Epicurus himself. However, it is clear that the question of the divine government of the world did not cease to be a main issue between Epicureans and Stoics in particular, and we may regard Lucretius as presenting the latest Epicurean contribution to a continuing debate.

We return to the question of the primal condition of the earth and the development of human civilization, and it is again to Lucretius that we are indebted for a fully developed account.[72] We have seen above that in speaking of the world experiencing successive periods of growth, maturity, and decay Lucretius drew an analogy with the living body. So in his treatment of the first stages in the earth's development he employs the same comparison, describing how the infant earth was first provided with a protective covering in the form of various grasses, then flowers, then trees, in the way that young animals and birds are provided with down, bristles, and feathers. Next the earth exercised its generative powers by bringing forth living creatures – first birds, which hatched from eggs which the earth had made, then various species of animals, including human beings, all issuing forth from moist wombs growing out of the earth and attached to it by roots.[73] This explanation of the origin of animal and human life, which has parallels in Anaximander, Anaxagoras, and Democritus,[74] Lucretius supports by referring to the supposed spontaneous generation of worms from the ground after it has been soaked by rain and warmed by the sun.[75] Just as the new earth was herself provided with protection, so now, as mother, she provided protection and sustenance for her young creatures – soft grass for a covering, sap from her pores, and a temperate climate.

Lucretius pursues his analogy with the human body by stating that at a certain point the earth reached the limit of her productive powers, at which time she was no longer capable of bringing forth the same creatures as before, producing instead various kinds of deformed beings which suffered early extinction because they lacked the means to propagate. There is a parallel here, of course, with Empedocles' theory of 'natural selection'.[76] But significant differences must be noted. First, Lucretius implicitly rejects the more fantastic elements in Empedocles' theory.[77] More importantly, while for Empedocles these deformed creatures represent nature's experiments which precede the emergence of perfectly formed specimens, for Lucretius they represent the products of a stage which follows the creation of perfect forms. To pursue the analogy which Lucretius himself employs throughout, we must think in terms of Down's syndrome. In addition, many other species of animals perished early because they were without the necessary cunning or swiftness to escape their natural enemies, or were too timid to protect themselves, or were insufficiently useful to humans to gain their protection. What Lucretius does not allude to explicitly, but what is certainly part of the Epicurean tradition, is that the earth's loss of direct productive power coincided with a transition to the propagation of species through sexual union.[78]

We have followed Lucretius' account of the primal condition of the earth and the appearance on it of living creatures. As far as the animal kingdom is concerned, the picture is an ambivalent one. As mother, the earth in the beginning provided her offspring with food and a mild climate. At the same time, the law of tooth and claw was harsh and caused many species to become extinct. Lucretius' picture of the early state of man and of his subsequent development is equally ambivalent, and has been variously interpreted. Some have seen Lucretius as a progressivist. Indeed, Dean Inge could say that we owe to Lucretius 'the blessed name of Progress in the modern sense'.[79] Bury would not go so far, but, despite his basic contention that no ancient source reveals a belief in continuing progress, allowed that

> Epicurean philosophers made indeed what might have been an important step in the direction of the doctrine of Progress, by discarding the theory of degeneration, and recognising that civilisation had been created by a series of successive improvements achieved by the effort of man.[80]

Margaret Taylor goes further. Focusing upon the importance which the Epicurean school attached to removing fear through understanding, she argues that in Lucretius' estimation 'man had

41

achieved the knowledge which was indispensable to the good life, and . . . the way was open for further development in the present and the future'.[81]

Others have read Lucretius' account differently. Robin was persuaded that Lucretius should be classified as a primitivist,[82] and this view has been partly endorsed by Green, for whom the dominant note in Lucretius' poem is one of pessimism: it is in the nature of things that this world will come to an end, and it is already in decline. He concludes that, while Lucretius can recognize that there have been advances in specific fields of endeavour, 'the five hundred lines which portray the history of civilization may better be taken to show that through all the changes of human experience there is no real progress, that is, no increase of happiness'.[83] Between the two extremes Lovejoy and Boas hold a middle ground, detecting in Lucretius 'two incongrous moods' expressive of a recognition that such progress as has taken place has been a mixed blessing. For, of the three stages of development which they distinguish in Lucretius' account, they regard Lucretius himself as favouring the second, when man had advanced beyond the primitive and savage state, but had not yet entered the more sophisticated world of the poet's own age.[84] Finally, before we turn to Lucretius himself, we should acknowledge the cautionary note sounded by Merlan, who warns against seeing Lucretius' account as an endorsement of either the earlier or the later stage in the development of human civilization. What we have, he suggests, is a chapter in Greek heurematology, for 'what Lucretius is primarily interested in is naturalism versus divine intervention, and not progressivism versus primitivism. On the latter problem Lucretius is simply non-committal.'[85]

We shall not present the details of Lucretius' exposition. Rather, we shall consider certain themes which run throughout the whole, and attempt to underscore the basic forces which Lucretius suggests were at work in the emergence of human civilization. We shall discover that what gives unity to his account and ties it closely to the purpose of the poem as a whole is the poet's strict application of Epicurean principles, and in particular the consistency with which he measures both the earlier and the later stages of man's develop-ment in terms of the ultimate Epicurean goal of attaining the happy life. We may begin with what has been the starting-point in the primitivist–progressivist debate, namely, the antithesis between man in his infant state and man as creator and product of an age of social, cultural, and technological maturity. The theme announces itself even before Lucretius begins his account proper of the successive discoveries in the mechanical and creative arts and of the development of social practices and institutions (V. 1011–1457). For he prefaces this concluding section of Book V with a vignette of life during the 'flowering newness of the world', and in the first lines strikes the comparative note: 'man was hardier in the fields, built as he was from larger bones'.[86] It is a note which is sustained throughout, though for the first two-thirds of the passage (V. 925–87) the comparison is implied rather than stated. Primitive man lacked knowledge of cultivation and of the planting and pruning of trees; he was without the use of fire; he had not learned the art of weaving garments or the technique of constructing dwellings; he lived a life little different from that of the animals of the forest, set apart from his fellows, living off acorns, berries, and wild pears, drinking from mountain streams, the woods and caves his dwelling-places. It is a simple life which Lucretius describes, but not the Golden Age experience which we find depicted in other classical writers.[87] Indeed, it is a harsh and demanding existence. Nature is sufficient but not bountiful, and death at the jaws of wild animals is never far distant. Yet, if primitive life is precarious and hard to sustain, there are aspects of primitive man himself which the poet clearly respects. He is hardy and self-reliant, and he is free from superstition. Darkness, for example, holds no terror, since he has learned by observing the regularity of nature that night will be followed by day.

It is when Lucretius considers the question of mortality that he becomes more explicit in his comparisons with his own age (V. 988–1010). As far as the rate of mortality is concerned he conjectures that it has changed little. For early man the chief causes of death were lack of food, ravaging by wild animals, and food poisoning. For Lucretius' contemporaries these dangers are less to be feared. On the other hand, early man was free from the large-scale disasters which modern man has brought upon himself through the practice of war and seafaring. Moreover, there is the irony that, while our ancestors accidentally poisoned themselves, we deliberately poison one another; while they died from scarcity of food, we die from overabundance. On balance, we may say that, if Lucretius is so far neutral with regard to the quality of life enjoyed by man at the earliest and most recent stages in his development, he is less so with

43

respect to human behaviour. Here, primitive man's lack of sophistication gives him the advantage.

When we come to Lucretius' account of man's discoveries we find
that the theme we have been following is present in the poet's mind
to a lesser degree. Moreover, since Lucretius is no longer concerned
with the primitive stage in man's development but with the stages
which succeeded it, the comparisons which he draws do not take the
same simple form. What we have, rather, are occasional reflections
upon the effects which man's advancement has had upon his
character and condition. The particular occurrences which draw
forth comment are the discovery of fire, the beginning of family life,
the institution of property, the growth of religion, and the practice of
war. The first two combined to rob man of his natural hardiness and
to weaken him emotionally by introducing him to the pleasures of a
softer life and by exposing him to the winsome charms of wife and
children.[88] More ruinous of man's character, however, was the
substitution of property for bodily strength and beauty as the
prerequisite for honour and prestige. Wealth became the pursuit of
all, but, far from bringing those who acquired it the security which
they had imagined would be theirs, it involved them in a life of
wasted ambition, since their power served only to provoke the envy
of others.[89] No less disruptive of human life has been the rise of false
beliefs about the gods. Indeed, Lucretius takes the opportunity to
include at this point a digression on popular religion which represents his longest connected treatment of the topic. Its effects have
been in every way pernicious and degrading. Man has become a
creature of fear, living in dread of the supposed power of the
immortals, cowering in terror at signs of their displeasure, ever
apprehensive of punishment at their hands. He has become dis-
trustful of his own reason, allowing himself to look no further for the
causes of natural phenomena than some unknown divine plan. In
short, false belief has robbed man of his dignity and taught him to
despise himself.[90]

Finally, Lucretius uses the discovery of metals to launch a review
of man's record in employing new methods of waging war. He
acknowledges that man has warred from earliest times, primarily for
self-protection, employing such crude weapons as lay at hand. The
discovery of bronze and iron, however, signalled the beginning of a
new and terrifying development by giving scope to man's inventiveness. For, after alluding to the fact that early man employed

these new metals for peaceful as well as warlike purposes, Lucretius moves into a description of man's use in battle of horses, elephants, bulls, lions, and boars. It is a passage which is regarded by many as the most troublesome in the entire poem. Some editors have sought to excise portions of it, and as judicious a commentator as Bailey finds it so disturbing that he wonders 'whether Jerome was not right, and that Lucretius' mind was from time to time deranged'.[91] What Lucretius describes is indeed startling, but we need not doubt that the lines are Lucretian. For what Lucretius is intent upon depicting is man possessed by a demonic lust for destruction. It is a madness which only Lucretius the poet can capture. If his verses seem to carry him beyond the limits of rational analysis into an insane world, it is a poetic insanity which mirrors the insanity of man himself as he is swept on by an uncontrollable passion for devising new means for procuring the annihilation of his own kind.[92]

It remains to note that there have been discoveries whose benefits Lucretius implicitly acknowledges. Man has improved his life in material ways through the introduction of new techniques in tilling, in planting, and in grafting fruit-trees, through the construction of the loom, through the establishment of laws, and through the building of roads. He has brought enjoyment to his leisure hours through the invention of music, dance, poetry, painting, and sculpture.[93] Yet, Lucretius insists, in certain of these areas too there have been unhealthy effects. In the case of clothing, for example, while primitive man was content with skins, now it is only the gold-embroidered cloak that will suffice. This Lucretius finds distressing because the demand for novelty fuels man's ambition and is a demand which can never be satisfied.

We concluded earlier that as far as human character is concerned Lucretius is conscious of a difference between primitive and modern man, and gives the advantage to the former. His account of man's development since primitive times suggests that he views man's decline in this regard not as a sudden and late phenomenon, but as a steady and cumulative process whose course can be plotted to some degree in terms of the successive discoveries and inventions which man has made. This does not mean, however, that Lucretius sees a simple cause and effect relationship, that he would condemn discovery and invention as being in themselves to blame for man's worsening moral state. Indeed, the reference to clothing to which we alluded contains an express indication that, if blame is to be

45

attached, it is to be attached in part, at least, to the nature of man himself: 'the fault, I think, lies more in us' (*quo magis in nobis, ut opinor, culpa residit*, l. 1425). Certainly, some editors, including Bailey, would tie this closely to the immediate context, taking 'us' to refer specifically to modern man. Others, however, accord the remark a more general reference – as in clothing, so in other things man has always been responsible for the anxiety and competition which accompanies the constant desire for novelty. This interpretation is certainly supported by what immediately precedes, namely, Lucretius' general observation that 'what is close at hand . . . delights the most and seems the best, until a better thing discovered later robs it of its place and changes our feelings towards all the old things' (ll. 1412–15). It is also supported by what immediately follows, namely, Lucretius' brief excursus on the limits of pleasure (ll. 1430–5). We would suggest then that Lucretius is noting the current craving for the latest fashions only as a manifestation of what has always been a weakness in man's nature, namely, a failure to distinguish between legitimate and illegitimate pleasures.

Now the question of the different types of pleasures is one that it will be instructive to pursue further. Epicurus' classification of pleasures is three-fold: those which are both natural and necessary; those which are natural but unnecessary; and those which are neither natural nor necessary.[94] As the scholion to *Principal Doctrines* 29 illustrates, the first class of pleasures are those which are produced by the simple removal of pain through the satisfaction of basic bodily needs, such as hunger, thirst, warmth, shelter. To deny these pleasures is to violate nature.[95] Pleasures of the second class do not depend upon the removal of pain and so are gratuitous rather than necessary. Further, since it is in the removal of pain that pleasure reaches its maximum limit, they cannot provide any increase;[96] they can only supply variation.[97] Hunger, for example, is removed through the plainest nourishment; rich food may vary the pleasure but in no way adds to its quantity. Moreover, while pleasures of the second class derive from natural impulses and may be harmless in themselves, they may be accompanied by painful effects which outweigh or nullify the enjoyment gained. Accordingly, what is required is a judicious calculation of pleasure and attendant pain so that indulgence is limited to those pleasures which can be enjoyed without destroying the equilibrium (εὐστάθεια) which the pure pleasures establish. Pleasures of the third class differ from the others in two respects: first, they are in no way natural, but require the fulfilment of desires which are prompted by 'empty imagination';[98] second, far from preserving the static pleasure which the satisfaction of primary desires affords, they are bound to disturb it, producing 'storms and blasts' which trouble body and mind alike.[99] Such, says the scholiast, are desires for crowns and statues.[100]

This threefold classification constitutes part only of the Epicurean theory of pleasure. Other aspects, in particular the dominant role of pleasure in determining the conduct of daily living, we reserve for separate consideration. But we have dwelt upon it at this point to suggest that it has a place alongside a theme which recurs throughout Lucretius' account of man's development, namely, the respective roles of nature, necessity, and human invention. This is a theme which Lucretius has good reason to stress. The primary purpose of Book V is to demonstrate that, just as the creation and operation of the world itself owe nothing to divine agency, so human society has evolved through various phases without divine intervention. Man's advance from a primitive state has been a response partly to certain instinctive desires and partly to the constraints of necessity. In certain particulars, such as the discovery of fire and metals, nature herself has given the lead. In others, such as cultivation, weaving, and the mechanical arts, man's native ingenuity has been the cause of improvements. In certain areas nature and human invention have combined forces. In the growth of language, for example, nature first provided a pattern of sounds, but it was man who recognized the utility of communication and his own inventive talents which enabled him to avoid confusion of speech by devising and imposing an accepted correspondence between words and objects. In certain areas it has been necessity which has played the dominant role. It was to avoid mutual destruction, for example, that men entered into a 'social contract'. There is no indication that Lucretius does not regard these and similar developments as improvements of the human condition.

However, Lucretius makes it clear that in some areas there have been developments whose effects have been for the worse, and that these developments have had a less legitimate base because they have been prompted by desires which exceed the limits of what is natural or necessary. Nothing, for example, has been more destructive of human happiness than man's desires for possessions beyond what are required for the preservation of life and the enjoyment of

47

natural comforts. The desire for honour and position has been similarly ruinous of man's happiness and security because it has been based upon a miscalculation or disregard of the troubles attendant upon their achievement. Man's domestication of animals has been a matter of necessity, but his desire to use them in warfare has represented an affront to nature. We would suggest, in short, that there exists this correspondence between the Epicurean classification of desires and Lucretius' analysis of the development of human society, that, where man has employed his inventive talents in adapting to his purposes the discoveries which nature herself has sanctioned, society has changed for the better, but, where man has been impelled by a desire for goals which lie beyond the limits of what is natural and necessary, the human condition has worsened.

Finally, to return to the primitivist–progressivist debate with which we began, we may make the following observations. That discovery and invention have brought about material improvements in man's condition is something which Lucretius would acknowledge. However, in terms of happiness and security of mind Lucretius clearly believes that man's desire for unnatural and unnecessary pleasures has prevented him from making a corresponding advance. To this extent, given that happiness and security are the primary goals of the Epicurean philosophy, we may conclude that in Lucretius' view human society is further removed now from a desirable state than it was in early times; in short, that the main thrust of Lucretius' account is anti-progressivist. However, to go further and suggest that Lucretius is altogether without hope for man's future would be to mistake his admittedly dejected tone for total resignation, and to deny him his faith in the Epicurean philosophy. For it is difficult to suppose that Lucretius' exposition of Epicurean teaching does not represent a firm belief in the power of its lessons to improve man's condition. We have suggested that for Lucretius not the least important of these lessons involves the proper understanding of the limits of pleasure. In this context we have not gone beyond mention of the Epicurean threefold classification. We must now undertake a more comprehensive review of the Epicurean theory of pleasure as a whole. It is a fact that the theory of pleasure was to become synonymous with the Epicurean philosophy itself. It is a fact too that no aspect of Epicurus' teaching was to be more misunderstood or more misrepresented.

'Pleasure is the beginning and end of the happy life.' Thus does Epicurus proclaim the cardinal principle upon which his entire theory of practical living is based.[101] We may consider first the basis of Epicurus' pronouncement, and begin by noting that in making pleasure the *summum bonum* Epicurus is not suggesting what ought to be man's goal, but observing what is a fact of human experience. For in his treatment of ethics no less than in his treatment of the physical world Epicurus is bound by the principles of his canonics. What is true is what is observed; and we observe that it is the first instinct of all living creatures to seek pleasure and avoid pain.[102] Moreover, the truth of the goodness of pleasure is not simply to be deduced from observation in others; it is as valid as any other item of our own immediate sensation. We noted in our treatment of Epicurean canonics that every sensation involves a readjustment of bodily atoms which results in an accompanying feeling (πάθος) of pleasure or pain, depending upon whether the atomic movement is agreeable or disagreeable. In this context pleasure and pain are to be regarded as criteria of truth alongside sensations themselves and general concepts, but in the functional sense that they identify which sense-experiences are welcome and which are not. Thus, it is the physiological status of pleasure as a concomitant of sensation which allows Epicurus to equate pleasure with good.[103] Accordingly, since there can be no dispute that good is a desirable end, he has no choice but to adopt pleasure as the primary and proper basis for action.

It is not the case, however, that, because every pleasure is good, all pleasures are equal. Some afford a greater degree of satisfaction than others. Being the most immediate, sensual pleasures are the most intense, and among these the pleasures of the stomach are the strongest.[104] And Epicurus does not hesitate to declare that 'he would have no means of knowing the good if he denied himself the pleasures of taste and sexual passion, hearing and sight'.[105] Now, if this were the whole of Epicurus' thinking, that is, if he viewed pleasure simply in terms of the momentary fulfilment of bodily desires, with the demands of the belly first in order, then Plutarch's charge that 'the Epicureans measure the amount of pleasures by describing a circle with the stomach at the centre' would not be unjust.[106] Nor would there be anything to distinguish Epicurus from Aristippus and the Cyrenaics, for whom pleasure consists solely in the immediate and fullest gratification of every bodily desire. In fact, this narrowly sensual view of pleasure falls so far short of representing Epicurus' position that it amounts to little less than a complete inversion of his true doctrine. For, while he admits that there is no pleasure which is not in itself good, he states firmly that, because certain pleasures are not without attendant pains, not all pleasures are to be chosen:

> Since pleasure is the primary good and is natural to us, for this reason we do not choose every pleasure, but sometimes pass up many whenever a greater discomfort may follow from them; likewise, we regard many pains as preferable to pleasures whenever we are likely to experience a greater pleasure through tolerating the pains over a long period. Therefore, while every pleasure is good by reason of its being by nature akin to us, not every pleasure is to be chosen; just as in the case of pains, while each one is an evil, not all are to be avoided. So we must make a judgment by weighing and considering both the advantages and disadvantages in every case.[107]

We are presented then with the general notion of a hedonistic calculus by which a proper choice of pleasures may be effected. But to understand more clearly the details of its application we must take account of the distinction which Epicurus makes between katastematic and kinetic pleasures, in which he clearly looks back to Aristotle's differentiation between pleasure 'at rest' (ἐν ἠρημίᾳ) and pleasure 'in motion' (ἐν κινήσει).[108] Diogenes Laertius introduces the distinction precisely in order to divorce Epicurus' views on pleasure from those of the Cyrenaics, and employs a citation from Epicurus' work *On Choice and Avoidance*: 'Freedom from disturbance (ἀταραξία) and absence of pain (ἀπονία) are pleasures defined in terms of a state or condition (καταστηματικαί), while delight (χαρὰ) and exultation (εὐφροσύνη) are regarded as active pleasures involving movement (κατὰ κίνησιν).'[109] Now, if we look to other Epicurean passages for an explanation of the relationship between these two kinds of pleasure, that is, between the static pleasure which is the enjoyment of complete absence of mental and bodily discomfort and those particular pleasures which presuppose the simultaneous experience of pain, we find confirmation of what is in the present passage only implied, namely, that it is the former kind of pleasure which represents the Epicurean goal: 'When we say that pleasure is the goal, we do not mean the pleasures of profligates and those which consist in sensual delights . . . but absence of bodily and mental disturbance.'[110]

If, then, the ultimate in pleasure consists of complete absence of pain, what role do momentary kinetic pleasures play? The answer lies in the fact that pain, in the form of a desire for something lacking, is natural and unavoidable, and its removal can be effected only through satisfying the desires which it calls forth. Thus, what makes kinetic pleasures legitimate is not the pleasurable experience which they afford as particular wants are being satisfied, even though this is real enough, but their role in making possible the static pleasure which obtains when the disturbance of particular desires is no longer felt.[111] Further, as we noted in the context of Epicurus' threefold classification, it is this role which determines the limits of kinetic pleasures. For, once the removal of pain has been accomplished, kinetic pleasures can do nothing to increase the static pleasure which supervenes. At most they can add variety.[112]

What Epicurean theory calls for, then, is not the random gratification of immediate desires which results in momentary enjoyment, but careful selection of pleasures based upon a calculation of attendant or consequent discomfort and designed to secure the true pleasure which consists in the complete absence of pain. The implications for daily living are clear. Certain activities will be engaged in sparingly, some avoided altogether, others promoted. The pleasures of eating and drinking and sexual intercourse, for example, will be indulged, but in moderation. Politics and other aspects of public life will be shunned as involving unwarranted mental stress. On the other hand, it will be of paramount importance to cultivate an intimate fellowship with others that will provide a secure and comfortable environment and one that holds the best promise of a fulfilling personal life.[113]

Important as it might be, however, for the external circumstances of life to be so arranged that they involve a minimum of physical discomfort and mental anxiety, the road to a truly happy life will lie open only when two particular misconceptions are overcome. One concerns the nature and activities of the gods, the other the meaning of death. For Epicurus is in no doubt that for the majority of men it is ignorance on the questions of religion and the human soul which constitutes the greatest obstacle to peace of mind. We shall consider religion first, and begin by noting that, contrary to the charge of Cicero and others, Epicurus was in no way intent upon discrediting religion as such.[114] It is the case, rather, that he regarded contemporary religious observance as based upon false beliefs which exercised an unhealthy influence upon men's minds, and was concerned to substitute a conception of the divine which would preserve human freedom by assigning to the gods their proper role in the universe.

Epicurus' concern embraced both popular belief and philosophical speculation. The citizen of the Hellenistic period was heir to a long tradition which placed success and failure in matters large and small in the power of supernatural agencies, whether these be the anthropomorphic deities of the Olympian pantheon or the various spirits and demons whose worship was a matter of local or family custom.[115] And the increasing popularity of foreign cults added a further dimension. One of the most humorous portraits in Theophrastus' *Characters*, the picture of the Superstitious Man who has scarcely a moment free from ritual observance, is certainly overdrawn, but it doubtless reveals symptoms which were real enough.[116] As Festugière comments:

> They [the masses] remained attached to their gods, and so imprisoned in fear and hope; in fear, because they always had to dread that by an omission, even involuntary, of some ritual observation they might have offended the divinity; in hope, because it was always possible to believe that . . . the heart of the gods might be touched.[117]

Prayers, sacrifices, purifications were clearly a regular part of the ordinary citizen's daily activity, and it was against this tyranny of superstition, rooted in a belief that the divine powers watch over the minutest details of human behaviour, that Epicurus reacted so strongly, convinced that it robbed man of his dignity and made him a cowering and abject creature, his fear unwarranted and his hope misplaced.

But it was not only for the generality of ordinary folk that Epicurus felt concern. Many of the educated minority, for whom belief in the effective power of the Olympians might no longer carry conviction, and who observed the simple acts of piety more perhaps through habit than serious attachment, were in their own way no less persuaded of the divine government of the world. For it was the message of the philosophical schools that the guarantee of cosmic order was to be sought in the divinity of the heavenly bodies.[118] In the *Timaeus* Plato points to the regular and unerring movement of the celestial bodies as evidence of their divinity and rationality, and in the *Laws* and *Epinomis* he makes it clear that, just as their own movements have the fixedness of necessity, so these astral gods regulate the affairs of men with a necessity no less absolute.[119] Aristotle is less explicit, but it is clear that he too regarded the heavenly bodies as rational and divine,[120] and it is fundamental to his system that all happenings are ultimately dependent upon his Supreme Being, the Unmoved Mover, which by acting upon the outermost sphere of the universe sets in train the orderly rotation of the stars around the earth.[121] Epicurus' response is predictable. A theology which seeks to impose divine beings which set human events on a course which is fixed and unswerving is for him as damaging to human happiness as a belief in gods whose will is arbitrary. With the latter, there is the possibility of hope, false though it may be, that the intentions of the gods might be swayed by prayer and sacrifice; with the former, there can be nothing but resignation. In the one case man is deceived, in the other he is totally enslaved.

How then did Epicurus himself conceive of the gods? For he did not dispute that gods exist. A concept of divine beings is common to all races of men and is based, Epicurus would argue, upon a clear vision of them.[122] In addition, as Cicero has Velleius argue, the Epicurean principle of *isonomia*, or equal distribution, demands that the number of mortals be balanced by a corresponding number of immortals.[123] Further, there is universal agreement as to their basic qualities: they are of human shape, perfectly happy, and immortal.[124] They must be of human shape because this is the only form in which they appear to us, there is no form more beautiful, and there is no other form which possesses reason.[125] Their happiness consists in complete freedom from pain and anxiety, and this because they dwell not in this or any other world, but in the interspaces between worlds (*intermundia*) –

> Where never creeps a cloud, or moves a wind,
> Nor ever falls the least white star of snow,
> Nor ever lowest roll of thunder moans,
> Nor sound of human sorrow mounts to mar
> Their everlasting calm![126]

As to their immortality, this is a condition of their structure, a question which clearly exercised the ingenuity of the Epicurean

school and which has caused considererable difficulty to commentators. First of all, the gods are physical beings composed of atoms
and void. But in what way do the bodies of the gods differ from other
compound structures? For if the gods are to be immortal their
composition must be in some way special, since it is the nature of
atomic compounds to suffer eventual dissolution.[127] Here we are
dependent upon a passage of Cicero's *De natura deorum* where
Velleius puts forward the Epicurean view that

> the power and nature of the gods is such that it is grasped not by
> the senses, but by the mind, and has no kind of solidity or
> numerical identity as do the objects which by reason of their
> firmness he [Epicurus] calls 'solids'; rather, it is grasped by means
> of identical images perceived as they pass through, since an
> infinite series of images exactly alike arises from innumerable
> atoms and flows towards the gods.[128]

This is a difficult passage and has been variously interpreted.[129]
What seems in general to be meant, and here we are heavily
indebted to Bailey's treatment, is first that the gods are distinguished from other material objects to the extent that, while their
form is perceived by means of atomic effluences emitted from their
bodies, as is the case with other objects, these effluences, as a
passage in Lucretius confirms,[130] are made up of atoms so subtle in
texture that they can be sensed only by the correspondingly subtle
atoms which constitute the human mind. Second, that the bodies of
the gods differ from other material objects in possessing formal
rather than substantial existence; that is, while other objects are
made up of atoms which join together to form a compound whose
material composition remains the same for as long as the compound
is preserved, we must imagine a god not as a persisting union of
atoms but as an atomic complex which is never for one instant
materially the same, but is being continuously replaced and renewed
by an endless stream of fresh atoms. In short, we may think, as
Bailey suggests, in terms of a waterfall, where the 'water composing
the fall is shifting from instant to instant, but the whole retains an
identity of form and by virtue of that identity remains the same
fall'.[131]

The gods, then, are to be imagined as immortal beings, possessing
human shape, self-sufficient, and enjoying a life of perfect tranquillity; undisturbed by the fear of death and untroubled by concern

over the human world; uninvolved in its operation and unaffected by its events. In short, these Epicurean gods enjoy and illustrate the blessed existence to which man himself, tutored in the principles of the Epicurean philosophy, is meant to aspire. It is for this reason that they are to be objects not of dread and suspicion but of admiration and gratitude. As for the form which expression of these feelings might take, Epicurus himself, by example and precept, encouraged regular participation in the traditional ceremonies and observances of the community.[132] For provided that such participation is accompanied by a conscious rejection of conventional belief and a proper understanding of the true nature of the divine, then the contemplation of the gods which it involves can be the source of the highest pleasure.[133]

We have stressed Epicurus' desire to free his contemporaries from fear arising from a false belief in divine control of human affairs. However, he was no less concerned to relieve them of the related fear that what awaited them after death was punishment at the hands of the gods for wrongdoings committed during life. And we need not doubt that he was combating a widespread belief. Pindar and Aeschylus provide evidence of such a belief in the fifth century, and we find references to *post mortem* punishments in the fourth-century orators.[134] Plato chastises those who make a living from peddling books of purifications,[135] even though the belief in a system of rewards and punishments after death is one which he himself perpetuates in more than one of his eschatological myths.[136] There is evidence too that punishments in the after-life were an appealing subject for painters of the Hellenistic period.[137] Now what such a belief presupposes is the continued existence of the human soul after death, and it is this assumption which Epicurus attacks: 'Death is nothing to us; for what is dissolved has no feeling; and what has no feeling is nothing to us.'[138]

What, in Epicurus' view, is the soul? We may begin with the definition which he gives in the *Letter to Herodotus*:

the soul is a body made up of fine particles and distributed throughout the whole structure, resembling most closely wind with some admixture of heat, in part similar to the one, in part similar to the other. There is a portion also which is composed of particles considerably finer even than these and which is for this reason even more capable of sharing feeling with the rest of the structure.[139]

The soul, then, is material in composition and is distinguished from other compound bodies by the extreme fineness of its constituent atoms. From the present passage these would seem to be of three kinds: those which approximate particles of wind, those which are like particles of heat, and those which are even more subtle in texture and to which no name is attached. It is clear, however, that Epicurus is here giving an abbreviated account, for other Epicurean sources agree in adding 'air' particles,[140] and in distinguishing between soul atoms which are mingled with body atoms throughout the body (*anima* is Lucretius' term) and pure soul atoms (*animus*) which remain set apart and unmixed and are the seat of thought and emotion.[141] Now Epicurus would not have been unaware that this view of the soul as a material substance was at variance with popular belief and particularly with the Platonic doctrine of soul as an immaterial existence. But in the *Letter to Herodotus* his only justification of his position involves no more than a rigid application of the basic principles of his physical theory: if the soul is incorporeal, it must be void; but void does not have the capacity to act or to be acted upon, in both of which, experience tells us, the soul has a part; therefore, the soul must be corporeal.[142]

We may now consider the function which Epicurus assigns to the soul thus constituted. In simplest terms the soul serves as the life-giving principle in the body by initiating and communicating sensation or feeling. This the soul is able to do by reason of the peculiar nature of its component atoms whose extraordinary fineness allows them to perform the appropriate sense-bearing movements. To understand the manner in which this comes about we must examine more closely the soul's atomic structure, for, while all its component atoms play a part, it is the 'unnamed' atoms which alone initiate the process. We have seen that in the *Letter to Herodotus* Epicurus distinguishes the 'unnamed' atoms from the other soul atoms in terms of their fineness and their greater capacity for sharing feeling with the rest of the body. Lucretius, working from a different Epicurean source, provides valuable elaboration.[143] Having explained that the atoms of which the soul is composed are exceptionally mobile because they are smooth, round, light, and exceedingly small, he argues that those which are akin to wind, heat, and air are still not tenuous enough to give rise to sense-bearing motions (*sensiferos motus*, III. 240). What are required are particles which are still corporeal but which are even further removed in fineness from the material of ordinary experience. It is the 'unnamed' atoms, or atoms of the 'fourth nature' (*quarta natura*, III. 241), which alone fulfil this requirement.[144]

Now what is meant by sense-bearing motions and the manner in which these arise and are communicated to the body may be summarized as follows. As we have noted, with the exception of those which form the *animus*, the soul atoms, including those of the fourth nature, are dispersed throughout the entire body. What occurs when something external impinges upon the body is that, if the impact is sufficiently strong, the soul atoms which lie closest to the body's surface at that particular spot are disturbed. However, because of their extraordinary mobility, it is the atoms of the fourth nature which are stirred first and experience the motion which is sensation (III. 246). This sensation they then communicate to the other soul atoms in order, first to those akin to heat, then wind, then air (III. 247–8). Finally, when the entire soul experiences the sensation, it communicates it to the body atoms with which it is mingled, again in order, the blood being the first to feel it, then the flesh, then the bones (III. 249–50). We can see, then, that both the soul and the body are dependent for sensation upon the sense-bearing motions of the atoms of the fourth nature, and it is for this reason that Lucretius says that the fourth nature is 'the soul of the soul' and 'lord of the whole body' (III. 279–81).

We have alluded more than once to the distinction between the *anima*, the soul atoms which are mingled throughout the body with body atoms, and the *animus*, those pure soul atoms which are localized in the area of the chest. As we have noted, it is a distinction which is not made in the *Letter to Herodotus*, but it is clearly a part of Epicurean doctrine, though we must be careful to note that it is one of function only and does not imply a physical or actual separation of the soul into two parts. So far we have concentrated upon the *anima* and identified its function as the seat of sensation or feeling. We must now consider briefly the role of the *animus*. Now, just as the atoms of the fourth nature, by reason of their unique role in the process of sensation, enjoy special distinction in relation to the other soul atoms, so the *animus* is accorded similar status in relation to the *anima* and the rest of the body. Indeed, Lucretius employs the same image when he calls the *animus* or the mind 'the head and master in the whole body'.[145] What qualifies the *animus* for its position of pre-eminence is the fact that it performs functions which are of a higher order than those performed by the *anima*, and this by reason of the fact that, while it is composed of the same four types of atoms as the rest of the soul, these atoms, separated as they are to a greater degree from contact with the grosser body atoms, are able to perform motions even more swift than those of the *anima*. One of the functions of the *animus* we have already alluded to in our review of Epicurean canonics, namely, its power to form general concepts (προλήψεις) or abstractions based upon sense-impressions stored away in the memory. We noted also that general concepts are used in the formation of judgments where the mind interprets particular sense-impressions by referring them to general concepts it has previously formed. This is the mind performing an act of comprehension (ἐπαίσθημα).[146]

The classification and interpretation of sense data, however, do not exhaust the operations of the mind. There are occasions when the mind 'perceives' directly without the intervention of the sense-organs. As we have already seen, sense-perception involves one of the sense-organs being touched by a series of images or idols (εἴδωλα) emanating from an object and forming a sense-impression (φαντασία). There are instances, however, when single images pass through the pores of the skin without disturbing the atoms on the body's surface and travel directly to the *animus* where they are peceived by an act of attention of the mind (ἐπιβολὴ τῆς διανοίας).[147] It is in this way, for example, that we are able to think of things even when we are unable to see them.[148] It is also the manner by which we gain mental concepts of Centaurs, Scyllas, and other strange creatures when stray idols of actually existing animals have accidentally combined to form a single image.[149] Or it may be a series of idols which have not combined to form a coherent pattern, such as the images seen in sleep or the visions experienced by madmen.[150] Further, there is the important instance of mind-perception which involves apprehension of the gods. Here it is not a case of single or unconnected idols; the gods give off a steady stream of images which properly reproduce their shapes. It is rather that the atoms from which these images are formed are so extraordinarily fine in texture that they escape contact with the sense-organs and penetrate directly to the *animus*.[151]

Finally, we must note the role which is assigned to the *animus* in the matter of action and will. Lucretius' account of the manner in which action or movement is initiated (and we are dependent upon

Lucretius for this aspect of Epicurean psychology) is straightforward enough.[152] Just as in the process of thought the *animus* is touched by images which have penetrated through the pores of the skin without arousing the atoms of the *anima*, so here in the same way the mind is presented with images of movement (*simulacra meandi*); at this point the mind decides whether or not to satisfy the desire which has been aroused (*inde voluntas fit*); if an affirmative decision is made the *animus* communicates this by arousing the atoms of the *anima*, which in turn stir the body atoms with which they are mingled until the body is set in motion. What we have, in short, is a chain reaction. Of greatest importance, however, is that this chain reaction is not wholly mechanical. Lucretius is insistent upon this both in the present passage in his repetition of the notion of 'will' (*volumus*, I. 878; *voluntas*, I. 883; *velit*, I. 886, 888), and more specifically in his discussion in Book II of the 'atomic swerve'.[153] There his principal concern is to argue that at undetermined times and places the atoms veer from their regular downward path through the void, and he adduces as support an observable fact of human experience, namely, that man is able, by exercising the volitional power of his mind, to control the movement of his body, even to the point of resisting the pressure of external force:

> You may see then that the beginning of movement takes its rise from the heart and proceeds first from the mind's will and is then transmitted through the entire body and limbs. This is quite different from when we move forward driven by a blow and under another's compulsion. For then it is clear that the entire mass of the body is seized and propelled against our wish until our will causes our limbs to resist. Do you not see then that although an external forces pushes many men forward, often forcing and sweeping them headlong against their wish, there is still something in the breast which is able to counter and resist?
>
> (II. 269–80)

Just as in nature, then, the chain of necessity is broken by the atomic swerve, so at the level of human behaviour provision is made for voluntary action by a corresponding deviation among the atoms of the *animus*. What is not so clear is whether we are to think in terms of a swerve accompanying every instance of voluntary action, or whether we are to suppose, as Furley argues, that a single swerve is sufficient to produce 'a break in the succession of causes, so that the source of an action cannot be traced back to something occurring before the birth of the agent'.[154] Whichever is the case, it is important to add that while the effect of the swerve is to ensure that a person's behaviour is not totally and inescapably determined by factors which lie beyond his control, the contribution of other factors is not wholly excluded. As internal factor is certainly the psychological disposition with which the person is born. As Lucretius explains, in atomic terms this is dependent upon the proportion in which the soul atoms are mixed in the *animus*.[155] A preponderence of atoms akin to 'heat', for example, will make a person naturally prone to anger. And we may assume that it is not only the mixture of soul atoms which is involved, but also their arrangement and motions. An external factor is the images which constantly impinge upon the atoms of the soul and produce reaction as they affect their arrangement and movement. In short, just as the pattern of the natural world is determined by the weight (*pondus*), blows (*plagae*), and swerve (*clinamen*) of the atoms, so in parallel fashion human behaviour is the combined result of three main atomic factors: natural disposition, external stimuli, and that element of free will which is represented by atomic deviation.[156]

We may now return to what prompted our discussion of the Epicurean concept of the soul, namely, Epicurus' concern to free man from the fear of death, and specifically his claim that the soul is mortal. Now we have alluded to the close connection which exists between the soul and the body. In sensation it is the action of the soul atoms, beginning with those of the fourth nature, upon the body atoms that causes the body to feel. Again, in will and action we have a similar chain of communication, this time initiated by the atoms of the *animus*. It is important to recognize, however, that because their extraordinarily fine nature prevents them from uniting in a self-preserving compound the soul atoms can perform the motions necessary for sensation and action only by reason of the fact that they are enclosed within the confines of the body. Thus the relationship between soul and body is one of mutual dependence:

> Moreover, you must recognize that the soul is the principal cause of sensation; yet it could not have acquired this prerogative if it were not in some way enclosed by the rest of the structure. Meanwhile, the rest of the structure, having afforded the soul this capacity, itself receives from the soul a share in it, though it does

not share all the powers which the soul possesses. So, when the soul is separated from the body, the body has no sensation . . . Moreover, when the whole structure is broken up, the soul is scattered, and no longer has the same powers, and does not move in the same way, so that it does not have sensation either.[157]

Epicurus is able to conclude, then, that far from being an event to be feared, either as robbing man of the pleasures of living or as a prelude to pain and punishment, death, if it is rightly understood as nothing more than the cessation of all feeling, is to be neither sought nor shunned, but accepted as the natural end:

Learn to accept that death is nothing to us. For all good and evil consists in feeling, and death is the cessation of feeling. Wherefore, a correct appreciation of the fact that death is nothing to us makes the mortal span of life enjoyable, not because it adds a whit to it in time, but because it takes away a desire for immortality. For there is nothing fearful in living for the man who has grasped firmly that there is nothing fearful in not living. So that he talks nonsense who says that he fears death not because it will cause pain when it comes, but because it pains in anticipation. For it is idle to feel pain in advance over something which causes no trouble when it comes. So death, the most horrifying of evils, is nothing to us, since, for the time that we are alive, it is not present, and, whenever it comes, we no longer exist. Therefore, death concerns neither the living nor the dead; for the former it does not exist, and the latter are no longer alive.[158]

3

THE INVASION OF ITALY

Italiam totam occupaverunt.
Cicero, *Tusculan Disputations* IV.7

When in 45 BC the Roman orator and statesman Cicero, his political
career over and his family life ruined, decided to devote his final
years to the composition of treatises on philosophy, he did so in the
belief that he would be rendering his countrymen valuable service
by instructing them in a subject which had been so much neglected
by Latin writers that its sole representatives were Amafinius and his
Epicurean followers, whose writings reportedly had so little to
recommend them that he himself could not be persuaded to read
them. Cicero had to acknowledge, however, that these Epicurean
tracts enjoyed astounding success, and it would appear that as the
Roman Republic drew to a close it was the Epicurean philosophy
which held the field in Italy. It is the purpose of this chapter to
examine the extent to which Epicureanism was indeed a vital force
in Roman society during the Republic, as well as under the Empire,
and we shall return to Cicero as an important witness. First,
however, we must give brief attention to the fortunes of the School at
Athens during the years following the death of Epicurus himself in
270 and to the spread of Epicurean teaching to centres outside
Greece proper.

We noted in the previous chapter that the years preceding the
establishment of the School at Athens in 306 BC were stormy ones for
Epicurus and his followers. At Mytilene in 311 BC Epicurus had met
with determined resistance from the first on the part of teachers
already resident, and, though his reception at Lampsacus in the

following year had been more encouraging due to the fact that he attracted the support of two leading citizens in Idomeneus and Leontius, he could not escape confrontation with the pupils of Eudoxus at neighbouring Cyzicus.[1] Epicurus had discovered, in short, that philosophical teaching was a competitive business. Nor were the years following the establishment of the School at Athens any less stormy. As we have seen, a steady activity at the School was publishing, and, while much of this was for the purpose of establishing and promulgating the fundamentals of Epicurean teaching, a good deal was called forth to answer attacks from rival schools. These attacks ranged from serious challenges on philosophical points to scurrilous attempts to malign the character of Epicurus and other members of the School, and attacks of this latter variety were to intensify after Epicurus' death, especially when Chrysippus assumed the headship of the Stoa in the latter part of the third century. More than this, the School had to contend with attack from within in the person of Timocrates, the brother of Metrodorus and one-time member of the Garden, whose malicious charges and innuendoes were to provide material for anti-Epicurean propaganda from the time of New Comedy onwards.[2]

That the School survived the early years is testimony to the loyalty and dedication which Epicurus inspired in his first followers. We have noted that during his lifetime Epicurus was the object of extraordinary devotion on the part of members of the Garden, and the large number of portraits of the Master, as well as of his closest associates Metrodorus and Hermarchus, executed at various periods in the School's history suggests that reverence of the School's founders was fostered to a greater extent than was the case with other major schools.[3] Indeed, it has been argued that the use of Epicurean images designed to convey both the personality of the Master and the philosophical message of the School played a prominent role in the recruitment of potential members.[4] The survival of the School also testifies to the ability of its spokesmen to give as good as they received in the cut and thrust of philosophical debate and personal invective. In addition, Epicurean teaching benefited from the start from effective presentation. The Epicurean system was relatively simple in outline, and a deliberate attempt was made to convey its essentials in the form of sayings both easy to memorize and convenient to transmit by word of mouth. Finally, there is the psychological attraction of the Garden itself, which offered a unique alternative community that was open to persons of every social standing, including women and slaves, a sheltered community where the stressful demands of the outside world might be laid aside for the enjoyment of friendship in the common pursuit of happiness and tranquillity.

We may speak of more, however, than the mere survival of the School. The very opposition which Epicureanism encountered among rival philosophies suggests in itself that, far from simply holding its own, it enjoyed considerable success in winning converts, and there is evidence that this was particularly so outside Greece proper. Certainly, the School at Athens continued to be the recognized centre of Epicurean activity, but after the third century the individual Epicureans mentioned in the sources are for the most part associated with centres in Asia Minor, Syria, and Egypt. After naming Hermarchus, Polystratus, Dionysius, and Basilides as Epicurus' first four successors at Athens, Diogenes Laertius introduces Apollodorus of Tyre, Zeno of Sidon, Diogenes of Tarsus, Ptolemy the White and Ptolemy the Black of Alexandria as among the most distinguished Epicurean spokesmen,[5] and we have the evidence of Cicero and others that Epicureanism flourished in these various places around the fringes of the Mediterranean world.[6] It is clear that of the four chief philosophical schools it was the Epicurean which approached almost missionary zeal in promoting the spread of its teachings, and it is not surprising that in the fast-growing and polyglot Eastern cities Epicureanism, with its emphasis upon community and its disregard for social distinctions, should have gained a strong foothold.

When we come to consider the introduction of Epicureanism into Italy we are presented with a more complex picture where factors which would seem favourable to the reception of Epicurean teaching are balanced by others which might be expected to prove a hindrance. It is certainly true, for example, that from the late third century onwards, when Rome's expansion brought her into closer contact with Greece and the East, the Romans proved quick to recognize foreign accomplishments and genuinely eager to assimilate foreign ideas. Lacking an intellectual and cultural tradition of their own, they were prepared to make good this deficiency by borrowing from the Greeks in particular. Thus it happened that Rome's earliest literature took the form of translations and adaptations of Greek epic, tragedy, and comedy. In education, Roman families began to abandon the time-worn tradition of home instruction and to look increasingly to Greek theorists and professional teachers to furnish training not only in rhetoric, grammar, politics, and science, but also in morals.[7] In religion, they were willing to give a place alongside their own spirits of the farm and the countryside to the anthropomorphic deities whom they discovered in Greek literature and art. Thus, despite the anti-Hellenic stance of such reactionaries as Cato the Censor in the middle of the second century, who saw in the new dependence upon Greece the certain erosion of traditional values, the Romans were receptive to Greek ideas, and the atmosphere was generally conducive to philosophical recruitment. Epicurean teachers, along with representatives of the other Greek schools, might be expected to enjoy some success.

However, if the anti-Hellenic movement represented by Cato was not strong enough to halt the general spread of Greek teaching, we must allow that it probably generated a greater degree of resistance to Epicurean ideas than to those of the other schools. For the traditional Roman values which Cato and others were striving to preserve – commitment to family life, active involvement in the affairs of the state, simple trust in the power and providence of the gods – were ones which Epicureanism would most seem to threaten. Indeed, there are clear enough indications of anti-Epicurean feeling. Two Greek Epicurean teachers, Alkios and Philiskos, were expelled from Rome in 173, and representatives of the Epicurean school were noticeably absent from the delegation of philosophers which the Athenians dispatched to Rome in 155.[8]

None the less, whatever initial obstacles Epicurean teachers may have encountered, the fact is that Epicureanism did not lag behind the other philosophies in gaining an Italian following. By the middle of the first century BC a flourishing Epicurean community had been established at Naples under the Greek teacher Siro, a community which was to claim the allegiance of the poet Virgil during his early years. At nearby Herculaneum the Syrian Epicurean, Philodemus of Gadara, was housed in the villa of his influential patron L. Calpurnius Piso Caesoninus, father-in-law of Julius Caesar, and was attracting a wide circle of students. Further, Epicureanism had distinguished itself from other Greek philosophies by having its own exponents in Latin – Amafinius, whose prose tracts enjoyed stunning success at Rome and in various Italian towns, and the poet

Lucretius, whose *De rerum natura* represents the most ambitious treatment of the philosophy of Epicurus since the founding of the School. Moreover, as Epicureanism took root in Italian soil it began to display its own distinctive characteristics and came to mean different things to different people. Whereas for many attachment to Epicureanism represented a serious philosophical commitment, for others it amounted to no more than a convenient cloak for a life of energetic pleasures in the parks and villas of Baiae or Puteoli. For some Epicureanism offered a welcome excuse for withdrawing from the public scene, for others it was to become a rallying-point for political action. And some of those who attached themselves to Siro and Philodemus were attracted not so much by the philosophical doctrines which these teachers were expounding as by the literary principles which they were helping to make fashionable.

At this stage in its development, then, Roman Epicureanism shows a varied face, and we shall be examining some of these aspects further in due course. First, however, there is the question of the relationship between the various Epicurean groups. Here the evidence allows us to go only so far. It is clear, however, that, if we are looking for the centre of most concentrated Epicurean activity, the Italian equivalent of the Athenian Garden, it is to be found in Siro's school at Naples. Precisely when Siro established an organized community at Naples we cannot be sure. Virgil's departure from Rome to Naples may be placed around 45 BC and it has been argued that Virgil left for Naples along with Siro himself and the rest of his pupils as a consequence of Caesar's laws against *luxuria* and the formation of new *collegia* in the city.[9] Of this, however, we cannot be certain. Indeed, we need not suppose that Siro was at any time formally resident in Rome. In fact, it is not unlikely that he settled first in Naples itself. Certainly, all of Cicero's references to Siro's group give it a Neapolitan location.[10] Moreover, as Tenney Frank rightly observes, 'Naples was the natural resort of all those Greek and Oriental rhetoricians and philosophers, historians, poets, actors, and artists who drifted Romeward from the crumbling courts of Alexandria, Antioch, and Pergamum.'[11]

In the absence of direct information we must assume that activity at Siro's school followed established Epicurean procedure and involved the formal instruction of pupils of varying levels of attainment in the general principles of Epicurean philosophy. What we cannot determine, however, is the extent to which the singularly successful efforts of Siro and his associates to enhance the appeal of their philosophy were balanced by an equal concern for the more technical aspects of Epicurean doctrine. In the case of Philodemus, for example, such scholarly interest is evident in the quantity of papyrus rolls recovered from Piso's villa at Herculaneum which are Philodemus' own compositions and which cover in detail an extremely wide range of Epicurean topics. This is not to suggest that Siro lacked Philodemus' philosophical depth. Cicero pronounced them both to be *doctissimus*.[12] Rather, it is to distinguish between their situations. To a large extent Siro's success at maintaining the school at Naples would depend upon his ability to attract a paying clientele. As house-philosopher of an extremely wealthy patron, Philodemus was freer to indulge his interests.

Of those who became members of Siro's *hortulus* the one who was to become the most illustrious was certainly the poet Virgil. He also seems to have been Siro's favourite pupil, for he inherited the villa when Siro died in 42 BC. We shall have more to say presently concerning Virgil's Neapolitan years. For the moment we may remark that the young Virgil was in many ways typical of the Neapolitan group, a group quite distinct from those numerous Epicureans whom Cicero characterizes as an undiscriminating crowd and whose teachers he dismisses as ignorant of style and so illiberal that they refuse to read anything beyond their own Latin texts.[13] We shall meet these Epicurean converts when we come to consider Amafinius and his fellow pamphleteers. Virgil's *contubernales* were of a different stamp. In the first place they were as comfortable in the Greek as in the Latin language, and part of the attraction of the 'garden', as of Naples itself, was that it provided a lively atmosphere in which to read and discuss the Greek authors. For it is clear that philosophical study was only part of the activity of the school and that the Neapolitan group escaped the charge which was traditionally levelled at Epicureans in general, namely, that they maintained a deliberate disregard for general learning.[14] What we may picture, in short, is a group of well-educated Romans who were bound together not only by an attachment to the Epicurean philosophy and a common enjoyment of the Epicurean life but also by a genuine love of the finest in both Greek and Roman culture. Moreover, in Virgil, L. Varius Rufus, Plotius Tucca, Quintilius Varus, Octavius Musa, Aemilius Macer, and possibly others we have an influential literary circle whose promotion of

Atticism earned for the school a strong role in the development of Latin poetry in the first century BC.

What has been said concerning the blend of philosophical and literary pursuits which characterized Siro's group at Naples applies in large measure to Philodemus and his circle at nearby Herculaneum. For Philodemus himself, despite his prolific activity as an Epicurean teacher and commentator, was perhaps as familiar to his contemporaries as a composer of Greek epigrams in the elegiac distich. Twenty-five of these epigrams survive in the *Anthologia Palatina* and the influence of Philodemus, especially through his treatment of the sympotic epigram and his handling of certain amatory motifs, may be seen in the poetry of Catullus, Horace, Tibullus, Propertius, and Martial.[15] Further, in his writings on literary theory, the Rhetorica and the Poetics, Philodemus provided critical support for the Atticist principles favoured by the poets of the Neapolitan group and ensured that the Epicurean position concerning utility and pleasure was given a strong voice in the contemporary debate on critical theory.

The nature and extent of Philodemus' philosophical activity were revealed by the recovery in 1752 from the remains of Calpurnius Piso's suburban villa outside Herculaneum of a large quantity of carbonized papyrus rolls which may reasonably be taken as the contents of Philodemus' library.[16] Some of this material consists of texts representing the teachings of the Stoic and other schools, and these Philodemus used for the systematic refutations of rival positions which form a regular component of his own works. The largest proportion, however, consists of Epicurean texts, and most of these are Philodemus' own compositions. These latter, which cover a wide range of Epicurean topics, reveal that Philodemus' grasp of Epicurean doctrine was secure and that he profited from the time he spent studying under Zeno, Phaedrus' predecessor as Head of the School at Athens. If in his manner of exposition Philodemus conceals the brilliance of which his epigrams show him capable, his treatises are generally precise and workman-like. There is little in them, however, which could be judged an original contribution to Epicurean doctrine, and Philodemus is to be regarded as essentially a transmitter of orthodox Epicurean teachings. None the less, it is clear that as a philosopher he commanded respect. He enjoyed the steady and generous patronage of Calpurnius Piso and by extension acquaintance with others at the highest levels of Roman society.

Lucretius, whether he knew Philodemus personally or not, made use of his treatises for the *De rerum natura*, as did Cicero for the *De finibus* and the *De natura deorum*.

As for the relationship between Philodemus and Siro's group we have remarked above that the views which Philodemus expressed in his works on literary theory would have found an appreciative audience among the Neapolitan poets. In fact, we can go further. For two papyrus fragments of Philodemus, one from *On Flattery*, the other from *On Wealth*, make it reasonably certain that, of the poets of Siro's group, L. Varius Rufus and Quintilius Varus, and possibly Virgil and Plotius Tucca, were directly associated with Philodemus as well.[17] Moreover, another papyrus fragment of Philodemus reveals that discussions between Philodemus and his fellow Epicureans at Naples extended also to philosophical matters.[18] Hence, while we cannot determine the extent to which the two former pupils of Zeno co-ordinated their efforts in promoting Epicurean teachings, it is clear that the groups at Naples and Herculaneum enjoyed an open exchange of views.

Siro and Philodemus were the principal Greek-speaking contributors to the spread of Epicureanism in Italy during the first century BC, and we have seen that together they were successful in gaining the attention and patronage of a number of well-educated Romans and Italians whose interest in the philosophy of Epicurus complemented their commitment to Greek learning in general. However, Cicero's remark in the *Tusculan Disputations* (*totam Italiam occupaverunt*, IV. 7) suggests that far greater success was enjoyed by Epicurean teachers who popularized the sayings of the Master not in Greek but in Latin, and whose audience was a good deal less sophisticated. These teachers we know, at least by name. They are C. Amafinius, Catius Insuber, and Rabirius, and we may with reasonable certainty place them as contemporaries of Siro, Philodemus, and Lucretius.[19] Cicero's opinion of them is low. Writing as an apologist for the New Academy he puts into the mouth of his friend Marcus Terentius Varro a scathing indictment of Amafinius and Rabirius for presuming to write on philosophical matters without troubling to observe the fundamental requirements of formal philosophical exposition.[20] In the *Tusculan Disputations* Cicero again criticizes their lack of precision,[21] and, in a letter to Cicero, Gaius Cassius, himself an Epicurean, speaks disparagingly of Amafinius, Catius, and the like as 'poor interpreters' of Epicurus' teachings.[22]

More difficult is the question of the audience to which Amafinius and his associates appealed with such evident success. Cicero is again of assistance. In his judgment the crowd which flocked to Amafinius' teaching did so either because it was presented with an absurdly simplified version of the Epicurean philosophy, or because it was enticed by the prospect of a life of pleasures, or because there was simply nothing else available.[23] If we add to this Varro's remark in the *Academica* to the effect that anyone with a genuine interest in acquiring philosophical knowledge went to the Greek teachers,[24] it becomes clear that in Cicero's view Amafinius' converts represented a class of Italians who were willing to settle for second best, either because they knew no Greek,[25] or because they shied away from the intellectual rigour which serious philosophical study demanded. In all of this, of course, we must set against Cicero's low estimate his own distaste for Epicurean teachings and his desire to be regarded himself as the premier expositor of Greek philosophical thought in Latin. None the less, we have to recognize that in the case of Amafinius' followers the sweeping success of Epicureanism was owed as much to the fact that it was attractively marketed at a time when the other schools were hardly represented in the Latin language as to a discriminating evaluation of its merits.

There remains Lucretius, and an immediate difficulty. In the case of Siro, Philodemus, and Amafinius the supply of biographical testimony is not generous, but it is sufficient to enable us to assign them their relative places in the context of current Epicurean activity. What is lacking, at least for Siro and Amafinius, is a record of their actual teachings. With Lucretius the situation is quite the reverse. The *De rerum natura* presents a complete record of his philosophical output. About the man himself, however, we have scarcely a word. To be sure, later sources allow us to place his date of birth at some point in the 90s BC and his death around 55 BC.[26] Moreover, there is sufficient indication in his poem of familiarity with the sights and sounds of Rome for us to assume with some confidence that he was resident there. However, Lucretius' contemporaries maintain an almost total silence. 'Live unnoticed' was certainly an Epicurean motto, but Lucretius cannot have taken it quite so seriously. In fact, we know that he did not. The *De rerum natura* is dedicated to one of the most prominent Romans of the day, Gaius Memmius, praetor in 58 BC and then governor of Bithynia. Lucretius' references to Memmius are formal and betray little in the way of personal attachment. But it can hardly be sustained that Lucretius did not know him, and if he knew Memmius he must have been acquainted with others of Memmius' social standing. Moreover, the one contemporary reference to Lucretius, in a letter from Cicero to his brother Quintus in Gaul, dated February 54 BC, reveals that the *De rerum natura*, or at least selections from it, was the subject of literary gossip.[27] Yet Lucretius the man goes almost unmentioned in his lifetime. How are we to explain it?

Perhaps the most extreme theory is that Lucretius' failure to receive mention is not at all accidental but the result of a deliberate conspiracy of silence. This is advanced by Benjamin Farrington as an element of his more general thesis that Roman Epicureanism of the first century BC was more than a quietist philosophy favoured by certain members of the governing class; it was also at another level a widespread popular movement supportive of an active political underground committed to undermining a state religion which served as 'an instrument of oligarchic suppression'.[28] It was this latter manifestation of Epicurean enthusiasm which called forth the spate of anti-Epicurean propaganda of which Cicero was the chief author; and the tactic which Cicero adopted was to place the Epicurean ideas which he attacked in his formal works in the mouths of politically harmless Epicureans like Velleius, while completely ignoring the populist Epicurean writers and thereby denying them any advantage which the compliment of a frontal attack might afford.[29] Hence, outside Cicero's private correspondence the very existence of Lucretius is unacknowledged.

This explanation of Cicero's silence concerning Lucretius depends upon two particular factors: whether or not Roman Epicureanism is to be seen as an essentially populist movement; this we shall consider when we come to examine the role of certain known Epicureans of the period in the political process; second, whether or not Lucretius' contemporaries would have viewed his outbursts against *religio* as sufficiently focused upon current practice and beliefs as to constitute a serious political challenge. Here Farrington's position is strongly stated: in Lucretius' eyes the Roman state of his own day was a deliberate purveyor of superstition, attempting to control the masses by exploiting their natural fears, and it was the chief purpose of Lucretius' attack to expose what amounted to a 'noble lie'.[30] However, the principal sources upon which Farrington draws for support, the historian Polybius and the satirist Lucian, cannot be said to be decisive witnesses. It is true enough that in a well-known passage (VI. 56) Polybius speaks plainly of the manipulation of the common people of Rome through the introduction and maintenance of an elaborate state religion. But Polybius' observation refers to the mid-second century BC or earlier and cannot be applied without reservation to Lucretius' period. Similarly, Lucian's picture, in *Alexander the False Prophet*, of ardent Epicureans unmasking the charlatan oracle-monger Alexander of Abonouteichos, even before we allow for satiric exaggeration, is drawn from the second century AD, when fascination with foreign cults and rituals had reached a level not experienced under the Republic. In short, while Farrington makes a strong case for Lucretius' sincerity, he fails to overturn what may be called the traditional view of Lucretius' attack upon *religio*, namely, that it is in large measure an anachronism, a brilliant and powerful flourish, but without pertinence to his own generation;[31] that while the Roman calendar might be punctuated by an almost bewildering succession of festivals and rituals, often to deities and spirits, such as Robigus, god of the red mildew, which could have had little meaning for an urban dweller, the citizen was scarcely paralysed, as his Athenian counterpart of Epicurus' day might well have been, by a constant dread of divine punishment. Cicero's remark that one *haruspex* found it hard to pass another on the street without smiling gives us some measure of the seriousness with which the state religion was regarded.[32]

For a more likely explanation of Cicero's silence concerning Lucretius and his poem we need look no further than professional rivalry. It was late in his life that Cicero turned to philosophical writing. He could claim distinction as an orator, and he had enjoyed an active public career. Yet he had failed to realize his ultimate political goals. Events had become too large, ambitions too strong; he had witnessed the weakening of the Republic, and had found himself powerless to prevent its collapse. The writing of philosophical essays was a compensation for political failure, as it was a solace for family distress. But Cicero had been too long a competitor not to see it also as a challenge, another sphere where he might emerge to head the field. And so he did, enriching the Roman intellectual tradition with the best of Greek thought and in a style which added distinction to Latin letters. Yet it is a clear fact that Cicero was not alone in writing philosophy in Latin. Amafinius and his colleagues we may perhaps dismiss. They would seem to have had no literary pretentions. But, by the time that Cicero proclaimed, in the *Tusculan Disputations*, that philosophy had lain neglected and Latin literature had thrown no light upon it, Lucretius' poem had been published for a decade.[33] It would be too charitable to think that Cicero was guilty merely of an oversight. The *De rerum natura* was known to him; he had commented privately upon its merits. The truth seems inescapable. In his formal treatises, which he composed with his eye as much on the future as on the present, Cicero was anxious to present himself as the sole representative of philosophy in Latin, even if this meant leaving out of account the one writer whose contribution to the Roman philosophical tradition was arguably as decisive as his own.

If Lucretius was the victim of a less-than-honest distribution of credit on Cicero's part, the claim which he makes on his own behalf is not entirely without difficulty. His boast is simple enough, namely, that he was the first to translate Epicurean doctrine into Latin.[34] However, if it is true, as we suggested above, that Amafinius, Catius, and Rabirius were active before the mid-point of the first century, then their Latin renderings of Epicurean teaching may well have been circulating while the *De rerum natura* was in preparation. Lucretius' failure to acknowledge their efforts requires explanation. The same is true of his silence regarding Philodemus, Siro, or any member of the Epicurean community in South Italy.

As far as Amafinius and his company are concerned, a passage in the *De rerum natura* may provide the clue.[35] Towards the end of Book I, following a review of various pre-Socratic cosmogonies, Lucretius pauses to explain that just as doctors who must administer a bitter medicine to children find it useful to smear the rim of the cup with honey, so he has chosen to employ the charms of poetry; for he recognizes that his subject-matter may seem unpalatable at first taste, so unpalatable, in fact, that the crowd shrinks back from it (*vulgus abhorret ab hac*, 945). This last remark is generally taken to imply that Epicureanism had no following in Italy until Lucretius himself undertook his mission, and Howe remarks that it is difficult to reconcile Lucretius' statement here 'with Cicero's account of the popularity of Epicureanism after Amafinius'.[36] There is no discrepancy, however, if Lucretius is here alluding to the fact that the crowd has already shown its distaste for the technical aspects of Epicurean teaching by flocking in large numbers to the simplified version of Epicureanism that had been popularized by Amafinius and his associates. Throughout the *De rerum natura* Lucretius shows himself to be uncompromising in his determination to take his audience through the most abstruse details of Epicurean doctrine. There can be no doubt that his estimation of Amafinius and his followers was of a kind with that of Cicero and Cassius.

The nature of Lucretius' relationship with Philodemus and the Naples group is more difficult to determine. That he was aware of their activities can be assumed, though there is no evidence from either side of personal acquaintance. It is true that the language of the South Italian community was Greek but, as we have seen, to many educated Romans this was as much an inducement as a hindrance. In any case, Lucretius' command of Greek was secure enough. Nor can it be that Lucretius was lacking in respect for the Epicureans in South Italy. Both Philodemus and Siro were highly regarded as Epicurean teachers. If Lucretius kept a distance from his fellow Epicureans it was for reasons which we cannot now know. However, there is one factor which it may not be out of place to consider, and which may account in part for the isolation which Lucretius would seem to have maintained. For the Epicureans around Naples, true as they were to the spirit of the Garden, Epicureanism was more than anything a way of life, a human experience to be enjoyed and shared with others. If such it was for Lucretius, the *De rerum natura* does not reveal it. There are passages, it is true, which mark the poet's deep feeling for his fellow human beings, passages which speak with eloquence and passion of the joys which a proper understanding of things will bring, when the mind is delivered from error and delusion concerning the gods, death, and the human soul. It is clear, however, that the joy which the Epicurean philosophy brought to Lucretius himself was above all the pure intellectual joy of the natural philosopher to whom have been revealed the workings of the physical world. *Felix qui potuit rerum cognoscere causas!* Virgil understood Lucretius well.

We have examined the relationship between the principal representatives of Epicurean teaching in Italy during the first half of the first century BC and we may conclude that one of the chief reasons for the popularity of Epicureanism during the period is that its appeal was not restricted to a single class. For those who wished to combine a serious interest in philosophy with the pursuit of Greek literary studies the schools of Siro and Philodemus provided a pleasant residential atmosphere in which the discipline of study was balanced by the relaxed enjoyment of Epicurean fellowship. Those whose education did not extend beyond the Latin language, or whose concern for Greek studies was less absorbing, could find in the Latin prose works of Amafinius and his colleagues a version of Epicureanism which may not have exhibited the rigour and polish to satisfy Cicero and others, but which was sufficiently attractive to enjoy wide popular appeal. Of Lucretius' audience we cannot speak with certainty. The *De rerum natura* is dedicated to a man of prominence in Roman political life and this may suggest that in the main Lucretius was directing his appeal to an influential group of highly placed Romans whose conversion to the Epicurean philosophy could be expected to have a powerful effect upon every level of Roman and Italian society. Whatever the case, Lucretius made a significant contribution to the Epicurean cause by making available to the Roman reader an account of Epicurean teaching which was at once comprehensive in scope, scholarly in aim, and elegant in presentation.

The individual Epicureans whom we have mentioned so far have been those whose interest in philosophy brought them into contact with one or other of the established Epicurean teachers. There are others, however, who make their appearance in a different context. They are known to us for the most part from Cicero's correspondence, and they bring us back to the question of the role of Epicureans in Roman political life. This is an issue of some importance. Orthodox Epicurean doctrine discouraged active involvement in political affairs. If certain Roman Epicureans felt free to take a different path, what was their motivation and how did they justify their decision? Further, to what extent did a common commitment to the School result in a shared political allegiance? The most thorough and convincing study of these questions is still that offered by Momigliano in his discussion of Farrington's *Science and Politics in the Ancient World*, and we are content to review his findings.[37]

Dismissing Farrington's notion of Epicureans engaged in 'secret political activity', Momigliano characterizes Epicurean political involvement as open and essentially aristocratic, and at the same time challenges the view that Epicurean sympathies were almost exclusively Caesarean. On both counts his evidence is strong. Against those Epicureans who supported Caesar, with varying degrees of enthusiasm, around 45 BC (L. Piso Caesoninus and

Philodemus (Cicero, *In Pisonem* 68ff.), C. Vibius Pansa (*Ad fam.* XV. 19) and A. Hirtius, consuls in 43 BC, P. Cornelius Dolabella, *consul suffectus* in 44 BC (*Ad fam.* VII. 33, 2), the jurist C. Trebatius Testa (*Ad fam.* VII. 12), P. Volumnius Eutrapelus (*Ad fam.* VII. 33), and C. Matius (*Ad fam.* XI. 28)) must be set others whose opposition to Caesar is confirmed (L. Manlius Torquatus, consul in 65 BC, Aulus Torquatus (?) (*Ad fam.* VI. 1–4), L. Papirius Paetus (*Ad fam.* IX. 20), M. Fadius Gallus (*Ad fam.* VII. 26; IX. 25), Trebianus (*Ad fam.* VI. II, 2), and Statilius (Plutarch, *Cato* 65, 4; 66, 3; and *Brutus* 12, 2)). Most revealing for Momigliano, however, is the way in which Epicureans declared themselves following the assassination of Caesar in 44 BC. For a good many (L. Varius Rufus, T. Pomponius Atticus, Valerius Messalla), including some who had been moderately pro-Caesar (Piso Caesoninus, Hirtius, Pansa, Trebatius Testa, Matius), declared themselves not against the liberators but against Antony and the triumvirs. Just as the tyrannicide Gaius Cassius himself had turned Epicurean in 46 BC 'not to enjoy the *hortulus*, but to reach quickly the conclusion that the tyrant had to be eliminated' (p.151), so now it was the prospect of a second tyrant in the person of Antony which enabled Epicureans to set aside traditional doctrine – μὴ πολιτεύεσθαι – and take a political stand.

One of Cicero's most persistent charges against the Epicurean philosophy was that it did a disservice to Rome by discouraging men of talent from making a proper contribution to the state. The charge is not without truth. In general Roman Epicureans followed the precepts of the School in leaving to others the stresses of political life. We have seen, however, that there were some who did pursue public careers which brought them office at the highest levels of government. Moreover, we cannot dismiss the fact that at a critical moment in the history of the Republic there were not a few who remembered that they were Romans first and Epicureans second.

Epicureanism has enjoyed remarkable success in Italy during the first part of the first century BC. Its Greek teachers have earned the respect and patronage of many of Rome's most cultured and influential citizens; Amafinius and his colleagues have succeeded in spreading its teachings throughout the peninsula; and in Lucretius it has produced a poet who must be ranked among the finest in the Latin language. We now witness a decline. For it is clear that the middle years of the century mark the high point in the fortunes of the

Epicurean philosophy. It does not cease to have followers, and it continues to exert an influence upon Roman thought and literature. But the feverish Epicurean activity which characterized the first part of the century is no longer in evidence. The reasons why Epicureanism failed to sustain the level of popularity which it had enjoyed are varied, but we may begin by recalling one of the factors which Cicero regarded as important to its early success, namely, that the Epicureans had been able to capitalize upon the absence of competition from the other Greek schools. For, due in no small measure to the philosophical activity of Cicero himself, the situation changed.

Cicero did not claim originality as a philosopher. He was content to be regarded as no more than a translator of Greek thought.[38] And his knowledge of the Greek systems was wide. At Rome, Athens, and Rhodes he had studied under, or at least heard, the Stoics Diodotus and Posidonius, the Epicureans Zeno and Phaedrus, and Philo and Antiochus of the New Academy,[39] and his treatises, almost all of them arranged in dialogue form, offered a generous survey of the Greek philosophical tradition. However, the effect of Cicero's works was not simply to broaden his contemporaries' philosophical perspective. Though he expressed surprise that anyone should seek to discover in his writings his own views on the questions under discussion,[40] it was no secret that he favoured the stance of the New Academy, which set greater store by examining alternatives than arriving at firm conclusions, and what influence he exerted upon the philosophical attitude of his contemporaries was in the direction of eclecticism and a less exclusive adherence to the tenets of any one school. Thus, indirectly Cicero dealt Epicureanism a double blow, first by publicizing the views of its principal rivals, and second by undermining the claims of all dogmatic systems.

A third blow was direct. In his presentation of the views of the different schools on various philosophical questions, Cicero maintained only a degree of impartiality. Favouring as he did the sceptical approach of the New Academy, his expressed objective was to come as close as possible to the truth by arguing *in utramque partem*,[41] and in the course of his writings he registered criticism of the views of both the Stoics and the Epicureans. However, it was the Epicurean philosophy which he most consistently and harshly chastised, to the extent that one respected commentator has remarked that 'Cicero despised Epicureanism sincerely, and one of his chief aims in undertaking his philosophical works was to stem the tide of its popularity in Italy'.[42] We need not go so far, but it must be remarked that he made effective, and not too scrupulous, use of the dialogue form to present the Epicurean viewpoint in the least favourable light. If we take the *De natura deorum* as an example, we may note first that the allocation of space is decidedly disproportionate. In Book I the Epicurean spokesman Velleius is allotted thirty-four sections compared with sixty-seven for the Academic Cotta, while in Books II and III the Stoic Balbus is given one hundred and sixty-four sections and Cotta eighty-eight for his reply. In total, the space accorded the Epicurean spokesman is approximately one-fifth of that which is given to his opponents. Second, there is a noticeable difference in the quality of the presentations put into the mouths of the Stoic and Epicurean representatives. The exposition of Stoic theology, for which Cicero drew heavily upon Posidonius, is well ordered, comprehensive, and rich in detail and illustration. Velleius' presentation is inexcusably poor. More than two-thirds is wasted upon a historical review and refutation of the views of other schools, and, in the brief portion which is devoted to the Epicurean view of the gods, what is offered is little more than an outline, and one in which the points stressed are the very ones which any opponent would find it most easy to attack. Cotta does attack them, and with obvious relish.

Epicureanism had more to face, however, than Cicero's negative stance. It is clear from the amount of space which Lucretius reserves for the refutation of Stoic views that towards the middle of the century the Stoic school was gaining strength in Italy. During the first part of the century the Stoics had offered the Epicureans little challenge, at least in terms of professional teachers. This is surprising for two reasons. First, it is the case that of the Greek schools it had generally been the Stoics who rivalled the Epicureans in recruiting converts in centres outside Greece. It is a significant fact that none of the known pupils of the school's founder, Zeno, was of Athenian birth, and it was not until Dardanus and Mnesarchus assumed joint Headship of the School in 109 BC that the position was held by a native Athenian. Second, the Stoic philosophy had enjoyed a favourable early start at Rome. In 155 BC Diogenes of Babylon, who had succeeded Zeno of Tarsus as Head, accompanied Carneades of the New Academy and Critolaus of the Peripatetic School to Rome on a diplomatic mission on behalf of the Athenians. All three philosophers were well received, but the reception given to Diogenes was particularly enthusiastic. However, it was Panaetius, Head from 129 BC, who made the strongest impression in Roman circles through his acquaintance with Scipio Aemilianus. It is not known how the two met, but in 140 BC Scipio took Panaetius to Alexandria as an adviser, and later at Rome Panaetius became a regular member of the influential Scipionic circle.

There is no doubt that through his association with Scipio and other Romans of position Panaetius did much to gain Stoicism a respectable following at Rome during the latter part of the second century, but for whatever reason it is not until the closing years of the Republic that Stoic teachers again make a presence in Italy. Cato the Younger, who was rigid in his commitment to Stoic principles to the degree that he was to be regarded by later Romans as the ideal Stoic, was patron to three Stoic teachers, Antipater of Tyre, Apollonides, and Athenodorus of Tarsus; Cicero adopted the Stoic teacher Diodotus as a member of his household; and the young Octavian, who was later to find a place for the Stoic Arius Didymus as court philosopher, was tutored by a second Athenodorus of Tarsus. We must not overstate the effect which these house-philosophers may have had upon the general popularity of the Stoic philosophy, but it is at least apparent that it was becoming increasingly fashionable for noble families to turn to Stoic preceptors for philosophical guidance, and given the nature of the Roman patron-client system it would be surprising if this acceptance of Stoicism did not filter down to the middle and lower classes.

Finally, there is Posidonius of Apamea. Posidonius studied under Panaetius at Athens during the closing years of the second century before taking up residence as a teacher at Rhodes. A man of wide interests and impressive learning, he travelled widely around the Mediterranean engaged in scientific researches, and first came to Rome in 87 BC on a diplomatic mission on behalf of the Rhodians. His reputation in Roman circles was high. Cicero studied under him at Rhodes in 78 BC and he found a particular admirer in Pompey the Great. He was a prolific writer and the extent to which later writers quote his works or cite him as an authority on a wide range of matters is evidence of a lasting respect. What is impossible to judge is the extent of his influence upon popular thought at Rome. It is important to note, however, that Panaetius and Posidonius together were responsible for changes in emphasis and tone which clearly distinguished the Middle from the Early Stoa and which can only have had the effect of making the Stoic philosophy more appealing to the ordinary person. For the philosophy of the Early Stoa must have seemed in certain respects a forbidding system. Much emphasis was placed upon epistemology and the finer points of dialectic, particularly under Chrysippus, and at the centre of Stoic ethical theory was the extreme exercise of reason. Little allowance was made for emotional and aesthetic sensibilities, and it was only the absolutely wise man who was considered capable of virtue. With the Middle Stoa this almost unapproachable standard was modified to accommodate the realities of practical living, and at the same time greater stress was placed upon those active virtues which were of importance to those who were engaged in political or military life. When there is added orthodox Stoic belief in the value of family life and involvement in civic affairs, as well as confidence in the possibility of progress through human ingenuity and the workings of divine providence, then it becomes apparent that the Stoicism which was competing with Epicureanism for the allegiance of Rome's citizens was not a dry school system, but a living philosophy that was relevant to contemporary needs and much in tune with traditional Roman values and beliefs.

We have considered two factors which contributed to the decline of Epicureanism from the middle of the first century BC onwards: the antagonism of Cicero and the emergence of Stoicism as an attractive alternative to Epicurean teaching. A third has to do with the changed political and social atmosphere following the collapse of the Republic. The first half of the century, when Epicureanism was enjoying its considerable success, was an eventful period for Rome. Beyond the borders of Italy, in North Africa, Spain, and Asia Minor, there were potentially serious disturbances which required attention, and closer to home the Social War, the slave revolt headed by Spartacus, the persistent problem of piracy, and the abortive conspiracy of Catiline added their demands. All these crises, however, proved to be within the capacity of Rome to handle without undue strain upon her resources. It is true also that in the careers of Marius and Sulla were present the early signs of a new kind of power politics which would eventually see more ambitious and less disciplined men engage in the open conflicts which would signal the end of Republican government. But, for the present, individual power struggles were more or less contained within the established political framework. In short, the first part of the century was a period when the demands of the state were not so pressing that a man could not with reasonable conscience commit himself to a philosophy and a style of living which gave low priority to active involvement in the business of the state.

However, the tense political struggles of the 50s, the civil strife which consumed the early years of the 40s, and the dramatic events of 44 BC and after made detachment from the world of affairs a luxury which the Roman citizen could no longer afford, and we have noted the prominent Epicureans who declared themselves politically active during this period. This does not mean that Epicureanism was abandoned wholesale. There were undoubtedly Epicureans who remained unaffected throughout, and the school at Naples maintained its activities even after the death of Siro in 42 BC. It is safe to say, however, that given the political turmoil and the accompanying social upheaval whole-hearted commitment to the Epicurean life was a course which fewer Romans found it easy to justify for themselves or for others.

Now it would be reasonable to think that the return of political stability following the victory of Octavian at Actium in 31 BC might have signalled an improvement in Epicurean prospects. For a quarter of a century Romans had lived with the unique savagery of civil strife. Now that the turmoil was over, a philosophy which preached friendship and the quiet life might be expected to exercise a powerful appeal. However, if there was a natural impulse to celebrate release from the daily strain of civil war by surrender to a life of total ease, it was tempered by the stern reality that within a single generation Roman society had been brought to the brink of dissolution, and that what had been lost had been not simply the lives of Roman citizens but much of what lay at the heart of Roman society. We do not suggest that the prevailing mood was one of sober dedication and commitment to the rebuilding of Rome's past. It would require the deliberate effort of Augustus and his ministers to foster and sustain such a spirit of national renewal. However, their success would indicate that they were not beginning *ex nihilo* and that the will to recover lay not far beneath the surface.

If we require an example of the new spirit and an illustration of its effect upon the fortunes of Epicureanism we need look no further than the poet Virgil. We have seen that throughout his early years Virgil was at home with his Epicurean friends. The Garden School at Naples offered him an atmosphere in which he could indulge his interest in Greek studies and exercise his poetic talent on subjects drawn from the Greek tradition. If his study of Epicurean doctrine was general rather than scholarly, he was in this respect no different from others of the Neapolitan group, and it does not lessen his firm attachment to the School. However, Virgil's Neapolitan years were not wholly untouched by events at large. As northern Italy felt the shock of proscriptions following the victory of Octavian and Antony at Philippi in 42 BC, Virgil learned of the loss of the family farm near Mantua, and there are clear indications in both the *Eclogues* and the *Georgics*, which he was writing at Naples, of his concern over the political and social upheavals which threatened to overwhelm the world outside the Garden. Two sections from the *Georgics* are particularly revealing. The first (III. 470–566) is Virgil's account of a plague which ravaged cattle and horses in the Alpine region of Noricum. Nowhere in Latin literature, except perhaps in Lucretius, do we find a more graphic description of disease and death, and it is made all the more pathetic because what Virgil depicts is not the random loss of stock through injury or age, but the sudden and wholesale devastation of proud creatures of the fields after a life of effort on man's behalf. The setting may be localized and the reference the animal world, but there can be no doubt that on a different plane it is all of Italy and her human inhabitants that occupy Virgil's mind. The second is the finely wrought story which brings the *Georgics* to a close (IV. 315–558). Again it is a tale of loss, this time of the bee-farmer's hive. But, if the earlier account of the plague at Noricum is a dispiriting reminder of the cruel power of nature to frustrate the best efforts of men, the experience of the bee-keeper Aristaeus, reinforced by the inner tale of Orpheus and Eurydice, offers hope in the depths of despair. Just as Aristaeus and Orpheus are given the chance to regain what they have lost by visiting the realms of the underworld, so Italy's moment of destruction and death may be the prelude to life recovered and prosperity regained.

In the *Georgics* we see Virgil at a point of transition. The Epicurean colouring of much of the poem is strong. But there are telling contrasts. The happy farmer enjoying without toil the fruits of the earth, free from the anxieties and stresses of the busy life, is matched by the weary labourer barely surviving a grim struggle with his grudging patch of soil. Virgil's depiction of Italy, its climes and landscapes, its trees and vines, its rivers and pastures, its animals large and small, has awakened in him more than a poet's delight. He has become acutely aware that Italy's promise is threatened by destructive impulses more powerful than the forces of nature. Up to this point in his life Virgil has taken no part in the struggles which have divided his compatriots. As he brings the *Georgics* to a close, Octavian's victory at Actium has secured a breathing-space. Now Virgil will act. If it means that he must abandon his Neapolitan haven it is a sacrifice which the future of his country demands. In the *Aeneid* his hero will make the same sacrifice as he leaves behind the alluring shores of North Africa to follow the path which duty has set before him. So now Virgil journeys northwards from Naples to Rome, there to devote his energy and talent to the promotion of a social and political programme in which there will be little room for the Epicurean ideals which have sustained the first half of his life. For as a spokesman for the Augustan regime Virgil will be called upon to advocate the subordination of individual will to national need, to promote the revival of traditional religious practice and belief, and to inspire faith in a divine providence which has determined for Rome a manifest destiny as ruler of nations. It would be wrong to suggest, of course, that Virgil is typical of the Romans of his generation, or that commitment to Augustus' programme of renewal meant automatic and total rejection of the Epicurean way. But it is a fact that Virgil was not alone among Augustan writers in seeking to set Rome upon the path to recovery by reminding her citizens of forgotten values, and despite the clear presence in Augustan literature of Epicurean themes the values which find most urgent expression are not Epicurean, but Stoic.

We have suggested certain political and social factors which, added to the growing appeal of Stoicism, may explain why Epicureanism failed to maintain the clear hold which it had upon Romans during the early and middle years of the first century BC. Beyond these particular factors, however, there is the more general consideration that by the time the century began to draw to a close Epicureanism had simply served its purpose. Introduced into Italy at a time when Romans were awakening to the attractiveness of Greek ideas, Epicureanism had been fortunate in having advocates, both Greek and Roman, who succeeded in presenting its teachings in ways which appealed to a wide segment of Roman and Italian society. The activity of Philodemus and Lucretius confirms that serious interest in the theoretical aspects of Epicureanism was not lacking. However, what attracted most was less the philosophical detail than the general message, the promise of a secure and tranquil life, free from anxiety over death and the power of the gods, a life given over to the enjoyment of comfortable pleasures and the cultivation of friendship. During the first half of the century Rome's circumstances were such that it was a promise which might be realized, and even during the years of bitter political turmoil which brought an end to the Republic the Epicurean life could still provide a comforting ideal. However, after the harsh reality of more than two decades of civil war a philosophic ideal, no matter how attractive, could not hope to compete with the immediate presence of a living saviour. For what Epicurus promised, another seemed to have delivered: *deus nobis haec otia fecit*. So declared the young Virgil while still at Naples; and the 'god' was not Epicurus, but Octavian.

We have counted among the factors which worked against Epicureanism during the years which followed the collapse of the Republic the growing strength of Stoicism, and it cannot be denied that by the beginning of the Augustan period the Stoic philosophy would seem to have gained the upper hand. Stoic ideas were clearly in tune with Augustus' programme of religious and moral reform, Stoic sentiments inform much of Augustan literature, and Stoic teachers were enjoying success at Rome, both in the city and at the court.[43] As we move into the imperial era it is still the Stoic philosophy which exerts the greater influence. The less austere and forbidding brand of Stoicism preached by such writers and teachers as Seneca, Musonius Rufus, Epictetus, and later Marcus Aurelius, stressing as it did the indifference of the true believer to the external circumstances of life, was well calculated to provide comfort and assurance to the ordinary citizen at a time when those circumstances were frequently difficult to bear. Moreover, those aristocratic families who felt deeply the loss of political liberty under a succession of repressive emperors found in Stoicism a useful philosophic foundation for opposition.[44]

It would be wrong to leave the impression, however, that Stoicism exercised an exclusive hold upon the Roman mind. In the first place, we must recognize that from the Augustan period onwards philosophy itself came to occupy a less commanding place in Roman life, and that strict adherence to one particular sect was less important than general acquaintance with the basic tenets of all the schools with a freedom to adopt whichever ideas most suited the mood or occasion. In education it was rhetoric which came to occupy the chief place. Philosophy was useful only to the extent that it could supply material for argumentation or display. Finally, all the philosophies found themselves having to compete for favour with the various eastern religions which were so successful in capturing the imagination of the Italian populace. In the worship of Mithras, Isis, Sarapis, Ma, and Cybele, as well as the Christian God, Romans discovered an excitement which was missing from the traditional Roman religion and which the philosophical systems could not match. In short, while Stoicism could rightly claim to be the dominant philosophy at Rome during the imperial period, it was a claim which had lost some significance.

Furthermore, Stoicism had not succeeded in ousting altogether its traditional rival. For there is varied and widespread evidence that Epicureanism continued to enjoy a following and to exert an influence throughout most of the imperial era, at Rome and in numerous centres outside Italy. As far as the parent School at Athens is concerned, it prospered for some considerable time. In AD 121, during the headship of Popillius Theotimus, it received favourable attention from the emperor Hadrian, who acted upon a petition of Plotina, widow of his predecessor Trajan, in approving a revision of the rules of succession to allow for non-Roman citizens to assume the headship.[45] Later in the century the emperor Marcus Aurelius showed the School equal favour with the Academy, the Lyceum, and the Porch by endowing a Chair in the amount of ten thousand drachmas.[46] And we have the testimony of Diogenes Laertius that the School remained open into the third century when the other schools had closed.[47]

Of the vigorous enthusiasm for Epicureanism in the Greek cities of Asia Minor during the first century AD we have sufficient evidence in the Acts of the Apostles and in the efforts of St Paul to warn the Christian communities of its dangers.[48] That this enthusiasm continued into the second century and beyond, and not only in the large centres, is made clear by a remarkable Greek inscription from the small and remote town of Oenoanda in Lycia (south-western Turkey) dated to around 200 AD. It is a lengthy summary of the basic tenets of the Epicurean creed which a local man of substance,

Diogenes Flavianus, had inscribed upon the walls of a colonnade near the market-square as a testimony to the comfort which he had derived from a lifelong devotion to the philosophy of the Garden and as an inspiration to his fellow citizens.[49] The original dimensions of the inscription cannot now be determined, since it was dismembered at the time when the colonnade was taken down and the blocks used for building material in scattered parts of the town. However, as new stones are discovered it seems clear that the inscription ran for more than fifty metres in length.[50]

As might be expected, the lengthiest sections of the inscription are devoted to a summary of Epicurean physics and ethics. In material which would appear to be introductory to these two sections Diogenes sets the stage by expressing his compassion for those of his contemporaries who find themselves trapped in the competitive world of politics and business as well as his deep faith in the power of philosophy, especially the study of nature, to bring tranquillity of mind and to conquer the fear of death. The surviving fragments from the physics affirm the possibility of knowing the external world, offer a rapid survey of pre-Socratic and Stoic views of matter, and touch briefly upon the Epicurean theory of atoms, astronomy, perception, the development of civilization, the Epicurean position on the existence of gods, and the futility of fearing death. These fragments represent a small portion only of the whole, but they are sufficient to reveal that Diogenes commanded a wide range of Epicurean texts and sources, and possessed an accurate understanding of Epicurean doctrine. So much is true also of the section on ethics, to which is appended, in the form of a continuous ribbon of text underneath, a selection of Epicurus' *Principal Doctrines*. The surviving fragments of this section focus in the main upon what is central to Epicurean ethical teaching, the theory of pleasure, and again Diogenes displays a firm grasp not only of Epicurean doctrine but also of the ethical views of the other Greek schools, especially those of the Stoics, who come in for a good deal of criticism.

The remainder of the inscription consists of a 'Letter to Antipater' on the innumerability of worlds, from which it is clear that the concept was a matter of vigorous debate between contemporary Epicureans and their opponents; a further selection of Epicurean maxims, whether from the pen of Epicurus himself or one of his early Ionian pupils;[51] some personal instructions regarding Diogenes' will and the setting up of the inscription; a 'Letter to Mother', which may well be from a collection of Epicurus' letters;[52] and, finally, a short treatise on 'Old age' in which the author, probably Diogenes himself, seeks to defend old age against the slanders which are commonly directed at it.

As an Epicurean document the Oenoanda inscription is of particular value, and it is to be regretted that so little of it has been recovered. It is not that Diogenes is a highly original thinker. Rather, he is a faithful recorder of traditional Epicurean teachings. But the fragments of the inscription which survive do provide a useful check upon other Epicurean sources, and they have the added distinction of providing some Epicurean arguments which are not found elsewhere, most notably in the introductory section, where Diogenes declares the Epicureans' concern for future generations, and in the ethics, where he acknowledges the common citizenship of mankind, and where he prophesies a new Golden Age to be brought about by the Epicurean philosophy.[53] Moreover, the frequency with which Diogenes either defends Epicurean positions against Stoic criticisms or argues the falsity of Stoic views confirms that the two schools were still engaged in bitter dispute. More than anything, however, the Oenoanda inscription is eloquent testimony to the power of the Epicurean philosophy to bring peace of mind to an ordinary citizen of the Empire and to inspire in him a burning enthusiasm to share with his fellow man the blessings of his faith.

We have remarked that at certain points Diogenes is clearly intent upon defending Epicureanism against Stoic attacks, and with respect to one particular aspect of Epicurean doctrine we are provided with an example of such attacks from the *De motu circulari corporum caelestium* of the Stoic philosopher Cleomedes which may reasonably be dated to the second century AD.[54] This work is in the nature of an elementary résumé of opinions on astronomy for the use of Cleomedes' pupils in their study of Stoic philosophy, and contains a lengthy section devoted to the Epicurean thesis that the size of the sun is exactly what it appears.[55] Cleomedes' treatment of this thesis is peremptory: the arguments which the Epicureans advance in its support are useless in themselves, ridiculous in their consequences, and easily repudiated by reference to a variety of phenomena; in short, they do nothing except expose Epicurean ignorance in matters of science. However, forthright as Cleomedes is in his dismissal of the Epicurean claim, his tone is moderate compared with the virulence which characterizes the more general remarks with which he brings the section to a close, a virulence which prompted Epicurus' seventeenth-century apologist, Gassendi, to single out Cleomedes as the most malicious of Epicurus' detractors.[56] Intellectual arrogance, lack of learning, obscenity, depravity – all the familiar calumnies are trotted out and capped with a final flourish in which the degenerate Epicurean is matched against the traditional Stoic hero:

> philosophy has banned you in disgrace. Take yourself off to Leontion and Philaenis and the rest of your courtesans, indulge in your 'sacred rituals' with Mindyrides and Sardanopolis and the rest of your troop. It is men like Hercules that philosophy demands, not effeminates and debauchers![57]

If the Oenoanda inscription and the work of Cleomedes provide us with clear proof that some five hundred years after the founding of the School the Epicureans and Stoics were still locked in lively doctrinal debate, we may look to another source for evidence that both Epicureans and Stoics were themselves the targets of attack on the part of supporters of the Academy. This source is Plutarch. As a writer Plutarch is not easy to classify. His *Parallel Lives* makes him best known as a biographer, but the *Lives* represents less than one-half of the extant works. The remainder, the *Moralia*, contains a number of strictly philosophical works, but is for the most part a diffuse collection of pieces on topics ranging over education, criticism, government, health, antiquities, prophecy, natural history, science, religion, and more. In short, Plutarch is essentially a tireless collector and recorder of information, from books, from travels, from conversations. A good deal of it is trivial, much of it is fascinating, some of it touches upon matters of deep seriousness; all of it is offered in the simple conviction that it will be of interest to anyone who is curious about human experience and achievement past and present.

Plutarch's philosophical works, then, form only part of a diverse and prodigious output. Yet there is no doubt that philosophy was a lifelong interest. Indeed, Plutarch's main occupation was as a teacher of philosophy, and as such he gained a considerable reputation, not only in his native Chaeronia, where he opened his school, but also at Rome and other centres in Italy, where he lectured to large audiences.[58] His own philosophical training had been under Ammonius at the Academy in Athens, and, while there were certain aspects of the Platonic philosophy with which he found himself out of sympathy, it was the Academy which claimed his allegiance throughout his life, and it was as an apologist for the Academy that he composed the polemical works directed against the Stoic and Epicurean schools. The Lamprias Catalogue lists eighteen such works, nine directed at the Epicureans, eight at the Stoics, and one at both.[59] The works which are of particular interest to us here are no. 81 – *Adversus Colotem* (Reply to Colotes), no. 82 – *Non posse suaviter vivi secundum Epicurum* (It is not possible to live pleasantly following Epicurus), and no. 178 – *An recte dictum sit latenter esse vivendum* (Is 'live unnoticed' a wise precept?).

The last of these is by far the briefest and we may consider it first. The injunction λάθε βιώσας, a warning not to seek security in active involvement in the world of affairs, was important enough to find a place among Epicurus' *Principal Doctrines*, and it remained central to Epicurean teaching on the happy life.[60] Lucretius opens Book III of his poem with praise of the joy to be derived from being an onlooker while others push for position, and elsewhere he speaks of the distress which accompanies the striving for wealth and power.[61] But, while retirement from the arena was an aspect of the Epicurean ideal which held appeal for some, it was a feature of Epicurean teaching which others were quick to condemn. We have argued that one of the reasons for the decline of Epicureanism during the closing years of the first century BC is to be found in the sharp contrast between the Epicurean preference for a life removed from the busy world and the Stoic concept of duty to the state, and it had been one of Cicero's most strenuous complaints that Epicureanism discouraged men of talent from exerting their energy in the service of the Republic. Μὴ πολιτεύεσθαι was a concept which ran counter to everything which Cicero believed worth while. Plutarch's reaction is on a different plane. Cicero's indictment stemmed from a genuine and practical concern for the welfare of the Roman state. He was issuing a challenge to Epicureans to assume along with others the responsibilities of government. Plutarch's context is academic, and his arguments essentially those of the philosopher, not the statesman. He charges Epicurus with being inconsistent on the grounds that in making his pronouncement Epicurus is himself striving for recognition as a philosopher. As for the obscure life itself, Plutarch argues that it is unproductive for society as a whole, paralysing for the individual, and contrary to human nature. Finally, the desire for obscurity can only be interpreted as a cover for the gratification of illicit desires. What we have, in short, is not so much an urgent denunciation of the Epicurean life of retirement as a studied declamation with all the marks of a school-exercise, complete with appropriate *exempla* and richly furnished with the requisite quotations from the philosophers and the poets.

The other two pieces, though more substantial, are of the same kind. The *Adversus Colotem* reproduces a lecture delivered by Plutarch, presumably in his own school at Chaeronia, and the *Non posse* represents the discussion which followed in the gymnasium nearby. Colotes became a pupil of Epicurus while the latter was teaching at Lampsacus between 310 and 306 BC. Whether Colotes accompanied Epicurus to Athens when he established the School there or stayed on at Lampsacus is not known. However, it is clear that he played a very active role in the vigorous pamphleteering which was so much a part of the rivalry between the various schools, and it would appear that his chosen target was Plato. He wrote replies to Plato's *Lysis* and *Euthydemus*, as well as a criticism of the Myth in Book X of the *Republic*.[62] The work of Colotes to which Plutarch's lecture is a reply was entitled *Conformity to the Teachings of Other Philosophers Makes Living Impossible*, and although Colotes did not mention him by name it was essentially an attack upon Arcesilaus, head of the Academy from 268 BC onwards, and may have been designed to win his students over to the Epicurean camp. However, by treating Arcesilaus as little more than a borrower of other people's opinions Colotes managed to include Democritus, Parmenides, Empedocles, Socrates, Melissus, Plato, Stilpon, and the Cyrenaics in his attack. The particular point on which Colotes focused was an epistemological one, namely the criterion, and his general contention was that the doubts which these philosophers expressed concerning the reliability of the senses or the reality of the phenomenal would itself make it impossible for their followers to deal with objects, and so to live. The details of Colotes' arguments, as Plutarch represents them, need not detain us. Nor need we rehearse the charges of misunderstanding and distortion which Plutarch brings against Colotes, or the arguments which he adduces in support of his own contention that the points which Colotes raises against other philosophers count most heavily against Epicurus himself. It is enough to remark that the debate is not unimpressive in the range of views examined and in the subtlety of the argumentation. At the same time, Plutarch's lecture is recognizably a display piece, and, if Colotes was less than honest in his presentation of the opinions he attacked, Plutarch's own desire to uphold the Academic cause leads him into a similar failing with respect to the Epicurean position.

As we have noted, the *Non posse* represents the discussion which followed Plutarch's lecture, and it is throughout a good deal more temperate in tone. The principals, Aristodemus and Theon, two members of the school, take up the theme of the lecture by contending that the Epicurean philosophy makes a pleasant life unattainable. The first half of the discussion (1087 D–1100 D) is set against the background of Plato's tripartite division of the soul and Aristotle's three types of lives. Compared with the intellectual pleasures to be derived from the activities of the mind and with the pleasures afforded by the active or political life, the bodily pleasures which the Epicureans set as their goal contribute nothing to the good life. They are unstable, insubstantial, and of short duration compared with the pain which is attendant upon them, and they reflect the lowest aspirations of human nature. As far as the mental pleasure which the Epicureans claim to derive from the anticipation or recollection of physical pleasures, this is even less satisfying than the physical pleasures themselves. The second half of the discussion (1100 E – 1107 C) turns away from the Epicurean theory of pleasure as such to establish the failure of the Epicurean philosophy to provide what Epicurus himself considered a prerequisite for attaining a pleasant life, namely, a right opinion concerning the gods and the after-life. By denying the gods a role in human affairs in an effort to eradicate superstition, the Epicureans have succeeded in depriving all men of the pleasures and benefits which true religious belief can afford. Upright men are denied the expectation of rewards, and wrongdoers are left without the restraining influence which comes from the certainty of retribution. So, with respect to the after-life, by making the soul mortal and death the end of everything the Epicureans deprive their fellow men of the joy which comes from the prospect of a better existence ahead, while they remove from the upright and the wicked alike the healthy fear of punishment after death. In summary, the Epicurean philosophy, far from fulfilling its promise of a happy life, offers nothing more than counterfeit pleasures which are momentary at best, and in the place of a sustaining hope for a better life to come the dismal certainty of annihilation.

We have introduced Diogenes of Oenoanda, Cleomedes, and Plutarch as witnesses to the fact that during the second century AD Epicureanism was still influential enough to provoke lively response from representatives of the other philosophies. Diogenes and Cleomedes, the one indirectly, the other directly, confirm a continuing rivalry with the Stoics, and the very vigour of Plutarch's criticisms, even allowing for obvious rhetorical flourish, reveals a depth of feeling in the Academic camp. It is the case, however, that opposition to Epicureanism did not come exclusively from the other philosophical schools. In the next chapter we shall be examining the reaction to Epicurean teaching on the part of some of the early Christian writers and we shall discover that much of that reaction is hostile in the extreme. We may bring this chapter to a conclusion, however, with mention of an opponent who was neither a philosopher nor a Christian, and a bizarre affair which takes us into the colourful world of the mystics, astrologers, diviners, and fortune-tellers who plied a busy trade around the Graeco-Roman world.

The affair has to do with the extraordinary career of the Paphlagonian oracle-seller Alexander, who established himself as priest of a new shrine of Asclepius in his native Abonoteichos about the middle of the second century and achieved such a startling success that his reputation spread throughout the Empire, even to Rome itself. Our sole literary source for Alexander's activities is the account which the satirist Lucian gives in *Alexander the False Prophet* of his own campaign against what he regarded as a blatant and outrageous case of systematic fraud. The account is colourful indeed: the prophet Alexander himself, complete with wig and gilded thigh; the sacred serpent Glycon, the 'latter-day Asclepius', ingeniously fitted with a human head and a bogus mouthpiece worked by strings; hidden speaking-tubes for autophones; sealed scrolls secretly opened with hot needles; crooked oracles; fake nostrums; divining through dreams and the shaking of sieves; cursings and stonings of Epicurean enquirers; burnings of Epicurean books; [63] finally, the attempted murder of Lucian himself. It is a fascinating story brilliantly told in Lucian's usual sparkling style. How much of it is accurate reporting, however, is a difficult question.[64] Certainly, we must allow for the licence of Lucian the satirist. Furthermore, for a number of details there are literary parallels upon which Lucian may well have drawn, in particular the fourth book of Hippolytus' *Refutation of All Heresies* and Oenomaus' *Detection of Impostors*. Moreover, we must acknowledge the conventional nature of much of the invective which Lucian employs against his opponent. None the less, while it may contain a substantial amount of embroidery and invention there is no doubting that in broad outline the *Alexander* is factual. In particular, there is no need to question the animus which Alexander felt towards the Epicurean pupils of Timocrates of Heraclea, led by Lepidus of Amastris, who visited the shrine, or the sincerity of Lucian's praise for their attempts to expose the prophet as a fraud. The *Alexander* is not the only work in which Lucian inveighs against charlatans and impostors, and his attitude is constant enough to allow us to see him as a sincere opponent of the many superstitious beliefs and practices of his age.[65] It is not surprising, then, that Lucian would welcome as allies the followers of that philosophy which distinguished itself through its opposition to superstition in all its forms. Thus, when Lucian tells his Epicurean friend Celsus, for whom the *Alexander* was written, that his primary aim has been 'to strike a blow for Epicurus, that illustrious man whose holiness was not an imposture, who alone had insight into the good', we may take it as a commendation sincerely felt.

We are not permitted to conclude, however, on quite so positive a note. For it would be wrong to leave the impression that in Lucian Epicureanism found a constant supporter. To the contrary, the attitude which Lucian displays in other places is for the most part unenthusiastic and consistent with his depreciation of philosophy in general.[66] For it is the case that despite one or two remarks favourable to philosophic study, notably in the *Piscator* and the *Hermotimus*, and his admiration for particular philosopher friends, such as the Platonist Nigrinus and the Cynic Demonax, Lucian reserves some of his liveliest satire for the philosophic sects, making full use of both the literary tradition and his own personal observation. Peripatetics, Sceptics, Academics, Stoics, Cynics, Neo-Pythagoreans all provide him with abundant material for satiric humour as well as serious criticism, and the Epicureans are no exception. If in the *Alexander* Lucian is willing to praise the Epicureans it is not through any deep sympathy for the Epicurean philosophy itself, but because they happen to share his own negative stance against superstition. In the same way he can be fiercely critical throughout his works of the Sceptics and the Cynics, yet commend them both for their opposition to the dogmatists.[67]

4

THE CHRISTIAN REACTION

We have seen that at the beginning of the third century AD, some five centuries after the death of its founder, Epicureanism was still alive both in major centres and in remoter parts of the Graeco-Roman world. It is generally held, however, that its demise lay not far off, that by the middle of the fourth century it would have become a virtually forgotten creed, overwhelmed, along with Stoicism, by the spread of Christianity, fully justifying St Augustine's boast that 'its ashes are so cold that not a single spark can be struck from them'.[1] Now there is no denying that the spread of Christianity brought about a transformation in the life of cities and towns throughout the Roman Empire. It would be wrong to suppose, however, that this transformation was either immediate or total. As rapid as the growth of Christian communities was, especially in urban centres, at the beginning of the fourth century the proportion of the Empire's population that could be counted as Christian was probably less than one-tenth.[2] And, though the conversion of Constantine in 312 and the Edict of Milan of the following year marked the beginning of conversion on an altogether more massive scale, Christians still accounted for less than half the population of the Empire at the end of the fourth century.[3] Meanwhile, there is ample evidence of the tenacity with which non-Christians clung to cult and religious practices which offered comforts and assurances which the Church was not equipped or did not pretend to match.[4]

Moreover, the intellectual and cultural life of the Empire was too deeply rooted in the Hellenic tradition to be quickly transformed. Indeed, we see that tradition receive a fresh burst of energy with the flowering of the Second Sophistic, its galaxy of virtuoso performers and brilliant teachers so vividly portrayed in Philostratus' *Lives of the Sophists*.[5] It is true that the high point of the movement had been reached by the end of the second century, but the Greek rhetorical tradition which had provided the context for this brilliant flourish continued to exert a strong influence, particularly upon higher education, as training in rhetoric remained a prerequisite for a career in law or in the imperial service. Philosophy as well held on to its place in the curriculum alongside rhetoric and the reading of the major classical Greek authors. Moreover, philosophy continued to flourish outside the schoolroom. While few would claim that the third and fourth centuries AD represent the richest period in the Greek philosophical tradition, there is no denying that in Plotinus, Porphyry, and Iamblichus we have figures who are by no means negligible and whose reworking of the Platonic tradition had a profound effect upon the development of Christian and medieval thought. We must recognize, of course, that this was a period of syncretism in philosophy, as in religion, and distinctions between the schools were becoming a little less sharply drawn. At the same time, it is important to note that of all the philosophies Epicureanism was perhaps the least included in the syncretistic process.[6] Throughout the history of the School Epicurean spokesmen had preserved substantially unchanged the fundamental teachings of the founder.[7] Finally, we need not suppose that the tendency towards syncretism meant the end of philosophic rivalry and that representatives of the various schools no longer competed for followers. The competition may not have been as intense as in the past, but we may reasonably assume that in the major centres, at least, there were still those who kept the teachings of the individual schools alive through instruction and debate.

Now we noted above that in 410 St Augustine proclaimed just the reverse, that both Epicureanism and Stoicism were so far neglected that they posed no threat whatsoever to the Christian faith. We have offered some general considerations to support the view that, in fact, philosophy maintained a lively existence as part of the continuing vigour of Greek culture during the early Christian centuries. And in the case of Epicureanism, and the same holds true for the other schools, we have specific and recurring evidence that Augustine was guilty of overstatement at the very least. This comes in the writings of the Church Fathers, almost all of whom mention Epicurus or some aspect of his teaching, and in a manner which confirms that,

far from being dismissed as a forgotten creed, Epicureanism commanded close attention.

Now we might expect the Christian reaction to Epicureanism to
be universally hostile, though not simply because it was a pagan
philosophy. It is true that for some Christian writers Tertullian's
'*quid ergo Athenis et Hierosolymis?*' evoked only one answer: all of Greek
philosophy was to be dismissed either as an irrelevance or as
perniciously inspired by the devil to be the seed of the various
heresies which threatened the unity of the Church. For the majority,
however, many of whom were converts from one or other of the
Greek schools, the answer could not be so categorical, and for
various reasons. Some were encouraged by a genuine belief that
Greek philosophy represented a positive, if partial, contribution to
truth to work towards a synthesis of Greek and Christian thought, or
at least a Christianization of the Hellenic tradition. Others, recog-
nizing that they were called upon to promote and defend the gospel
in an age which demanded a degree of intellectual sophistication,
saw in Greek philosophy, used with discretion, a useful, perhaps
indispensable, ally. If Greek rationalism could enhance the appeal of
gnosticism, it would serve as well in the cause of true Christian
teaching. However, while Christian writers might find ways to
accommodate and utilize certain aspects of the metaphysics of Plato
and Aristotle or the ethical teachings of the Stoics, Epicureanism
was a different matter. After all, a philosophy which postulated a
wholly material and mechanistic universe shaped without divine
participation, which denied the gods a providential role in the affairs
of mankind, which preached the mortality of the soul and the finality
of death, and which looked to pleasure as the first and ultimate goal
of human existence would seem to stand at variance with the very
fundamentals of Christian teaching. And it is true that none of these
tenets escaped criticism. At the same time, there are certain aspects
of the Epicurean philosophy which drew more favourable, if not
enthusiastic, comment. It is this ambivalence which we shall
attempt to articulate, an ambivalence which is owed in part to the
still emerging state of Christian thinking and in part to ambiguities
inherent in Epicureanism itself.

Rather than attempt to offer an exhaustive catalogue of all the
references to Epicurus and his teachings which appear in the
patristic literature, we shall do better to focus upon a number which
reflect certain representative and significant features of the patristic

attitude.[8] We may begin with a feature which is certainly characteristic and, as we have suggested, altogether natural, namely, the
almost wholesale rejection of Epicurean theology. Here, over and
above a general confusion as to Epicurus' true opinion concerning
the existence of the gods, we meet with keen criticism of a number of
aspects of conventional Epicurean doctrine concerning the nature of
the gods and their attributes. Aristides, Origen, and Augustine
attack the notion that the gods are endowed with human form.[9]
Theophilus, Lactantius, and Tertullian reject the view that the gods
are never touched by anger.[10] Tertullian, Eusebius, and Basil echo
Epicurus' non-Christian opponents in ridiculing the concept of gods
whose sole occupation lies in the enjoyment of pleasure.[11]

All of these criticisms, however, are relatively minor compared
with the outcry raised against the Epicurean denial of divine
providence. Christian writers were not the first, of course, to take
issue with Epicurus on the question of providence. As Book I of
Cicero's *De natura deorum* illustrates, it had long been an area of
fundamental disagreement between Epicureans and the Stoics, for
whom Providence served along with Spirit, Reason, Destiny, Law,
and Fire as a name for the creative and ruling principle of the
universe. Moreover, Plutarch's *Adversus Colotem* and *Non posse* serve
as evidence that the Stoics were not alone in opposing the Epicurean
view.[12] Accordingly, given the protracted history of the debate, it is
not surprising if the arguments adduced by the Fathers have a
familiar ring. Indeed, they well illustrate the fact that patristic
apologetic in general relied far more heavily upon arguments
supplied by the philosophical schools than upon purely theological
arguments drawn from the Scriptures, and on this particular issue it
was the Stoic position which the Christian writers found the most
useful and the most congenial.[13] So, from Athenagoras in the second
century to Augustine in the fifth, we find repeated the familiar
appeal to design as proof of the hand of an intelligent creator and
controller of the universe as against the random union and configurations of atoms posited by the Epicureans.[14] Traditional too are
the repeated declarations that divine providence extends also to the
daily condition of man despite the presence in the world of seeming
injustices, the existence of harmful animals and poisonous plants,
and the apparent weakness of man in comparison with the animal
kingdom.[15] In short, we look in vain for anything more than slight
variations on a well-worn theme. However, this lack of inventiveness

in no way diminishes the importance which the question of providence assumed for the Christian writers or the strength of their
opposition to the Epicurean view. After all, what was at issue was
not something on the fringes of Christian doctrine or merely
incidental to the Christian life. The denial of divine providence
struck at the very heart of the Christian message, the proclamation
of man as the special object of the love of God.

Given that God's love of man was seen to culminate in the
Incarnation and in the prospect of redemption and eternal salvation,
it is to be expected that Christian writers should pay close attention
as well to Epicurus' views concerning the soul and that their
reaction should be negative. This is not to suggest that the Fathers
themselves came anywhere close to agreement as to the nature of the
soul or its destiny. The soul's origin, its relation to the body and to
the mind, whether it is corporeal or incorporeal, rational or irrational, corrupt or incorrupt, its location, its functions, whether it is
mortal or immortal, these were questions which provoked lively
debate, subtle argument, and deep controversy. What is to be noted,
however, is that, while the Christian writers relied heavily upon the
Greek philosophical tradition in their examination of these and
related questions, and the influence of Plato, Aristotle, the Stoics,
and the Neoplatonists is marked, even if certain aspects of their
theories did not escape censure, the Epicurean view of the soul is
singled out for unanimous rejection. It is not simply that Epicurus
held the soul to be corporeal in nature. Tertullian, for example, for
whom the soul must be in some sense corporeal if it is to experience
the penal sentences of the final judgment, expressly calls upon
Epicurus, along with the Stoics and the writers of the Gospels, to
support his view.[16] What presents the greater difficulty is the
Epicurean view that the soul is an agglomeration of atomic particles
with the necessary corollary that being composed of parts it is
subject to dissolution. To refer again to Tertullian, he insists that
since the soul is immortal it must be simple or uniform in structure,
and he goes out of his way to list those Greek thinkers who have
rightly maintained the material unity of the soul even while dividing
it into parts.[17] In the context it does not serve his purpose to mention
the contrary case of Epicurus, but elsewhere he does relate the
mortality of the Epicurean soul to its atomic composition.[18]

What was decisive for Christian writers, then, was Epicurus'
insistence that the soul is mortal, that it is dissolved as completely as

the body upon death. Their concern is not difficult to appreciate. The Christian certainly lived in this world, but he regarded his temporal life not as the sum total of his existence but as a preparation for a life to come that would endure for all eternity. The conditions of this future existence might be unknown to him: the terrors of hell were his haunting dread, the vision of paradise his sustaining hope. But of some sort of personal survival he was certain. Death was not an end, but a beginning. The notion that beyond death there was a total nothingness was not a philosophical quibble: it was a negation of God's purpose, a denial of man's special place among God's creatures.[19] Hence, in addition to frequent conventional denials of the soul's mortality, we find more than one of the Fathers undertaking a more detailed refutation of the principal Epicurean arguments. In the *De anima*, an anti-heretical treatise written during the early years of the third century, Tertullian focuses upon two of them. The first is that cases of gradual paralysis, where the person loses sensation limb by limb, can be taken as evidence that the soul is divided and leaves the body little by little, and so as proof that it is mortal. This argument is reproduced in Lucretius, though we cannot be sure that Tertullian had the passage directly in mind since he offers as his response the very answer which Lucretius anticipates and rejects, namely, that the affected parts lose their sensation because the soul has voluntarily withdrawn to another place.[20] The second, which is again found in Lucretius, is that sleep is proof of the soul's mortality, for the following reason: sleep is nothing other than the cessation of sensation resulting from the expulsion of a certain number of soul atoms from the body; the recovery of sensation is possible only because some soul atoms remain; since at death the loss of soul atoms from the body is total, further sensation is an impossibility. Tertullian responds by asserting that in sleep the soul has not ceased to function; it has ceased only to activate the body, and is itself still active; in short, sleep is, as the Stoics contend, 'a temporary suspension of the activity of the senses'.[21]

In the *Divinae institutiones*, written almost exactly a century later, Lactantius extends the range by challenging eight of the fifteen Epicurean 'proofs' adduced by Lucretius. He agrees with Lucretius that the body and the soul are united from birth, but argues that they are of quite different natures and that the fact that the body endures for a period of time after death proves Lucretius false in maintaining that body and soul die together. As to Lucretius' claim that since the body and the soul mature together they must grow old and perish together, Lactantius insists that it is the body and the mind which proceed in tandem, the soul remaining the same throughout. Further, when the faculties begin to fail this is due to the progressive weakening of the body, not, as Lucretius would have it, a deterioration of the soul. To Lucretius' contention that in order for the soul to have an existence outside the body it would need its own sense-organs Lactantius replies that since it is the soul which gives sensation to the body it is more than capable of experiencing sensation on its own. Lucretius is in error too in claiming that cases of gradual physical paralysis confirm that the soul is gradually torn apart; the affected parts lose their sensation only because, as Tertullian had argued, the soul has withdrawn to another place. Finally, Lactantius counters Lucretius' observation that if the soul were immortal it would not sound in complaint at the moment of death by pointing to countless individuals in his own experience who far from bemoaning the approach of death rejoice in it, regarding it not as the soul's annihilation, but only as its separation from the body in preparation for a new journey.[22] We have reviewed the debate between Tertullian and Lactantius on the one side and Lucretius on the other not for any intrinsic merits which the arguments themselves might have. The point is rather that on the question at issue the 'proofs' are really secondary. Starting from completely contradictory presuppositions neither party can hope to convince the other. For the Epicurean the survival of the soul is a denial of its very nature; for the Christian it is an article of faith.

So far we have noted the Christian concern over Epicurus' denial of the soul's immortality only as it affects the prospect of an eternal life. There was equal concern, however, over its implications for the conduct of the present life. This concern is expressed succinctly by Gregory of Nyssa at the opening of the *De anima et resurrectione* (*Macrina*): 'How can virtue have a place among those who hold that this present life is the total sum of existence and that beyond it nothing is to be looked for?' Gregory is voicing a sentiment which is echoed variously by others. In the second century Athenagoras, coupling the Epicureans' rejection of the soul's immortality with their denial of divine providence, comments

For if no judgment whatever were to be passed on the actions of men . . . a life after the manner of brutes would be the best, virtue would be absurd, the threat of judgment a matter for broad laughter, indulgence in every kind of pleasure the highest good, and the common resolve of all these [the Epicureans] and their one law would be that maxim, so dear to the intemperate and lewd, 'let us eat and drink, for tomorrow we die'.[23]

For Arnobius at the beginning of the fourth century it is not the fear of punishment as much as the hope of reward which is the decisive factor:

But again, if souls draw near to the gates of death, as is laid down in the doctrine of Epicurus, in this case, too, there is no sufficient reason why philosophy should be sought out . . . it is not only a very great mistake, but shows stupid blindness, to curb innate desires, to restrict your mode of life within narrow limits, not yield to your inclinations, and do what your passions have demanded and urged, since no rewards await you for so great toil when the day of death comes, and you shall be freed from the bonds of the body.[24]

For Augustine fear of punishment and hope are of equal importance:

Some indeed, but not all, of your authors have said that death is the end of all evils: that is indeed the opinion of the Epicureans, and of such others as believe the soul to be mortal. But those philosophers whom Cicero designates 'consulares' . . . are of the opinion that when our last hour on earth comes the soul is not annihilated, but removes from its tenement, and continues in existence for a state of blessedness or of misery, according to that which a man's actions, whether good or bad, claim as their due recompense.[25]

In setting moral conduct so firmly in the context of incentives and restraints these Christian writers, and they are not untypical, reveal a profoundly pessimistic evaluation of man's natural disposition, and this is interesting in itself. Of immediate importance, however, is the clear connection which they draw between Epicurus' metaphysics and his ethics. It is a connection, of course, which Epicurus himself would readily have acknowledged, for while he was less concerned than some of the Greek thinkers with articulating a comprehensive and structurally integrated philosophical system, he was none the less convinced that his teachings were all of a piece. The proper conduct of daily life depended upon a true understanding of the gods, the soul, and the meaning of death. For Epicurus these were the issues which, if wrongly perceived, represented the most serious obstacles to the attainment of happiness. For Christian writers, however, Epicurus, far from liberating man from erroneous beliefs which obstructed his well-being, had succeeded only in removing all basis for acceptable human behaviour. It will be no surprise, therefore, if patristic references to Epicurus' ethical theory are found to be for the greatest part decidedly negative. Indeed, it is here that the Christian writers become their most vituperative. At the same time, as we shall see, it is on the question of ethics that they show themselves least understanding of true Epicurean doctrine.

The name-calling and slander begin early and continue late. Already in the second century Justin Martyr places Epicurus in the company of Sardanapalus, the Sotadists, the Philaenidians, and the Dancers.[26] For Jerome in the fifth Epicurus is an Aristippus and an Alcibiades.[27] And throughout the period in between Epicurus and his latter-day disciples are credited with a colourful array of depravities and perversions in their single-minded pursuit of carnal satisfaction: swinish gluttony, drunkenness, fornication, adultery, homosexuality, sodomy, incest – Theophilus, Clement, Pseudo-Clement, Ambrose, Epiphanius, Peter Chrysologus, Filastrius, and Augustine each contributing a little to the list.[28] We need not dwell upon this aspect of the patristic treatment of Epicurus. It offers nothing novel. The Fathers are simply repeating the calumnies which had originated with Epicurus' earliest detractors and had been put to effective use by later opponents of the School, not least by Cicero in the *In Pisonem*. At the same time, we must recognize that these outbursts were not wholly rhetorical. We have remarked that the Christian lived in the world. He was not blind to its attractions or proof against them, and the devil appeared in many guises. Finally, we must observe that in associating Epicurus with the excesses and depravities of their age the Fathers were influential in perpetuating and sharpening that image of the Garden as a *hortus deliciarum* which was to persist throughout the Middle Ages and beyond.

When we come to the Fathers' more serious treatment of Epicurean ethics we have to reckon with a factor of some importance, namely, the selective and incomplete nature of their acquaintance with Epicurean doctrine. To an extent this is a factor too with respect to the issues upon which we have already touched, namely, the gods, providence, and the soul. There, however, the difficulty is less acute, since Lucretius' *De rerum natura* and Cicero's *De natura deorum*, both of which were well known during the patristic period, offer fairly detailed and comprehensive expositions. On the subject of ethics, however, the situation is less satisfactory. There is little evidence that the Fathers benefited from a firsthand knowledge of Epicurus' writings,[29] and Lucretius does not offer so concentrated or full a treatment of Epicurean ethical doctrine, leaving Cicero as the principal indirect source. The difficulty here, however, is that, while Cicero examines Epicurus' ethical views in a number of his philosophical treatises, he is not altogether unbiased in his interpretations, even where he employs an Epicurean 'spokesman'. Moreover, not all of Cicero's philosophical works received equal attention from patristic writers. Lactantius, for example, though he employs a number of Cicero's philosophical works, seems not to have known the *De finibus*, which contains Cicero's most thorough treatment of Epicurean ethics.[30] Augustine, who makes greater use of Cicero than of any other Latin writer, certainly knew the *De finibus*, but makes only modest use of it.[31] We have to recognize, then, that to an appreciable extent the Fathers derived their knowledge of Epicurean ethical doctrine not so much from reasonably complete and faithful accounts as from quotations, paraphrases, and summaries found in florilegia and handbooks. Accordingly, we shall be disappointed if we look to the patristic literature for any sustained or comprehensive critique of Epicurean ethical doctrine which takes into account its complexities or relates it to other aspects of Epicurus' philosophy. What we find, rather, are comments, for the most part brief, upon particular Epicurean sayings either taken in isolation or treated as representing the whole of Epicurus' teaching. When these are added up, it is clear that the major components of Epicurus' ethics have indeed filtered through the sources, but in a way that has left his ethical theory as a whole out of proportion, certain elements, and these not necessarily the most important, outbalancing others. There is an irony of sorts. Part of the reason for the success of Epicureanism has been the fact that the system could be readily transmitted through memorable sayings. Herein also lay the seeds of its distortion.

Clement of Alexandria provides an illustration. His references to Epicurus' ethical views come in a chapter of the *Stromateis* which consists entirely of a cursory review of the opinions of various philosophers on the chief good. Thirty individuals or schools are included in the list.[32] He notes that for Epicurus the chief good is pleasure, but makes no distinction between Epicurus and the Cyrenaics, and implies that what Epicurus meant by pleasure was the simple gratification of bodily desires; again pairing Epicurus with the Cyrenaics he records their view that virtues are to be sought not for themselves but for the sake of pleasure, but does not mention Epicurus' ancillary contention that virtue is so necessary to a pleasant life that no man can live pleasantly without living virtuously; he notes the Epicurean definition of pleasure as absence of pain, first associating Epicurus with the Cyrenaics in this regard, then reversing himself later in the chapter, but shows no awareness of Epicurus' insistence upon a legitimate role for active pleasures in securing this desired condition. What we witness, in short, is the simple procedure on Clement's part of selecting from his handbook sources those Epicurean sayings which he found useful for his context with no attempt to co-ordinate them into anything like a full or accurate statement of Epicurean doctrine.

The nature of the *Stromateis* may make Clement an extreme example of the kind of distorted treatment which Epicurus' ethical views received. However, the general tendency which Clement displays is followed to a lesser degree by others. Augustine, for example, consistently characterizes the Epicurean concept of pleasure as nothing more than surrender to the desires of the flesh.[33] Ambrose, in a lively tirade against sensualism, in which he chastises two 'Epicurean' apostate monks Sarmatio and Barbatianus, offers a similarly narrow presentation.[34] Elsewhere, in a review of philosophers' opinions on happiness modelled closely on a passage from Cicero's *De finibus*, he restrict Epicurus to the bare pronouncement that happiness consists in pleasure, and attributes the concept of pleasure as absence of pain not to Epicurus, to whom it rightly belongs, but to one of the heads of the Peripatetic school.[35] Nemesius does recognize Epicurus' claim to the concept of pleasure as absence of pain, but in viewing it as the basis of the Neoplatonist notion of pleasure as genesis which he is attacking he quite misrepresents its proper Epicurean connotation.[36]

In fact, there is only one element of Epicurean ethical doctrine which is not is some way misrepresented by the Christian writers, and that is the threefold classification of desires into those which are both natural and necessary, those which are natural but not necessary, and those which are neither natural nor necessary. This was a concept which was familiar enough from a number of Epicurean sources and from Cicero's *De finibus*, and was clearly one which the Fathers did not find objectionable in itself.[37] It lies behind the distinction which Tertullian draws between the unnatural desires occasioned by the maturing of sexual instincts and the one natural desire sanctioned by God, namely, the desire for nourishment.[38] Clement finds the distinction useful in a somewhat different context. Having argued for marriage as a holy estate, he wishes to admonish the later followers of the Gnostic Basilides for departing from the precepts of their teacher by promoting a life of rigid celibacy which, in Clement's view, leads them into the practice of the grossest indecencies. Accordingly, he cites an apposite passage from Basilides' son Isidorus which closely echoes the Epicurean distinction between natural and unnatural desires.[39] Finally, in a chapter of the *De natura hominis* devoted to pleasure, Nemesius employs the Epicurean threefold classification, of which he gives a particularly full account, as the basis for his defence of Christian asceticism.[40] What is interesting in these three instances is not so much that a Greek concept is put to Christian use. This is very much part of the pattern. It is, rather, that by none of these writers is the concept credited to the Epicurean school. It is an irony indeed that, when Epicurus has emerged as the *bête noire* of the Greek moral tradition, the one aspect of his doctrine upon which the Fathers looked favourably should seem to have become so much a part of accepted ethical thought as to have lost its Epicurean identity.

We have focused so far upon Christian reaction to the Epicurean view of the gods, divine providence, and the soul, and to Epicurean ethical teaching, and we have found it to be almost universally negative. This is not the extent of patristic criticism of the Epicurean school, but it is in these areas in particular that Christian writers saw in Epicureanism a philosophy which was at variance with the fundamentals of Christian doctrine. Moreover, while it is proper to acknowledge the degree to which criticism of the Greek schools entered Christian apologetic as a purely formal element, it would be a mistake to assume that the patristic attack upon Epicureanism was wholly in the nature of a rhetorical or intellectual skirmish. The Christian writers recognized well enough that Epicureanism was damaging in real terms to the spread of the Christian faith, that for many thousands of ordinary citizens of the Empire, the targets of the Christian mission on the ground, the Epicurean message, especially in its popular garb, had considerable appeal. It spoke of a world which was not managed by any unseen power, of a life in which a man's actions were free from divine scrutiny, a life which within the bounds of society a man might shape according to his own will, securing himself against discomfort, acknowledging his natural instincts, relieved from the nagging fear of an unknown beyond the grave by the certainty of death as the final end. It was an appeal which had proved its power. For the Christian advocate, Epicurus was the enemy outside the gates.

But there was also the enemy within. If the early Christian writers saw it as their mission to shape Christian doctrine and to promote the Christian message among the unconverted, they saw it as no less their responsibility to safeguard authentic Christian teaching against the doctrinal aberrations which from the second century onwards began to lay equal claim to authority, in particular against the various forms of Gnosticism, that imaginative, if often bizarre, amalgam of Jewish, Christian, Hellenistic, and Oriental philosophy, mythology, and astrology which threatened to destroy the unity of the Church. The anti-heretical literature which this crisis provoked reveals something of that ambivalence towards Greek philosophy which we have already noted, though it is an ambivalence which does not extend to all writers. One of Hippolytus' principal strategies in the *Refutation of All Heresies* is to expose the falsity of the various heresies by tracing their origins to the teachings of one or other of the Greek schools.[41] Similarly, in the fourth century it is the Hellenization of Christian teaching which forms the basis of Epiphanius' vehement denunciation of Origen in the *Panarion*.[42] In fact, Epiphanius treats Hellenism itself as one of the five 'mother-heresies' from which all subsequent heresies were born.[43] In others, however, the ambivalence is marked. Justin Martyr, for example, is adamant that perfect truth is to be found only in the divine Scriptures, yet he reveals a decidedly warm attitude towards the Greek tradition. Greek philosophy, in particular Platonic philosophy, while it is not free from the most serious inadequacies, does contain something of the truth, and for the reason that it is at points divinely inspired or derived from the writings of Moses.[44] It is an attitude which is paralleled to an extent in Justin's near contemporary Athenagoras. In the *Legatio*, a spirited attempt to exonerate Christians in the eyes of the secular authorities

from charges of atheism and immorality, Athenagoras relies primarily upon the divine writings of the prophets to confirm the Christian
concept of God. However, the *Legatio* is by design a conciliatory
piece and Athenagoras finds it strategically useful to associate
Christian belief as closely as possible with the best of pagan thought.
Accordingly, while he makes much of the great divergence of
opinion in the pagan tradition concerning the nature and role of God
and appeals for the same tolerance to be shown towards the
Christian view as is shown towards others, he goes out of his way to
stress that the views of the most respected Greek thinkers are in fact
in essential harmony with the Christian concept. 'Athenagoras'
philosophical theology . . . bears witness to the desire of a segment of
Christians in the second century to exploit the most prestigious
elements of Greek culture.'[45]

But the ambivalence is perhaps best seen in Clement. As Chadwick has pointed out, Clement was cognizant of two competing
forces at work in Alexandrian Christianity at the beginning of the
third century: on the one side, the appeal for educated Christians of
the intellectual colouring of Gnosticism and the mental gymnastics
performed by its exponents, and on the other the staunch illiberal-
ism which Gnostic extravagances provoked in more simple-minded
believers. Clement's task was to point a path between the two
extremes, between 'the Scylla of obscurantist orthodoxy and the
Charybdis of heretical reinterpretation of the faith'.[46] Accordingly,
Greek philosophy is not to be denied, and Clement is fervent in
arguing its value in much the same terms as Justin; it is provi-
dentially inspired to serve as a propaedeutic to the acceptance of
Christian teaching:

> we shall not err in alleging that all things necessary and profitable
> for life came to us from God, and that philosophy more especially
> was given to the Greeks, as a covenant peculiar to them – being,
> as it were, a stepping-stone to the philosophy which is according
> to Christ.[47]

However, Clement proceeds immediately to caution that 'tares were
sown' by certain of the Greek thinkers, and by drawing an analogy
between these 'tares' and the heresies which have sprung up in the
Church he indirectly confirms the legitimacy of looking to the Greek
tradition as one of the sources of heretical doctrine. Moreover, by
singling out as an example of the tares which corrupted Greek

thought the teachings of Epicurus, Clement hints clearly enough that Epicureanism might well repay investigation.

In fact, no hint was needed. The association of Gnostic error with the philosophy of Epicurus was one which commended itself readily to a number of anti-heretical writers from Irenaeus in the second century to Salvian in the fifth. The instances divide themselves into two main groups. First there are those where the writer is examining a specific heresy and makes reference to a particular aspect of Epicurean teaching. Tertullian, for example, introduces Epicurus at three points into his denunciation of Marcion, on each occasion with respect to the nature of the second god which Marcion's doctrine introduced as superior to the god who is responsible for the creation of the world. In Tertullian's view this second god possesses none of the attributes of a true god. In particular, he cannot accept as a god one who is so indifferent to the affairs of the world that he is incapable of showing any emotion over them. Marcion may as well confess that his god is none other than the sluggish and unfeeling god of Epicurus.[48] Tertullian also characterizes the Valentinians' supreme being, the first member of the group of eight highest Aeons, as no different from Epicurus' 'placid and stupid god', in this following Irenaeus, who had charged the Valentinians with having discovered for themselves 'the god of Epicurus, who does nothing for himself or for others'.[49] However, this is not the only connection which Irenaeus and Tertullian make between Valentinian doctrine and Epicureanism. The Valentinians have borrowed the very basis of their system, the distinction between the Pleroma and the Kenoma, the world of being and the world of non-being, from the Epicurean concept of atoms and void.[50] Quite a different aspect of Gnostic teaching provides Tertullian with another opportunity to attack both Marcion and Valentinus through Epicurus, and this time Basilides and Apelles are added to the list. For denying the survival of the body after death all four heretics are branded as latter-day Sadducees, a sect which Tertullian views as 'allied more closely with the Epicureans than with the prophets'.[51] It is an association which would appeal much later to Filastrius, who regards the Sadducees as a Jewish–Gnostic sect which in its devotion to the pleasures of the flesh 'follows the madness of Epicurus rather than the principles of divine law'.[52]

To the second group belongs an equal number of instances where Epicurean tendencies are attributed to various heretics not with respect to their adoption of any particular element of Epicurean doctrine but as a general indictment. Jerome's treatment of Jovinian provides a revealing example. Jerome composed the *Contra Jovinianum* in 393 AD, three years after Jovinian's writings had been condemned in synods at Rome and Milan, and his attack centres around Jovinian's claim that virginity is no better than marriage in the eyes of God and abstinence no better than thankful eating. Against both of these propositions Jerome adduces a series of scriptural arguments which were to be an important factor in the debate over asceticism within the Church. In addition, after parading a number of historical examples of virginity honoured, Jerome offers a review of Greek and Roman writers who counselled against marriage, and here Epicurus is enlisted as an ally along with Chrysippus, Aristotle, Plutarch, and Seneca.[53] Moreover, the alliance is sustained when Jerome proclaims the merits of a simple diet and Epicurus' recommendation of vegetables and fruits is duly cited.[54] However, it is an alliance of convenience and easily broken. For Jerome's underlying strategy throughout the work is to undermine Jovinian's credibility by presenting him as a fanatical advocate of total sexual freedom and luxurious living, and to this end Epicurus is conscripted into Jovinian's camp. Jovinian is 'the Epicurus of Christianity', 'our modern Epicurus debauching in his gardens with his favourites of both sexes', attended by his coterie of profligates chanting, 'we follow vice, not virtue; Epicurus, not Christ; Jovinian, not the Apostle Paul'.[55] The *Contra Jovinianum* is remarkable only to the extent that Jerome presents Epicurus' true image and its distortion in the same work and uses both to his own advantage. In employing the popular conception of Epicureanism as a means of discrediting an adversary it is typical. In his debate with Bishop Julian over Pelagianism Augustine labels his opponent an 'Epicurean', and Julian does not hesitate to hurl the epithet back.[56] To Jerome the worldly clergy at Rome are 'Epicuruses', as are Ambrose's two renegade monks, and Salvian's leisured Gallic gentry in the fifth century.[57]

We have been concerned to put on record as a feature of orthodox reaction to the emergence of heretical movements within the Church the strategy of exposing certain doctrinal aberrations by linking them with the philosophy of Epicurus. It is important, however, to see this in perspective as part of a general pattern. There are few Greek thinkers who are not linked with some aspect of heretical teaching, and some of them command more frequent attention than Epicurus. If the role of Epicureanism is distinctive, it is because it has a double aspect. In common with the other Greek philosophies it is seen as a possible source of particular heretical doctrines. In addition, however, 'Epicureanism' has clearly emerged in a unique way as a symbol for the antithesis of Christian morality, and has 'acquired the force of a *Schimpfwort*, a convenient label to pin on any sort of opponent whatever in a theological controversy'.[58]

Up to this point we have focused upon the negative side of the Christian reaction to Epicureanism, and, given the range of the criticism which has been levelled at Epicurean teaching and the vehemence with which a good deal of it has beeen expressed, it might be surprising that there should be anything to record on the other side. However, this would be to mistake the nature of the patristic attitude and approach. For what was of primary import-ance to the Fathers was not the overthrow of Epicureanism, or indeed of any of the pagan philosophies, but the promotion and preservation of Christian doctrine. To this end, certainly, the Christian spokesmen found it incumbent upon themselves to oppose those aspects of pagan teaching which stood at variance with the fundamentals of Christian belief, and Epicureanism took its place alongside the other Greek systems in this regard. At the same time, the Fathers recognized that Greek philosophy contained much that could be usefully accommodated to Christian teaching and were not slow to use this advantage. Accordingly, Epicureanism, albeit to a far lesser degree than Platonism or Stoicism, found itself the object of some favourable comment.

Some instances we have already noted: in the *De anima* Tertullian calls upon Epicurus to confirm his view of the soul as corporeal, quoting an apposite line from Lucretius;[59] Jerome makes use of Epicurus' strictures against marriage, as well as his recom-mendation of a simple diet.[60] Again in the *De anima* Tertullian looks to Epicurean doctrine for support, this time with reference to his defence of the reliability of the senses. Tertullian is concerned that to question the reliability of sense-perception is to repudiate divine providence which has endowed man with senses so that he may accomplish God's purpose in civilizing the world; furthermore, to disparage the evidence of the senses opens the way for the denial of certain of Christ's experiences and of the actuality of his miracles.

The chief culprits, in Tertullian's view, are the Platonists and the Sceptics, and it is against the traditional Sceptic arguments, such as the oar which appears bent in the water and the square tower which seems to be round from a distance, that he adduces the Epicurean view that it is not the senses which are deceived, it is the image rather which is distorted by the medium before it reaches the eye.[61] Another aspect of Epicurean epistemology is appealed to by Clement in support of his contention that faith is a precondition of all knowledge.[62] What Clement means is that it is impossible to advance in any area of investigation, knowledge of God being the most important, without possessing a preconceived idea of what one is aiming at, and what he finds it useful to point to in this regard is Epicurus' theory of general concepts or preconceptions, which are formed by abstraction from particular sense-impressions and stored in the mind as criteria of truth.[63]

Further sporadic approval of Epicurean doctrine stems from the Fathers' deliberate practice of undermining Greek philosophy by setting the schools against one another. Epicureanism is more often the victim of the tactic,[64] but benefits more than once. Lactantius, for example, employs Epicurus against Aristotle to argue that the world had a beginning, and against both Aristotle and Plato to argue that it will have an end.[65] Again, he cites with approval a passage from Lucretius which is critical of the Stoics for affirming that God created the world for man's benefit but failing to produce adequate reasons why God should have done so.[66] For Augustine Epicurus is a useful ally in his battle against the Sceptics.[67]

The instances which we have cited from Tertullian, Jerome, Lactantius, Clement, and Augustine confirm the occasional readiness of Christian writers to draw upon Epicurean doctrine either as a means of bolstering particular theological arguments or as a way of refuting the views of one or another of the philosophical schools. It is a matter of convenience, and does not betoken any degree of commitment to Epicurean principles in general. There is one area, however, where Christian approval of the Epicurean school is based upon a genuinely shared attitude, namely, a firm opposition to all forms of superstition. The Epicurean view was well known and had drawn both criticism and praise from pagan writers. Plutarch sees the Epicureans' rejection of divination and the worship of the heavenly bodies as one more example of their disruptive influence in society.[68] The satirist Lucian, on the other hand, welcomes the

Epicurean stance as supportive of his own. In *Alexander the False Prophet* he can imagine no more suitable opponent for the charlatan oracle-seller, whose chicaneries called for the vigilance of an Epicurus, a man 'whose sceptical mind was proof against such trickeries, and who, even if he would not pinpoint the precise nature of the deception, would be convinced beforehand that the entire business was a fraud and an imposture'.[69] Moreover, Lucian presents Epicureans and Christians joining ranks in a common cause: 'Christians, out! Epicureans, out!' is the refrain which prefaces Alexander's mantic rituals.[70]

It is natural, then, that in their polemic against pagan superstition and polytheistic ritual Christian writers should either draw upon Epicurean arguments, or at least make reference to the Epicurean view. An example of the former is provided by Clement's *Protrepticus*, where the affinity with Philodemus' *De pietate*, both in matters of detail and in the general sequence of arguments, warrants the conclusion that Philodemus and Clement are dependent upon the same Epicurean source, perhaps Phaedrus, Head of the School at Athens at the beginning of the first century BC.[71] Despite his indebtedness Clement does not actually mention Epicurus, but others do, even where they make no use of Epicurean arguments. At several points in his debate with the pagan Celsus Origen finds himself called upon to defend the unique validity of Old Testament prophecy against his opponent's claims on behalf of the Greek oracular shrines. He takes a double approach, drawing upon the Scriptures to confirm the efficacy of divine revelation, and subjecting the Greeks' acceptance of the mantic arts to a thoroughgoing rational critique. For this latter he chooses to employ only his own arguments, but in two places he freely acknowledges that solid arguments had already been advanced by two of the Greek schools – the Peripatetic and the Epicurean.[72] In his polemic against Greek and Roman religious practices Lactantius too declines to record the Epicurean arguments, but for a different reason: he does not regard them as valid, undoubtedly because they involved in part the denial of divine providence. However, the Epicurean attitude he is quite prepared to applaud, and on three occasions he quotes with approval appropriate passages from Lucretius.[73] For the most unreservedly enthusiastic commendation, however, we must turn to Eusebius. He acknowledges that among the Greeks the Aristotelians and the Cynics were firm opponents of oracular practices, but he singles out for special praise the Epicureans –

> in whom what I most admire is, how, after being brought up in the customs of the Greeks, and having been taught even from the cradle, son from father, that those of whom we speak are gods, they have not been easily caught, but proved with all their might that even the renowned oracles, and the seats of divination which were sought after among all, had no truth, and declared that they were useless, nay rather mischievous.[74]

Finally, against the conventional representation of the Epicurean School as an academy of vices, and its founder as a *patronus voluptatis*,[75] we must set a few instances where Christian writers follow the lead of such classical authors as Seneca in crediting Epicurus himself, as distinct from his later followers, with a commendable standard of personal morality.[76] Ambrose, who is generally a hostile witness, in the same letter to the congregation at Verceil in which he denounces the renegade monks, Sarmatio and Barbation, as 'Epicureans', is prepared to concede that Epicurus' own standards were meritorious:

> But as to that Epicurus himself . . . what if we proved him to be more tolerable than these men? He declares . . . that neither drinking, nor banquets, nor offspring, nor embraces of women, nor abundance of fish, and other such like things which are prepared for the service of a sumptuous banquet, make life sweet, but sober discussion.[77]

Similarly, in the same work in which he characterizes his opponent Jovinian as the 'Epicurus of Christianity', Jerome applauds Epicurus himself for his sage remarks on the advantages of moderate eating and drinking.[78] Finally, Gregory of Nazianzus praises Epicurus' 'temperance', and remarks that his character and mode of living served as a corrective for those who might be tempted to interpret his theory of pleasure as a call to licentiousness.[79]

In outlining the Christian response to Epicurus and his philosophy we have been examining a conscious reaction. Quite apart from such questions as finding and defending its place within the secular structure, organizing and sustaining its communities, and carrying its message to the unconverted, two particular challenges faced the

Church, and particularly its appointed spokesmen, during its earliest centuries. One was the pressure to win intellectual respectability by offering a rational articulation of Christian beliefs, and to a very great extent this meant meeting the Greek philosophical tradition on its own terms. As we have seen, the stance adopted by most, though by no means all, of the Fathers was not a categorical or wholesale dismissal of Greek philosophy, but an admission that it had succeeded, to a limited extent at least, in anticipating Christian truth, either through being in places divinely inspired, or because its exponents had plagiarized divine writings. As for the individual schools, it became a matter of rejecting those teachings which most threatened Christian doctrine and assimilating those which might be most usefully adapted to the Christian context. In the case of Epicureanism the former outweighed the latter, so that the overall response was preponderantly negative. The second challenge came from those teachers within the Church itself whose impulse towards intellectualism had led to the emergence of the numerous splinter movements which fall under the term Gnosticism. More conservative spokesmen took it in hand to outlaw the doctrines which the various Gnostic teachers elaborated as being aberrations from true Christian teaching resulting in large measure from a misapplication of pagan thought, and here Epicureanism took its place alongside the other Greek philosophies as a likely source of error. On the positive side, it was only where particular aspects of Epicurean doctrine could be made to support a theological argument, or where Epicurean teaching could be used strategically to disqualify another philosophical position, that Epicureanism was accorded favourable mention. As for Epicurus himself, save for a few discriminating notices, his name became a byword for the moral degeneracy which in the popular mind Epicurean philosophy as a whole had come to represent.

In large measure, then, the philosophy of Epicurus became an object of attention for patristic writers because it was part of a tradition which could not be ignored. As we have already noted, however, the Epicurean philosophy was also an object of attention at an equally important level, namely, as a rival for the allegiance of ordinary citizens throughout the empire, and here, given the insistence with which successive Fathers emphasize the radical differences in Christian and Epicurean doctrine, there is some irony in the fact that in many ways the appeal of the Christian and

Epicurean messages was fundamentally similar. We have already drawn attention, for example, to the common resistance which Christians and Epicureans mounted against superstition, especially the claims made for oracles and divination. At root was the rejection by both groups of determinism and their shared commitment to the doctrine of human free will. In this the Epicureans were perhaps the more consistent. They believed in a mechanistic universe whose workings were saved from rigid necessity by an arbitrary atomic swerve which accounted also for freedom of action at the human level. The Christian position, on the other hand, was complicated by two factors: the belief in divine providence and the acceptance of scriptural prophecy. None the less, despite the obvious difficulty of reconciling these views with the principle of free will (and attempts to do so were not always convincing), the Christian insistence upon man's control over his choice of actions was uncompromising.[80] Hence, in a world where every action and experience might seem to bear the mark of compulsion, dictated or imposed by secular power or through the determining influence of stars and planets, what the Christian message and the Epicurean philosophy offered the individual was the liberating assurance of self-determination, the dignity of responsibility.

A recurring criticism levelled against Epicureans since the time of Cicero and taken up with insistence closer to the Christian period by Plutarch was their reluctance to take an active part in the business of the state. Nor was the complaint wholly unjustified. Withdrawal from the world of affairs was an important element in the Epicurean search for the untroubled life.[81] The same criticism was also directed at Christians, and, while many Christians accepted their full share of civic responsibilities, there were those who were prepared to acknowledge its truth. For some, withdrawal was a matter of seeking seclusion as a relief from the stresses of the busy world, an impulse which was to find its most extreme expression in the monastic life.[82] For others, it was a conscious rejection of the Roman way:

I owe no obligation to forum, campus, or senate. I stay awake for no public function, I make no effort to monopolise the platform, I pay no heed to any administrative duty, I shun the voter's booth, the juryman's bench . . . I serve neither as magistrate nor soldier, I have withdrawn from the life of secular society . . . My only concern is for myself, careful of nothing except that I should have no care.

– so Tertullian in clear Epicurean tones.[83] Perhaps the most basic impulse, however, is signalled by Origen in his response to Celsus' complaint that Christians avoid the burdens of public office:

> If Christians do avoid these responsibilities, it is not with the motive of shirking the public services of life. But they keep themselves for a more divine and necessary service in the Church of God for the sake of the salvation of men.[84]

For it must be recognized that, when he accepted the faith, the Christian, for all that he was a citizen of the empire, became a citizen of a larger state; from now on the *civitas Romana* took second place to the *civitas Dei*.[85]

In short, then, what Epicureanism and Christianity both offered the individual was membership in an alternative community. Certainly, they were communities of a different order, and in terms of demands they were far apart: for the Epicurean withdrawal from society was a renunciation, for the Christian an exchange of service. Yet the similarities are striking. During the earliest years of the Church especially, when Christian practices and beliefs were very much subject to suspicion and misunderstanding and members of Christian communities the targets of much odium and abuse, a factor critical in sustaining individual commitment to the Christian life was the sense of belonging to a group which was united by a special bond of friendship which was extended to all its members regardless of status or class. Similarly, of all the Greek schools it was the Epicurean which was the least exclusive and which, in its cultivation of *philia*, came closest to anticipating Christian *agape*. Moreover, both movements satisfied a psychologically powerful impulse by projecting in the person of their founders the figure of a saviour. Indeed, two Christian writers look back consciously to Lucretius' celebrated hymn to Epicurus in composing their own eulogies of Christ.[86] In suggesting that the Christian opposition to the philosophy of Epicurus was not without irony we implied an unawareness of similarities. It may be rather that it was owed to an awareness all too conscious.

116

5

MEDIEVAL INTERLUDE

The fortunes of the Epicurean philosophy during the ten centuries or so between the collapse of the Roman Empire in the west and the end of the Middle Ages are bound up closely with the fortunes of classical culture itself. We have seen that during the early Christian centuries the attitude of the Church Fathers towards pagan learning was an ambivalent one. There were influential Christian spokesmen whose determination to safeguard the integrity of Christian teaching led them to declare all pagan writing a contrivance of the devil designed to thwart God's purpose, and to pronounce against the Greek philosophers in particular as sowers of the seeds of heresy. At the same time, there were others, no less zealous in their promotion of the Christian faith, for whom the classical authors still held a powerful appeal, and who were perceptive enough to recognize that there was much in pagan thought which might be used to advantage in support of Christian teaching, and on their part we witness a quiet approval of certain classical writers and a willingness to grant limited sanction to the study of Greek philosophy in particular as a preparation for the reception of divine truth.[1] Thus, even as the Christian mission enjoyed increasing success throughout the Roman Empire, pagan letters continued to hold their place.

Nor did the collapse of the empire mean the obliteration of the classical heritage. It is true that in general creative literary activity of the highest order came to an end, but the Roman educational system, which had proved effective in providing a suitable training for all levels of government administration, survived as an instrument which the invaders were neither equipped nor inclined to replace, and there is evidence of the continued operation during the fifth and sixth centuries of schools on the Roman model throughout the various barbarian kingdoms.[2] In such major centres as Rome, Milan, Ravenna, Avignon, Lyon, Bordeaux, Cordova, and Carthage the teachers of grammar and rhetoric, in imparting the basic rules for reading and writing the Latin language and equipping their more advanced students with the skills appropriate to the performance of legal and administrative functions, went some way towards perpetuating the classical tradition by drawing upon the standard Latin writers for examples and exercises – Virgil, Silius Italicus, Terence, Ovid, Tibullus, Statius, and Lucan among the poets, and Cicero, Sallust, Caesar, and Valerius Maximus among the prosewriters.[3] Indeed, the fragmentary contents of surviving fifth-century manuscripts attest to the fact that there was still sufficient interest to warrant the copying of a good part of Latin literature.[4]

There are a number of factors, however, which rendered the survival of classical culture as a whole far from certain. In the first place, among Romans formal education was limited for the most part to members of the senatorial class, and among even these privileged few knowledge of Greek was a rarity.[5] Further, there is little evidence that among the invaders training in the Latin language was encouraged for any but the immediate members of the royal families and those who were looking to an administrative career. As for the barbarian aristocracy, they would seem to have been little inclined to abandon their own culture in favour of the Roman. The education which they preferred for their youth was one that was grounded in their own native traditions, essentially military in character and stressing the moral qualities celebrated in tribal legend and song.[6] What the barbarians chose to exploit from the Roman legacy was what answered to their immediate and practical needs. Thus it was in such areas as law, medicine, husbandry, architecture, and administration, rather than in the realm of humanistic pursuits, that the Roman civilization had its most pronounced effect upon the newcomers.

A second factor has to do with a growing antagonism towards classical antiquity on the part of such influential Christian scholars as Caesarius of Arles, who viewed paganism as a continuing threat to the Christian faith. In warning of the dangers of classical poetry and philosophy in particular they were reviving themes which many of the Church Fathers had already rehearsed with vigour and they did little more than repeat the standard patristic criticisms.[7] However, this renewed onslaught against Greek and Roman letters was more than just a rhetorical outburst. What Caesarius and others were rejecting was the liberal attitude of such contemporary Christian scholars as Boethius, Cassiodorus, and Fulgentius, who sought a deliberate accommodation between classical and Christian culture and showed no hesitation in incorporating in their writings classical motives and allusions. For Caesarius and others this was a compromise which could only damage the integrity of Christian scholarship. Further, it was more than the substance of Christian teaching that was at stake. As Riché has well illustrated, Caesarius and his fellow 'rigorists' were equally concerned that attachment to classical forms and fondness for stylistic embellishment and literary allusion had rendered contemporary Christian writing an ineffective vehicle for promoting the Christian message, especially among an urban public whose knowledge of classical Latin itself was probably rudimentary.[8] What was demanded from scholars and preachers alike was a manner of expression which was simple and direct and owed as little as possible to the classical tradition.

For a number of reasons, then, there was a renewed call for a complete break with the antique past, and, while we cannot suppose that this brought about an end to the study of the ancient authors, there is evidence that the appeal was not without effect. Certainly, pressure was exerted upon bishops to honour the traditional injunction against the reading of pagan authors,[9] and such influential bishops as Ennodius of Pavia, Sidonius of Clermont, and Avitus of Vienne did set an example by renouncing their former attachment to liberal studies. More generally, the concerns expressed by Caesarius and others led to a sustained effort during the sixth century to increase the opportunities for elementary religious education in monasteries, episcopal schools, and parish schools, and to a recognition of the need for centres of higher religious studies, as evidenced most notably by Cassiodorus' design for a Christian 'university' at Rome.[10]

Finally, it is the case that by the end of the fifth century a greater abundance of Christian literature lessened the need for turning to the profane authors for material. Christian poets such as Prudentius, Sidonius Apollinaris, Paulinus, Sedulius, and Arator had mastered the classical metres and offered a substitute for Virgil, Ovid, and the rest. In the realm of general knowledge Martianus Capella's *De nuptiis philologiae et Mercurii* presented a comprehensive survey of the seven liberal arts; and the sixth century would add Cassiodorus'

Institutiones and Isidore of Seville's *Etymologiae*. Thus, the layman was provided with reference works which had the legitimacy of Christian authorship and which were encyclopedic enough in scope to render the direct reading of their Latin sources unnecessary.

Yet, important as this vigorous promotion of Christian studies was, it did not mean the end of classical learning. The antique schools continued to function alongside their Christian counterparts, and traditional secular education, particularly the study of grammar, rhetoric, law, and medicine, was to receive added impetus after 533 from the Emperor Justinian's efforts to revive antique culture in regions recovered from the barbarians, and his specific proposal to fund the teaching of liberal studies at Rome.[11] As a result, up to the end of the sixth century at least, the Latin language and antique culture in general were far from overwhelmed by Christian and barbarian influences. And not only in Italy. There is ample evidence that in the southern part of Merovingian Gaul, as well as in Visigothic Spain, Roman institutions and customs were kept alive, and cultivated groups and individuals maintained a lively interest in Latin letters.[12]

The beginning of the seventh century marks a decisive turning-point. Certainly, liberal studies continue to be promoted at Rome and other Italian cities, as well as at certain centres in Visigothic Spain, but generally the seventh and eighth centuries witness the almost complete disappearance of the antique schools and the virtual eclipse of the traditional culture which they had helped to perpetuate. It was the completion of a process which had been set in train by the social and political disruption attending the wars between the Frankish kingdoms and hastened by the upheaval of the Lombard invasions after 568. Where culture survived the crush of barbarism it was ecclesiastical, not secular.[13] The flame of classical learning had been all but extinguished.

The long and slow process of rekindling would take its start at the rim of civilized Europe and work gradually inwards towards the centre. For it was in Ireland and Britain that the Latin, and to a lesser extent the Greek, legacy was kept alive to be transmitted across the Channel into Gaul and Italy as successive missionaries and teachers set about establishing on Continental soil the instructional centres which they had developed in their own lands for the understanding and promotion of the Christian faith. It is a just irony that the Latin language, which had been instrumental in assisting the spread of Christian teaching, should now be reliant upon the Church for its own survival. For it was the need for a Latin-reading clergy that motivated the Irish and Welsh monks at such foundations as Clonard, Kells, Darrow, Llan-Carvan, and Llan-Iltud to devote their energy first to acquiring and then to imparting a knowledge of Latin, without which there could be no serious study of the Bible and the Psalter. Not that we must suppose that the Latin which they and their pupils came to command was anything more than rudimentary. After all, Roman culture had barely penetrated these Celtic outposts; Latin was an alien language to be learned not through familiarity with the spoken idiom or the Latin authors themselves, but artificially through the use of grammars and word-lists.[14] Yet, if the level of grammatical training which the Celtic monasteries provided was at best elementary and the result a Latin far removed from classical idiom, they may take credit for being the first to respond to the challenge of teaching the language of the Scriptures to Christianized communities with few surviving links with the antique past.

Towards the close of the seventh century the same challenge was taken up by the Anglo-Saxon cathedral schools, and with even greater urgency. For the Roman Church in Britain faced the double task of promoting Christian studies among a newly converted barbarian people and making up lost ground against the Celtic Church, which had been taking full advantage of the Latin training provided by Irish teachers.[15] The important date is 669 when Pope Vitalian dispatched Theodore of Tarsus to succeed Deusdedit as Archbishop of the English Church. What distinguished the work of Theodore and his associate Hadrian was not the introduction of any new system of organizing Christian education or any new method of teaching the Latin language. The important and successful innovations in these areas would be made by various of their pupils. Rather, it was the breadth of learning which Theodore and Hadrian offered their students. To the teaching of Latin they added training in Greek, and this was supplemented by reading in selected sacred and profane authors, as well as instruction in metrics, astronomy, and ecclesiastical computation.[16] Study of the Scriptures was to be part only of Christian education. Of parallel importance was acquaintance with some of the main currents of ancient learning.

Theodore and Hadrian, though they travelled extensively throughout Britain in organizing a national English Church and attracted pupils wherever they went, concentrated their instructional efforts at Canterbury and around East Anglia, bringing new life to the bishop's schools which had been established in that region since the time of Augustine around 600.[17] Through a number of their first- and second-generation pupils, however, they exercised a wide and lasting influence as important centres of study and teaching were established in other parts of the country. At the abbey of Malmesbury in Wessex, Aldhelm, the most gifted pupil of Theodore and Hadrian, produced a variety of compositions in both prose and verse which reveal a wide reading in both sacred and profane authors. At the Wearmouth–Jarrow monastery in Northumbria, founded in 674 by Benedict Biscop, who had accompanied Theodore and Hadrian on their journey to Britain, and who had furnished the monastery with many manuscripts, the Venerable Bede wrote numerous exegetical works and made a substantial contribution to martyrology and ecclesiastical history, displaying at every turn a close familiarity not only with the Scriptures themselves, but also with the writings of the Fathers and a number of Latin and Greek authors. At York, Bede's pupil Egbert began a tradition of scholarship which continued with his successors Elbert and Alcuin. And to these we may add Daniel at Winchester, Winfred at Nursling, and Tatwine at Canterbury. It was indeed the work of this generation of scholars which made England an acknowledged centre of scriptural studies in the eighth century.[18]

Yet, if scholarship was an important activity at the English monasteries and cathedral schools, so was teaching, and it was during the first half of the eighth century that the pattern of Christian education in England was set. In his poem *On the Bishops and Saints of the Church of York* Alcuin gives a summary of his own preparation under his master Elbert, and it is clear that the course of study was very much in the spirit of Theodore and Hadrian. At the centre stood close reading of the Scriptures, but this was supplemented by instruction in those liberal arts which might serve as aids to proper understanding and interpretation and as guides in matters of doctrine and ritual – grammar, rhetoric, law, poetry, astronomy, natural history, arithmetic, geometry, and music.[19] Thus, since a good deal of the material for these ancillary subjects was most readily available in the encyclopedic works of Martianus Capella, Cassiodorus, and Isidore, themselves largely dependent upon Greek and Roman sources, classical learning came to occupy an important place in English education in the eighth century.

The Anglo-Saxon scholars whom we have mentioned are the most notable among a number of individuals who together gained for the eighth-century English Church a wide reputation for learning. They were gifted and industrious men who were taught and themselves taught at foundations which placed a high value upon scriptural studies, encouraged training in the liberal arts, and through the collection, copying, and exchange of manuscripts brought within reach the learning of the past. It would be a mistake to assume, however, that the likes of Aldhelm, Bede, and Alcuin were at all representative of the general class of monks and clerics, or that the foundations with which they were associated were typical. Already in 734, in a letter to Egbert of York, Bede expressed concern over the state of the Northumbrian Church, and elsewhere complained of a general lack of commitment to studies in the monasteries.[20] Boniface expressed similar concern in a letter to Cuthbert of Canterbury.[21] Finally, we have confirmation of official concern over the general decline of moral and intellectual discipline in the thirty Canons of the Council of Clovesho summoned by Archbishop Cuthbert in 747 at the prompting of Pope Zacharias. Certainly, the picture we get of monastic and priestly life is a sorry one: bishops and priests negligent of their pastoral duties, particularly preaching; priests failing through slackness or ignorance to perform the basic offices; candidates admitted to the priesthood without examination; widespread neglect of scriptural studies; monasteries becoming the resort of travelling poets, musicians, minstrels, and buffoons; excessive eating and drinking; a consuming passion on the part of monks, nuns, and mynchens for elaborate dress and adornment; a preoccupation with secular activities at the expense of the established festivals of the Christian calendar.[22]

The summoning of the Council of Clovesho is itself, of course, an indication of the readiness of the English Church to attempt to reform abuses and stimulate learning, and further resolutions were made at the Council of Chelsea in 787.[23] However, time was not on the side of renewal. From the closing years of the eighth century successive Viking invaders overwhelmed the greater part of Britain. Many monasteries, among them Wearmouth–Jarrow and Lindisfarne, were ravaged, their libraries and scriptoria sacked; others were reduced to a shadow of their former selves. A remarkable period in the history of the Anglo-Saxon Church, a period in which the fusion of the Celtic and Roman traditions brought forth three generations of renowned scholars and teachers, came to an end. The observation of Alfred the Great less than a century later tells the tale:

> So clear fallen away is learning now in the Angle race, that there are very few on this side Humber who would know how to render their service-book into English, or read off an epistle out of Latin into English, and I ween there would not be many on the other side of Humber.[24]

The Anglo-Saxon Church would recover and Britain would regain a place in the world of learning, thanks in no small part to the efforts of Alfred himself. In the mean time, it is on the Continent that the Latin language and with it the essentials of ancient learning are being fostered. By the time of the earliest Viking invasions around 793, Alcuin of York was already at the court of Charlemagne assisting in the grand educational design which Charlemagne had inaugurated. That Charlemagne should have looked to an Anglo-Saxon to aid him in his enterprise is fitting, since it had been the Continental missionary efforts of the Anglo-Saxon Church that had laid the groundwork. Since the second half of the seventh century the likes of Wilfrid of York, Willibrord, Suidbert, Boniface, Albert of York, Willihad, and Leofwin, aided by scores of zealous and energetic men and women from all parts of the kingdom, had devoted their energies to Christianizing and educating Friesland and Central Germany, thus preparing the way for the revival of learning with which Charlemagne's name is associated.[25]

Yet much remained to be done. The missionary labours of the Anglo-Saxons had resulted in the establishment of many new monastic houses, the rejuvenation of others, and the building up of numerous libraries and scriptoria. In addition, there had been set in motion a much needed process of ecclesiastical reform. None the less, under the Merovingian rulers the cultural decline throughout the Frankish Empire had been so complete that Charlemagne inherited a Church whose clergy were barely equipped to perform correctly the basic offices, still less to apply themselves in any meaningful way to the study of the sacred texts. Charlemagne announced his intention to remedy these deficiencies in his First Capitulary of 769, again in the General Admonition of 789, and most particularly in the *Epistola de litteris colendis* sent sometime between 780 and 801 to Abbot Baugulf of Fulda for distribution to all abbots and bishops.[26]

The Palace School, which Alcuin served as head from 782 to 796, was central to Charlemagne's design. Under Alcuin's supervision and following methods devised by him during his teaching years at York, training not only in Latin grammar and orthography, but also in the elements of arithmetic, geometry, versification, rhetoric, and dialectic, was given to pupils of all ages, as well as to those who were to be responsible in their turn for providing the Church with an adequate supply of clergy, readers, singers, copyists, and administrators, and for effecting an improvement in general culture and education. While it is to be admitted that the results of the enterprise fell short of the universal education for which Charlemagne may have hoped, the School did turn out scores of successful teachers and served as a model for more modest monastic and episcopal schools throughout the Empire. Moreover, as at the Palace School, so in these centres training progressed beyond the rudiments of the Latin language to embrace more advanced study in the liberal arts. Thus, Charlemagne's educational initiative had the effect not only of preserving and extending a knowledge of correct Latin, but also of establishing a secure place for important elements of the classical tradition.[27]

No less important, however, for the preservation of the classical heritage was the role played by Charlemagne's court as an 'academy' for the appreciation and emulation of the literary traditions of Greece and Rome. Partly, no doubt, to add lustre to his rule, but also from a genuine enthusiasm for learning, Charlemagne surrounded himself with some of the most accomplished and stimulating talents of the age from all parts of Europe. From England, as we have seen, came Alcuin ('Flaccus'), from Ireland Dungal, from Italy Peter of Pisa, Paulinus of Aquileia ('Timotheus'), and Paul the Deacon, from Spain the Goth Theodulph ('Pindar'), future Bishop of Orleans, and from Francia itself the young Angilbert ('Homer'). These were the men who formed the Emperor's entourage as he moved his court between the various royal residences before the completion of the palace at Aachen in 794. They were busy scholars and teachers, some were men of affairs in politics and the Church, but for brief periods they formed an intimate circle around their 'David', displaying their poetic talents through half-playful, half-serious rivalry in public display and private correspondence. By the time the palace at Aachen was completed, some members of the circle had left the royal retinue to take up important positions, but the court continued to provide a stimulating environment for the creative spirit as new poets, prominent among them Moduin of Autun ('Naso') and Einhard ('Bezaleel'), joined the coterie.[28]

The biblical and classical nicknames which this first generation of Carolingian poets assumed speak of their double patrimony. They were all dedicated servants of the Church and it is natural enough that a good deal of their poetry should have drawn its inspiration from the Bible and the liturgy, and that for models they should have looked to the early Christian Latin poets. Sedulius, Nemesian, Prudentius, Juvencus, Arator, Avitus, Venantius Fortunatus were the authors of their reading and reminiscences abound.[29] Yet the secular tradition exerted a powerful influence. Just as they were keen to celebrate their royal patron as the 'new Augustus' and Aachen as a 'second Rome',[30] so they were unashamedly conscious of their own poetic efforts as a contribution to the renewal of ancient learning which Charlemagne's rule promised.[31] The range of genres which they attempted was wide – verse epistle, satire, elegy, lyric, epic, epyllion, pastoral, epigram – and one does not read far before becoming aware of their debt in matters of style, vocabulary, and cadence to Virgil, Statius, Lucan, Ovid, Homer, Calpurnius Siculus, and Martial. Even the most generous critic would be reluctant to claim that the Latin poetry of these early Carolingians merits high regard when measured by the best from the classical period. Yet, compared with the host of mediocre versifiers which the Carolingian age produced, these poets display in many of their pieces a fluidity of diction, a freshness of imagery, and a sureness of style which make them worthy representatives of the tradition which they strove to renew and perpetuate.

The testimony of Walafrid Strabo and Lupus of Ferrières, both writing during the reign of Charlemagne's successor, Louis the Pious, would suggest that the death of Charlemagne in 814 marked the beginning of a dramatic decline in learning throughout the Frankish Empire.[32] Certainly, Louis the Pious was preoccupied more with monastic reform than with the advancement of polite studies. He did engage a few scholars and teachers, among them Walafrid Strabo, who served as tutor to young Charles the Bald; and we cannot discount the intellectual interests of Louis's second wife, Judith.[33] However, the royal court under Louis was no longer the vibrant centre of scholarly and literary activity which it had been under Charlemagne. As for Louis's immediate successors, Lothar, Louis the German, and Charles the Bald, only the last made any serious effort to patronize scholarship.[34] However, the admittedly modest commitment of the emperors is misleading, for what we witness during the ninth century is not so much a decline in learning as a shift away from the court as the focal point of intellectual activity in favour of monastic and cathedral centres in different parts of the empire. Hence, it is with such places as Reichenau, Ferrières, Fulda, Corbie, Liège, St Gall, and Auxerre that prominent figures like Walafrid, Gottschalk, Hraban Maur, Paschasius Radbertus, Sedulius Scottus, Servatus Lupus, Heiric, and Notker are associated.

One of the major factors in this transformation is the energy displayed by various abbots and masters in securing for their libraries collections of books sufficient to support the scholarly work of their houses, and as far as the survival of classical culture is concerned this is by far the most important aspect of ninth-century monastic activity. This is not to say that the recovery and reproduction of classical texts was of first importance. The largest bulk of manuscripts copied were of patristical works and of biblical and liturgical books. None the less, it is evident that the texts of the Latin authors were in great demand and that the search for them was widespread and enterprising.[35] The results are staggering. The copyists at Charlemagne's court scriptorium around 800 had made an important beginning, producing texts of Lucretius, Vitruvius, Justinus, the Elder Pliny, the Elder Seneca, Calcidius, and a Latin Euclid.[36] By the end of the ninth century, the monastic scriptoria, principally those at Tours, Fleury, Ferrières, Auxerre, St Armand, Corbie, Rheims, Lorsch, Reichenau, and Fulda, had produced copies of the larger part of Latin literature.[37] Even if the ninth century cannot boast a single towering figure who stamped his character upon the development of European culture, none the less, in keeping alive the spirit of Carolingian humanism and in recovering a substantial portion of ancient literature, it played no small part in laying the foundations for the more impressive advances in learning which lay in the future.

Taken as a whole the tenth and eleventh centuries might be seen to constitute a period of stagnation, a dreary hiatus between the shining promise of the Carolingian age and the brilliant burst of intellectual activity ushered in by the twelfth century. Yet here and there patches of radiance relieve the gloom. Certainly, by the mid-point of the tenth century the flame of the Carolingian 'renaissance' was fading as Charlemagne's descendants wrangled over the remains of his empire and struggled to find a leader strong enough to hold off the heathen. To the north, the Norsemen swept up the peaceful rivers, sacking towns and cloisters. In Spain and Asia Minor Islam was expanding, and in eastern Europe the Magyars advanced as far as Augsburg. It was Otto I, the heir to Saxony, who preserved an area where trade could continue and where the arts were fostered. He stopped the Magyars at the battle of the Lech in 955 and consolidated his holdings with his coronation as Emperor of the Holy Roman Empire in Rome in 962.

The Ottonian dynasty lasted until the death of Otto III in 1002 and from the beginning the court of the Ottos was a cosmopolitan affair with embassies from as far afield as Italy, Spain, and Byzantium. Having by his own marriages formed links with powerful European interests, Otto I allied his throne with the Eastern Empire by arranging for the marriage of his heir to Theophanu, daughter of the former Byzantine Emperor Romanus II. There was a corresponding cosmopolitan flavour to the educational and intellectual activity which the Ottos sponsored. Otto I brought to the court Deacon Gunzo and Stephen of Novara. He engaged the diplomatic services of the brilliant scholar and linguist Liutprand of Pavia, whom he created Bishop of Cremona. From Lorraine he brought Rathier, whose humanistic interests embraced the teaching of many of the Roman authors. Theophanu engaged John Philagathos, a Greek scholar from Rossano in Calabria, as tutor for her son Otto III. And in 997 Otto III himself invited to the court his father's former teacher, the gifted and versatile Gerbert of Rheims, later to become Pope Sylvester II.

This importation of talent, however, was not designed primarily to make the court the centre of intellectual life as it had been under Charlemagne. It is to be seen, rather, as a deliberate move towards enhancing the already close alliance between the monarchy and the imperial Church by placing under royal patronage the educational and cultural endeavours of the major episcopal seats. To this end Stephen of Novara was appointed Bishop of Würzburg with express instructions to build up the school there, as Bruno, the brother of Otto I, had done at Cologne. Similarly, Rathier and, later, Notker were appointed to Liège, and Gerbert to Rheims. Further, cathedral schools were founded or revived in Magdeburg, Hildesheim, Mainz, Worms, and Paderborn. Since the immediate purpose in upgrading the cathedral schools was to strengthen the Church by ensuring a ready supply of educated clergy and efficient administrators, the training offered was practical rather than literary, but, given the interests of those who played a leading role, we may assume that reading of the ancient authors was not wholly neglected.[38]

However, it was in the liberal environment of the French cathedral schools, especially those of the Loire valley, that the reading of the classical authors most bore fruit. In Godfrey of Rheims, Adalbero of Laon, Hilderbert of Lavardin, Marbod of Rennes, and Baudry of Bourgueil we have the emergence of a group of poets who were inspired by their schoolroom acquaintance with Juvenal, Persius, Martial, and especially Ovid to recreate something of the literary atmosphere of the early Carolingian period, and in lively response to the fashionable milieu in which they lived to attempt new subjects which were to find their full expression in twelfth- and thirteenth-century lyric.[39]

When we turn to the monasteries we find that the copying tradition of the Carolingian period is being maintained, particularly at Reichenau, Echternach, Freising, Tegernsee, St Emmeram, Regensburg, and St Gall. Liturgical books dominate, but steady attention was also being paid to the reproduction of classical texts, not only in the German scriptoria, but also in those at Fleury, Gembloux, Lobbes, and especially Montecassino, which had made a remarkable recovery from the destruction visited upon the abbey and its possessions by the Saracen raids of 883.[40]

At the same time, it is proper to note that, despite this continuing interest in adding to the stock of classical texts, there still persisted something of the same reserve towards secular literature which we noted with respect to the early Christian period, and which had been expressed in extreme terms around the middle of the ninth century by Paschasius and Paulus Albarus.[41] At the convent of Gandersheim, founded by the great-grandparents of Otto I, and presided over during the latter half of the tenth century by Otto's learned niece Gerberga, the nun Hrosvitha was provided with the opportunity to read the plays of Terence. Her response, however, was not one of unreserved enthusiasm. Indeed, though she imitated Terence in form and style in the composition of her six Latin dramas, she was careful in the preface to warn against the corrupting influence of his

129

subject-matter.[42] Othlo, monk of St Emmeram between 1032 and 1070, attributed to his preoccupation with Lucan a persistent illness and a terrifying dream in which his clothing and his bed dripped with blood.[43] Around the middle of the eleventh century Peter Damian unleashed a furious onslaught against a whole range of ancient authors – Plato, Aristotle, Pythagoras, Euclid, the tragic and comic dramatists, the orators, the satirists – banishing them all to the darkness and filth of their earthly wisdom.[44] It would be rash to extrapolate from one or two instances: Hrosvitha's protestations may be no more than conventional; Othlo was a man obsessed with 'visions'; and the extravagant outbursts of Peter Damian have the ring of fanaticism. None the less, the spiritualism which spurred the reforming zeal of the Cluniac movement cannot be discounted as an important feature of the tenth- and eleventh-century monasticism, and the examples we have cited may well be symptomatic of a growing reaction against secular reading.

From a point around the beginning of the seventh century when there was every chance that antique culture would disappear altogether we have seen it not only survive but flourish to the degree that at the beginning of the twelfth century it had become woven into the very fabric of medieval society. The major factor has been the Latin language, which has come to enjoy privileged status as the speech of common currency throughout Europe. It is the language of the Church, of secular administration, diplomacy, law, and business, the vehicle for public and private communication. As such it occupies a commanding place in the curriculum of the schools, and the standard Latin grammars, Priscian's *Institutiones* and the *Ars maior* and *Ars minor* of Donatus, in addition to instructing in the rudiments of the language, offer generous selections from a variety of classical Latin authors. Thus, an acquaintance with antique literature has become an inescapable element in general education, and for those whose interests extend beyond the bare requirements of literacy a wide range of Latin authors is available for reading or imitation, either in complete texts or in one or other of the florilegia which have become a feature of the age.[45]

The fact remains, however, that, deeply as the antique past has stamped its character upon the medieval world, there are large areas of classical learning which have been more or less neglected or which the absence of Greek texts and general ignorance of the Greek language have rendered inaccessible. From the twelfth century onwards changed conditions and fresh needs serve to bring some of these areas into greater focus, and the emergence of certain professional classes, together with the development of new intellectual centres, stimulates a wider and more systematic exploitation of ancient learning. This is especially the case in the areas of law, medicine, science, and philosophy. The repository of Roman law was the *Corpus iuris civilis*, compiled in the sixth century under the auspices of Justinian and comprising the *Code*, the codification of imperial legislation, the *Digest*, a summary of the prominent Roman jurists, the *Institutes*, a textbook for legal training, and the *Novels*, Justinian's later legislation. Between the seventh and the eleventh centuries the *Corpus* would seem to have been little used, even in areas where Roman law survived. From the twelfth century, however, reliance upon customary law and local usage became inadequate to meet the demands of an increasingly complex society and the need was recognized for lawyers professionally trained in the art of jurisprudence. Reponse was most immediate in northern Italy where Bologna emerged as the leading centre for legal studies. First under Irnerius, and then under his successors Bulgarus, Martinus, Hugo, and Jacobus, the 'Four Doctors', the *Corpus* came into its own as the basic text for research, teaching, and practical application. Professional centres were soon established in other Italian cities, as well as in Spain and France, thus ensuring for Roman legal theory and practice an enduring place in the European tradition.

Faced with the task of establishing jurisprudence as an independent branch of study twelfth-century scholars were able to employ the simple expedient of turning to a readily available body of texts which preserved the fruits of Rome's experience as an imperial power and the accumulated wisdom of her finest legal minds. In the case of medicine, science, and philosophy it was again the classical past that would furnish the essentials, but the route to the sources was not so direct. In each of these areas the substantial contributions had been made by the Greeks rather than the Romans. Further, while the Romans leaned heavily upon Greek learning and consciously imitated Greek models in shaping their own literary tradition, they did little in the way of direct translation of Greek texts into Latin. As a consequence, the almost complete absence of Greek manuscripts in the Latin west during the early medieval period meant that the sole available repositories of general knowledge were the works of the Latin encyclopedists Boethius, Isidore of Seville, Martianus Capella, Cassiodorus, and Bede.[46] These were certainly successful enough in catering to the limited needs and interests of the period, and we have already noted the role which they played in liberal studies. However, as purely derivative compilations which observed little distinction between the factual and the fanciful, the significant and the merely curious, they could not hope to serve as a lasting substitute for the rich deposits of original material which Greek learning promised, and it was the recovery of this material that the twelfth century initiated. As a result of the efforts of a large number of translators, working for the most part in Italy, Sicily, and Spain, Latin versions of scores of Greek writers were made available, some from Greek originals, some from intermediate Arabic translations, not a few from both. In addition, Latin translations were made of a large number of important Arabic texts, as well as of Arabic commentaries on Greek works. Moreover, the rate at which the work of translation proceeded was exceedingly rapid. So much so that by the middle of the thirteenth century the medieval world had access for the first time to the larger part of Greek and Arabic medicine, mathematics, astronomy, natural science, astrology, alchemy, and literature, as well as significant parts of Greek philosophy. A partial listing of works and authors would include the following: the *Aphorisms, Prognostics,* and *De regimine morborum acutorum* of Hippocrates; numerous works of Galen; the *Elements, Data, Optica,* and *Catoptrica* of Euclid; the *Almagest, Quadripartitum,* and *Planisphera* of Ptolemy; the *De motu* and *Elementatio physica* of Proclus; the *Analytica priora, Sophistici elenchi, Topica, Analytica posteriora, Physica, De anima, Parva naturalia, Meteorologica (I–IV), Metaphysica (I–IV), Ethica Nicomachea* (part), and *De generatione et corruptione* of Aristotle; the *Meno* and *Phaedo* of Plato; the *Pneumatica* of Hero of Alexandria; the *Algebra* and the trigonometrical and astronomical tables of al-Khwarizmi; the *De scientiis* of al Farabi; the *De anima* and other works of Avicenna; the *De motu et tempore* of Alexander of Aphrodisias; the *De mensura circuli* of Archimedes.[47]

The assimilation of the new learning was not a rapid process, and there is little enough evidence of immediate impact. Lambert of St Omer's encyclopedic *Liber floridus,* published around 1120, is another gathering together of the traditional Latin sources, and Bartholomew the Englishman's widely popular *On the Properties of Things,* written about a century later, is very much in the same mode. Yet an increasing number of references to new works testifies to the gradual diffusion of the new translations throughout Europe.[48] Certainly, scholars in such major intellectual centres as Salerno, Bologna, Toulouse, Montpellier, Chartres, and Paris became increasingly aware of Greek and Arabic learning, and during the thirteenth century it was more and more the new logic and science, especially the works of Aristotle and his commentators, which came to dominate the university curricula.

The task of accommodating so vast an amount of new information, however, was not without complications. Indeed, it was to tax the ingenuity of successive generations of scholars, and on one front in particular. This involved the potential which much of this material had for disrupting orthodox Christian teaching. It was in the area of natural philosophy that the danger was seen to be most acute, and it was the Neoplatonic and Aristotelian world views which posed the most pressing challenge. From the time of Augustine certain Platonic and Neoplatonic elements had found a place within the Christian framework, and during the twelfth century Bernard and Thierry of Chartres, William of Conches, Bernard Sylvestris, and others had drawn heavily upon the Neoplatonic tradition in their efforts to reconcile pagan and Christian cosmological concepts. During the twelfth century it was left to the Franciscans Alexander of Hales and Bonaventura to attempt to complete this grand synthesis, though the condemnation of Bonaventura's pupil Petrus Olivi serves to underscore the serious difficulties posed by the inherent mysticism of Neoplatonic thought.

In the case of the Aristotelian philosophy the path towards accommodation had to some extent already been prepared, and the recent increment in Aristotelian learning would seem to have every chance of ready acceptance. Aristotle himself enjoyed an unequalled reputation as the undisputed authority in so many branches of knowledge, and such Christian scholars as Anselm and Peter Lombard had demonstrated that the Aristotelian logic, if judiciously employed, could be of immense value as a critical tool in theological exegesis and debate. In the area of natural philosophy, however, the situation was complicated by the fact that much of the 'new' Aristotle did not arrive alone but was accompanied by a mass of Arabic commentary whose orthodoxy was highly suspect. Official concern expressed itself early in the thirteenth century. In 1210 the

provincial council at Paris banned both public and private reading
of Aristotle's books on natural philosophy, along with their commentaries.[49] In 1215 the ban was repeated and the *Metaphysics*
singled out for special mention.[50] In 1231 Pope Gregory IX restricted the ban to those books which had not been declared free from
error and established a commission to oversee the process. Whatever
the thoroughness of the commission's work, in 1255 the whole of the
'new' Aristotle was prescribed for the degree of Master of Arts at the
University of Paris.

However, this cleansing of individual Aristotelian texts as a
condition of their use was no more than the shaving of the head and
the paring of the nails which St Jerome had prescribed with respect
to all pagan writings.[51] The greater challenge lay in reconciling the
essentials of Aristotelian metaphysics with Christian theology to
achieve a lasting and acceptable synthesis, and the response to this
challenge on the part of various thirteenth- and fourteenth-century
scholars, most notably St Thomas Aquinas, represents an essential
characteristic of the whole scholastic movement. The details of the
various contributions need not detain us. For our purpose it is
important only to underscore the preoccupation of late medieval
thinkers with the works of Aristotle and his commentators, and
not only in the area of theology. In the field of science Robert
Grosseteste, Albertus Magnus, and others were busy analysing and
interpreting the large amount of new technical learning which the
work of the translators had made available. Similarly, in the wider
field of general knowledge men like Vincent of Beauvais, whose
Speculum Maius, written around the middle of the thirteenth century,
stands as a supreme example of the scholastic impulse, were
perpetuating the encyclopedic tradition (represented in the ninth
century by Hraban Maur and in the twelfth by Thierry of Chartres
and Hugh of St Victor) in an attempt to bring the vast bulk of new
information into intelligible and manageable compass.[52]

Now this is not to suggest that the entire contribution of the later
medieval period lay in the reformulation of ancient learning. It was
after all the age of Chaucer, *Piers Plowman*, the morality play, the
vagantes, *Carmina Burana*, *Sir Gawain and the Green Knight*, Thomas the
Rhymer, *Parzival*, the *Roman de la Rose*, Dante, Petrarch, Boccaccio,
Salisbury Cathedral, the Palazzo Vecchio, Giotto, Duccio's *Maesta*,
and the *ars nova*. It is fair to say, none the less, that within the strictly
scholarly domain the thirteenth and fourteenth centuries constitute

a period of consolidation where the preservation of the Christian order through the adaptation of inherited learning was of greater urgency than the acquisition of new knowledge or the pursuit of original and independent enquiry. Dante asks the apposite question: 'who would strive to expound again felicity, which Aristotle has already expounded, or who would undertake again the apology of old age, which Cicero has already accomplished?'[53] Moreover, it is a frame of mind which affected the attitude towards classical learning itself to the extent that, while a good deal of effort was directed towards gathering into omnibus collections what had already been recovered from ancient sources, there was little inclination to extend the boundaries by exploring untrodden paths.[54] The reawakening of that impulse awaited the infusion of a new energy and conditions of a different order.

We began by suggesting that during the ten centuries or so between the collapse of the Roman Empire in the west and the end of the Middle Ages the fortunes of the Epicurean philosophy are bound up with the fortunes of classical culture itself. It will now be apparent that the correlation is a negative one. The medieval response to the culture and learning of the ancient past follows a clear pattern whose lines were drawn by St Augustine; the 'spoils of the Egyptians' have been duly gathered up.[55] The Latin language has been preserved as a prerequisite for Christian teaching and scholarship and as the most effective medium for ecclesiastical and secular administration. The ancient authors have been selectively cultivated as practical models of style and expression and as exemplars of literary taste. The ancient sources have been mined to enlarge the store of technical and general knowledge. Greece, Rome, and the Arab world have supplied the essential texts for the professions of medicine and law. The logic of Aristotle has furnished the critical basis for theological debate, and his natural philosophy has been adapted to secure the metaphysical foundations of the Christian world-view.

The first half of this chapter has been an attempt to sketch the main lines of this development as it unfolded, and we have touched upon a wide range of classical authors and texts. The name of Epicurus has been conspicuous by its absence. Nor is it the case that we have been keeping Epicurus in the wings only to produce him with a dramatic flourish at the last to take his place alongside the principals. The plain fact is that Epicurus commands a place only among the supporting cast, and this for reasons which are simple to state. In the process of sifting through the ancient spoils utility was only one of the criteria to be used for distinguishing the silver from the dross. Another was acceptability. In the case of most of the ancient authors all that was required in order to bring their work into conformity with orthodox Christian teaching was a greater or lesser degree of adjustment. Epicurus was a different matter. The essential tenets of his philosophy were so at variance with the fundamental principles of the Christian faith that there existed a gulf which no degree of ingenuity could hope to span. Moreover, as the sifting of the spoils continued, the more the silver accumulated, the more readily could the dross be disregarded. Thus, Epicurus fell victim not only to his own extreme unorthodoxy, but also to the abundance of riches which the rest of the classical tradition was yielding up. Yet produce Epicurus we must, since he is not totally absent from the stage. Indeed, if the role he plays is substantially smaller than those of some of his classical rivals, it at least has the distinction of being a double one. For, as we shall see, the Middle Ages knew not one Epicurus, but two.

The extent to which medieval readers might have become acquainted with Epicurean teaching through direct access to Epicurean texts is difficult to assess. The two principal Epicurean sources, Diogenes Laertius and Lucretius, were certainly known. In the Greek east Diogenes' *Lives of the Eminent Philosophers* was known to Stephanus of Byzantium and Hesychius of Miletus in the sixth century, to Photius in the ninth, to the compiler of the *Suida* in the tenth, and to Tzetzes and Eustathius in the twelfth, and copies of the work found their way to the Latin west. The two principal extant manuscripts (codex Borbonicus Neapolitanus Gr. iii. B. 29 and codex Parisinus Gr. 1759) attest to an interest in the work during the twelfth and thirteenth centuries, an interest which is confirmed by the fact that around the middle of the twelfth century Admiral Maio and the Archbishop of Palermo requested a translation from Henricus Aristippus, Archdeacon of Catania and first Latin translator of Plato's *Meno* and *Phaedo*.[56] Around 1335 the Englishman Walter Burley responded to a heightened interest in the ancient philosophical tradition by drawing heavily upon Diogenes for his *De vitis et moribus philosophorum*, and in 1431 Diogenes received his first Latin translation at the hands of Ambrosius Traversarius Camaldulensis.

In the case of Lucretius' *De rerum natura* the period of keenest activity would seem to be the ninth century when the two oldest extant manuscripts, O and Q, were written.[57] O (Leiden: Voss. Lat. F 30) was written shortly after 800 at Charlemagne's Palace School at Aachen, with corrections entered by the resident Irish scholar Dungal.[58] Its subsequent whereabouts are unclear, but by the end of the fifteenth century it had found its way to St Martin at Mainz. Q (Leiden: Voss. Lat. Q 94) was written later in the ninth century in north-east France, and may have been housed at Saint-Bertin.[59] Selections in two ninth-century florilegia from Reichenau and St Gall indicate that the *De rerum natura* was circulating in the Lake Constance region, and a letter written from St Gall by Ermenrich of Ellwangen around 850 contains a quotation. The French abbeys of Lobbes and Corbie had obtained copies by the twelfth century, [60] and Bobbio owned a copy already in the ninth.[61]

Finally, to Diogenes Laertius and Lucretius we must add Cicero, even if, or perhaps no less because, his presentation of Epicureanism is in places deliberately unflattering. The treatises which contain the most extensive treatment of Epicurean teaching are the *De natura deorum* and the *De finibus*, and of these the former was in circulation in France from the beginning of the ninth century and in Italy from the last half of the eleventh, while the latter was known in Germany in the eleventh century and in France from the twelfth.[62]

A record of the transmission of Epicurean sources takes us only so far. Certainly, texts were not copied for no reason. Maintaining an active scriptorium entailed a certain amount of expenditure in terms of time, materials, and expertise, and it might seem reasonable to suppose that texts which were copied were also studied. Yet we cannot be certain that the copying of a given manuscript did in fact signify a serious interest in its contents. We must allow that the business of copying could acquire a certain momentum of its own with the result that a manuscript might be copied for no other reason than that it happened to be at hand. Further, enough is known about the movement of scholars and teachers among the various abbeys, monasteries, and schools to allow us to assume that some manuscripts were copied only to provide a stock for purposes of borrowing, exchange, and presentation. Moreover, in the case of the Epicurean sources we have mentioned there are particular considerations. Only Book X of Diogenes' *Lives* deals with Epicurus, so that an interest in the work cannot necessarily be equated with an interest in Epicurean teaching. Interest in the *De rerum natura* may reflect the attraction of Lucretius the poet as much as Lucretius the Epicurean spokesman. Finally, the reputation which Cicero enjoyed during the medieval period is sufficient in itself to account for the copying of any of his works which became available. In short, therefore, the currency of Epicurean source materials cannot be taken as conclusive evidence of a serious and sustained interest in Epicurean teaching.

Moreover, there is little about the nature of the scattered references to Epicurean doctrine in medieval writers which would suggest that they derive from critical examination of extended Epicurean texts. It would seem to be the case, rather, that Epicurean ideas gained currency largely through citations from Lucretius in the grammatical and lexicographical writings of Valerius Probus, Nonius Marcellus, and Priscian, whose works occupied a standard place in the medieval curriculum, and from references in the writings of the Fathers. What we witness, in short, is a process of distillation whereby Epicurean concepts filter through the sources in sufficient number to provide medieval scholars with some notion at least of Epicurean doctrine together with supporting text for a few key Epicurean positions. Thus, in his *Etymologies*, composed around the beginning of the seventh century as an attempt to reduce the accumulated knowledge of the past to manageable scope, as well as in his *De natura rerum*, Isidore of Seville is able to cull from his rich store of secondary sources Epicurean material relating to a range of questions concerning natural phenomena. In some cases what he offers is no more than a summary statement of the Epicurean view to be listed in catalogue fashion alongside the views of the other Greek schools. In others, he is equipped to offer a paraphrase of Lucretian material, supplemented at times with a brief quotation.[63] What we do not find in Isidore is any critical appraisal of Epicurean views or any attempt to provide a co-ordinated and comprehensive account of Epicurean teaching. Isidore is a compiler, and Epicurus is just one of a line of ancient thinkers whose opinion on various topics is to be recorded in order to render the account as complete as possible.

Isidore's treatment of Epicurus derives its importance from the fact that it set the pattern for subsequent encyclopedists. In his *De natura rerum*, written a century after Isidore, Bede makes similar use of Lucretian extracts, and in the ninth century Hraban Maur's *De universo* reproduces the greater part of Isidore's Lucretian material.

138

With respect to the fortunes of Epicureanism in general these encyclopedic works may be said to have had both a positive and negative effect. On the one hand, their popularity as basic reference works guaranteed an acquaintance, albeit superficial, with some of the elements of Epicurean science. Moreover, the fact that their authors were Christian scholars and had given their Lucretian references the appearance of conformity with Christian teaching gave Epicurus the scientist a degree of legitimacy. On the other hand, the fact that these works were expressly designed to serve as substitutes for the texts from which they had been compiled inhibited independent reading of Epicurean sources. Indeed, this reliance upon compendia was in a wider sense symptomatic of a general tendency to regard the boundaries of knowledge as fixed. It was an attitude which served to arrest the course of intellectual exploration and one which would persist in the area of science until the discovery of fresh deposits of ancient learning in the eleventh and twelfth centuries. As we have seen, however, the science which these deposits yielded was in largest part the science of Aristotle. Epicurus *philosophus* must wait in the wings. Centre stage is occupied.

In the mean time, another Epicurus is making his way through medieval Europe. He is not the proponent of a mechanistic universe or the advocate of a corpuscular theory of matter, but the champion of sensuality, the proprietor of the kitchen, the tavern, and the brothel. Familiar enough from classical and early Christian appearances he makes his medieval debut in costume in Martianus Capella's *Marriage of Mercury and Philology*, trailing roses and violets and all the enticements of pleasure.[64] He is the same Epicurus whom Boethius denounces a century later.[65] He is the Epicurus who prompted Giovanni Villani to explain the Florentine fires of 1115 and 1117 as acts of God against the 'luxurious and gluttonous sect of Epicureans';[66] and the Epicurus who accompanied the *vagantes* on their merry ramblings through Europe –

Alte clamat Epicurus:
venter satur est securus;
venter deus meus erit,
talem deum gula querit,
cuius templum est coquina
in qua redolent divina.[67]

He is Chaucer's franklin on the road to Canterbury:

> A Frankelyn was in his company;
> Whyt was his berd, as is the dayesye.
> Of his complexioun he was sangwyn.
> Wel loved he by the morwe a sop in wyn.
> To liven in delyt was ever his wone,
> For he was Epicurus owne sone.
> That held opinioun, that pleyn delyt
> Was verraily felicitee parfyt.[68]

He is the servant of 'fool's delight' in John Gower's *Mirour de l'omme*:

> Trop fuist du Foldelit apris
> Uns philosophes de jadys
> Qui Epicurus noun avoit:
> Car ce fuist cil q'a son avis
> Disoit que ly charnels delitz
> Soverain des autres biens estoit
> Et pour cela trestout laissoit
> Les biens del alme et se donnoit
> A sa caroigne; dont toutdis
> Depuis son temps assetz om voit
> De ses disciples qui toutdroit
> Suiont s'escole a tiel devis.[69]

He is the Epicurus who is depicted in book illuminations in the company of Nero, Holophernes, Sardanapalus, Herod, Judas, and Arius being trampled underfoot by the seven cardinal virtues.[70]

We need not follow this second Epicurus further. He leaves a clear trail. Let us note, however, what is clearly the case, namely, that in popular usage the term 'Epicurean' has little to do with any serious philosophical commitment to Epicurean doctrines. It is no more than a label to be attached to anyone whose primary concern is for worldly delights. John of Salisbury is explicit when he declares that 'the world is filled with Epicureans for the reason that in its great multitude of men there are few who are not slaves to lust'.[71] Yet this popular identification of Epicureanism with sensual living only mirrors the extent to which even among serious students of ancient learning Epicurus' theory of pleasure has come to overshadow all other aspects of his teaching. We may turn again to John of Salisbury, than whom there is nobody in the tenth century more conversant with the philosophic tradition. In more than one place in the *Policraticus* he does allude to other features of Epicurean doctrine, and in the matter of personal morality he is discerning and charitable enough to distinguish Epicurus himself from his later followers. None the less, what commands his almost exclusive attention is the Epicurean commitment to pleasure, narrowly interpreted as the satisfaction of desires, and his description of the Epicurean paradise may be taken as representative of the medieval view:

> the garden of the Epicureans has as its source lust, which also produces rivers which irrigate the whole of this vale of tears . . . . One stream is, as it were, the love of possession, by which wealth is sought for sufficiency and in which avarice labours to possess or to know more than is lawful; a second spreads the enticements of self-indulgence and flows down into a variety of delights as it strives to attain the joys of tranquillity and pleasure; the third gathers strength with which to protect natural liberty and to ward off the injury of any discomfort whatsoever, and after it has acquired abounding strength it bursts forth into the odious stream of tyranny; the fourth, as a result of its striving for celebrity and respect, in the struggle for eminence becomes swollen with trickery. These are the four rivers which pour out upon and surround the whole world and gush forth from the spring of ill will which has its origin from the slime of vanity.[72]

6

THE HUMANIST DEBATE

Epicurus' final medieval appearance is not in the part of *patronus voluptatis*, but in a role with which he was no less familiar – the arch-heretic. Against the harrowing backdrop of Dante's *inferno* we see him confined to the sixth circle in the company of Farinata, Frederick II, and others of Dante's unbelievers waiting for the lid of the coffin to be sealed for all eternity –

> Suo cimitero da questa parte hanno
> Con Epicuro tutti i suoi segauci,
> Che l'anima col corpo morte fanno.[1]

However, Epicurus' incarceration was to be far shorter in duration than Dante had anticipated. For within a hundred years he experienced a symbolic resurrection with the rediscovery of Lucretius' *De rerum natura* and its migration southwards across the Alps to the sunnier climate of its native Italy. The agent was the indefatigable collector of Greek and Latin manuscripts Poggio Bracciolini, who took advantage of his attendance as Papal Secretary at the Council of Constance to scour the neighbouring libraries in search of classical authors.[2] Precisely where he came upon the manuscript of the *De rerum natura* in the spring of 1417 he does not tell us. 'Locus satis longinquius' is the only clue.[3] The copy which he had made he sent for transcription to his Florentine friend and fellow book-hunter Niccolo Niccoli, though what happened to this copy is not known. Poggio requested its return repeatedly for the next twelve years, stressing again and again how much he desired to finish his reading of Lucretius' poem.[4] So anxious was he, indeed, that he had his travelling companion Bartolomeo da Montepulciano searching for another manuscript version.[5] In the mean time, Niccoli made a copy, now housed in the Laurentian Library (Codex Laurentianus 35,30), which became the parent of the many further copies of the poem made during the fifteenth century.[6]

Poggio's discovery of the *De rerum natura* certainly marks an important moment in the history of the Epicurean tradition. At a time when the early Italian humanists were passionately eager to broaden their knowledge of the classical authors and to enrich their discussions with as wide a sampling as possible of ancient opinion, it made available the principal Latin presentation of Epicurean teaching. It would be a mistake to conclude, however, that Poggio's discovery was itself the cause of a sudden reawakening of interest in Epicurean thought. It is the case, rather, that Poggio's clear excitement at discovering Lucretius reflects an interest already present. In requesting from Niccoli the return of his copy of the *De rerum natura* Poggio expressly states that there are many others besides himself who will be grateful for the opportunity to read it.[7] Moreover, we have the statement of one of Poggio's closest friends, Bartolomeo da Montepulciano, writing to Ambrogio Traversari in 1418, that he was acquainted, either personally or through correspondence, with a large number of individuals who had committed themselves to the Epicurean cause.[8]

Furthermore, Epicurus has already featured in humanist writings. In the 1390s Coluccio Salutati published the revised and expanded edition of his *De laboribus Herculis*, an allegorical treatment of the career and attributes of the mythical hero written very much in the medieval mode.[9] In the first part of Book IV Salutati prepares the way for an interpretation of Hercules' descent into the underworld by offering a general excursus on the katabasis theme illustrated by an examination of the descents of Orpheus, Theseus, and Amphiaraus. It is in the presentation of the Orpheus story that Epicurus makes his appearance, in the role of Orpheus himself. For, according to Salutati's elaborate interpretation, descent into the underworld represents the Epicurean's lowering of himself to a subhuman level in pursuit of worldly delights (*delectabilia*).[10] Having stated his general thesis Salutati pursues his identification of Orpheus with the Epicurean man through an elaborate series of associations and fanciful etymologies: Orpheus' connection with music links him closely with the Epicureans, who place the sounds of music among the most pleasurable delights.[11] Eurydice's name, transliterated into Latin, yields the idea of choosing among fleeting pleasures *(bonorum fluentium iudicium)*, an art in which the Epicurean is practised.[12] Virgil's depiction of Orpheus' severed head floating downstream still crying forth Eurydice's name represents the tenacity with which the Epicurean clings even to the memory of sensual delight.[13]

There is little in any of this, and we have offered only a minimum of illustration, which contributes either to a deeper understanding of the Orpheus myth or to a more informed appreciation of Epicurean teaching. What it does reveal is the extent to which the patristic and medieval characterization of Epicurus' concept of pleasure as active gratification of sensual desires would seem to have become standard even among individuals as well read in the classical tradition as Salutati. Not that the medieval view went totally unchallenged. In October of 1400 Francesco Zabarella put the finishing touches to a brief treatise entitled *De felicitate*, dedicated to his friend Pier Paolo Vergerio in commemoration of the discussions which they had shared during the summer months on the subject of happiness. In a format similar to the one which Valla would adopt for his *De voluptate*, the Epicurean, Stoic, and Peripatetic views on happiness are reviewed and rejected in favour a concept, medieval in its ascetic and mystical overtones, which places happiness in the understanding, possession, and enjoyment of God. In his treatment of Epicurus' theory of pleasure Zabarella shows himself fully aware of the medieval interpretation. However, while he can only condemn the pursuit of pleasure as ruinous of human life, he argues that Epicurus himself has been largely misunderstood, and goes so far as to suggest that Epicurus should rightly be included among those for whom mental pleasures are of greater importance than physical ones.[14]

Zabarella's generous judgment certainly marks a refreshing change from the customary slander. However, the treatise remained unpublished until 1640, when it was edited by Giacomo Zabarella, one of the author's descendants, and it is doubtful whether at the time of its composition it had much effect. What Epicureanism needed was the benefit of the fresh and wholly partisan presentation which Poggio's discovery of Lucretius promised. Yet, despite the evident excitement surrounding the event, there is little indication that Poggio's discovery had any immediate impact. As we have already noted, Poggio himself, having sent his copy of the *De rerum natura* to Niccoli in 1417, had no access to the poem for at least another twelve years, and, although Niccoli had a copy made, we cannot be sure how widely he allowed the poem to circulate at

Rome. Indeed, it has been suggested that his own aversion to Epicurean doctrine prompted him to deliberately suppress the work.[15] Whatever the truth of the matter, it is the case that the most expansive humanist treatment of Epicurean teaching, Lorenzo Valla's *De voluptate*, was composed without reference to Lucretius' poem or to Ambrogio Traversari's Latin translation of Diogenes Laertius' *Lives of the Eminent Philosophers*, published around 1430.

The *De voluptate* was first published at Pavia in 1431, though it was conceived during Valla's earlier years at Rome and Piacenza. It was published again in 1433 with certain changes. One was in the title, which became *De vero bono* (On the true good). Another was in the setting of the dialogue and the identity of the participants. The work is in the form of three set speeches delivered by representatives of the Stoic, the Epicurean, and the Christian viewpoints. In the original version the setting was a supposed discussion among the papal secretaries at Rome, and Valla chose as spokesmen for the respective parties the historian Leonardo Bruni, the Sicilian poet Antonio Beccadelli (Panormita), and the Florentine scholar Niccolo Niccoli. In the 1433 edition the venue changes from the Mons Jordanus at Rome to the porch of the Church of San Gregorio in Pavia, and the speeches are assigned to the Pavian jurist Catone Sacco, the distinguished poet Maffeo Vegio, and the Franciscan monk Antonio da Rho. In general, these modifications reflect changes in Valla's personal relationships, especially his recent rift with Panormita, as well as a desire on Valla's part to bring recognition to the Pavian intellectual community of which he was by now a leading member.[16]

The question of the intention of the *De voluptate* and Valla's own position with respect to Epicurean teaching has produced an extensive bibliography and judgments divergent in the extreme. At different times Valla himself has been viewed as a champion of Christian orthodoxy and as an Epicurean crusader, and the dialogue has been taken as a justification of contemporary Christian morality, a barely concealed exhortation to the sensual life, and a programme for achieving a sort of 'Christian Epicureanism'.[17] Valla's own statement of intent is explicit enough: it is to come to the defence of the Christian Republic against those who look to ancient philosophy, expecially Stoic ethics, rather than to Christian teaching as the source of virtue. As to his method, he will attack the enemy on a triple front: just as David and Jonathan defeated the Philistines by employing their own weapons against them and by turning them

145

against themselves, so Valla will cause the Stoics to be vanquished out of their own mouths, will enlist their traditional opponents, the Epicureans, as auxiliary forces in the skirmish, and, finally, will employ Christian arguments not only to inflict upon the Stoics the final blow, but to undermine the Epicureans into the bargain.[18] In the end, Epicurean *voluptas*, like Stoic *honestas*, is to be set aside.

Valla is at pains to establish at the outset, then, that his use of Epicurean arguments is to be regarded as a strategic device adopted *ad occasionem*, and that in and of themselves these arguments have no value beyond their usefulness in assisting the overthrow of the enemy camp. Yet, insistent as this initial declaration may sound, it is not his final statement. In the middle of Book I, after the Epicurean spokesman Vegio has presented an outline of the case which he will make against the Stoic position, Valla (through Lorenzo) is almost effusive in expressing the pleasure which Vegio's performance will give him.[19] Moreover, it is undeniable that in the selection of arguments Valla consistently puts the Epicurean at a clear advantage, and in the composition of the speeches he draws upon his considerable rhetorical and literary skills to imbue Vegio's presentation with a force and charm beyond what mere strategy would require.

Accordingly, without going so far as to contend that for Vegio we should substitute Valla, it seems reasonable enough to suggest that Valla's prefatory protestations are not to be taken strictly to the letter; that notwithstanding the fact that the Christian spokesman is given the victory over both the Stoic and the Epicurean, there are elements of Vegio's 'Epicureanism' which, in Valla's opinion, if they are not wholly acceptable in the light of Christian experience, are none the less to an important degree valid in any discussion of the nature of man. For, despite the crowning position given to the Christian view, and notwithstanding Valla's undoubted commitment to the Christian faith, it is important to place the *De voluptate* in its proper context as a discourse on human nature rather than a religious tract. As such, it can be seen not simply as a Christian's rebuttal of pagan philosophy, but as a contribution by a leading humanist to an established topic of humanist debate, a contribution which, despite its formal structure as a response to the claims of two ancient schools, addresses positions which are very much part of contemporary humanist thought.[20] Accordingly, it is entirely consistent that the 'Stoicism' and 'Epicureanism' which Catone and Vegio

respectively represent is in neither case an accurate reflection of true
classical doctrine. They are, in fact, no more than terms of convenience designed to cover two polar views of human nature which
certain of Valla's contemporaries have assumed as the basis for
ethical theory and behaviour.

On the one side, certainly, Valla has in mind those of his
contemporaries whose ethical views coincided largely with those of
Leonardo Bruni, who was assigned the part of the Stoic spokesman
in the 1431 version of the dialogue. We do not suggest that the
sentiments expressed by the Stoic spokesman bear total correspondence with Bruni's published views, or that Bruni would have
regarded himself as an adherent of classical Stoicism. In moral
philosophy Bruni looked to Aristotle as the source of wisdom (he
translated Aristotle's *Nicomachean Ethics* and *Politics*), just as he looked
to Cicero as the fount of eloquence. Rather, what Valla is attacking
under the term 'Stoicism' is a contemporary tendency, best represented by Bruni and inspired by an intellectual attachment to
ancient moral theory, be it Stoic, Peripatetic, Platonic, or a synthesis
of all three, to regard moral excellence not only as a goal sufficient in
itself for the production of happiness, but also as one which can be
achieved by adopting an abstract hierarchy of values constructed
on purely a priori principles.[21]

Valla's objections are twofold. First, while he can only commend
the virtues themselves as being entirely consistent with the highest
Christian values, he regards their cultivation outside the context of
the Christian experience as a denial of Christ's coming.[22] Second,
the extreme austerity which the 'Stoic' programme of moral perfection imposes ignores what is an undeniable factor in human
motivation, namely, the impulse towards the gratification of those
instincts and desires which are stimulated through daily contact
with the sensual world.[23] In short, 'Stoicism' is both un-Christian
and contrary to nature.

On the other side, Valla takes issue with those of his contemporaries, whether or not they are conscious adherents of Epicurean
teaching, for whom the sensual life, to which Vegio has given
eloquent exhortation, has become the *raison d'être* of human existence. Valuable as this stance may be as a corrective to 'Stoic'
asceticism in its recognition of the pleasure instinct as a primary fact
of human psychology, it too is to be rejected because it fails to
distinguish between the limited and fleeting pleasures of the mortal

147

world and anticipation of the boundless and lasting pleasures reserved for the life to come, as well as the highest virtue which consists in the love of God as the efficient cause of all earthly joys.[24]

It is clear that it would be a mistake to regard the *De voluptate* as a serious exposition of historical Epicurean teaching, or to speak of Valla as a committed Epicurean advocate. Rather, in a manner quite in accord with humanist fashion, the ancient secular tradition is introduced into a topic of contemporary interest as a point of departure, and Valla's presentation of Epicurean, and for that matter Stoic, teaching is deliberately coloured, at times to the point of serious distortion, to serve strategic or rhetorical ends. This is not to say that Valla saw nothing of worth in Epicurean thought. On the contrary, he plainly believes that of the pagan schools it is the Epicurean which has most of value to say concerning human nature. Yet, if Valla's Epicurean man is projected in a more favourable light than Salutati's Orpheus/Epicurus, this is incidental rather than a matter of primary intent, and, despite a degree of contemporary suspicion to the contrary, the *De voluptate* cannot be interpreted as a conscious contribution to the rehabilitation of Epicurus without a serious misreading of Valla's true purpose.

It is the case also that with one notable exception, which we shall examine in due course, we look in vain for any unconditional endorsement of Epicureanism on the part of Valla's fellow humanists. At the same time there is evidence, reflecting perhaps a closer acquaintance with Epicurean teaching gained from Lucretius and Diogenes Laertius, of a continuing relaxing of the traditional prejudice against Epicurus himself, and of a somewhat more discriminating appraisal of Epicurean moral theory. Francesco Filelfo, collector of manuscripts (he brought forty from Constantinople in 1427), translator of Aristotle, poet, prolific writer of letters in both Greek and Latin, reveals in the dedication of his *De morali disciplina* that he is aware of the traditional distortion of Epicurean ethical doctrine and is intent upon restoring a proper perspective:

Nam de Epicureis difficile est dictu, quanta in caligine eorum versetur opinio; culpa fortassis adversiorum, quod secus quam illi senserint, quae sunt ab Epicuro scripta, vel interpretentur vel falso insimulent plura. Nam et sapientem Epicurum et vitae continentissimae exstitisse constat.[25]

148

Further, in a letter to Andrea Alamanni, dated 18 December 1450, Filelfo draws an explicit distinction between the Cyrenaic Aristippus, for whom *voluptas* resided solely in bodily pleasure, and Epicurus, who made room also for the mental pleasure which comes from the pursuit of wisdom and virtue.[26]

Cristoforo Landino, Professor of Eloquence and Poetry at Florence, member of the Platonic Academy, poet, and commentator on Dante, expounded Epicurus' personal qualities in almost Stoic terms. Clearly aware that intemperance was only one among the failings with which Epicurus had been charged by his detractors, he argued in his Commentary on *La divina commedia* that Epicurus-

> . . . visse con somma temperanza
> e ne' cibi e nelle cosa veneree.
> Sopportò con grand'animo i dolori.
> Fu osservantissimo della fide.
> Fu fidelissimo nell amacitie,
> e hebbe molti amici. Fu molto
> liberale e clemente; ed è molto
> e in molto luoghi lodato da
> Seneca filosofo gravissimo.[27]

Leonardo Bruni, as we have noted, was drawn to the Peripatetics on questions of moral philosophy. In general, however, convinced that too much stress had been laid upon the differences between the ancient schools and too little upon their similarities, he was concerned to effect some kind of accommodation between them, and despite the natural distaste of a man of affairs for a philosophy which advocated withdrawal from the public arena, his attitude towards Epicurean ethics reveals something of this conciliatory spirit. In his *Isagogicon moralis disciplinae*, for example, he remarks that so much attention has been paid to Epicurus' promotion of *voluptas* as the *summum bonum* that it has been forgotten that he was one with other philosophers in insisting that *voluptas* is an unattainable goal as long as the traditional virtues of justice, prudence, and temperance are neglected.[28] Further, in a short work which became attached to his translation of Aristotle's *Nicomachean Ethics* as an Introduction, he reviews the claim that virtue is something to be pursued not for its own sake but for the sake of *voluptas* without adverse comment, and is careful to discriminate, as had Filelfo, between Aristippus' promotion of bodily pleasures and the value placed by Epicurus

upon the pleasures of the mind.[29] Finally, in a precious *Canzone* in
which Bruni the poet searches for the key to the happy life, both
language and mood are strongly Epicurean:

> Chi negar può adunque giù tra noi
> Quel del huomo essere il felice stato
> Ch'è più assimigliato
> Alla felice vita degli dei?
> Voluptà gaudiosa colli suoi
> Piacere suavi, il cor contento e grato
> E in sé appagato
> D'ogni disio e vôto d'ogni omei?
> Certo, quand'io ricerco i pensier miei
> s'altri san chiedere, e'diventan muti
> E stan come perduti
> Che viprovar gli argumenti egli è duro
> E questa oppinion fu d'Epicuro.[30]

There were clearly private moments when the man of affairs was not
insensitive to the Epicurean appeal.

If we cannot look to Filelfo, Landino, and Bruni for an
endorsement of Epicurean teaching, we can at least credit them
with a genuine concern to remove some of the confusion surrounding Epicurus' moral doctrine and absolve Epicurus himself from
some of the malicious charges levied against him by a hostile
tradition. In Cosma Raimondi, however, we meet a humanist
whose defence of Epicurus stems not from a simple desire to set the
record straight but from a passionate commitment to Epicurean
teaching. Raimondi, who was born at Cremona around 1400, was
one of those less fortunate humanists, of whom there must have
been many, who failed to secure a permanent position in public or
private service and spent their lives moving from one temporary
appointment to another.[31] From 1421 to 1422 he studied oratory
and philosophy under Gasparino Barzizza in Milan, but in a letter
to Giovanni Corvino expresses his regret at having attended the
lectures only fitfully.[32] It was for Barzizza that he deciphered and
transcribed three books of Cicero's *De oratore* from the difficult
manuscript discovered at Lodi by Bishop Gerardo Landriani. He
was in Milan again some five years later in search of employment,
but frustrated in his efforts he left Italy for Avignon, where he
published in 1431 a short treatise entitled *De laudibus eloquentiae*.

He opened a school at Avignon, but for whatever reasons success and security eluded him, and in 1435 or early 1436 he hanged himself.[33]

Raimondi's interest in Epicurus is signalled by a brief but spirited defence of Epicurean teaching composed in 1430.[34] It takes the form of a reply to a letter from Ambrogio Tignosi in which Tignosi, who has deserted the Epicurean fold and is acting as a spokesman for the Stoics, the Academics, and the Peripatetics, has levelled charges which Raimondi, as a committed Epicurean, feels honour-bound to refute. He begins his reply, which is concerned exclusively with Epicurus' theory of pleasure, by arguing that since every person is a composite of mind and body any theory of pleasure which neglects the one or the other is incomplete. It is in this regard that the Stoics and the Aristotelians have erred. By placing happiness in virtue alone and in disregarding physical well-being, they neglect the very things in which happiness consists. No matter how virtuous a person may be, bodily discomfort can but make him the most wretched of creatures.[35] To separate mind from body and call a man happy who has cultivated the former to the disadvantage of the latter is as ridiculous as a man who sits on a throne calling himself king when he has not a single slave or subject.[36]

Having thus dismissed the Stoic and Aristotelian ideal of happiness through virtue (the Academics he dismisses with the bare comment that any philosophy which holds nothing as certain can hardly be taken seriously), Raimondi enters upon a defence of the Epicurean view. His principal argument, reminiscent of Maffeo Vegio in Valla's *De voluptate*, with which Raimondi may have been familiar, is taken from nature. That nature has provided so many things which stimulate pleasure, and has equipped man alone with all the faculties (both sensual and intellectual) necessary for satisfying his natural impulse for taking delight in them, can only be regarded as proof that Epicurus was correct in regarding *voluptas* as the highest good:

> Haec vero qui attenderit et diligenter animo contem-
> plabitur, quot et quantas res, quanta copia et
> varietate natura hominis unius causa procreavit,
> dubitare poterit quin et voluptas maximum sit
> bonum, et propter illam omnia sint comparanda.[37]

151

This is not to admit, however, that virtue has no role to play. Indeed, it is in this regard that Epicurus has been most consistently misunderstood. Virtue is that which both guides and constrains us in our choice of which pleasures to seek and which to avoid, thus assuring us of attaining true happiness.[38] Anyone who imagines that Epicurus maintains that happiness is to be found simply in eating, drinking, gambling, wenching, and other such pastimes is guilty of the most serious distortion of his real intention.[39]

To say that what Raimondi offers in his letter is a penetrating analysis of Epicurean theory would be an exaggeration. His treatment is, in fact, narrow and simplistic. His correspondent has deserted Epicureanism for the more subtle arguments of the Stoics and the Aristotelians, and if subtlety is his preference Raimondi is unlikely to win him back. What makes the letter worth reading, however, and more than compensates for its lack of philosophical depth is the obvious sincerity and genuine warmth of Raimondi himself. His unabashed enjoyment of the sights and sounds and smells of nature is more effective than any coldly dialectical diatribe. If in the end Raimondi found life more than he could bear, we have evidence enough in this brief letter that it once held great joy.

We may fairly say that during the first part of the quattrocento Epicureanism has fared reasonably well. It is true that it has failed to win the allegiance of any of the leading humanists, but Epicurean views have none the less gained a secure place alongside those of the other ancient schools in humanist ethical discussion. Moreover, while there is little evidence that the newly available texts of Lucretius and Diogenes Laertius have exerted much influence, certain humanists, as we have seen, have combined a more positive reading of Cicero and Seneca with a willingness to distinguish true Epicurean moral teaching from the Cyrenaic hedonism with which it had been more or less consistently confused. Finally, in Raimondi the Epicurean philosophy found an ardent supporter, and we may infer from his appeal to Tignosi to re-enlist in the Epicurean camp that Raimondi was by no means alone in his allegiance to the Garden.

It is the case, however, that despite these encouraging signs Epicureanism found it difficult to shed its 'popular' image as a philosophy which sanctioned, indeed promoted, the unfettered pursuit and enjoyment of worldly delights. In the first place, not all those who were in a position to make a fair judgment were as discriminating or as generous in their assessment of Epicurean ethical doctrine as those whom we have been considering. In 1458, for example, Giovan Battista Buoninsegni, son of an established Florentine commercial family and member of Ficino's circle, in a letter *(Epistola de nobilioribus philosophorum sectis et de eorum inter se differentia ad. . .)* addressed perhaps to Ficino himself, presents a historical survey of ancient philosophy in which he gives evidence of reasonable knowledge of the tradition.[40] In the case of the Epicurean School he displays a fair grasp of the range of Epicurean doctrine, and with respect to ethical theory he remarks specifically upon the distinction drawn by Lactantius between *voluptas* as understood by the Cyrenaics and *voluptas* as understood by Epicurus. However, having noted the distinction, he promptly ignores its implications and roundly criticizes Epicurus for having made the virtues subservient to pleasure.[41]

Second, the word 'Epicurean' continued to be employed as a general term of reproach to be applied to anyone whose primary preoccupation was with the business of pleasurable living. When Buoninsegni, for example, reports that 'the Epicurean sect is growing daily', and Filippo Beroaldi relates that 'the educated and uneducated alike are flocking to it in droves', they are not referring to a dramatic shift of allegiance in favour of Epicureanism and away from the other schools based upon serious philosophical grounds; they are commenting upon what they see as an alarming trend in contemporary Italian society towards a life of immorality and indulgence.[42] Similarly, when in 1468 the Milanese ambassadors to Rome, Agostino de' Rossi and Giovanni Blanco, report to Galeazzo Maria Sforza on the activities of the leading members of the Roman Academy, notably Pomponio Laeto, Bartolomeo Platina, and Callimacho Esperiente, detailing their rejection of established religious practices and beliefs and their studied cultivation of sóphisticated hedonism, they characterize them baldly as 'sectatori de Epicuro e de Aristippo'.[43] For some, clearly, 'Epicureanism' has become, and not for the first time in its history, synonymous with the steady corruption of not just the individual but society as a whole.

Nor were Italians themselves the only ones to associate what they regarded as the degeneration of Italian society with the Epicurean philosophy. For more than one Englishman of the following century 'Italian' and 'Epicurean' were identical terms. Witness Thomas Nashe, whose *The Unfortunate Traveller* is quite specific in warning of the dangers attending upon visitors to 'Epicures heaven':

Italy, the Paradice of the earth and the Epicures heaven, how doth it forme our yong master? It makes him to kis has hand like an ape, cringe his necke like a starveling and play hey passe repasse come aloft, when he salutes a man. From thence he brings the art of Atheisme, the art of epicurising, the art of poysoning, the art of sodomitrie.[44]

And we may compare Roger Ascham in *The Scholemaster*:

> The marke they shote at, the end
> they look for, the heaven they desire
> is onelie, their own present pleasure,
> and of what Religion they be: Epicures
> in living and in doctrine: this last
> word is no more unknowne now to
> plaine English men, then the Person was
> unknown somtyme in England, untill
> some Englishe man took paines to fetch
> that develish opinion out of Italy.[45]

These are scattered pieces of testimony, but there can be no doubting that the general identification of Epicureanism with gross self-indulgence, coupled with the fact that the Epicurean philosophy was one which was grounded in a materialist conception of nature and preached the mortality of the soul, was sufficient to discourage the orthodox from taking too open an interest in Epicurean teachings.

This would seem to be confirmed also by the Italian fortunes of Lucretius' *De rerum natura* during the fifteenth and sixteenth centuries. The *editio princeps* was printed by Thomas Ferrandus at Brescia in 1473, the second by Paulus Fridenperger at Verona in 1486, and the third by Thoedorus de Ragazzonibus at Venice in 1495. The first Aldine edition appeared at Venice in 1500, the Juntine edition was produced by Pietro Candido at Florence in 1512–13, and the second Aldine by Andrea Navagero at Venice in 1515. In addition, there were twenty-five further printings of the poem before 1600.[46] Now, while this activity might seem to indicate that there was interest enough in Epicurean material during the period, there are other considerations which would demand a more sober judgment. First, as far as the number of editions is concerned, Lucretius places low on the list of classical Latin authors. For example, against the four fifteenth-century editions of the *De rerum natura* we must place nineteen of Virgil, fifteen of Horace, and twenty-four of Juvenal.[47] Second, while there was clearly a market for quarto plain texts of Lucretius in university circles at Paris and Louvain around the middle of the sixteenth century, as well as some demand for sextodecimo portable editions after 1540, no edition of the *De rerum natura* was printed in Italy between the production of the second Aldine in 1515 and the appearance of the Nardi edition in Florence in 1647. Moreover, the only two annotated editions of the *De rerum natura* to appear between 1511 and 1631, those of Lambinus (1563–4) and Gifanius (1565–6), were printed not in Italy, but in France and Belgium respectively. Finally, no translation of the *De rerum natura* into Italian was printed until Alessandro Marchetti's in 1717, by which time the poem had already been translated into French, English, and Dutch.[48]

It is fair to say, then, that the *fortuna* of the *De rerum natura* does not point to widespread popular interest in Epicurean teaching in Italy during the fifteenth and sixteenth centuries. Certainly, there is no evidence that the poem found a place in the school curriculum alongside the standard Latin authors. Indeed, in 1517 the Florentine synod expressly prohibited the reading of Lucretius in the schools because of his vigorous arguments in favour of the mortality of the soul.[49] It is true that Lucretius did inspire two poems in imitation of his own during the sixteenth century, the *De principiis rerum* (1534) of Scipione Capece and the *De immortalitate animorum* (1536) of Aonio Paleario. However, neither of these authors was motivated by any sympathy for the Epicurean philosophy. Both poems are strongly supportive of Christian teaching and explicit in their rejection of Epicurean views. It was the language and style of Lucretius the poet which provided the impulse.[50] Similarly, such poets as Politianus, Marullus, and Pontanus were filled with admiration for Lucretius' poetic talent, as their own Latin verses reveal, but they remained untouched by his Epicurean message.

It would be misleading, then, to speak in terms of an Epicurean 'renaissance' in Italy during the two centuries following Poggio's discovery of the *De rerum natura* in 1417. In debate on the question of the happy life Epicurus' theory of pleasure has been accorded a hearing, but, despite evidence of some softening of traditional prejudice and of a more generous appraisal of Epicurus' personal morality, this aspect of Epicurean doctrine has failed to gain the endorsement of leading members of the intellectual community.[51]

Moreover, the availability of Diogenes Laertius and Lucretius as new Epicurean sources would appear to have done little to generate interest in other aspects of Epicurean teaching. Certainly, if the discovery of the *De rerum natura* in particular might be expected to have sparked interest in Epicurean views in the areas of natural science and epistemology, such was not the outcome. Lucretius the poet was embraced as both a model and a challenge; Lucretius the Epicurean spokesman was largely ignored. In short, Italian interest in Epicurus during the fifteenth and sixteenth centuries, far from being popular and widespread, was limited to a rather narrow circle and concerned itself with but one aspect of his teaching. Some of the groundwork for an Epicurean revival may well have been laid, but the revival itself still lies in the future.

Nor can the situation in France during the same period be described in greatly different terms, even though the *fortuna* of Lucretius might seem to warrant a more positive assessment. In a prefatory letter to the first French printing of the *De rerum natura*, a Paris reprint of the 1514 Bologna edition of Joannes Baptista Pius, Nicolas Bérault confirms that the appearance of Pius' text has already gained Lucretius an enthusiastic readership. Around the middle of the century there was a demand for quarto plain texts as well as for sextodecimo portable editions. Finally, it was at Paris that there appeared the first truly important critical text of the *De rerum natura*, the 1563 quarto edition of Denys Lambin. In 1565 a sextodecimo pocket edition was issued, omitting Lambin's copious notes but retaining his dedications, and 1570 saw the publication of Lambin's definitive second quarto edition. This publishing activity certainly attests to a reading public for the *De rerum natura*.[52] However, it is important not to confuse a taste for Lucretius with sympathy for Epicurean doctrine. In his prefatory letter of 1514 Bérault commends Lucretius on the charm of his poetry, but is careful to distance himself, as Pius had done throughout his notes on the text, from the substance of the *De rerum natura*. Lambin too, for whom Lucretius was 'omnium poetarum Latinorum . . . elegantissimus et purissimus, idemque gravissimus atque ornatissimus', disowns Lucretius' Epicureanism.[53] In his dedicatory epistle to Charles IX he regrets that Lucretius should have chosen to argue against the immortality of the soul, against providence, against religion, and in favour of pleasure as the highest good, though, in addition to dissociating himself from Epicurean teaching, Lambin attempts to excuse Lucretius as well by arguing that responsibility lies not with Lucretius but with Epicurus.[54] Moreover, there was every reason for Lambin's insistence, for in order to gauge the strength of hostility towards Lucretius in some quarters we have only to refer to the violent attack which Pierre Galland made against Ramus for instructing his pupils in the *De rerum natura*, accusing him of 'vomiting forth a throatful of pus and poison'.[55]

As in Italy, then, so in France it was for the most part not Lucretius the philosophical spokesman who commanded attention, but Lucretius the artist. This is not to say that Lucretius the poet was universally admired, or that he came close to rivalling Virgil, Horace and Ovid as the favourite Latin poets among sixteenth-century French writers. For example, the leaders of the Pléiade express at best a lukewarm appreciation of Lucretius' poetry. Joachim du Bellay's sole critical reference to Lucretius consists of a comparison with Virgil in which Lucretius emerges clearly second-best.[56] And Pierre de Ronsard, while allowing that certain of Lucretius' verses are 'non seulement excellents mais divins', refuses to grant him the rank of poet.[57] Yet, several members of the Pléiade, including Ronsard himself, did find in the *De rerum natura* certain choice passages for imitation, notably the 'Invocation to Venus' at the beginning of the poem and the prologue to Book II ('Suave, mari magno').[58]

In addition, the *De rerum natura* was known to and utilized by a number of authors of poems dealing with cosmology and various aspects of natural philosophy. The *L'Univers* (1557) of Pontus de Tyard, the *Microcosme* (1562) of Maurice Scève, the *Le Premier des météores* (1567) of De Baïf, the *L'Encyclie* (1571) of Le Fèvre de la Boderie, the *Amours et nouveux eschanges des pierres précieuses* (1576) of Rémi Belleau, the *Louanges* (1581) of Jacques Pelletier du Mans, the *Première sepmaine* (1578) and *Seconde sepmaine* (1580) of Guillaume Salluste, Sieur du Bartas – all of these poems borrow in varying degrees from Lucretius, whether it be from his treatment of the development of primitive man in Book V, as with Scève and Pelletier, or from his explanation of colour in Book II, as with Belleau.[59]

It is important to recognize, however, that, while the *De rerum natura* was acknowledged, as it had been in Italy, as the principal ancient example of the scientific poem, Lucretius was not among the major sources for these sixteenth-century representatives of the genre. Plato, Aristotle, Seneca, Pliny the Elder, the Neoplatonic writers, medieval encyclopedias, and the literature of alchemy, astrology, and the hermetic tradition supplied far more. Moreover, with the exception of the more general theme of the condition of early man, the Lucretian borrowings were for the most part confined to matters of small detail. At the level of cosmology and metaphysics the anti-Christian implications of the Epicurean system rendered it unacceptable even as a starting-point.[60] Simon Goulart, the first commentator on the works of Du Bartas, sums up the general view:

> C'est un Ancien Poëte latin qui a escrit en beaux et doctes vers six livres *de Rerum Natura*, qui se lisent encores aujourd'hui et où il a expliqué beaucoup de beaux secrets fort dextrement, ayant tiré des Philosophes Grecs ses discours Poëtiques Latins. Vray est qu'il suit les opinions de Democrite, d'Epicure et de leurs semblables, en divers etroits; au moyen de quoy et à bon droit il est detesté des Chrestiens, comme soustenant beaucoup de choses qui contredisent directement à quelques principaux point de la pure doctrine. Mais au reste ç'a esté un grand esprit, et de qui les hommes de jugement peuvent apprendre et pour la langue latine, et pour la Philosophie naturelle.[61]

In general, it is fair to say that despite the fact that the *De rerum natura* was made available to the reading public in a variety of editions, Lucretius exercised only a moderate influence upon French thought and literature during the sixteenth century. His impact upon the Pléiade was tangential compared with that of a number of other Latin poets and his contribution to scientific poetry only scant. Further, he commanded a very minor place in the handbooks and anthologies of the period. In the *Sententiae et proverbia ex Plauto, Terentio, Vergilio, Ovidio, Juvenali, Persio, Lucano, Seneca, Lucretio, Martiali, . . .,* edited by Robert Estienne in 1536 and reissued in 1540, Lucretius is accorded a single page compared with twenty-two for Horace, thirty-three for Ovid, and forty-one for Plautus; in Estienne's *Sententiae veterum poetarum in locos communes digestae per Georgium Maiorem* of 1552 his allotment is equally scant; and Antoine du Verdier, in his *Prosopographie ou description des personnes insignes* of 1573, takes care of Lucretius with the terse 'Lucrèce, poète, florit de ce temps.'[62]

Finally, it is the case that there are certain writers, most notably Etienne Dolet and François Rabelais, whose liberal temper might be expected to have embraced Lucretius' rationalist spirit with some enthusiasm, who express no interest at all in the *De rerum natura*. Labelled by his opponents an 'atheist' and an 'Epicurean',[63] and finally burned as a heretic, Dolet had ample opportunity at different stages in his life to become well versed in the poetry of Lucretius. As a young student in Paris in 1525 he had as one of his teachers Nicolas Bérault, who had first introduced the *De rerum natura* into France with his edition of 1514. From Paris he went to Padua, where he enjoyed a close relationship with the free-thinking circle of the 'Epicurean' Pietro Bembo, and from Padua to Venice, where he studied Lucretius under J.-B. Egnazio.[64] Further, from 1534 he was employed as a corrector by Sébastien Gryph of Lyon, who published five editions of the *De rerum natura* between 1534 and 1558. Yet, whatever impression the poem made upon Dolet, his work betrays nothing of it. Lucretius' name appears in his writings only once, and that of Epicurus not at all. So too with Rabelais. That he did not know the *De rerum natura* is hardly conceivable. His familiarity with a number of the standard Latin authors is attested by citations in his works, and he was on familiar terms with the same individuals who were in large part responsible for promoting Lucretius in France. He was a fellow guest with Nicolas Bérault at a banquet held in 1537 in honour of Dolet, and was a visitor to Lyon during the period when Gryph, who published two of Rabelais's own works, was busy issuing his editions of Lucretius' poem. Furthermore, as Fusil has noted, in a work so full of classical anecdotes and scientific oddities as the *Gargantua et Pantagruel* it would seen natural enough that Rabelais would enrich his borrowings from so many of the ancient authors with material from Lucretius.[65] Yet there are no Lucretian echoes, and nowhere in Rabelais's writings does the name of Lucretius occur. Unless we accept the view that Rabelais's silence concerning Lucretius was a matter of design, a deliberate ploy calculated to conceal a secret attachment to libertinism and irreligion,[66] we must conclude that to Rabelais, as to Dolet, the *De rerum natura* was of little more than passing interest.

Dolet and Rabelais are representative of a notable indifference towards Lucretius the poet on the part of sixteenth-century French writers generally. Michel de Montaigne is the exception. For in Montaigne we have an author whose reading of Lucretius was both thorough and constant and whose citations from the *De rerum natura* are carefully integrated into the fabric of his writings. The statistics are impressive. There occur one hundred and forty-nine citations in the *Essais*, representing some four hundred and fifty-four verses from the *De rerum natura*. Forty-eight of these citations appear in the 1580 edition of the *Essais*, three are added in the reissue of 1582, a further ninety-seven occur in the 1588 edition, and one more in the 'Bordeaux' edition of 1595.[67] The non-scientific parts of the poem are clearly favoured, one hundred and seventeen citations coming from Books III, IV and V of the poem, against twenty-nine from the more technical Books I and II.[68] Further, in addition to citing from Lucretius more frequently than from any ancient author except Plutarch and Seneca, Montaigne leaves us in no doubt as to his high opinion of Lucretius' poetry. It is Virgil, to be sure, whom he places first among the Latin poets, expressing particular admiration for the *Georgics*, but Lucretius is not far behind; indeed, he confesses that there are passages in Lucretius which even tempt him to reverse the order.[69]

However, it would be a mistake to view the frequency of Montaigne's citations from Lucretius and his clear admiration of Lucretius' poetic talents as indications of sympathy for Lucretius' message. In fact, there are few aspects of Epicurean doctrine which Montaigne finds himself able to endorse. The Epicurean notion of a world formed through the union of atomic particles, together with the concept of an arbitrary atomic 'swerve', he classes among the 'asneries de l'humaine prudence'.[70] Epicurus' theory of knowledge fares only slightly better. Montaigne agrees with Epicurus that sense-experience is the source of all knowledge: 'Or toute coignoissance s'achemine en nous par les sens: ce sont nos maistres.'[71] However, he labels the Epicurean claim that the senses never err a 'conseil desesperé', and employs the entire range of traditional sceptical arguments to demonstrate that, in fact, the information provided by the senses forms a completely unreliable basis for certain judgment; the senses, in short, 'sont incertains et falsibliables à toutes circonstances'.[72] As for Epicurean teaching concerning the nature of the human soul, Montaigne is prepared to accept the analogy which Epicurus draws between the growth and decline of the soul's powers and the pattern of growth and decline observable in the physical body;[73] but on the question of the ultimate fate of the soul Montaigne sets himself squarely in the Christian camp.[74]

Montaigne's criticism of key elements in Epicurean doctrine is not out of character. It is registered for the most part in the *Apologie de Raimond Sebond*, where his vigorous defence of Pyrrhonian scepticism leads him to condemn all dogmatic philosophizing, indeed all claims to certain knowledge on any scale, as insupportable and presumptuous.[75] However, since it is also in the *Apologie* that more than half of Montaigne's Lucretian citations occur, the question of his use of Lucretius takes on added significance. Certainly, in the *Apologie*, as elsewhere, many of the Lucretian citations are no more than ornamental, adding richness and colour to Montaigne's own prose style, and in this respect Lucretius takes his place alongside Virgil, Horace, Ovid, and others of Montaigne's Latin favourites. In addition, there are numerous instances where Montaigne draws upon Lucretius, as he does upon others, not simply for the purpose of embellishment but in order to strengthen the force of a particular argument or observation. The citations are generally apt enough, and even though the context has been changed no violence is done to Lucretius' original meaning or intent.[76] More troubling are those instances where Lucretian lines are removed from their context and employed to bolster positions which Lucretius would certainly not accept, or which are the very opposite of those which the lines were originally meant to support. To illustrate the uncertainty of human knowledge Montaigne points to the mass of differing opinions on any given topic and the tendency of people to give their assent always to the newest, and he cites Lucretius' observation that 'the finer thing more recently discovered destroys and changes our feelings towards all the old things'.[77] In their original context, however, these lines refer not to human opinion but to changing fashions in clothing and food, and Montaigne's claim that judgment must be suspended is one which Lucretius would certainly dispute. Similarly, in support of the Pyrrhonist condemnation of those who claim to know that knowledge is unattainable Montaigne cites Lucretius' observation that 'the man who thinks he knows that nothing is known does not know whether this itself can be known, since he admits that he knows nothing'.[78] In the original context, however, Lucretius, far from accepting the Pyrrhonist view, goes on to argue that in fact sense-experience is a reliable criterion of truth.

Now, this kind of dislocation and distortion is so regular a feature of Renaissance treatment of classical sources that its occurrence in Montaigne need cause no undue surprise. Moreover, in the case of

Lucretius the surprise should be even less when it is remembered that, for all that he might be admired as a poet, his association with Epicurean teaching made him an author to be treated with particular care, and of this Montaigne could not fail to be aware. As we have already noted, Lambin, in his edition of 1563, the edition which Montaigne used, attempted to solve the dilemma by expressly dissociating the poet from the contents of his work. Montaigne is less direct, but no less effective. For the overall impression which Montaigne's Lucretian citations leave upon the reader of the *Essais*, more especially upon a reader who might be unfamiliar with the *De rerum natura* as a whole, is of a poet who, despite an unfortunate attachment to an ill-conceived philosophy, might be read with both enjoyment and profit.[79]

In embracing Lucretius the poet while rejecting the Epicurean message Montaigne sustains a pattern which is both familiar and ironic. Lucretius himself felt an artist's joy in his own poetic achievement, conscious that, out of the paucity of the Latin language and on a theme as yet untried, he had fashioned a poem 'touched by the Muses' charm'.[80] Yet, the sweetness of the verse was meant only to beguile, to serve like honey around the rim of the cup to induce the reader to drink deeply of the teachings of the Epicurean school. During the sixteenth century, in France as in Italy, artist has recognized artist and responded; the honey has retained its sweetness; the Epicurean message is unpalatable still.

It remains only to record that in Germany and the Low Countries Epicurus attracted a degree of attention during the sixteenth century, for the most part in the context of a heated theological controversy which brought little enough credit to the protagonists and little more to Epicurus himself. First, a preliminary skirmish. As Professor of Greek at Wittenburg the Tübingen theologian Philip Melanchthon (1497–1560) was among the most influential in fostering humanism in post-Reformation Germany, and more particularly in promoting the cause of Aristotle.[81] Towards Epicurus, however, he was decidedly unsympathetic, though no more so than towards the Stoics and the Cynics. It was the Epicurean theory of pleasure which disturbed him most. In the *Philosophiae moralis epitomes*, reacting against what he regarded as Valla's approbation of Epicurus' promotion of pleasure as the highest good, he argues strenuously that this opinion must be exposed as a perversion of the true nature of man, and in particular by Christians, who have been taught by Christ that, while physical pleasures must be acknowledged, they are to be placed always beneath the pursuit of virtue.[82]

Melanchthon's view is cast in the humanist mould. The approach of his master Luther is of a much different order. Luther's understanding of Epicurean teaching is derived in the main from Cicero's *De natura deorum* and from the writings of the Fathers, and it is accurate enough in those essentials which concern him most, namely, the denial of immortality[83] and the denial of providence.[84] At the same time, he errs in claiming that Epicurus denied the existence of the divine altogether,[85] and with respect to the Epicurean concept of pleasure he is guilty of repeating the traditional distortions with characteristic vigour. However, the exactness of Luther's grasp of classical Epicurean doctrine is of little importance. For Luther's concern is not with the philosophic tradition but with the contemporary scene – the integrity of the Christian faith, his own reforming crusade, and the state of public and private morality. If his portrait of the Epicurean philosophy is less than faithful, it is because in Luther we have a throw-back to the patristic age as 'Epicurean' becomes once again no more than a ready insult to be hurled at theological opponents, and 'Epicureanism' a convenient label for all the moral ills which afflict contemporary life. The Pope is an 'Epicurische Sew' and his entourage his 'Borfaren';[86] the theologians of Louvain are 'crassissimos porcos Epicuri';[87] eating, drinking, gambling, dancing, fornicating, these are the indulgences of the modern 'Epicurean' which render him indistinguishable from the beasts of the field.[88] Moreover, this 'Epicureanism' is spreading like a disease across Europe at so alarming a rate that it not only threatens the end of Germany,[89] but is the surest sign that the end of the world is at hand.[90]

Luther's use of the terms 'Epicurean' and 'Epicureanism' amounts to little more, then, than an example of the colourful hyperbole which characterizes much of sixteenth-century theological debate, and it would have been recognized as such by his contemporaries. However, in the case of one of his opponents, the charge of being an 'Epicurean' would seem to have been taken more seriously. This opponent was Erasmus. Luther makes the charge more than once in the *De servo arbitrio* which he composed in 1525 in answer to Erasmus's *De libero arbitrio* of the previous year, itself a response to Luther's *Assertions* of 1520: in minimizing the importance of enquiry into the question of free will, Erasmus 'breathes forth full-strength the drunkenness of Epicurus';[91] in ridiculing those who firmly believe in a providential God, he shows that he 'harbours in his heart a Lucian or some other pig from Epicurus' sty';[92] and, in appearing to question the truth of the gospel and the immortality of the soul, he is 'Epicurus' ally'.[93] As the sequel shows, Erasmus was distressed. In the first book of his *Hyperaspistes diatribae adversus servum arbitrium Martini Lutheri*, published in 1526, he refers to Luther's slur no less than a dozen times,[94] and in letters to Joannes Faber, John Elector of Saxony, and Luther himself he protests vehemently against what he clearly regarded as particularly offensive behaviour on Luther's part.[95] Yet Luther showed no inclination to desist. In a 1529 letter to Wenceslas Linc he refers to Erasmus as 'hunc Atheon, Lucianumque Epicurum',[96] and references in the *Table-talk* reveal that the identification was sustained until as late as 1533.[97]

Erasmus's response was a surprising one in that it took the form not of a denial of Epicurean leanings, but of a presentation of Epicurean hedonism whose sympathetic tone is in marked contrast to that of his earlier Epicurean references in the *Enchiridion* (1503,1518) and the *Antibarbari* (1520).[98] It came in the dialogue entitled 'Epicureus' printed in the 1533 edition of the *Colloquia familiaria*.[99] The interlocutors are Spudaeus and Hedonius, and the subject of their colloquy the proper end of living. Spudaeus, who has been reading Cicero's *De finibus* in his search for an answer, is shocked that Hedonius should recommend the opinion of Epicurus, which all men protest is the 'voice of the brute beast, not of man'.[100] For the rest of the dialogue Hedonius takes his companion through an analysis of pleasure for the purpose of demonstrating that this general condemnation of Epicurus is unjustified, because it attributes to him a desire for the kinds of base pleasures which he would in fact reject. Such are 'shameless love, unlawful lust, over indulgence in food and drink', which the true Epicurean knows bring only 'the ague, the headache, the gripes, dullness of wit, disgrace, forgetfulness, vomiting, gastric ulcers, and the tremors'.[101] Once a distinction is made between these indulgences and those higher pleasures which bring true enjoyment, and once it is recognized that no one lives more enjoyably than those who live righteously, then it may be said that 'none are more truly Epicureans than Christians who live a reverent life'.[102]

The 'Epicureus' is not a defence of Epicureanism. The dialogue is decidedly meant to promote the Christian way of life. Erasmus's strategy is to show that a life devoted to the righteous pursuit of virtue, far from entailing a denial of pleasure, is commensurate with true pleasure itself. To this end Epicurus, duly dissociated from the perverted creed which bears his name, is pressed into service. In the process Erasmus has also devised a neat and effective means of answering Luther. If Luther insists upon calling Erasmus an 'Epicurean', so be it. To Erasmus it is a compliment.[103]

The affair between Luther and Erasmus revolved around issues of serious theological import which our account does not explore. We have been concerned only to examine what may be described as the exploitation of Epicureanism by two controversialists for strategic ends. For it is clear that Luther's repeated use of 'Epicurean' jibes was designed simply to embarrass his adversary and discredit his theological positions by association, while Erasmus's final 'Epicurean' pose was equally a calculated ploy to disarm his attacker. In short, Epicurus has become a rhetorical shuttlecock to be batted back and forth between opponents as a side-show to the main event. Yet, if Epicurus finds himself playing a minor part, it is a role for which he would seem to have been cast. For during the fifteenth and sixteenth centuries he really plays no other. However, as we move into the seventeenth, the stage takes on a different aspect, lead players gradually relinquish their parts, and Epicurus emerges much closer to the footlights.

FRENCH REVIVAL

We began the previous chapter with a picture of Dante consigning Epicurus and his followers to lidless coffins, there to remain for all eternity. We may begin this chapter with an image of rebirth: 'E tumulo eum exsuscitas.' The writer is Louis Emmanuel de Valois, Comte d'Alais, Governor of Provence, in a 1645 letter to Pierre Gassendi,[1] and such is the dominant role which Gassendi played in the seventeenth-century revival of Epicureanism that the major portion of this chapter must be devoted to it.[2]

By the time that de Valois's letter was written, Gassendi had dedicated almost twenty years to Epicurus, and he would spend a further ten bringing his 'grand dessein', a comprehensive exposition of the entire Epicurean philosophy, to a conclusion. Thus, in Pierre Gassendi we shall meet someone whose interest in the philosophy of the Garden was not incidental, but consuming, one, in fact, which defined his life. More importantly, this interest in Epicureanism, while it would see Gassendi sequestered for long periods within the sheltered walls of the library, confronting with the scholar's persistence the exacting task of correcting, editing, and translating Epicurean texts, and taking through revision after revision his own exhaustive commentaries, was not simply the interest of the philologue, the antiquarian, or the closet humanist. Gassendi knew the world beyond the study door, and he made his mark upon it by securing for Epicurean psychology and logic a prominent place in contemporary philosophic enquiry and by encouraging seventeenth-century men of science to look to Epicurean atomism as a reasonable hypothetical foundation for the investigation of nature. In short, it is due to Gassendi's efforts that late in its history, after a long period during which it has attracted only intermittent attention and exerted only moderate influence, Epicureanism emerges to play a formative role in the development of post-Renaissance scientific and philosophic thought.

However, this is to signal the result of Gassendi's work. Our immediate concern is to examine in turn the circumstances which initially prompted Gassendi to turn his attention to the Epicurean philosophy, the nature of his Epicurean researches, the challenges which the promotion of Epicureanism posed and the strategies which Gassendi employed to meet them, and, finally, the status which Gassendi accorded his own modified version of Epicurean teaching.

In 1624, two years after he was forced to relinquish his position as Professor of Philosophy at Aix, Gassendi published at Grenoble his *Exercitationes paradoxicae adversus Aristoteleos*, containing Book I of seven which he planned to write. This work, which was based upon notes which he had compiled during his six years at Aix, is a spirited indictment both of the Aristotelian philosophy and of the Aristotelian professors who monopolized the teaching positions in the universities and flooded the bookstalls with an ever increasing number of commentaries on the Master. Since detailed criticism of particular aspects of Aristotelian teaching is to be reserved for the projected later books, Gassendi limits himself to general charges, beginning with what he regards as the grave disservice which the latter-day Aristotelians have done to philosophy itself. They are, in fact, pseudo-philosophers whose tiresome disputations have turned philosophy into a childish game.[3] The search for truth has given way to a display of verbal juggling designed merely to draw the crowds.[4] Moreover, such is the premium which is placed upon mastering one's opponent in debate that serious philosophers, such as Plato, Cicero, and Seneca, are completely ignored in the Schools, with the result that when the student comes to face the real issues of life he is utterly helpless.[5]

Yet this is not Gassendi's most serious charge. More damaging is the fact that the Aristotelians have made themselves, and would make others, slaves to the Master, to the extent that they 'would rather be mistaken with Aristotle than correct with anyone else'.[6] However much they may protest that they have the liberty to be Thomists or Scotists, they are like birds in a cage to which Aristotle holds the key; they may jump through hoops, but are denied the freedom to try their wings in the open air.[7] Gassendi is no more caustic than here. For what is at stake is the very freedom to philosophize. Gassendi's is a *cri de cœur* expressive of a frustration which he has long felt. Having looked to philosophy to provide something useful and profitable, he has been introduced to the philosophy of the Schools and found it barren and stifling. Indeed, as he reveals in the Preface to the *Exercitationes*, it was only his reading in such classical authors as Cicero, Lucretius, and Sextus Empiricus, and in such moderns as Vives, Charron, Gian Francesco Pico della Mirandola, and Montaigne that enabled him to maintain his faith in intellectual enquiry.[8] For his reading in these authors has served to strengthen his conviction that truth is not the prerogative of any one school but the object of free enquiry and open discussion. In short, if he has gained anything from his reading in philosophy, it has been a determination to battle against dogmatism,[9] and it is this more than anything which fuels his desire to topple the Aristotelianism of the Schools from its position of authority.

Book I of the *Exercitationes paradoxicae* represents a first volley in Gassendi's frontal attack. It was also the last. Gassendi himself had been reluctant from the first to confront the Aristotelians in so open and direct a fashion, well aware how vigorously they would rush to Aristotle's defence.[10] His misgivings proved to be well founded as the publication aroused considerable stir. As he says in a letter to the Tübingen professor Schickard in 1630, the book came close to 'provoking a tragedy',[11] and a note in the hand of Gassendi's secretary, La Poterie, in the manuscript version of Book II confirms that the strength of the Aristotelians' reaction was a decisive factor in Gassendi's decision not to continue publication.[12] Gassendi had no intention, however, of abandoning his goal. One method of attempting to dislodge a philosophy from a position of authority is to subject it to criticism. For the moment this approach has served only to cause the Aristotelians to become even more entrenched in their support of Aristotle.[13] Another is to promote the cause of a rival philosophy. It is this strategy which Gassendi now adopts, and the philosophy is to be the philosophy of Epicurus.

That Gassendi's initial interest in Epicurus was indeed a strategic one is confirmed by a letter to Erycius Puteanus (Van de Putte), dated 24 March 1628, in which Gassendi congratulates Puteanus on his *Epicuri sententiae aliquot aculeatae ex Seneca*, published at Louvain in 1609, and declares that he has himself completed an Apology for Epicurus and has it in mind to include an expanded version of it as part of the *Exercitationes paradoxicae*.[14] A year later, in a letter written to Jacques Gaffarel, historian to Cardinal de Richelieu, Gassendi confirms his intention, adding only that other commitments have prevented him from making much headway.[15] By the following year, however, Gassendi's plans have changed. In a letter to Marin Mersenne, dated 30 April, 1630, Isaac Beeckmann expresses surprise at Mersenne's news that Gassendi is no longer planning simply an apology for Epicurus and an account of Epicurean ethics, but a comprehensive account of the entire Epicurean philosophy (*totam illam philosophiam*).[16]

The turning-point would seem to have been Gassendi's extended visit to Flanders and Holland, begun in December 1628 in the company of François Luillier, to whom he had been introduced in Paris earlier in the year. For during the course of their tour Gassendi had the opportunity to widen his circle of acquaintances through meetings with a number of the leading intellectual figures of the day: the Leyden Professor of Oriental Languages Golius, Erycius Puteanus, the noted philologian Daniel Heinsius, the scholar and physician Henri Reneri, the humanist Vossius, and the scientist and physician J.-B. Van Helmont. However, it was his conversations with the atomist Isaac Beeckmann, whom he met at Dordrecht, which proved decisive.[17] For it was shortly after these conversations, which focused upon Epicurean physics, that Gassendi's enlarged design began to take shape. Gassendi has found a new role. From this point on he will be no longer simply the opponent of Aristotle; he will be the champion of Epicurus.

The work begins in earnest. Even before his return to Paris in 1629 Gassendi writes to Peiresc requesting him to send from Aix his notes on Epicurus;[18] on 28 August he tells Peiresc that the packet is in his hands;[19] on 14 September there is a flurry of correspondence as Gassendi writes to no fewer than five of the people he had met on his tour, requesting their assistance on matters of dates, sources, and textual readings, and expressing confidence that his Epicurus will soon be ready for the press.[20] However, Gassendi has underestimated the labour involved. In November he tells Peiresc that he is spending most of his time in de Thou's library, but is not nearly through;[21] in December he tells Puteanus that the general scheme has been worked out, but that he is becoming concerned at the mass of material he is accumulating;[22] in March 1630, the date by which he had hoped to have the work ready for publication, he is still revising what he has written and researching additional material.[23]

Gassendi has been busy, but now the work slows. In October he is taxed by his friend Naudé for neglecting Epicurus,[24] and it is not until April 1631 that Gassendi reports any progress. In a letter to Peiresc, dated 28 April, he gives the most detailed account to date of the overall scheme and contents of the commentary, and the most precise indication of the stage he has reached.[25] Treatment of the Epicurean philosophy itself is to be preceded by an *Apology* for the life of Epicurus in seven chapters, and this part is now complete. The doctrine is to be treated in three parts, logic, physics, and ethics, of which the logic, in five chapters, is also complete. Four separate books are to be devoted to the physics, comprising a total of forty-two chapters, and Gassendi is at about the mid-point, having completed Book I (twelve chapters) and Book II (eight chapters). As for the ethics he will give details at a later date. In August Gassendi tells Naudé that he is still occupied with Book III of the physics and entertains little hope of finishing it by the end of the year.[26] In March 1632, he reports that Epicurus 'proceeds as slowly as ever, like an old grandfather', and that he has not yet completed the physics;[27] by May he has advanced only as far as Chapter Three of Book IV.[28] In October Gassendi leaves Paris for Provence, and it is not until February 1633 that he finds time to resume the work.[29]

Gassendi has been occupied with the commentary now for almost exactly three years and still has work to do on the physics before he can turn his attention to the ethics. If progress has been slow, Gassendi's determination to make his account of Epicurean teaching as comprehensive and exact as possible has been partly responsible. For he has needed to consume an inordinate amount of time in de Thou's library searching the shelves for requisite materials, seeking out references, emending and restoring Greek sources. Moreover, he has not been able to devote himself exclusively to Epicurus. His ecclesiastical responsibilities have demanded his attention, especially during the months he has spent in Provence, and his correspondence, particularly his communications on scientific and astronomical matters with people like Schickard, Kepler, Galileo, and Scheiner, has made an additional call upon his time. Finally, during this period Gassendi has published three works not connected with his commentary. The first is the *Examen philosophiae Roberti Fluddi medici*, an apology on behalf of Marin Mersenne against the writings of the English Rosicrucian Robert Fludd. The second is the *Parhelia sive soles quatuor spurii qui circa verum apparuerunt Romae die 20 Martii anno 1629*, an account of the phenomenon of sunspots originally appended to a letter sent to Peiresc on 14 July 1629, and published later in the same year at Amsterdam. The third is the *Mercurius in sole visus et Venus invisa* of 1632, in which Gassendi announced his confirmation at Paris on 7 November 1631, of Kepler's prediction of 1629 that Mercury would pass across the sun in 1631.

Meanwhile, despite his lack of progress, Gassendi's friends encourage him to press ahead with the commentary. Mersenne had asked Gassendi to compose a second reply to Fludd, but this time Peiresc advised Gassendi not to comply, urging him to give whatever time he has to his Epicurus.[30] In April Gassendi tells Luillier that he is determined to complete the physics before going to Aix to stay with Peiresc.[31] Again, however, he finds it impossible to make much headway, and it is not until the end of 1633 that he can devote his entire effort to the project. Now, however, his plan has changed: he intends to revise the entire commentary from the beginning, setting himself a schedule which would result in one 'cahier' each week.[32] The 'cahiers' are to be sent to Peiresc at Aix and by Peiresc to Luillier at Paris. The first is sent on 13 January 1634 and by 21 February six have been dispatched.[33] On 18 March Gassendi arrives at Aix to stay with Peiresc, but by May no further progress has been made. In August, the story is much the same.[34] In fact, it is not until two years later, in the autumn of 1636, that Gassendi finds time to continue with his revisions. For he is occupied with other things: ecclesiastical business; an excursion through the Provençal Alps; astronomical observations and recordings; and work on a response to the *De Veritate* of Herbert of Cherbury undertaken at the request of Mersenne, Peiresc, and Elie Diodati.

When Gassendi finally resumes work in November 1636, he expresses confidence, in a letter to Galileo, that another year will see the project through.[35] He passes from the logic (now the canonics) to the physics. In April 1637, Peiresc announces to Bouchard that Gassendi 'a achevé sa philosphie', but adds that he is introducing new refinements every day![36] Then, on 24 June, Peiresc dies. Gassendi is distraught. The work stops. It will be four years before it is resumed. In the mean time, there is little to report. Gassendi writes only one letter during the two years following the death of his 'fidèle ami' – to Galileo, consoling him over the loss of sight in one eye. He travels around Provence. On two occasions he is taken ill. Then, in 1638, he meets the new Governor of Provence, Louis Emmanuel de Valois, who takes an immediate interest in his work, urging him to resume the task and requesting him to submit regular reports of his progress. It is the spur Gassendi needs. In 1641 he leaves Provence for Paris to stay with his friend Luillier, and a new stage begins. In September his life of Peiresc is published, and in October he is at work again on Epicurus, picking up at the point where he had left off four years before.

By October he has advanced as far as Book XVII of the physics; by midsummer of 1642 he has finished Book XVIII; the remainder of 1642 and 1643 sees the completion of Books XIX–XXIII; Book XXV was finished during the early months of 1644, and, by the time he is appointed Professor of Mathematics at the Collège Royal in November 1645, this second *rédaction* of the commentary, which has occupied him since 1 January 1634, has been brought to a conclusion.

The four-year period since Gassendi's return to Paris in 1641 has been one of intense activity. In addition to working strenuously on the commentary, Gassendi has maintained a steady correspondence, written the life of his friend Peiresc, published three works on astronomical matters (*Proportio gnomonis, Novem stellae circa Jovem visae, Institutio astronomica*), three on physics (*De apparente magnitudine solis humilis et sublimis, De motu impresso a motore translato, De proportione*), and written his lengthy *Objections* to Descartes's *Metaphysics*. Moreover, he has been conscientious in honouring his commitment to Louis Emmanuel de Valois by sending him regular reports of his progress on the commentary.[37]

These reports present only the essentials of Epicurean doctrine without the mass of supporting material which would be included in the commentary, and their composition provided Gassendi with an opportunity to look at the philosophy of Epicurus from a wide angle. Stress is laid upon those features of Epicurus' general approach to scientific investigation which Gassendi considers to be particularly appropriate to the seventeenth-century context, and from his presentation we learn much concerning Gassendi's own attitude towards the study of the natural world. In particular, in full accord with Epicurus' reliance upon sensory information as the foundation of all knowledge, Gassendi underscores the primary importance of experience as the touchstone of truth, a point which he will elaborate in his treatment of Epicurean logic. Further, Gassendi takes the opportunity to confront an issue which has been a concern to him for some time, namely, the problem of reconciling certain key aspects of Epicurean doctrine with the teachings of the Church. In 1632 Gassendi had skirted the issue. In two letters written in May and July of that year Campanella, while congratulating Gassendi on certain astronomical observations, had objected strenuously to Gassendi's promotion of the Epicurean philosophy because of Epicurus' claim that the world is governed by chance and not by reason.[38] In his reply, Gassendi defended himself by stating that, while as a Christian he must oppose positions which are contrary to the teachings of the Church, as a commentator he was bound to put forward whatever arguments might help to elucidate his author, adding that this was a procedure which Campanella had himself followed in his *Atheismus triumphatus*.[39]

In the letters to de Valois Gassendi is less equivocal and identifies a number of areas where the Epicurean view must be rejected. At the most general level, he can agree with Epicurus that one of the aims of scientific enquiry is to attain tranquillity of mind through understanding, but he cannot accept Epicurus' insistence that this tranquillity can only be realized through the recognition that the world is not governed by divine forces beyond our comprehension. In Gassendi's view, the limits to our knowledge must not lead us to despair, since as Christians we are assured that God ordains nothing which is not ultimately for our benefit.[40] As to specifics, Gassendi feels constrained to reject certain elements in the Epicurean atomic theory. He is convinced by Epicurus' arguments in favour of the existence of void, and does not object to Epicurus defining it as 'incorporeal nature'. What he must challenge is Epicurus' contention that void is the only incorporeal nature, since this leaves no room for the divine being or the human soul, both of which must be regarded as incorporeal.[41] As for atoms, Gassendi has two objections. First, Epicurus is mistaken in regarding their number as infinite, since to admit that the number of atoms is infinite is to accept that the world itself is infinite, a position which runs counter to the Christian view that the only infinite being is God.[42] Second, Epicurus errs in claiming that the atoms are eternal and uncreated, since this removes the role of God as creator of all things.[43] The letters to de Valois make it clear, then, that Gassendi does not

173

consider his role as an Epicurean commentator to be such that it obliges him to accept uncritically the whole of Epicurean doctrine, and give fair warning that the Epicurean philosophy which Gassendi will present to his seventeenth-century audience will be in certain key areas radically different from its classical parent.

The commentary has been revised now for the second time, but Gassendi is in no haste to publish. In June 1642, Samuel Sorbière had pressed Gassendi to release some of his material for publication, and in August repeated his plea.[44] Gassendi resisted, unpersuaded that his 'trifles' were weighty enough to commit to the public at large.[45] Sorbière made another attempt in May 1643, but again to no avail.[46] In fact, it was not until 1647 that Gassendi would permit anything of his commentary to see the light, and then only the Apology, which had been ready since 1631. As for the rest, there was to be yet another revision.

The Apology was published at Lyon under the title *De vita et moribus Epicuri* and differs from the original draft only in arrangement.[47] The 1631 plan announced to Peiresc called for a treatment in seven 'chapters', while the 1647 edition is divided into eight 'books', the first 'chapter' having become two 'books'. The first two books, which make up almost one-third of the whole, document in turn Epicurus' place of birth, his family, the places where he spent his boyhood and youth, his initial interest in philosophical studies, the founding of the School of Athens, his close friends and pupils, his writings, his last hours, his time of death, his will, his successors as Head of the School, and so forth. It is not entertaining reading, so crammed full are the pages with references to all the available ancient sources. However, the very documentary nature of the treatment has a strategic purpose. Epicurus emerges not as a shadowy figure from the ancient past whose biography is a matter of speculation, but as a known figure the details of whose life and career have been placed beyond dispute.

For the remainder of the work Gassendi examines in turn four general charges which have been brought against Epicurus by his detractors – impiety, lack of respect for others, the promotion of bodily pleasure as the highest good, and contempt for intellectual pursuits. The details of Gassendi's treatment need not detain us.[48] Suffice it to say that Gassendi continues with his documentary approach. On each count Epicurus' chief accusers are identified and the charges elaborated with reference to as much of the ancient evidence as Gassendi has been able to uncover. As spokesman for the other side, Gassendi promises to be as objective as possible, stating that he has no intention of defending his client on points where he is clearly guilty of error. Indeed, if the charges brought against Epicurus are found to be true, he will be the first to condemn him; his intention is only to present certain considerations which would persuade him, if not others, that in some matters there is room for doubt.[49] However, despite his protestations, Gassendi is throughout as partial as Epicurus' opponents. It is true that he chastises Epicurus for denying divine providence, and he expresses regret that Epicurus did not pay greater attention to the mathematical sciences; but for every other charge, and the list is long, he manages to produce a counter, either by presenting contrary testimony from the ancient sources, or by advancing mitigating circumstances.

This is not to suggest that Gassendi's performance is a sparkling one. In fact, he is uncompromisingly pedestrian, matching citation with citation, even pausing at times to discuss the merits of various textual readings. Again, however, the strategy is clear. The issue must be settled on the level of fact; half-truth, misrepresentation, and innuendo have been the weapons of Epicurus' opponents; Gassendi's standards must be seen to be higher. For the purpose of the Apology is two-fold: as the opening section of the commentary it is designed to gain a fair hearing for Epicurus and his teachings; it is also designed to establish Gassendi himself as a conscientious and reliable commentator.

Publication of the *De vita et moribus Epicuri* served to intensify expectations among Gassendi's friends and associates that he might now be prepared to release more of the commentary. The most pressing request came from François Barancy, Doctor of Law and celebrated copy-editor of Lyon, who had seen the *De vita et moribus Epicuri* through the press. What Barancy proposed was the printing of a work which Gassendi had completed in 1629. This was a Latin translation, augmented by historical and critical notes, of the Greek text of Book X of Diogenes Laertius' *De clarorum philosophorum vitis*, which Gassendi had originally intended to bring out with the German publisher Tampach.[50] Gassendi was not enthusiastic. He was already annoyed with Barancy for proceeding with the *De vita et moribus Epicuri* without receiving express permission, and, as he reveals in a letter to Pierre Seguier, Chancellor of France, he had misgivings over his own command of the Greek language.[51] Finally, however, under pressure from his friends, Gassendi relented and released to Barancy the 1629 work, together with much of the material he had been accumulating on Epicurean philosophy during the intervening years. Thus, in July 1649, there was published at Lyon the three-volume *Animadversiones in decimum librum Diogenis Laertii*.

The work was well received in the world of learning.[52] Gassendi himself was far from pleased. The one hundred pages of Greek text and Latin translation are buried under a mass of more than sixteen-hundred pages of cluttered philological annotations and ill-arranged philosophical commentary. We have followed Gassendi's preparation of the commentary closely enough to appreciate the importance which he attached to careful arrangement of the material, and it would be surprising if he had viewed the patchwork nature of the *Animadversiones* with anything but distress. Certainly, when he came to prepare his final exposition of Epicurean philosophy, the *Syntagma philosophicum*, he did not hesitate to dismember the *Animadversiones* completely, and the only parts of it reprinted intact in the 1658 edition of the *Opera Omnia* are the Greek text, the Latin translation, and the strictly grammatical annotations.[53]

In the hope of alleviating a recurring lung ailment Gassendi spent the four years following the publication of the *Animadversiones* in the milder climate of his native Provence. This prolonged and relaxed stay effected some improvement in his health, to the extent that he was able to scale the cliffs at Toulon, and in April 1653, he felt restored enough to return to Paris, where he would spend the last two years of his life. He took up residence at the house of Henry-Louis Herbert de Montmor on the Rue Saint-Avoye, and before long he was busy writing: a life of the Danish astronomer Tycho Brahe, which included a historical survey of work in astronomy up to the time of Tycho's death; biographies of Copernicus, Puerbach, and Regiomontanus (Johann Müller); and pamphlets on coinage, music, the Roman calendar, and his diocese of Digne. In addition, he began preparation of a final version of the commentary, twenty-five years exactly after he had begun the first. For this he turned to the manuscript version of the *Animadversiones* (Tours, *mss.* 707, 708). Some of this material he decided to use unchanged; some he completely revised; some he discarded altogether. At the same time he made numerous additions based upon his most recent researches, including a fresh treatment of Epicurean ethics. Most importantly, he transformed the very nature of the work itself. The title which Gassendi had assigned to the work in the earlier manuscript versions, *De vita et doctrina Epicuri*, accurately reflected his original intention, namely, to present an account of Epicurus' life, character, and philosophical teachings based upon an independent analysis of the ancient testimony and supplemented by such interpretative and illustrative commentary as might render the whole as clear, authoritative, and comprehensive as possible. Already in the letters to de Valois, however, Gassendi had added the role of corrector to that of commentator, and now the role of commentator is dropped altogether. At the same time the title of the work is changed to *Syntagma philosophicum*. Gassendi's final offering will be a compendium of his own philosophical thinking.

The preparation of the *Syntagma philosophicum* was a project, however, which would be left to Gassendi's editors to complete.[54] On 17 November 1654, Gassendi was stricken with a fever which kept him confined to bed until early in January 1655. On 22 February the fever returned and his pulmonary condition worsened. His friend Guy Patin immediately carried out a phlebotomy which gave Gassendi temporary relief. However, in late August he fell ill once again with a fever which ran unabated for more than two months. He was bled a total of fourteen times, until on 24 October it became evident that he would not recover. He made his confession and died early in the afternoon of the same day.

In following Gassendi through the successive stages of his 'grand dessein' we have touched only in passing upon the challenges which confronted him along the way. An immediate obstacle, certainly, was the state of the Epicurean sources upon which he had to rely. Lucretius' *De rerum natura*, upon which he depended heavily, quoting more than five thousand of its approximately seven thousand lines, posed no problem. Lambinus's 1563 and 1570 quarto editions provided not only an adequately restored text, but also an abundance of critical commentary. Diogenes Laertius, however, was another matter, as Gassendi himself testifies. Writing to Peiresc in 1629 concerning his own efforts to produce a serviceable Latin version of Book X, he complains over the corrupt state of Giffen's text and is irritated at the amount of time he is required to spend comparing various manuscripts, translations, and notes.[55]

The obstacles which faced Gassendi in the matter of texts and references should not be minimized. He enjoyed the advantage of having access to de Thou's library while he was in Paris, and he received a good deal of assistance from a variety of his correspondents, but there is no doubt that the basic requirements of scholarship cost him a great deal in time and energy. These obstacles do not compare, however, with a challenge of a different order to which we have already alluded, namely, the problem of rendering acceptable a pagan philosophy many of whose principal tenets ran counter to the teachings of the Church. We have already touched upon Gassendi's attempt in the *De vita et moribus Epicuri* to allay suspicion and create a receptive climate for an exposition of Epicurean doctrine by correcting certain long-standing misconceptions concerning Epicurus' personal life and moral principles. In addition, with reference to the series of letters to de Valois, we have identified some specific aspects of Epicurean physical theory which Gassendi agrees must be rejected on theological grounds. It is important, however, that we set these observations in a wider context by taking stock of the overall strategy which Gassendi adopted. It is a strategy which has more than one dimension and which reveals something of importance concerning the nature of Gassendi's commitment to Epicurean teaching.

A critical element in this strategy is a readiness on Gassendi's part to expose and condemn those features of Epicurean doctrine which are patently at variance with Christian teaching. It is a policy which he enunciates in clear terms in the dedicatory letter to Luillier placed at the head of the *De vita et moribus Epicuri*, and reiterates, as we have noted, in his correspondence with de Valois.[56] The advantages of the approach are clear. At one and the same time Gassendi is able to affirm his own commitment to safeguarding the Christian faith and to imply that those aspects of Epicurean doctrine which he leaves intact pose no threat to orthodox beliefs. Moreover, while he may give the appearance of sacrificing vital elements of Epicurean teaching, in reality he need make only a slight adjustment to retain the effect, at least, of the original formulation. In the area of physical theory, for example, orthodox belief requires him to reject the Epicurean position that atoms are uncreated, eternal, and infinite in number and variety, and that they move incessantly as a result of an innate motive force independent of any other cause. However, he is saved from having to jettison the entire notion of atoms as the primary units of matter by positing that in the act of creation God brought atoms into being in sufficient number and variety and at the same time endowed them with the power to perform the motions necessary for the formation of the phenomenal world.[57] In short, by taking a pragmatic view of Epicurean theory and introducing God as efficient cause, Gassendi is able to satisfy the demands of orthodoxy without abandoning what he regards as the essentials of Epicurean doctrine.

Gassendi's strategy also provides him with the opportunity to give his treatment of Epicurus a degree of historical sanction. For, as he points out in the *De philosophia universe*, which forms a brief introduction to the *Syntagma philosophicum*, the procedure which he proposes to follow with respect to the un-Christian elements in Epicurean philosophy is in no way novel, but identical with that which the early Church Fathers adopted with respect to the philosophy of Aristotle. It is a matter of legitimacy by association, and at various points throughout the *Syntagma philosophicum* Gassendi takes pains to foster the association by stressing certain similarities between Epicurean and Aristotelian doctrine, and by pointing out that in a number of places where Epicurus contradicts Christian teaching he does so in company with Aristotle.[58] At the same time, if there are occasions when Gassendi finds it strategically useful to stress the similarities between Epicurean and Aristotelian doctrine, there are others when he is confident that Epicureanism can be shown to be not equally consistent with Christian teaching but more so, and here Gassendi takes pains to divorce Epicurus from Aristotle, effectively combining his immediate objective of portraying Epicureanism as a philosophy which can be suitably accommodated to Christian theology with the more general objective of discrediting Aristotelianism at every possible turn.[59] For it is important to recognize that the ultimate success of Gassendi's Epicurean programme depended in large part not only upon rendering Epicurean teaching theologically respectable but upon overthrowing what was the reigning philosophy, and it was from the Aristotelian camp that keenest opposition came.[60]

The need to accommodate Epicureanism to the teachings of the Church was one which Gassendi recognized as imperative if he was to be successful in persuading his contemporaries to entertain an alternative to the Aristotelian philosophy, which he considered both faulty and outmoded, and the fact that his work escaped the Index and he himself at no time suffered embarrassment with the ecclesiastical authorities is a measure of his success in purging Epicurean doctrine of offending elements. In the process, however, classical Epicureanism has suffered a radical sea-change. From a purely materialist and mechanistic system in which divine power is expressly denied a creative or operational role it has been transformed into one in which the immaterial is preserved as an essential element and God placed at the very centre. It is a transformation which raises an important question. If Gassendi can feel free to manipulate traditional Epicurean doctrine to the point where in certain essentials it becomes the antithesis of itself, what status does he accord his own modified version? If it is to be considered as tentative and as open to improvement as its parent, what utility can be claimed for it? If, on the other hand, it is offered as a now true and definitive explanation of the nature of things, how does this square with Gassendi's repeated pronouncements against dogmatic philosophizing?

The answer lies in a proper evaluation of Gassendi's remarks concerning the possibility of certain knowledge and in a consideration of the support which he found in Epicureanism itself for advocating a 'middle path' between the extremes of assertive dogmatism on the one hand and destructive scepticism on the other. In the preface to the *Exercitationes paradoxicae adversus Aristoteleos* Gassendi states his position on the possibility of knowing in plain terms with a resounding endorsement of the Sceptics' dictum *nihil sciri*.[61] Similarly, in an early draft of the commentary dealing with logic (Carpentras *ms.* 1832), written in 1636, Gassendi again looks to the traditional sceptical modes to illustrate the Sceptics' position, and it is clear that in the fifteen years which separate the two documents Gassendi's position has not changed: truth lies hidden and it must be counted a gain if we can attain so much as probability.[62]

What has changed, however, is the tone of Gassendi's remarks and the value which he is prepared to place upon that knowledge of appearances which sense-experience affords. In the *Exercitationes paradoxicae adversus Aristoteleos* Gassendi betrays a clear sense of satisfaction at being able to marshal the entire sceptical armoury in support of the *nihil sciri* position. In the Carpentras manuscript, on the other hand, while the sceptical tropes are granted the same force, they are brought forward in a spirit of reluctance as irritating constraints upon a too generous hope for the advancement of knowledge in the future. For there is also a difference in tone attached to the remarks contained in the two works concerning the possibility of progress. In the *Exercitationes paradoxicae adversus Aristoteleos* Gassendi is eloquent enough in proclaiming that the moderns may be expected to add to the discoveries of the past.[63] Yet his remarks are for the most part rhetorical, designed merely to add to the list of criticisms which may be levelled against the Aristotelians by charging that in their slavish attachment to the pronouncements of the Master they undermine man 's freedom to philosophize. In the Carpentras manuscript, on the other hand, Gassendi's remarks on progress are of a different order. For throughout the intervening years he has been busy as an observer and experimenter. He has written the *Parhelia sive soles quatuor spurii* (1629), the *Mercurius in sole visus* (1632), the first of four letters *De apparente magnitudine* (1636), and the first two of three letters comprising the *Proportio gnomonis* (1636). Moreover, his correspondence during these years has constituted a busy exchange of information with fellow researchers throughout Europe. To Gassendi the active scientist the prospect of adding to the sum of human knowledge has become a matter of vital concern, for without such a prospect

> our inborn desire for knowledge would be a cruel mockery, all instruction and learning pointless, the discovery of new instruments fruitless, and the efforts of all those who strain to acquire a deeper, more complete, and richer understanding of things than is granted the common man no more than an empty pastime.[64]

The most significant factor, however, has been Gassendi's work as an Epicurean commentator, in that his researches into Epicurean science have introduced him to a physical theory which fully satisfies his epistemological demands. For unlike the Aristotelian science, which pretends to a knowledge of the real nature of objects, Epicurean atomism lays claim only to a descriptive knowledge of appearances to which the sceptical arguments do not apply. At the same time, it is a theory which enables Gassendi to put a much more positive value upon his own scientific investigations. For what atomism offers is a conceptual framework within which sensory information concerning qualities and effects can be analysed and co-ordinated in a way that reduces the observable world to a meaningful pattern. Moreover, Gassendi has become convinced by

Epicurus' arguments concerning the value of indicative signs that there are instances where sensory experience can be used as the basis for probable conclusions concerning matters which lie beyond the level of immediate obervation. Accordingly, although we cannot hope to reveal completely the inner nature of all things, or indeed to penetrate the deepest recesses of any single thing, we may be confident that the more we uncover the qualities and properties an object possesses, the closer we come to complete understanding of its real nature.[65]

If this process of adding little by little to the stock of information concerning the external attributes of things seems a modest substitute for the acquisition of certain knowledge of the inner workings of nature, it none the less provided Gassendi with sufficient incentive to maintain a steady programme of research and observation throughout the last twenty years of his life. Moreover, while his enthusiasm for the corpuscular theory was only strengthened as a result of his own enquiries and by the promise of further advances with the refinement of scientific instruments, particularly the microscope, his refusal to grant it more than limited and provisional status remained constant. Indeed, so faithful did he remain to the position which he adopted during the Carpentras period that when he came to prepare his final formulation of the logic for inclusion in the *Syntagma philosophicum* he kept the Carpentras version firmly before his eyes. Thus, when he declares in the *Syntagma philosophicum* that 'in light of the extreme positions which have been adopted on the question of the criteria of truth . . . we must follow a path midway between the Sceptics on the one side and the Dogmatics on the other', he is merely reaffirming a conviction of long standing.[66] Gassendi's commitment, then, to Epicurean physics has not caused him to reverse his opinion that demonstrably certain knowledge of the inner workings of nature lies beyond human grasp, and to this extent he would class himself among the Sceptics. At the same time, he is confident that in the corpuscular theory he has discovered a hypothetical explanation of the constitution and behaviour of matter which not only accords best with the information derived from the close study of the phenomenal world, but also holds the surest promise of success in penetrating the hidden world beyond the senses.

Pierre Bayle reserved high praise for Gassendi, declaring him to be 'philosophorum maxime literatissimus, literatorum maxime philosophus'. By reason of both temperament and training Gassendi found himself divided between two traditions. On the one side, through his early reading in the ancient authors and in the works of such moderns as Vives, Charron, and Montaigne he was drawn to the humanist goal of creating out of the inheritance of the past. Moreover, the whole character of his writing – his use of the Latin language, the accumulation of references from the widest possible range of ancient sources, the patient attention to the minutiae of textual restoration and analysis – is eloquent of a temperament ideally suited to the the humanist's task. On the other side, born as he was into a lively Provençal tradition of observation and experiment, Gassendi developed an early fascination for the mysteries and challenges of the physical world and a determination to read with understanding the living book of nature. It is understandable, therefore, that he should have found Epicureanism appealing. Of the major classical phil-osophies it was Epicureanism whose teachings had received the least attention and whose textual sources stood most in need of critical scrutiny. As such Epicureanism presented a ready challenge to Gassendi's humanist impulses. At the same time, as a philosophy which placed the highest premium upon experience as the touchstone of truth it complemented Gassendi's own commitment to observation as the key to expanding man's understanding of the natural world. It is this double nature of Gassendi's allegiance that accounts for both the strengths and the weaknesses of his Epicurean programme. As an observer and experimenter Gassendi was in tune with the science of his day, and this enabled him to appreciate the significance of the Epicurean corpuscular theory in the context of current scientific issues and to articulate its potential to a wide community of fellow investigators. However, Gassendi's talent for assimilating and com-municating new ideas was not matched by an equal capacity for original scientific thinking. As a result, his treatment of Epicurean physical theory remained for the most part descriptive and left untouched certain problems which demanded solution. In particular, he advanced no convincing explanation of the actual mechanics of matter in motion in the void and devised no experiments which might provide a clear link between the sensible qualities of things and their inner atomic composition. As a consequence, the Epicurean atomic theory remained at the ideological level with no more positive support than the alternative mechanical system advocated by Descartes or the Aristotelian theory of substantial forms.

On the other side, Gassendi's presentation of the entire range of
Epicurean teaching, with its patient reconstruction and analysis of
the ancient testimony, both Greek and Latin, is a tribute to his
commitment to the highest standards of humanist scholarship.
However, it has to be recognized that Gassendi's very thoroughness
carries its own penalty. For in his determination to render his account
of Epicurean doctrine as complete as possible, Gassendi is too often
willing to sacrifice economy and falls easily into the habit of piling
illustration upon illustration and dwelling to excessive length upon
matters of grammatical and philological detail. It is a failing whose
baneful results Gassendi was quick to recognize in the *Animadversiones
in decimum librum Diogenis Laertii*, yet one which he did not altogether
avoid in the *Syntagma philosophicum*. The result is that when it is
compared, for example, with Descartes's *Meditations*, which is a model
of economy, Gassendi's Epicurean synthesis presents a forbidding
aspect even to a readership brought up in the tradition.

By design we have focused exclusively in this chapter upon the
work of Pierre Gassendi. While this leaves out of account a number of
individuals such as Samuel Sorbière, Jean François Sarasin, and
François Bernier, who associated themselves with Gassendi in the
preparation and publication of his work and in the general promotion
of Epicurean ideas during the first half of the seventeenth century,[67] it
is a concentration which underscores the fact that Epicurus' 'French
revival' was due in far the largest measure to Gassendi's sustained
commitment. For, if we have pointed to certain shortcomings in
Gassendi's Epicurean programme, it has not been to diminish the
magnitude of Gassendi's contribution to the Epicurean cause. At the
close of the sixteenth century the philosophy of Epicurus, despite a
degree of sympathetic treatment on the part of certain humanist
scholars, was still for the most part the object of suspicion on both
theological and moral grounds. By the mid-point of the seventeenth
century, pared of its most obviously objectionable elements and
accommodated to the demands of Christian teaching, it had become a
philosophy which no longer affronted the sensibilities of orthodox
believers. If this has been accomplished only through a ruthless
distortion of certain key Epicurean doctrines, this was the price which
Epicurus has finally been required to pay in order to be admitted into
the company of respectable philosophers. Most importantly, if
Epicureanism has not dislodged the Aristotelian philosophy from its
position of dominance, Gassendi has succeeded in bringing it to a

position from which it might challenge, along with Cartesianism, for the allegiance of the intellectual community. The arena, however, will change. The sequel will be played out not on French but English soil.

8

EPICURUS BRITANNICUS

Then fly, false Thanes, and mingle with the English Epicures.
Shakespeare, *Macbeth* v.iii

On 12 May 1656, the English diarist John Evelyn recorded that 'little of the Epicurean philosophy was then known amongst us'.[1] This was on the occasion of the publication of his *Essay on the First Book of T. Lucretius Carus, De Rerum Natura*, and in the same year that Dr Walter Charleton presented the English public with a systematic defence of Epicurean ethics in his *Epicurus's Morals*. Certainly, if we are to go by the amount of Epicurean material published in England prior to 1656, there would seem to be some justification for Evelyn's admittedly self-congratulory declaration. Despite the fact that English presses had supplied the reading public with editions and translations of a wide variety of ancient authors, a Latin edition of Lucretius' *De rerum natura* had yet to be printed on English soil, and Lucretius had yet to find an English translator. Moreover, references to Epicurus or Lucretius in standard late Elizabethan and early Jacobean literary works are scant indeed compared with the frequent allusions to Plato, Cicero, Ovid, Horace, Homer, and Virgil.[2]

This does not mean, however, that Epicurus was altogether unknown to Englishmen of the sixteenth and early seventeenth centuries. Some knowledge, albeit scanty and vague, of certain features of Epicurean doctrine had filtered through. Certainly, Epicureanism is marked down more than once as a foe to true religion: George Joye, in *The Exposicion of Daniel the Prophete* (1545), asserts that his author 'describeth the furye of the Epicures . . . even

186

to contempne the very God'; Thomas Cooper, in *An Admonition to the People of England* (1589), assures his readers that 'the school of Epicure, and the Atheists, is mightly increased in these days'; Henry Smith, in *An Arrow against Atheists* (1593), attests that 'there seemeth small difference between Epicurisme, Atheisme, and Mahometisme'; and Bishop Hugh Latimer, in *A Sermon before Edward VI* (1549), challenges the irreligious to 'beleve (as ye Epecurs do) that after this life ther is neither hel nor heaven'.[3] As for the nature of the human soul, Sir John Davies rightly declares in 1599 that the 'Epicures do make them swarmes of atomies'.[4]

However, the Epicurus whose name was most clearly imprinted upon the popular mind was that hardy perennial, Epicurus the *patronus voluptatis*. He is the champion of the 'voluptuous Worldlings' in John Vander Noodt's catalogue of temporal vices:

> Withdraw yourself then, (if you will be counted wise before God) from the vanitie of this present worlde, and caste aside all manner of voluptuousness, pleasure, and Carnall Concupiscence . . . . Be not Ye abashed or displeased, for consideration of temporall felicitie, which God gyveth here upon earthe unto the ungodly, wicked, and carnall libertines, to Epicures, bellygods, and other . . seeing that they shall consume lyke smoake, and perish like the herbe and floure of the fieldes.[5]

He is the model for Brathwaite's degenerate English gentry, 'whose Epicureall mindes, are only set upon prodigall expence', and in whom Sir John Ferne detected 'not the notes of Nobilitie, but the marks of Epicurisme, and companions to effeminancie'.[6] He is the pride of King Lear's entourage whose 'Epicurisme and Lust' make Goneril's court 'more like a Taverne, or a Brothell Than a grac'd Pallace'.[7] He is the arbiter of fine taste in whose honour 'another, out of his epicurious humor, made a kind of oration in the praise of a goose pie'.[8]

It is fair to say, then, that during the sixteenth and early seventeenth centuries Epicurus was known to the general English public almost exclusively in his medieval role as the champion of sensual living, and we look in vain for evidence of any comprehensive and coherent grasp of the Epicurean philosophy as a whole. Yet, this does not mean that we are without evidence of the influence of Epicurean ideas. Indeed, it is during the closing years of the sixteenth century that we witness the beginnings of an especially

187

lively English interest in atomism. At the same time, it must be recognized that it was not a uniform atomism faithful to the Epicurean model and derived exclusively from Epicurean sources. Certainly, acquaintance with the texts of Diogenes Laertius and Lucretius contributed to the general interest in atomist theory and supplied something to the substance of the varying versions. But the range of influences was wider. Witness, for example, what is the first publication by an English writer devoted, in part at least, to the corpuscular theory, namely, Nicholas Hill's *Philosophia Epicurea, Democritiana, Theophrastica*, brought out at Paris in 1601. The title of the work gives only a hint of its real contents. Its atomism is Epicurean in little more than name only, while the treatment of cosmology, psychology, physiology, optics, and theology which takes up the greater part is a pastiche of ideas derived from Aristotle, Hermes Trismegistus, Nicholas of Cusa, Giordano Bruno, and Copernicus. In short, it is misleading to say that the *Philosophia Epicurea* is 'the first modern work to urge actively the atomic theories of Leucippus, Democritus, and Epicurus',[9] if by this it is meant that its author was intent upon promoting the acceptance of atomism in its original Epicurean form. What interests Hill is the concept of atomism itself and the variations which his imaginative mind can weave around it. Epicurus is important primarily because he provides atomism with a lineage.

What is true of Hill is to some extent true also of the other atomist members of the circle of scientific theorists and experimenters who gathered around their patron Henry Percy, Earl of Northumberland, during the last two decades of the sixteenth century and the first two decades of the seventeenth. To document the careers and interests of the various members of the Northumberland circle, which included, in addition to Hill, Thomas Hariot, Robert Hues, Walter Warner, Nathaniel Torporley, and Thomas Allen, would be to duplicate the serviceable treatment given by Kargon.[10] It is important, however, that we at least identify the attraction which atomism held for them in their scientific endeavours and to signal the effect which their attachment to atomism had upon the fortunes of Epicureanism in England during the first half of the seventeenth century.

Although for our purposes Henry Percy himself is not the most important member of the group (that place is reserved for Hariot), he does provide an instructive starting-point in that he reveals something of the importance which atomism assumed for many members of the group not so much as a focus of study in itself, but as an ancillary dimension of other more central preoccupations. Percy's range of interests was broad, embracing optics, astronomy, medicine, mathematics, physics, and alchemy, and it is in connection with the last two that he declares, in his *Advice to His Son* (1595), that the necessary conceptual framework is supplied not by the Aristotelian theory of 'substantial forms' but by atomism:

> The Doctrine of Generation and corruption unfoldeth to our understanding the method general of all atomical combinations possible in homogeneal substances, together with the ways possible of generating of the same substance . . . with all the accidents and qualities rising from these generated substances, as hardness, softness, heaviness, lightness, tenacity, fragibility, ductibility, sound, colour, taste, smell, etc. the application of which doctrine satisfieth the mind in the generation and corruption . . . which part of philosophy the practice of alchemy does much further, and in itself is incredibly enlarged, being a mere mechanical broiling without this philosophical project.[11]

The form which Percy's 'atomism' took, and the precise nature of its application to physical questions, it is impossible to know. However, with respect to the most distinguished member of the Northumberland circle, Thomas Hariot, we are better placed. Like Percy's, Hariot's range of interests was wide. In astronomy, where he was an early supporter of Kepler, he employed the telescope as early as 1609, and his sightings of sunspots in 1610 are the earliest known extant;[12] he made useful contributions to navigational science and ballistics; and as a mathematician he did pioneering work in algebraic theory. His most original work, however, was in physical optics, and it is in this connection that his dependence upon corpuscular theory is most clear. Indeed, in a 1606 letter to Kepler on the problem of the reflection and refraction of light striking a transparent object he invites Kepler to become an 'atom' if he wishes to enter 'nature's house'.[13] It is the case, however, that for Hariot, more than for others of the Northumberland circle, the utility of atomist theory was not exhausted with its application to particular physical problems. For Hariot, 'nature's house' was not simply the world of optics but the whole of reality. Atomism became the very foundation of his entire natural philosophy.[14]

The members of the Northumberland circle were at the centre of experimental scientific activity in Elizabethan England, and their general commitment to atomism, even though their formulations of it differed in important respects from the classical prototype, showing the more immediate influence of Giordano Bruno's *De triplici minimo et mensura* (1591), might be expected to have had some positive effect upon the fortunes of Epicurus during the early years of the seventeenth century. That this was not the case is the result of a combination of factors. In the first place, the members published little during the life of the circle. Hariot is an example. He published only one work, *A Briefe and True Report on the New Found Land of Virginia* (1588), and upon his death in 1621 left a mass of unedited scientific and mathematical material. In his will he named as his literary executor his close friend Nathaniel Torporley, expressing the hope that he would 'separate the chiefe of them from my waste papers, to the end that after hee doth understande them hee may make use in penninge such doctrine that belongs unto them for publique uses'.[15] Torporley was well suited to the task, having served as secretary to the French mathematician François Vieta while he was preparing his *Algebra nova* for publication in 1591, and he resigned his post as Vicar of Salwarpe in order to assume the assignment. However, ten years later nothing had been made ready for publication, and the task was taken over by another of Hariot's associates, the mathematician Walter Warner, who quickly put in print the *Artis analyticae praxis* (1631), a slim volume presenting only Hariot's work on algebraic equations. However, Warner failed to secure resources for further publication and in 1632 Hariot's papers were locked away in a trunk and deposited in the Earl of Northumberland's library at Petworth House.[16] Thus, the major part of Hariot's scholarly work, and consequently the details of his atomism, remained in manuscript form.

This does not mean that Hariot's attachment to atomism was not generally recognized. However, whatever benefit the atomist, and by association the Epicurean, cause might be expected to have gained from the support of a prominent scientific figure was minimized by the fact that as a result of a variety of circumstances Hariot found himself suspect as a holder of unorthodox beliefs. Indeed, his known atomist views only added to the concern. It is likely, for example, that a factor in Torporley's tardiness in preparing Hariot's papers for publication was his concern over Hariot's atomist leanings. For among Torporley's papers is the title-page of a proposed pamphlet (*The Analytical Corrector*) in which he planned not only to correct what he regarded as Warner's flawed presentation of Hariot's algebra, but also to offer 'a refutation of the pseudo-philosophic atomic theory revived by him [Hariot] and, outside his other strange notions deserving of reprehension and anathema'.[17]

But it was through his association with Walter Raleigh that Hariot became the subject of adverse public comment. In 1591 Raleigh was temporarily out of favour with Elizabeth I as result of his concealed marriage to Elizabeth Throckmorton. He was summoned to court from Sherborne in Dorset, where he was busy establishing a residence for his family, and promptly confined, along with his wife, to the Tower. Meanwhile, he was the target of a campaign designed to discredit him further. In 1592 the Jesuit Robert Parsons published in Germany a commentary on Elizabeth's 1591 edict against the Catholics, entitled *Elizabethae, Angliae reginae haeresim Calvinianum propugnantis saevissimum in Catholicos sui regni edictum . . . cum responsione*, in which Raleigh, along with others, was accused of atheism, and Hariot identified as 'Raleigh's teacher', and an 'Epicurean and Magus' who called into question the existence of God, the immortality of the soul, and the life eternal.[18] In the abbreviated English version published shortly after the Latin original and entitled *An Advertisement Written to a Secretarie of my L. Treasurers of England, by an Inglishe Intelligencer*, the author speaks of

> Sir Walter Rawley's Schoole of Atheisme by the waye, and of the Coniurer that is M. thereof, and of the diligence used to get young gentlemen to this schoole, where in both Moyses, and our Saviour, the olde and the new Testamente are iested at, and the schollers taught amonge other thinges to spell God backwarde.[19]

Hariot's name also surfaced in another context. In May 1593 Christopher Marlowe was summoned to appear before the Privy Council on suspicion of atheism and a report was submitted by one of the Council's investigators, Richard Baines, a report which included in a long list of accusations the charge that Marlowe had affirmed that 'Moyses was but a Jugler, and that one Heriots being Sir W. Raleighs man can do more than he'.[20]

Meanwhile, the campaign against Raleigh had taken on an additional dimension. In 1594 an ecclesiastical commission was appointed to look into alleged heresies in Dorset, and it is clear that

Raleigh was the target. In the course of the sittings, which were held at Cerne Abbas in March, depositions were taken from fifteen individuals, and most implicated Raleigh either directly or indirectly. Moreover, Hariot was implicated by three of the witnesses. John Jessop, minister of Gillingham, said that 'he hath hearde that one Herryott of Sr Walter Rawleigh his house hath brought the godhedd in question, and the whole course of the Scriptures'; Nicholas Jefferys, parson of Wyke Regis, swore that 'he hath hearde that one Herriot attendant on Sr Walter Rawleigh hath ben convented before the Lordes of the Counsell for denyinge the resurrecion of the bodye'; and Thomas Norman, minister of Melcombe Regis, said that 'he harde of one Herryott of Sr Walter Rawleigh his house to be suspected of Atheisme'.[21]

No formal proceedings resulted from the Cerne Abbas enquiry, but Hariot's reputation for impiety persisted. In delivering his judgment at Raleigh's trial for treason in 1603 Chief Justice Popham implored Raleigh to 'aske God forgivenesse' for his atheistic beliefs and 'lett not Heriot nor any soul Doctor perswade you that there is no Eternity'.[22] Finally, not even Hariot's death from cancer in 1621 escaped the malicious attention of the gossips. For, as Aubrey records:

> The Bishop of Sarum (Seth Ward) told me that one Mr. Haggar (a countryman of his), a gentleman and a good mathematician, was well acquainted with Mr. Thomas Hariot, and was wont to say, that he did not like (or valued not) the olde storie of the Creation of the World. He would not believe the old position; he would say *ex nihilo nihil fit*. But sayd Mr. Haggar, a *nihilum* killed him at last; for in the top of his nose came a little red speck (exceeding small), which grew bigger and bigger, and at last killed him.[23]

For all the imputations of impiety there is no evidence that Hariot himself was ever formally investigated. The real target was Raleigh, and it was a case of discrediting him through his associates. Hariot was not the only one so used, but he was ideal for the purpose.[24] For, as the substance of the allegations shows, it was an easy matter to equate his scientific commitment to atomist theory with attachment to all the heterodox views generally associated with Epicurean teaching.[25] Thus, instead of Hariot having some positive impact upon the fortunes of the Epicurean philosophy during the early decades of the seventeenth century, it is Hariot himself who is damaged because of his 'Epicurean' associations. But then, as we have seen, 'Epicurean' became a convenient label of disparagement early in the tradition.

If the support of members of the Northumberland circle did less than might have been expected to advance the cause of atomism, promise of support was forthcoming from a more respectable source in the person of Francis Bacon. Bacon's earliest references to atomist theory, which date to a period during the first decade of the seventeenth century when he was becoming acquainted with the experimental work of the Northumberland circle, are decidedly positive. He opens the *Cogitationes de natura rerum*, which was written prior to 1605, with the declaration that the

> doctrine of Democritus concerning atoms is either true or useful for demonstration, for it is not easy either to grasp in thought or to express in words the genuine subtlety of nature, such as it is found in things, without supposing an atom.[26]

In the *De principiis atque originibus*, composed around 1612, he suggests that the atomist teaching of Democritus deserved far more than did the philosophies of Plato and Aristotle to survive the destructive forces of barbarism, since 'in most things it agrees with the authority of the early ages';[27] and in *On Atheism*, printed in the 1612 edition of the *Essays*, he illustrates his submission that depth of philosophical learning is an aid to religion by singling out the atomist philosophy:

> Most of all, that which is most acused of Atheisme doth demonstrate Religion. That is, the schoole of Leusippus, and Democritus, and Epicurus. For it is a thousand times more credible, that foure mutable Elements, and one immutable fifth essence, duely and eternally placed, neede no God: then that an Army of infinite small portions of seeds unplaced, should have produced this order, and beauty, without a divine Marshall.[28]

It is the case, however, that the *Cogitationes de natura rerum* and the *De principiis atque originibus* did not see publication until 1653, and in the mean time Bacon's attitude changed. As he deliberated concerning the goals of scientific enquiry and refined his thoughts concerning scientific method, his enthusiasm for 'fruits and works' increased and his enthusiasm for 'speculations and glosses' waned, with the result that by the time he came to publish the *Novum organum* in 1620 his attitude towards classical atomism had become more reserved. He was still prepared to grant that among the ancients it was the atomists who progressed furthest in dissecting nature into her parts (*naturum secare*).[29] He was not convinced, however, that their hypotheses, regardless of whether they are true or not, have much to contribute to the welfare of mankind.[30] The reason lies in the faultiness of their method. For, in Bacon's view, they would have made more progress of a useful kind if, instead of leaping to establish on the basis of a minimum of observation the existence of certain primary qualities, and focusing their attention exclusively upon these, they had concentrated rather upon secondary, third, and fourth qualities, patiently working up to general maxims by orderly observation and experiment, employing, in short, the method which Bacon himself advocated.[31]

On general grounds, then, classical atomism is to be dismissed as methodologically unsound and barren of serviceable results. But it is the case that Bacon's attitude towards atomist theory has changed at the level of particulars as well. For when in Book II of the *Novum organum* he comes to consider the question of analysing the texture and configuration of bodies by reducing them to their simple natures, it is no longer atoms which he has in mind:

> Nor shall we thus be led to the doctrine of atoms, which implies the hypothesis of a vacuum and that of the unchangeableness of matter (both false assumptions); we shall be led only to real particles such as really exist.[32]

For Bacon it will be a matter of analysing bodies in terms of the constituent elements of 'spirit' and 'material essence', discovering, through a combination of reasoning and experiment, as much as can be known about their precise natures, their relative proportions, and their modes of interaction.[33]

It is fair to say that during the early years of the seventeenth century in England the atomist cause suffered not so much from lack of attention as from attention which for a variety of reasons had a negative rather than a positive impact. The pro-atomist members of the Northumberland circle published little of their experimental work with the result that atomist theory was left without the benefit of illustrative support. As well, the involvement of a number of the members, Hariot in particular, in the affairs of prominent persons who were at one time or another politically or morally suspect led to a revival of traditional prejudices against atomist teaching. Finally, in the person of Francis Bacon atomism gained an ally whose support was to prove short-lived as early enthusiasm turned to cold contempt.

Yet the fact remains that atomism, and by association Epicureanism, continued to be a topic of lively discussion during the 1630s and 1640s. As testimony we may look to the first English translator of Lucretius, Mrs Lucy Hutchinson. Born in 1619 in the Tower of London, where her father, Sir Allen Apsley, was Lieutenant-Governor, she was educated with Puritan regard for serious studies. She learned French along with English, could read by the age of four, and was proficient in Latin by the age of eight. In 1637 she married John Hutchinson (later Colonel), who became Governor of Nottingham Castle and fought on the side of the Parliament during the Civil War. Shortly after the Restoration her husband was confined in Sandown Castle in Kent and died there in 1664, and she was left to spend her widowhood in reduced circumstances, devoting her energy to the composition of the *Memoirs* of her husband.

What concerns us, however, is a far different composition from her earlier years. In 1675 she sent to the Earl of Anglesey, Lord Keeper of His Majesty's Privy Seal and a patron of letters, the manuscript of an English version of the *De rerum natura* which she had completed some thirty years earlier at a time when she was fired by a 'curiosity to understand things I heard so much discourse of at second hand'.[34] What form this discourse concerning Epicurean teaching took, and whether the sentiments expressed were favourable or otherwise, we do not know; but the very fact that it took place at all, and presumably not infrequently, in the Hutchinson's Puritan household, where Lucretius evidently had a place upon the library shelves, is of interest in itself. However, as she confesses to the Earl in her prefatory epistle, Mrs Hutchinson's youthful fascination played upon her conscience and she became 'convinced of the sin of amusing myself with such vain philosophy', which cannot be distinguished from that of 'the other fardle of philosophers who in some pulpits are quoted with divine epithets'. As for the 'dog' Lucretius, only his 'lunacy can extenuate the crime of his arrogant ignorance', and

> 'tis a lamentation and horror that in these days of the Gospel, men should be found so presumptuously wicked to study and adhere to his and his master's ridiculous, impious, execrable doctrines,

reviving the foppish casual dance of atoms, and denying the sovreign wisdom of God in the great design of the whole universe.

Her only excuse for having preserved the evidence of her failing is the hope that 'having by rich grace scaped the shipwreck of my soul among those vain philosophers', she might set up a 'seamark, to warn uncautious travellers . . . that those walks of wit which poor vain-glorious scholars call the Muses' groves, are enchanted thickets'.

Lucy Hutchinson's youthful dalliance with Lucretius did nothing either to advance or to hinder the reception of Epicureanism in England, since she did not allow her Roman poet to parade before the general public in his new English clothes. However, it was not just in England that Epicurus was engaging the attention of English minds. Around the time that Mrs Hutchinson was busy with the *De rerum natura* a small circle of English enthusiasts found themselves at the centre of lively Epicurean discussions in Paris, and the return of some of their number to England around the mid-point of the century had a significant impact upon Epicurean fortunes. We refer to the group of royalist *émigrés* who, with their protector and patron William Cavendish, Marquis of Newcastle, sought refuge on the Continent after the battle of Marston Moor in 1644. The 'Newcastle circle' had been in existence since the early thirties and had included at that time, in addition to William Cavendish, his brother Sir Charles Cavendish, Thomas Hobbes, the mathematicians John Pell and Walter Warner, and Sir Charles's secretary, Robert Payne. The augmented group consisted of the Cavendish brothers, Hobbes, who had been in France since 1641, Pell, who kept in close touch from his post at the University of Breda in the Netherlands, William Petty, Sir Kenelm Digby, and, finally, Margaret Lucas, who became Marchioness of Newcastle upon her marriage to William Cavendish in 1645.

It is important to recognize that, as with the 'Northumberland circle', so with the 'Newcastle circle' a shared interest in natural philosophy did not result in the adoption of a common atomistic world-view on the classical Epicurean model: Charles Cavendish, while he was doubtless interested in atomist theory, was more deeply involved in practical problems in optics, mechanics, and mathematics;[35] during the 1640s, when he was in close contact with Gassendi, Hobbes was prepared to admit the existence of atoms and

196

void; however, by the time he came to record his mature reflections on the mechanical philosophy in the *De corpore* of 1655, while he had retained his commitment to one of the twin pillars of classical atomism, indivisible particles, he had rejected the second, the vacuum; Petty's atomism, while reflecting in its general outlines the Epicurean atomism of Gassendi, introduces elaborations concerning the characteristics of individual atoms, such as their magnetic nature and their rotational motion, which are quite foreign to the Epicurean model; Digby's atomism represents an attempt to bring contemporary corpuscular theories in line with traditional scholastic minimist doctrine;[36] and, finally, Lady Margaret's atomism, whatever it owes to Epicurean teaching, is far more the product of her own fantastic imagination.[37]

Clearly, then, we do not have to do with serious attempts to revive classical atomist doctrine. These were speculative and independent minds, and Epicurean theory served at best as a starting-point for their own idiosyncratic variations on a theme. However, the importance of the members of the Newcastle circle for the promotion of Epicurean science does not rest upon the degree to which they adhered to traditional Epicurean doctrine. It rests, rather, upon the extent to which their French contacts, and here we must include Descartes as well as Gassendi, bolstered their enthusiasm for the mechanical philosophy in general, and the extent to which they in turn communicated that enthusiasm to their compatriots upon their return to England. For from 1650 onwards the mechanical philosophy, and Epicurean atomism in particular, began to attract increasing attention in English intellectual circles.

This was due in no small part to the publication in 1649 of Gassendi's *Animadversiones in decimum librum Diogenis Laertii* which, despite Gassendi's own reservations, enjoyed considerable success in England as on the Continent. In addition, in 1653 Isaac Gruter, working from manuscripts bequeathed by Bacon to William Boswell, an associate of the Newcastle circle, published Bacon's early pro-atomist works in a volume entitled *Scripta in naturalia et universalia philosophiae*, thus adding the weight of Bacon's considerable authority to the atomist cause.

However, if the return to England of some of the members of the Newcastle circle coincided with a quickening interest in atomism, it coincided also with an increasing disquiet among the orthodox over the moral and theological implications of atomist teaching. This concern had been sharpened by the printing in Amsterdam in 1644 of a pamphlet authored by Richard Overton, close friend of General John Lilburne, founder of the Levellers. Overton's heretical tract, entitled *Mans Mortalitie*, was designed to demonstrate, by appeal to both the Scriptures and natural reason, that the concept of an immaterial soul separable from the body is false, and that at death it is the material body alone which is raised above to a life eternal.[38] Overton does not rely heavily upon Epicurean arguments, but from among the ancient philosophers from whom he draws support he does single out the atomists Democritus, Leucippus, and Epicurus, and these references, together with the unorthodox thrust of his arguments, were enough. In 1645 Alexander Ross, in *The Philosophicall Touchstone*, assailed Overton as 'a pig from Epicurus' stye', and in the following year John Bachiler directed his *The Soules Own Evidence, for its Own Immortality* against 'Atheists, Epicuruses, etc.'.[39] It was also during the 1640s that the Cambridge Platonist John Smith signalled his concern in two discourses, *A Discourse Demonstrating the Immortality of the Soul* and *A Short Discourse on Atheism*, in which the Epicurean arguments for the soul's mortality are accorded lengthy treatment.

In this apprehensive atmosphere the publishing activities of two of the returning *émigrés* did little to dispel concern. In 1651 Hobbes, whose materialism and moral philosophy were readily equated in the popular mind with Epicurean teaching, brought out his *Leviathan*, which provoked prompt and strident protest from a wide range of English readers.[40] And in 1653 Lady Margaret published her *Poems and Fancies*. It is true that the majority of her atomist verses contained little that could occasion serious alarm, and they were doubtless taken as nothing more than the harmless musings of a rambling mind. However, given the prevailing nervousness and given her close association with Hobbes, the reader must have been rendered not a little uncomfortable at being assured that 'small Atomes of themselves a World may make'.[41]

What Epicureanism needed at this point in its English journey was an advocate who commanded respect in intellectual circles, whose moral, religious, and political views were beyond suspicion, and who was equipped to present the English public with an account of Epicurean teaching which would relate the parts to the whole in comprehensive fashion. What Epicureanism needed, in short, was a

'Gassendi *anglais*'. Such an advocate appeared, ironically perhaps, in the person of a friend of Hobbes and Lady Margaret, Dr Walter Charleton. Charleton was born into a clerical family in 1620 (his father was the rector of Shepton Mallet in Somerset) and educated at Magdalen Hall (later Hertford College), Oxford, matriculating in 1635. He decided upon a medical career, was appointed physician-in-ordinary to Charles I in 1643, and remained a staunch royalist throughout the period of the Commonwealth. He was elected Fellow of the Royal Society in 1663 and Fellow of the Royal College of Physicians in 1676, serving as its President from 1689 to 1691.[42] Charleton's interest in natural philosophy was awakened early through his studies with John Wilkins, whom Aubrey described as 'the principall reviver of experimentall philosophy at Oxford', and for a time he was much taken with the medical and chemical theories of Johannes Baptista Van Helmont. Indeed, two of his earliest publications, the *Deliramenta catarrhi* (1650) and *A Ternary of Paradoxes* (1650), were English adaptations of works by Van Helmont.[43] At what point he first became acquainted with the atomist theory is difficult to determine. He spent the early part of the 1640s at Oxford where philosophical debate was lively and wide-ranging, and he may well have encountered discussion of atomist doctrine in that context. However, it is clear that the development of a serious interest in atomism coincided with his introduction around the mid-point of the century to the ideas of the French natural philosophers. The precise occasion of this introduction is unclear. He may well have visited Paris for a period in 1651 and gained access through his friends John Evelyn, Kenelm Digby, and Hobbes to French intellectual circles.[44] Or it may be that the ideas of the French philosophers were communicated to him by members of the Newcastle circle on their return to England. Whatever the case, the years between 1650 and 1652 produced a transformation in Charleton's philosophical orientation. From this point on he not only became a convert to the new science, he determined to bring the Epicurean atomism of Gassendi in particular to the attention of the English public at large.

His first 'Epicurean' publication, *The Darkness of Atheism Dispelled by the Light of Nature: A Physico-theologicall Treatise* (1652) reveals a close dependence upon Gassendi's *Animadversiones in decimum librum Diogenis Laertii* of 1649. It also reveals that Charleton has not underestimated the importance of presenting a version of Epicurean atomism which would least offend the moral and religious sensibilities of his English public. An extract from Nathaniel Culverwell's *An Elegant and Learned Discourse of the Light of Nature*, published in the same year as Charleton's *Darkness*, gives the measure of the kind of anti-Epicurean prejudice which Charleton had to overcome:

> The whole summe of *Epicurus* his Ethicks . . . is this, that pleasure was the alpha and omega of all happinesse. To this purpose he wrote a multitude of books, and scattered them like so many of his Atomes, and the greedy appetite of his licencious followers was easily caught with these baits of pleasure, which made his opinions to be stiled meretricious doctrines that curl'd their locks, that painted their faces, that open'd their naked breasts, that cloth'd themselves in soft and silken apparel, to see if they could thus entice the world.[45]

The strategy which Charleton adopts is to disarm potential critics by divorcing himself, and his 'new' Epicurus, from those contemporary materialists whose atomistic discourses he considered injurious to true religion. For, as he admits to his reader: 'England . . . hath of late produced, and doth at this unhappy day foster more swarms of Atheisticall monsters . . . then any age, then any Nation hath been infected withall.'[46] In particular, he denounces the notions that the soul is mortal, that motion is inherent in matter, and that God has no providential role in the creation of the universe and its 'constant Conservation and Moderation'. As long as these errors are corrected, there is no 'justifiable ground, why atoms may not be reputed *Mundi materies*, provided that we allow, that God wanted first Matter out of nothing; that his wisdom modelled and cast them'.[47] Indeed, says Charleton, appealing to the same argument from design which Bacon had employed in his *On Atheism* exactly forty years earlier, atomism, far from threatening religion, may be seen as a powerful proof of God's existence:

> Is it possible to imagine, or by any specious argument to hope to persuade that so many minute bodies or Atoms, by the rash and undeterminate conduct of their own innate propensity to motion, could . . . meet and unite in just that number which was sufficient to . . . exactly accommodate to the great body of the world whose bounds we know not and whose dimensions are immense?[48]

Having set the stage by advertising the 'new' atomism as a philosophy which the most orthodox minds may safely entertain, Charleton turns his attention in his second work to the task of educating his English public in its physical details. This work is the *Physiologia Epicuro-Gassendo-Charltoniana or A Fabrick of Science Natural, upon the Hypothesis of Atoms, Founded by Epicurus, Repaired by Petrus Gassendus, and Augmented by Walter Charleton* (1654), whose extended title offers the reader further reassurance that it is a 'corrected' atomism that he will encounter.[49] The *Physiologia* is an imposing volume of some five-hundred closely packed pages, and again Charleton draws heavily upon Gassendi, offering what is essentially a translation and amplification of the physical part of the *Animadversiones*. Following a general survey of the principal ancient schools, Charleton presents two lengthy sections in support of the twin pillars of the atomist system, void and atoms, supplementing the traditional Epicurean arguments with an array of references to modern physical and chemical observations and experiments. Detailed treatment of the essential properties of atoms, size, shape, and motion, leads to an examination of the origins of qualities, an explanation of the physiology of vision, and a discussion of the nature of colours, light, sound, odour, taste, etc. Finally, in an attempt to demonstrate that the so-called 'occult qualities' are dependent upon known causes, Charleton treats the reader to a discussion of an assortment of curiosities in the course of which he may learn, *inter alia*, 'why shellfish grow fat in the Full of the moon, and lean again at the New', or 'why such as are empoysened by the biting of a Tarantula, fall into violent fits of Dancing, and cannot be Cured by any other Remedies, but the Harmonous Straines of Musick alone'.

The *Physiologia* does not make easy reading. Charleton allows his reader little relief from scientific detail, and the mass of illustrative material and the frequent references to passages in ancient and modern authors leave the main points of the presentation too often lost to view. In short, Charleton imports from Gassendi's *Animadversiones* along with much of its material many of its faults. None the less, the essentials of the 'new' atomism are faithfully recorded and Charleton deserves the credit for furnishing the English reading public with its first authoritative and comprehensive account.

In dedicating the *Physiologia* to Mrs Elizabeth Villiers Charleton expressed confidence that her patronage would give his writings 'not only an Estimation among Good Men; but also a full Protection from the Malevolence of Evil'. It would seem, however, that this confidence was ill-founded. In the dedicatory epistle to Mrs Villiers he promised, as 'the Remaining Moity of this Physiologie', a work on the human soul, and this duly appeared in 1657 as *The Immortality of the Human Soul Demonstrated by the Light of Nature*. In the previous year, however, he brought out a work which he had not intended, entitled *Epicurus's Morals . . . Collected Partly out of his owne Greek Text, in Diogenes Laertius, Partly out of the Rhapsodies of Marcus Aurelius, Plutarch, Cicero, and Seneca . . . and Faithfully Englished*, which offers a vindication of Epicurus' personal morality and a sympathetic account of Epicurean ethics. Now it may be that Charleton had only recently come into possession of the two works on which the *Epicurus's Morals* is largely based, Gassendi's *De vita et moribus Epicuri* of 1647 and Jean François Sarasin's *Apologie pour Epicure* of 1651. However, a more likely reason for Charleton's abrupt change of plan is suggested by his statement in *The Immortality of the Human Soul* that 'from the time I published that Physiology you mentioned, even to this very day, I have been embroil'd in as many troubles and distractions, as malice, persecution, and sharp adversity could accumulate upon me'. We know that some of these difficulties stemmed from disagreement with fellow members of the medical profession, but it is not impossible that others were related to the *Physiologia* itself, and that what prompted Charleton to interrupt his proposed sequence of writings with the publication of *Epicurus's Morals* was in part a realization that there were those whose concerns over the implications of atomist doctrine had not been wholly allayed by his careful assurances and that the ground needed to be more thoroughly prepared.

The *Epicurus's Morals* is neatly structured and written in a pleasing prose style. While the largest part of the substance is freely taken from Gassendi and the ancient authors identified in the subtitle, with references duly supplied in the margins, Charleton does not simply present a random collection of testimonies relating to Epicurean ethical teaching. Rather, he has taken care to draw his material together into a complete and integrated ethical system. Happiness is established at the outset as the supreme good and defined in terms of the pleasure which consists in tranquillity of mind. Fears and desires are introduced as the principal obstacles to the realization of this state, and the practice of the traditional virtues is identified as the only means by which these obstacles may be removed. The result is an ethical scheme which neatly combines the pursuit of the Epicurean ideal with the cultivation of the highest Christian values.

Of equal importance with the substance of the essay are the contents of the lengthy 'Apologie for Epicurus' which is prefixed to the work in the form of 'A Letter, to a Person of Honour', and in which Charleton addresses the 'three Capital Crimes' of which Epicurus has been accused, namely, his denial of the soul's immortality, his refusal to grant God an active role in human affairs, and his approval of suicide as an acceptable end to life. Charleton's response to each of these charges is of the same kind. As a Christian he cannot but condemn the Epicurean view as contrary to the teachings of the Church. At the same time, he feels constrained to advance certain considerations which, if they do not absolve Epicurus from guilt, at least justify a more charitable judgment. First, it has to be remembered that Epicurus had the misfortune to be born into a pagan world, and it must be asked with what justice he

> is so highly condemned, for being ignorant of that unattainable Truth, when he could steer the course of his judgment and belief by no other star, but that remote and pale one of the Light of Nature, that bright North-Star of Holy Scripture appearing not at all to the Horizon of Greece, till many Ages after his death?

Second, it has to be acknowledged that Epicurus was far from being the only philosopher among the ancients to hold these particular views. Lastly, it has to be admitted that on the plane of reason alone the positions which he advances are difficult, if not impossible, to refute, and it is only by the light of Holy Scripture that Christians have been led to a position of truth. There is little in Charleton's appeal which cannot be found in Gassendi and Sarasin. What is important is that Charleton's audience was for the first time granted the opportunity to hear the arguments in its own language.

To say that Charleton's *Epicurus's Morals* 'added little or nothing to the acceptance of atomism' is to underestimate the degree to which any expression of interest in atomist teaching was considered suspect in orthodox circles.[50] It is a fact of which further illustration is given by the disclaimers which John Evelyn felt constrained to incorporate into his *Essay on the First Book of T. Lucretius Carus, De Rerum Natura*, published in the same year as Charleton's *Epicurus's*

Morals. Evelyn was given reason to feel nervous early on. In 1653, three years before the *Essay* was published, he sent a manuscript version to his cousin Richard Fanshawe. Fanshawe, himself a translator, congratulated Evelyn on the exactness of his rendering of Lucretius' verses, but went on to rejoice that, since the likeness was so remarkable, Lucretius could entertain no hope of escaping his accusers, like a runaway criminal, by disguising his voice.[51] In April 1656, when the *Essay* was in the hands of the printer, Evelyn's friend Jeremy Taylor, later Bishop of Down, was more direct, expressing regret that Evelyn should have been prevailed upon to busy himself with his *Lucretius* and demanding that he also 'prepare a sufficient antidote'.[52] Evelyn sent his assurances by return:

> My *Essay upon Lucretius*, which I told you was engaged, is now printing, and (as I understand) near finished: my animadversions upon it will I hope provide against all ill consequences, and totally acquit me either of glory or impiety. The captive woman was in the old law to have been head-shaven, and her excrescences pared off . . . I hope I have so done with this author, as far as I have penetrated; and for the rest I shall proceed with caution, and take your counsel.[53]

The *Essay* issued forth from the press in May 1656, heralded by commendatory verses by a number of Evelyn's contemporaries. These laudatory flourishes, however, tell us more about the conventions of friendship than their authors' poetic judgment, since by the most generous estimate Evelyn's translation is entirely forgettable. Nor does the rest of the volume have much to recommend it. The promised animadversions, which take up three times more space than the translation itself, are perfunctory, and Evelyn's 'defence' of Epicurus is a repeat of arguments by now familiar. Indeed, Evelyn himself was distressed at the result of his labours, and not least by the book's appearance. He had engaged his friend Dr Triplet to see it through the press in his absence, and makes plain his disappointment at Triplet's efforts in his own copy of the book housed in Christ Church Library, Oxford:

> Never was book so abominably misused by printer, never copy so negligently surveied by one who undertook to looke over the proofes with all exactnesse and care, namely Dr. Triplet . . . . This good yet I received by it, that publishing it vainely, its ill

success at the printers, discourag'd me from troubling the world with the rest.

In fact, as he told Meric Casaubon in 1674, 'shame and indignation' prompted him to prepare a second edition, but he thought better of it, and 'it still lies in the dust of my study where 'tis likely to be for ever buried'.[54]

The immediate impact which the works of Charleton and Evelyn had upon the acceptance of Epicureanism in England is difficult to assess. We have noted that Charleton's *Physiologia* met with a certain amount of adverse criticism, and Evelyn was less than ecstatic about the merits of his *Essay*. It is true to say, however, that after 1656 the English public had ready access to ample detail concerning Epicurean physical and ethical theory and could feel encouraged by the unquestioned orthodoxy of Charleton and Evelyn to approach Epicurean teaching with some degree of assurance that in its new guise it no longer posed a threat to Christian beliefs. Moreover, there appeared in 1660 a work which, while it was not designed to promote Epicureanism, offered yet another comprehensive account. This was the third volume of Thomas Stanley's *The History of Philosophy, containing the Lives, Opinions, Actions and Discourses of the Philosophers of every Sect*, which allotted to Epicurus by far the largest section of the whole work, amounting to more pages than those devoted to Plato and Aristotle combined. Stanley's account takes the form of a descriptive exposition of Epicurean doctrine derived in the main from Diogenes Laertius, whom he cites frequently, but relying heavily as well upon Charleton and Gassendi. Indeed, Stanley's account of Epicurus' life is translated directly from Gassendi's *De vita et moribus Epicuri* and his presentation of Epicurean ethical theory is virtually a word-for-word reproduction of Charleton's *Epicurus's Morals*. If Stanley added nothing new to the Epicurean material already available in English, he did provide yet another respectable source for Epicurean teaching, and the *History* enjoyed considerable success. It received a second edition in 1687, a third in 1701, and a fourth in 1743. In addition, a Latin version was put out in 1711 and reprinted in 1731.

To say that the 1650s represent a turning-point in the fortunes of Epicureanism in England is an exaggeration if by this it is meant that by the time of the Restoration it had succeeded in capturing the allegiance of a substantial part of the scientific and intellectual community. What can be said is that as a result of the publications of Charleton, Evelyn, and Stanley, as well as those of Gassendi, the details of Epicurean science were known to a wider public and that some modest progress had been made towards alleviating traditional concerns over the anti-Christian implications of Epicurean theology and ethical theory. In sum, at a time when a general disillusionment with Aristotelian science, particularly among members of the Royal Society, which received its first charter in July of 1662, was giving impetus to the search for alternative models and new modes of enquiry, Epicurean science would seem to be reasonably well placed to enter the lists. In the event, however, whatever hopes may have been entertained of securing for the Epicurean philosophy a place within the main stream of English thought were to prove illusory. For during the two decades following the Restoration Epicurus was to become the target of a series of spirited attacks and be disowned by the very element in the English intellectual community which owed him most.

The attacks came for the most part from staunch defenders of Christian orthodoxy, for whom, despite the apologetics of Gassendi and Charleton in particular, Epicureanism continued to represent a serious danger to established religion. In a number of his sermons John Tillotson, future Archbishop of Canterbury, rhapsodizes at length upon the splendid design of the world and all its creatures as evidence of God's providence, and inveighs strenuously against 'Epicurus with his followers, who ascribe the regular and orderly frame of nature to a happy casualty and fortunate concourse of atoms'.[55] For Tillotson is concerned that 'by denying that God either made or governed the world' the Epicureans are determined 'to strip the divine nature of most of its perfections . . . his being the first cause and original of all things, and his goodness likewise, and wisdom, and power, and justice'.[56] For a fellow divine, Richard Baxter, it is the materialist aspects of Epicurean doctrine which cause alarm, and in a vigorous defence of the soul's immortality against the arguments of the Epicurean school he takes direct aim at the new generation of atomists, referring to those 'who in this age adhere to the *Epicurean* (or *Cartesian*) Hypothesis' as 'the younger sort of ingenious men . . . who reduce all to *Matter* and *Motion* because nothing but *Matter* and *Motion* is thoroughly studied by them'.[57] The most sustained attack, however, came from the pen of the Anglican controversialist Meric Casaubon. For Casaubon Epicurus is 'the arrantest brute . . . that took upon him the name of philosopher', and the current revival of his doctrines is 'of all things of that nature this age hath pro- duced . . . the most prodigious and incredible', and 'that so many, professing Christianity, should entertain the attempt with so ready an assent and applause – an argument to me, with many others, of the inclination of the age'.[58]

It is important, however, to place these anti-Epicurean outbursts in their broader context. For Baxter and Casaubon especially the real target was not Epicurus but the Royal Society, and it was a matter of attempting to embarrass the members by suggesting that their commitment to the 'new science', and by implication Epi- curean atomism, was proof in itself of their irreligion. It was a strategy which aimed at a particularly vulnerable spot. From its inception the Society's soundness in matters of religion had been so repeatedly questioned that Thomas Sprat devoted Part III of his *History of the Royal Society* to a vindication of the Society's record, beginning with the statement:

> I will now proceed to the weightiest, and most solemn part of my whole *undertaking*; to make a defence of the *Royal Society*, and this new *Experimental Learning*, in respect of the *Christian Faith*. I am not ignorant, in what a slippery place I now stand.[59]

Moreover, other Fellows, notably Joseph Glanvill and Robert Boyle, had already been at pains to stress the harmony between the new philosophy and religion. In 'An Adress to the Royal Society' prefixed to his *Scepsis scientifica* of 1664, Glanvill sums up the work of the Society as

> the improving of men's minds in solid and useful things, helping them to such theories as may be serviceable to common life, and the searching out of the true laws of Matter and Motion, in order to the securing of the Foundations of Religion against all attempts of Mechanical Atheism . . . So that 'tis not conceivable how a more suitable remedy could have been provided against the deadly influence of that Contagion, then your Honourable Society, by which the meanest intellects may perceive, that Mechanick Philosophy yields no security to religion, and that those that would be gentilely learned and ingenious, need not purchase it, at the dear rate of being atheists.[60]

Boyle, meanwhile, devoted a good part of *The Usefulness of Natural Philosophy* (1663) to arguing that the study of natural philosophy was a sure inducement to a belief in God's existence and perfection, concluding that 'he, that could bring philosophical devotion into the request it merits, would contribute as much to the solemnising of God's praises, as the benefactors of choristers and founders of chauntries'.[61]

Yet the insinuations continued. In 1669 Casaubon warned that the '*Natural* or *Experimental* philosophy' was 'very apt to be abused and to degenerate into Atheism',[62] while in the following year Henry Stubbe, who was prepared to use any pretext to pursue his relentless attack upon the aims of the Royal Society, suggested that the new science was part of a Papist plot, a charge elaborated upon by Bishop Thomas Barlow in 1675:

> It is certain this New-Philosophy (as they call it) was set on foot, and has been carried on by the Arts of *Rome*, and those whose *Oath* and *Interest* is to maintain all her superstition . . . *Papists* (especi-ally the Jesuites) have promoted this New-Philosophy (and their design to ruine us by it), for the writers and Promoters of it were of the Roman religion: (such as Des Cartes, Gassendus . . .) and what divisions this new Philosophy has caused among Protestants in *Holland* and *England*, cannot be known to any considering person.[63]

The Royal Society could not but continue to respond, and so it did with a flood of books and pamphlets, including Glanvill's *The Friendly Agreement between Reason and Religion* (1670), *Philosophia Pia: or, a Discourse of the Religious Temper and Tendencies of the Experimental Philosophy which is Profest by the Royal Society* (1671), and *Essays on Several Important Subjects in Philosophy and Religion* (1676), and Boyle's *The Excellence of Theology Compared with Natural Philosophy* (1674), *Some Considerations about the Reconcileableness of Reason and Religion* (1674), and finally *The Christian Virtuoso* (1690).

What we have been sketching has been the effort on the part of the Royal Society to defend itself against criticism, not widespread perhaps, but certainly vocal and persistent, that its promotion of the new science was damaging to established religion, and we have drawn attention only to the most general feature of the Society's response, namely, the assertion that reason and religion are wholly compatible and the repeated assurance that in searching out nature's secrets the Society's purpose was only to illustrate and magnify the power and providential care of the Creator. It was an inescapable fact, however, that the conceptual framework for much of the Society's scientific work was supplied by a hypothesis which was linked, and by many identified, with the name of Epicurus. It was essential, therefore, that the Society do more than offer general assurances of its theological soundness, more even than expressly discountenance the anti-Christian elements of Epicurean doctrine, which the publications we have listed certainly did. It was essential also that the Society dissociate its 'atomism' as markedly as possible from the Epicurean model.

This was a task which fell largely to the Society's most active promoter of the new science, Robert Boyle, and at the very opening of his *Of the Excellency and Grounds of the Mechanical Hypothesis* (1674) he registers the point in clear terms:

> But when I speak of the corpuscular or mechanical philosophy, I am far from meaning with the Epicureans that atoms, meeting together by chance in an infinite vacuum, are able of themselves to produce the world, and all its Phaenomena . . . . I plead only for such a Philosophy, as reaches but to things purely Corporeal, and distinguishing between the first original of things, and the subsequent course of nature, teaches, concerning the former, not only that God gave motion to matter, but that in the beginning he so guided the various motions of the parts of it, as to contrive them into the world he design'd they should compose . . . and estab-lish'd those rules of motion and that order amongst things corporeal, which we are wont to call the laws of nature . . . . And now having shown what kind of corpuscular philosophy it is that I speak of, I proceed.[64]

What Boyle proceeds to is a brief review of those features of the corpuscular hypothesis which render it eminently serviceable to the natural scientist, namely, the simplicity, clarity, and, in particular, the comprehensiveness of its principles. However, the majority of Boyle's works in support of the corpuscular philosophy, of which *The Origin of Forms and Qualities* (1666) and *Experiments, Notes, etc. about the Mechanical Origin and Production of Divers Particular Qualities* (1675) are the most noteworthy, are concerned with the application of corpu-scular theory to particular physical and chemical questions, and are designed not so much to argue that the corpuscular hypothesis is

necessarily and demonstrably the only true explanation of the
constitution and behaviour of matter as to illustrate that it renders
reliance upon explanations based upon Aristotelian and alchemical
concepts quite unnecessary. Boyle's aim, in short, is to do

> no unreasonable piece of service to the corpuscular philosophers
> by illustrating some of their notions with sensible experiments,
> and manifesting that, the things by me treated of may be at least
> plausibly explicated without recourse to inexplicable forms, real
> qualities, or so much as the three chymical principles.[65]

Allowing for continuing discussion over matters of detail, especially between the supporters of the Cartesian and Gassendist positions, it is a fact that by the turn of the century the mechanical
philosophy, to the extent that it explained the physical world in
terms of the size, shape, motion, and configurations of indivisible
particles, had attained the dominant position in natural science. In
1715 Bernard Nieuwentijdt allows for no dispute:

> That all visible bodies do consist of an unconceivable number
> of . . . little parts, is already admitted by all Philosophers, and
> demonstrated too by so many Experiments and Proofs, that no
> Body who had taken the least trouble of examining the Nature of
> Creatures, can entertain any kind of doubt therefor.[66]

It is equally the case that in the process Epicurus' claim to
parentage has been effectively disqualified, largely justifying the
advertisement of the publisher of Boyle's *The Origin of Forms and
Qualities* that 'though the most noble author hath herein, for the
main, espoused the atomical philosophy . . . yet considering the
several alterations and additions . . . made therein, I may not
scruple to call it a new hypothesis, peculiar to the author'.[67] With
Boyle it is a matter of 'alterations and additions'. Cudworth is more
ingenious. In a desperate attempt to render the 'Atomick Physiology' a 'Sovreign Antidote against Atheism', he provides it with a
new and respectable genealogy stretching as far back as Moses:

> we are of the opinion that neither Democritus, nor Protagoras, nor
> Leucippus was the first Inventour of this Philosophy; and our
> reason is, because they were all three of them Atheists . . . we have
> also good Historical probability for this opinion . . . first because

Posidonius, an Ancient and learned Philosopher . . . did avouch it for an old Tradition, that the first Inventour of this Atomical Philosophy was one Moschus a Phoenecian, who, as Strabo also notes, lived before the Trojan wars. Moreover it seems not altogether Improbable, but that this Moschus a Phoenecian Philosopher, mentioned by Posidonius, might be the same with that Mochus a Phoenician Physiologer . . . . Mochus or Moschus is plainly a Phoenecian Name . . . and Mr. Sheldon approves of the Conjecture of Arcerius, the Publisher of Iamblichus, that this Mochus was no other than the celebrated Moses of the Jews.[68]

The image of Cudworth's 'Moses' leading the tribes of men into a new atomistic world is perhaps as appropriate as any to bring us to the close of what has been a long story. Not that the tale is told. Epicurus will make further appearances, but not any more at centre stage. It has been a story not without its ironies, and it is with a recurring one that we may conclude. For it is again the case that at the very time when Epicurus is struggling for survival, his teachings openly abused on one side and studiously disavowed on the other, his chief classical exponent, Lucretius, is enjoying a notable popularity. For between 1675 and 1685 the text of the *De rerum natura* was brought out in a Latin edition and favoured by the attention of two very different translators, the one a young graduate of Oxford, the other the Poet Laureate of England.

The edition, a reprint of Tanneguy Le Fèvre's Saumur edition of 1662, was issued by John Hayes of Cambridge in 1675, almost exactly two hundred years after the *editio princeps*, complete with Le Fèvre's notes and textual emendations, a 'life' of Epicurus by Gifanius, and Lambin's index. It was not a landmark edition except in so far as it was the first to issue from an English press, but it testifies to a demand for a locally available text, and was popular enough to earn a second printing in 1686.

Of greater importance are the translations. The first, Thomas Creech's *Lucretius Carus the Epicurean Philosopher, His Book De Natura Rerum, Done into English Verse, with Notes*, appeared in 1682 and is noteworthy not least because it represents the first published English version of Lucretius' complete text. The first printing was accompanied by congratulatory verses by two of Creech's Oxford associates and subsequent editions carried many more. Even by conventional standards these offerings were effusive in the extreme. Mrs Aphra Behn's is untypical only in its emphasis upon the service which Creech has performed for the women of the age:

> So Thou by this Translation dost advance
> Our Knowledge from the State of Ignorance
> And Equal'st Us to Man! O how shall We
> Enough Adore, or Sacrifice enough to Thee!
> The Mystick Terms of rough Philosophy
> Thou dost so plain and easily Express.[69]

The popularity of the translation was immediate. Two more printings were issued in 1683, one at Oxford, the other at London, and further printings followed in 1699, 1700, and 1714. Lucretius became the vogue and Creech himself a celebrity. Indeed, if we may believe Cibber, the translation 'succeeded so well, that Mr. Creech had a party formed for him, who ventured to prefer him to Mr. Dryden, in point of genius'.[70]

If the Poet Laureate was concerned, he had little need. Creech's translation was decidedly uneven, its merits falling somewhere between the extravagent praises of his early admirers and the devastating judgment of Nathan Drake, who declared in 1798 that Creech preserved so little of 'the dignity, sublimity, and descriptive powers of the poet, that it is impossible to form any idea of the beautiful original from his coarse and ill-executed copy'.[71] Dryden's translations of five selections from the poem, which appeared in his *Sylvae* of 1685, are of a different order. Admittedly, Dryden started with every advantage. Unlike Creech, he selected only those passages which, as he says in the preface, 'most affected me in the reading'. Moreover, in accordance with his own principles of translation he took a less confining approach to the original, a point which he candidly acknowledges in comparing his own efforts with Creech's:

> The ways of our Translation are very different; he follows him more closely than I have done; which became an Interpreter of the whole Poem. I take more liberty, because it suited best with my design, which was to make him as pleasing as I could.

Whether Dryden's rendering would have been so far superior to Creech's in sections of the poem less congenial to his temperament and talent we can only speculate. What is beyond question is that there is little in Creech that approaches the level which Dryden attained.[72]

We introduced the translations of Creech and Dryden to illustrate one half of an irony which finds Lucretius the Epicurean poet the focus of admiring attention while Epicurus himself is besieged by bitter criticism on all sides. In differing degrees they illustrate the other half as well. For both Creech and Dryden are careful to register their rejection of the poet's Epicurean message. With Dryden it is a case of affirming his belief in the immortality of the soul; with Creech it is a matter of furnishing his translation with some sixty pages of scathing commentary which leaves hardly any aspect of Epicurean doctrine untouched.

A final irony. One of the passages which affected the Poet Laureate in his reading was the opening of Book II:

Suave, mari magno turbantibus aequora ventis,
e terra magnum alterius spectare laborem;
non quia vexari quemquamst iucunda voluptas,
sed quibus ipse malis careas quia cernere suave est.

He renders them thus:

'Tis pleasant, safely to behold from shore
The rowling Ship; and hear the Tempest roar:
Not that another's pain is our delight;
But pains unfelt produce the pleasing sight.

They are the Lucretian lines most often quoted in the tradition. They capture in an image the Epicurean ideal. In our story it is an experience which Epicurus himself rarely enjoyed.

NOTES

CHAPTER 1   MAN FOR A SEASON

1 Thucydides II. 53. Translations of Greek and Latin texts are mine, except where indicated.
2 Thucydides III. 84.
3 Cf. Thucydides III. 40: 'I urge you now, as before . . . to guard against the three errors most fatal to a ruling power – to feel pity, to be swayed by a pretty speech, and to act in accordance with decency' (Cleon); III. 44: 'For if we are prudent, the question we shall ask will not be whether they are guilty, but whether we are best serving our own interests' (Diodatus). Cf. the Melian Dialogue (V. 85–113), the whole of which is a starkly cynical defence of 'interest' as the basis for action.
4 For a penetrating study of the 'rationalistic' element in Thucydides' concept of history, see F. M. Cornford, *Thucydides Mythistoricus* (London, 1907), esp. ch. V, from which we may quote the following:

> The great contrast, in fact, between ancient and modern history is this: that whereas the moderns instinctively and incessantly seek for the operation of social conditions, of economic and topological factors, and of political forces and processes of evolution, – all of which elements they try to bring under laws, as general and abstract as possible, the ancients looked simply and solely to the feelings, motives, characters of individuals or of cities. These, and (apart from supernatural agencies) these only, appeared to them to shape the course of human history. (p. 66)

5 Plato, *Gorgias* 463 e 5 – 466 a 3. See the instructive comments of Dodds in *Plato, Gorgias*, ed. E. R. Dodds (Oxford, 1959), pp. 226–32.
6 *Antigone* 332–66.
7 In general see T. B. L. Webster, *Hellenistic Poetry and Art* (London, 1964); J. Onions, *Art and Thought in the Hellenistic Age* (London, 1979).
8 H. D. F. Kitto, referring to *Electra, Orestes, Iphigeneia in Aulis*, and *Phoenissae*, remarks that 'the new drama deals with matters of purely private interest', *Greek Tragedy* (London, 1939), p. 344.
9 On Greek comedy in general, see F. H. Sandbach, *The Comic Theatre of Greece and Rome* (London, 1977).

10 On Hellenistic comedy in general and Menander in particular, see
   T. B. L. Webster, *Studies in Later Greek Comedy* (Manchester, 1953);
   Studies in Menander (Manchester, 1950; 2nd edn 1960); *An Introduction
   to Menander* (Manchester, 1974).

11 ἐπισφαλῆ μὲν πάντα τ' ἀνθρώπει' (*Menander: the Principal
   Fragments*, ed. and trans. Francis G. Allinson (The Loeb Classical
   Library, Harvard, Cambridge, Mass., 1959), p. 25).

12 ὦ Μένανδρε καὶ βίε, πότερος ἄρ' ὑμῶν ποτερον ἀπεμιμήσατο.

13 See D. J. Furley, 'The purpose of Theophrastus' characters', *Symbolae
   Osloenses* 30 (1950) 56ff.; R. G. Usher, 'Old comedy and character',
   Greece and Rome 24 (1977) 71–9.

14 Albin Lesky, *A History of Greek Literature*, trans. James Willis and
   Cornelis de Heer (London, 1966), p. 639.

15 On Greek portraiture, see G. M. A. Richter, *The Portraits of the Greeks*,
   2 vols (London, 1965); M. Bieber, *Alexander the Great in Greek and
   Roman Art* (Chicago, 1964); Martin Robertson, *A History of Greek Art*
   (Cambridge, 1975), vol. I, pp. 504–27.

16   it would be difficult to envision a more effective picture of the tense and
      temperamental Athenian orator – idealistic but querulous, frail but brave,
      with a haunted and even neurotic look which conjures up his disastrous final
      years and his ignominious death.

      (J. J. Pollitt, *Art and Experience in Classical Greece* (Cambridge, 1972), p. 183)

17 On Hellenistic sculpture in general, see M. Bieber, *The Sculpture of the
   Hellenistic Age* (rev. edn, New York, 1961).

18 The following studies are particularly useful: Martin P. Nilsson, *A
   History of Greek Religion* (2nd edn, Oxford, 1949), trans. from Swedish
   by F. J. Fielden; *Greek Popular Religion* (New York, 1940); *Greek Piety*
   (Oxford, 1948); A. J. Festugière, *Personal Religion Among the Greeks*
   (Berkeley and Los Angeles, 1954); *Epicurus and His Gods* (Paris,
   1946), trans. C. W. Chilton (Oxford, 1955); Gilbert Murray, *Five
   Stages of Greek Religion* (3rd edn, New York, 1951).

19 For an assessment of the value of Diogenes' *Life* we may quote the
   judicious remarks of Cyril Bailey in *Epicurus: the Extant Remains*
   (Oxford, 1926), pp. 401–2; having noted that Diogenes was working
   with source material which had already suffered from the less than
   methodical treatment of a succession of doxographers, and having
   concluded that the book is 'not an intelligent compilation, but a
   growth', he continues,

   When it has grown from so many sources, unknown to us, whose validity
   cannot now be estimated, what importance can be attached to its statements?
   The answer seems to be that it is of value, if used with discretion. In the first
   place, there is no reason to doubt the main statements about Epicurus' life:
   with the exception of one or two minor discrepancies as to dates, they tally well.
   In the second, the 'Life' embodies a very considerable number of quotations
   from Epicurus' writings, which, couched as they are in language very similar to
   that of the *Letters*, we may fairly accept: they are in many instances confirmed
   from other sources. . . In short, though the process of its construction has made
   the book almost intolerable as literature, it has not impaired the value of its
   contents if duly sifted and compared with what is otherwise known.

In addition to Bailey, the following are the important editions and translations of Epicurean texts: H. Usener, *Epicurea* (Leipzig, 1887; repr. Stuttgart, 1966); G. Arrighetti, *Epicuro: Opere* (Turin, 1960); E. Bignone, *Epicuro* (Bari, 1920). The best edition of Diogenes Laertius is that of P. von der Muehll (Leipzig, 1923; repr. 1966).

20 Diogenes Laertius 10. 13.

21 *Epicurus and His Gods*, p. 21. It is worth remarking that Festugière is generally cautious in filling gaps where firm information is wanting. Other scholars have been less hesitant. It must be said, for example, that N. W. De Witt, in chapter 2 of a book which otherwise contains much of value (*Epicurus and His Philosophy*, Minneapolis, 1954), constructs an account of Epicurus' early years which borders upon romance.

22 See De Witt op. cit., pp. 60ff.; J. M. Rist, *Epicurus: an Introduction* (Cambridge, 1972), pp. 3ff.

23 For Epicurus' poor opinion of Nausiphanes, see Diogenes Laertius 10. 8, and Sextus Empiricus, *Adversus mathematicos* 1. 4 (Usener 114) – 'lung-fish', 'prostitute', 'ignoramus', 'impostor' are among the abusive terms Epicurus chooses to employ.

24 For details, see *Cambridge Ancient History* (Cambridge, 1927; repr. 1969), vol. VI, pp. 495–8.

25 Diogenes Laertius 10. 8 (Usener 238).

26 Diogenes Laertius 10. 6 (Usener 163).

27 Diogenes Laertius 10. 120.

28 Plutarch, *Non posse* 1095 c.

29 Cicero, *De natura deorum* I. 33. 93.

30 ibid.

31 Diogenes Laertius 10. 8. Cf. Athenaeus VIII. 354b and Aristocles, *Eusebii praep. eu.* XV. 2 p. 791ª (Usener 171).

32 For *testimonia* on Nausiphanes, see *Die Fragmente der Vorsokratiker*, ed. H. Diels and W. Kranz, II, 75 A/B.

33 Rist, op. cit., p. 6.

34 Cf. Diogenes Laertius 10. 17; Plutarch, *Non posse* 1098 b.

35 See De Witt, op. cit., pp. 90ff., and 'Organisation and procedure in Epicurean groups', *Classical Philology* 31 (1936) 205–11.

36 Philodemus, *On Frankness* fr. 45. 9–11.

37 De Witt, *Epicurus and His Philosophy*, p. 95; Diogenes Laertius 10. 21.

38 Cf. Diogenes Laertius 10. 5–8.

39 Cicero, *Orator* 151.

40 *Principal Doctrines* 29 and scholion.

41 *Vatican Sayings* 51. Cf. Diogenes Laertius 10. 118; Plutarch, *Quaestionum convivalium* 654B (Usener 62).

42 Cf. Plutarch, *Quaestionum convivalium* 653F–654B (Usener 61).

43 Diogenes Laertius 10. 9; Cicero, *De finibus* I. 20. 65 (Usener 539): 'de amicitia . . . Epicurus quidem ita dicit, omnium rerum quas ad beate vivendum sapientia comparaverit nihil esse maius amicitia, nihil uberius, nihil iucundius, nec vero hoc oratione solum, sed multo maius vita et factis et moribus comprobavit'.

44 Cf. frags 30, 35, 50 (Bailey).

CHAPTER 2   SCHOOL IN THE GARDEN

1 In addition to those noted in the previous chapter the following monographs will be found useful: C. Bailey, *The Greek Atomists and Epicurus* (Oxford, 1928); E. Bignone, *L'Aristotele perduto e le formazione filosofica di Epicuro* (Florence, 1936); T. Cole, *Democritus and the Sources of Greek Anthropology*, American Philological Association Monographs, no. 25 (1967); B. Farrington, *The Faith of Epicurus* (London, 1967); D. J. Furley, *Two Studies in the Greek Atomists* (Princeton, 1967); D. J. Furley, *The Greek Cosmogonists* vol. 1: *The formation of the atomic theory and its earliest critics* (Cambridge, 1987); P. Merlan, *Studies in Epicurus and Aristotle* (Wiesbaden, 1960); R. D. Hicks, *Stoics and Epicureans* (London, 1910); A. A. Long, *Hellenistic Philosophy* (London, 1974); J. M. Rist, *Epicurus: an Introduction* (Cambridge, 1972). For bibliography, see H. J. Mette, 'Epikuros 1963–1978', *Lustrum* 21 (1978) 45–114, W. Schmid, 'Epikur', in *Reallexicon für Antike und Christentum*, vol. 5 (Stuttgart, 1962), cols 816–19 and A. A. Long and D. N. Sedley, *The Hellenistic Philosophers* (Cambridge, 1987), vol. 2 pp. 480–90.
2 Cf. Diogenes Laertius [DL] 10. 85 (Pythocles).
3 DL 10. 122 (Menoeceus); cf. Usener [US] 219 (Sextus Empiricus, *Adversus mathematicos* [*Adv. math.*] 11. 169).
4 DL 10. 37–8 (Herodotus); Bailey, *The Greek Atomists and Epicurus* [*Atomists*], p. 232.
5 DL 10. 38.
6 On Epicurus' theory of knowledge the following should be consulted: Rist, op. cit., pp. 14–40; A. A. Long, 'Aisthesis, prolepsis, and linguistic theory in Epicurus', *Bulletin of the Institute of Classical Studies* 18 (1971) 114–33; D. J. Furley, 'Knowledge of atoms and void', in *Essays in Ancient Greek Philosophy*, ed. J. P. Anton and G. L. Kustas (New York, 1971), pp. 607–19.
7 DL 10. 31.
8 DL 10. 147.
9 Cf. Sextus, *Adv. math.* 8. 9.
10 DL 10. 32. Cf. Plutarch, *Adversus Colotem* [*Adv. Col.*] 1121; Sextus, *Adv. Math.* 7. 203–16; 8. 9.
11 DL 10. 51–2 (Herodotus).
12 Clement, *Stromateis* 2. 4 (US 255). Cf. Sextus, *Adv. math.* 1. 57.
13 It is this aspect of general concepts which is stressed by Clement, *Stromateis* 2. 4 (US 255): πρόληψιν δὲ ἀποδίδωσιν ἐπιβολὴν ἐπί τι ἐναργὲς καὶ ἐπὶ τὴν ἐναργῆ τοῦ πράγματος ἐπίνοιαν.
14 Cf. DL 10. 33.
15 Cf. DL 10. 34.
16 DL 10. 50 (Herodotus).
17 DL 10. 34; Sextus, *Adv. math.* 7. 216 (US 247).
18 DL 10. 32.

19 Cf. Sextus, *Adv. math.* 7. 213 (US 247).
20 DL 10. 87 (Pythocles).
21 Cf. Sextus, *Adv. math.* 7. 213 (US 247).
22 Cf. DL 10. 8; 10. 13.
23 DL 10. 37.
24 DL 10. 38–9.
25 Cf Lucretius, *De rerum natura* [*DRN*] I. 159–214.
26 Cf. Lucretius, *DRN* I. 217–64.
27 Cf. Lucretius, *DRN* II. 304ff.
28 DL 10. 39–40; cf. Lucretius, *DRN* I. 419–48.
29 DL 10. 41.
30 DL 10. 42; cf. Lucretius, *DRN* I. 958–64.
31 DL 10. 42; cf. Lucretius, *DRN* I. 984–91.
32 DL 10. 54–5.
33 DL 10. 55–6.
34 DL 9. 44; Aëtius 1. 12. 6; Rist, op. cit., pp. 44–5.
35 DL 10. 55–6.
36 DL 10. 56–9. Cf. Lucretius, *DRN* I. 599–634. For a detailed
   examination of this difficult aspect of Epicurean atomism, see
   D. J. Furley, *Two Studies in the Greek Atomists*, Study I.
37 DL 10. 42, 56; cf. Lucretius, *DRN* II. 333–80; II. 478–99.
38 Lucretius, *DRN* II. 500–21.
39 DL 10. 42; Lucretius, *DRN* II. 522–31.
40 Bailey, *Atomists*, pp. 128ff.; Rist, op. cit., Appendix B, pp. 167–8;
   W. K. C. Guthrie, *A History of Greek Philosophy* (Cambridge, 1969),
   vol. 2, pp. 400–2.
41 Plutarch, *Plac.* 1. 3. 26 (US 275).
42 DL 10. 61.
43 DL 10. 60. For Plato, see *Timaeus* 62 d.
44 Lucretius, *DRN* II. 216–93.

> Illud in his quoque te rebus cognoscere avemus,
> corpora cum deorsum rectum per inane feruntur
> ponderibus propriis, incerto tempore ferme
> incertisque locis spatio depellere paulum,
> tantum quod nomen mutatum dicere possis.

(216–20)

   Cf. Cicero, *De finibus* I. 6. 18; *De fato* 10. 22; 20. 46; *De natura deorum*
   I. 25. 69; Diogenes of Oenoanda fr. 32 (Chilton); Aëtius 1. 12. 5; 1.
   23. 4.
45 Lucretius, *DRN* II. 112ff.
46 DL 10. 43; Lucretius, *DRN* II. 95–108.
47 Cf. DL 10. 46 b and 47 b; for a fuller discussion see Bailey, *Atomists*,
   pp. 330–8 and *Epicurus: the Extant Remains* [*Epicurus*] (Oxford, 1926),
   ad loc.
48 DL 10. 74 (Herodotus); 10. 89 (Pythocles).
49 Cf. Lucretius, *DRN* VI. 160, 200, 206, 213, 217, 271, 275, 316, 497,
   507, 520, 863, 867, 876, 883; in other places *semina* is used to mean
   individual atoms, e.g., I. 59, II. 755, 988, III. 187, V. 456.

50 DL 10. 68.
51 DL 10. 69.
52 ibid. Cf. DL 9. 72, 106; Sextus, *Adv math.* 7. 135–6.
53 DL 10. 54.
54 Lucretius, *DRN* II. 398–407.
55 Lucretius, *DRN* II. 410–17.
56 Lucretius, *DRN* II. 730–841.
57 τὸ ὅλον σῶμα καθόλου μεν <ἐκ> τούτων πάντων τὴν ἑαυτοῦ φύσιν ἔχον ἀίδιον (DL 10. 55). Cf. DL 10. 59. For an analysis of these passages, see Bailey, *Atomists*, pp. 300–4.
58 DL 10. 45; 73–4 (Herodotus); 10. 88–90 (Pythocles). In general see F. Solmsen, 'Epicurus on the growth and decline of the cosmos', *American Journal of Philology* 74 (1953) 34–51.
59 DL 10. 89–90 (Pythocles).
60 DL 10. 89 (Pythocles).
61 Lucretius, *DRN* V. 432–94.
62 DL 10. 73 (Herodotus).
63 Lucretius, *DRN* II. 1105–74. Cf. V. 235–415.
64 Lucretius, *DRN* II. 1105–17. Cf. DL 10. 89 (Pythocles), where Epicurus employs the image of 'watering' (ἐπαρδεύσεις) to illustrate this constant feeding of the world's body.
65 Lucretius, *DRN* I. 1042–4.
66 Lucretius, *DRN* II. 1139–45.
67 Lucretius, *DRN* II. 1150–74; V. 107–9.
68 DL 10. 76–7 (Herodotus).
69 Lucretius, *DRN* V. 110–235. Cf. III. 167–83; V. 73–90; 1183–93; VI. 43–95.
70 Cf. Lucretius, *DRN* III. 784–99.
71 Cf. Cicero, *De natura deorum*, I. 9. 21–3.
72 Lucretius, *DRN* V. 772–1457.
73 Lucretius, *DRN* V. 783–92; 801–8.
74 Hippolytus, *Ref.* i. 66, Diels A 11 (Anaximander); idem i. 8. 12, Diels A 42 (Anaxagoras); Aëtius 5. 19, Diels A 139 (Democritus).
75 Lucretius, *DRN* 797–8. Cf. II. 871–3, 898–901, 928–9, where Lucretius uses the same erroneous observation to support his argument that atoms may combine to form sentient beings even though they are themselves without sensation. We may note that Censorinus attributes Lucretius' theory of earth-born animals directly to Epicurus himself (*De die nat.* 4. 9 (US 333)). Cf. Diodorus Siculus i. 7. 10.
76 For Empedocles, see Diels B. 57; B. 58; B. 61; A. 72.
77 We must note too that Lucretius insists that there can never have existed such mythological beasts as Centaurs, Scyllas, and Chimaeras, since the individual species from which these hybrid creatures are supposed to have been formed mature and decay over different periods (V. 878–924).
78 Cf. Diodorus Siculus i. 7. 6.
79 Dean W. R. Inge, *Outspoken Essays, Second Series* (London, 1923), p. 159.

80 J. B. Bury, *The Idea of Progress* (London, 1920), p. 19.
81 Margaret Taylor, 'Progress and primitivism in Lucretius', *American Journal of Philology* 68 (1947) 180–94.
82 L. Robin, 'Sur la conception Épicurienne au progrès', *Revue de Métaphysique et de Morale* 23 (1916) 697–719.
83 William M. Green, 'The dying world of Lucretius', *American Journal of Philology* 63 (1942) 51–60.
84 Arthur O. Lovejoy and George Boas, *Primitivism and Related Ideas in Antiquity* (Baltimore, 1935), pp. 222–42.
85 Philip Merlan, 'Lucretius – primitivist or progressivist?', *Journal of the History of Ideas* 11 (1950) 364–8. Merlan is followed by Rist, op. cit., p. 71. The following works may also be consulted: J. Bayet, 'Lucrèce devant la pensée grecque', *Museum Helveticum* 11 (1954) 89–100; C. R. Beye, 'Lucretius and progress', *Classical Journal* 58 (1963) 160–9; J. P. Borle, 'Progrès ou déclin de l'humanité? La conception de Lucrèce', *Museum Helveticum* 19 (1962) 162–76; A. C. Keller, 'Lucretius and the idea of progress', *Classical Journal* 46 (1951) 185–8; M. Ruch, 'Lucrèce et le problème de la civilisation. *De rerum natura*, chant V', *Les Études Classiques* 37 (1969) 272–84; Philip de Lacy, 'Lucretius and Epicureanism', *Transactions of the American Philological Association* 79 (1948) 12–23; Jean-Claude Fredonille, 'Lucrèce et le "double progrès constrastant"', *Pallas* 19 (1972) 11–27; D. J. Furley, 'Lucretius the Epicurean: on the history of man', *Entretiens sur L'Antiquité classique 24, Lucrèce* (Geneva, 1978), pp. 1–27; Antoinette Novara, *Les Idées Romaines sur le Progrès* (Paris, 1982) vol. 1 pp. 313–83.
86 Lucretius, *DRN* V. 925ff.
87 Cf. Empedocles B. 130 (Diels); Plato, *Politicus* 271 d – 272 e.
88 Lucretius, *DRN* V. 1011–18.
89 Lucretius, *DRN* V. 1113–35.
90 Lucretius, *DRN* V. 1161–240.
91 C. Bailey (ed.), *Lucretius: De rerum natura* (Oxford, 1947), vol. 3, p. 1529.
92 We may note that as a poet Lucretius is doing only what Wordsworth would recommend:

> It will be the wish of the Poet to bring his feelings near to those of the persons whose feelings he describes, nay, for short spaces of time, perhaps, to let himself slip into an entire delusion, and even confound and identify his feelings with theirs. (Preface to *Lyrical Ballads*)

93 Lucretius, *DRN* V. 1350–60 (weaving); 1361–78 (arboriculture); 1379–403 (music, dance); 1448–51 (law, roads, poetry, painting, sculpture).
94 DL 10. 149. Cf. DL 10. 127 (Menoeceus); *Vatican Sayings* 20; Pap. Herc. 1251, cols 5–6 (Schmid); Cicero, *Tusc. disp.* V. 33. 93 (US 456); *De finibus*, I. 13. 45.
95 Cf. *Vatican Sayings* 21, 33.
96 *Principal Doctrines* 3.

97 *Principal Doctrines* 18. Cf. Plutarch, *Contra Epicuri beatitudinem* 3, 1088 c (US 417).
98 *Principal Doctrines* 29.
99 Cf. Plutarch, *Contra Epicuri beatitudinem* 5, 1090 b; Athenaeus XII. 546ª (US 413).
100 Scholion to *Principal Doctrines* 29 (DL 10. 149). Cf. Pap. Herc. 1251, col. 15 (Schmid), where beauty, riches, and marriage are added to the list.
101 DL 10. 129 (Menoeceus).
102 DL 10. 137. Cf. Sextus, *Hyp. Pyr.* 3. 194; *Adv. math.* 11. 96; Cicero, *De fin.* II. 31. We may compare the similar observation attributed by Aristotle to his contemporary Eudoxus (*EN* X. 1172 b 9).
103 DL 10. 129 (Menoeceus); DL 10. 34; Plutarch, *Adv. Col.* 27, 1122 d; Cicero, *De fin.* I. 9. 30; II. 12. 36.
104 Athenaeus XII. 546ᶠ (US 409).
105 DL 10. 6.
106 Plutarch, *Contra Epicuri beatitudinem* 17, 1098 d (US 409).
107 DL 10. 129 (Menoeceus). Cf. *Principal Doctrines* 8; Aristocles, *Eusebii praep. eu.* XIV. 21. 3 p. 769ª (Usener 442) and Seneca, *De otio* 7. 3 (US 442).
108 Cf. Aristotle, *Nicomachean Ethics* 1154 b 28. On the relationship between Epicurus and Aristotle on the question of pleasure, see Merlan, *Studies in Epicurus and Aristotle*, pp. 1–37; Bignone, op. cit.; on Aristotle's theory of pleasure, see W. F. R Hardie, *Aristotle's Ethical Theory* (Oxford, 1968), pp. 294–316; J. O. Urmson, 'Aristotle on pleasure', in *Aristotle: a Collection of Critical Essays*, ed. J. M. E. Moravcsik (London, 1968), pp. 323–33.
109 DL 10. 136.
110. DL 10. 131 (Menoeceus).
111 Cf. Cicero, *De finibus* I. 37: 'Non enim hanc solam sequimur, quae suavitate aliqua naturam ipsam movet et cum iucunditate quadam percipitur sensibus, sed maximam voluptatem illam habemus, quae percipitur omni dolore detracto' (Torquatus); Diogenes of Oenoanda, J. William (ed.), *Diogenis Oenoandensis fragmenta* (Leipzig, 1907), p. 38, frags 9–13.
112 Cf. *Principal Doctrines* 3, 9, 18. See also Rist, op. cit., pp. 106–14; C. Diano, 'Note epicuree', *Studi Italiani di Filologia Classica* 12 (1935) 61–86, and 'Quaestioni epicuree', *Reddiconti dell'Accademia dei Lincei* 12 (1936) 819–95; Ph. De Lacy, 'Limit and variation in the Epicurean philosophy', *Phoenix* 23 (1969) 104–13.
113 Cf. *Principal Doctrines* 7 and 14 (retirement from public life); 27 and 48 (friendship); *Vatican Sayings* 23 and 52 (friendship), 58 (politics), 51 (sexual indulgence).
114 Cicero, *De natura deorum* I. 43. 44; Plutarch, *Adv. Col.* 31.
115 For a useful examination of popular Greek religion, see Martin P. Nilsson, *Greek Piety* (Oxford, 1948) and *Greek Folk Religion* (New York, 1961); H. J. Rose, 'The religion of a Greek household', *Euphrosyne* 1 (1957) 95–116.

116 The following excerpts (translated from the text of R. G. Usher, *The Characters of Theophrastus*, London, 1960) will give a sense of the whole:

> Superstition, we might say, is cowardice before the supernatural. The superstitious man is the kind who washes his hands if anything dirty touches him, who sprinkles himself with water from a holy fountain, and goes about all day stuffing his mouth with bay leaves . . . when he sees a snake in the house, if it is harmless he makes a prayer to Sabazius, if it is poisonous he has a shrine built right away to mark the spot . . . if he hears an owl hoot when he is out for a walk, he says 'Athena, save us!'. . . every month he's off for his session with the Orphic teachers, with his wife and little ones in tow.

117 A. J. Festugière, *Epicurus and His Gods* [Epicure et ses dieux], trans. C. W. Chilton (Oxford, 1955), pp. 53–4.
118 Cf. DL 10. 81 (Herodotus).
119 Cf. *Timaeus* 47 b–c; *Laws* X. 902 b–c; VII. 818 b; *Epinomis* 982 b–c. For a comprehensive treatment of Plato's theology, see F. Solmsen, *Plato's Theology* (Ithaca, 1942).
120 Cf. *De caelo* 285^a 29; 292^a 20, b. 1.
121 Cf. *Metaphysics*, Book Λ and *Physics*, Book VIII.
122 Cf. DL 10. 123 (Menoeceus); Lucretius, *DRN* V. 1161ff.; Cicero, *De natura deorum* I. 43.
123 *De natura deorum* I. 50.
124 Cicero, *De natura deorum* I. 45–6.
125 Cicero, *De natura deorum* I. 48.
126 Tennyson, *Lucretius*, echoing *De rerum natura* III. 18–22:

> Apparet divum numen sedesque quietae
> quas neque concutiunt venti nec nubila nimbis
> aspergunt neque nix acri concreta pruina
> cana cadens violat semper [que] innubilus aether
> integit, et large diffuso lumine ridet.

127 *DRN* II, 1139–40.
128 *De natura deorum* I. 49:

> [Epicurus] docet eam esse vim et naturam deorum, ut primum non sensu, sed mente cernatur, nec soliditate quadam nec ad numerum, ut ea quae ille propter firmitatem στερέμνια appellat, sed imaginibus similitudine et transitione perceptis, cum infinita simillimarum imaginum series ex innumerabilibus individuis exsistat et ad deos adfluat.

> Cf. I. 105: 'Sic enim dicebas, speciem dei percipi cogitatione non sensu, nec esse in ea ullam soliditatem, neque eandem ad numerum permanere, eamque esse eius visionem ut similitudine et transitione cernatur neque deficiat umquam ex infinitis corporibus similium accessio', and scholion to Epicurus, *Principal Doctrines* 1.

129 See Bailey, *Atomists*, pp. 444–67 and Appendix VI; R. Philippson, 'Zur epikureischen Götterlehre', *Hermes* 51 (1916) 568–608; G. Pfligersdorffer, 'Cicero über Epikurs Lehre vom Wesen der Götter (*nat. deor.* i. 49)', *Weiner Studien* 70 (1957) 235–53; C. Diano, 'Quaestioni epicuree', *Giornale Critico di Filosofia Italiana* 30 (1949)

205ff.; G. Freymuth, *Zur Lehre von den Götterbildern in der epikureischen Philosophie* (Berlin, 1953); K. Kleve, *Gnosis Theon*, Symbolae Osloenses, Supplement 19 (Oslo, 1963).

130 *DRN* V 148–9: tenuis enim natura deum longeque remota/sensibus ab nostris animi vix mente videtur.

131 Bailey, *Atomists*, p. 450.

132 Cf. DL 10. 10; fr. 57 (US 387); P. Oxy.^{2} 215 (ed. H. Diels, 'Ein epikureisches Fragment über Götterverehrung, Oxy. Pap. 2. 215', *Sitzungsberichte der Kgl. Preuss. Akademie der Wissenschaften* (1916) 885–909); Philodemus, *De pietate* 2, col. 108, 14, p. 126 (Gomperz); col. 108, 9, p. 126; col. 110, 25, p. 128. Cf. G. D. Hadzits, 'The significance of worship and prayer among the Epicureans', *Transactions of the American Philological Association* 39 (1908) 73–88; W. Schmid, 'Götter und Menschen in der Theologie Epikurs', *Rheinisches Museum* 94 (1951) 97–156.

133 Cf. Cicero, *De natura deorum* I. 50; Philodemus, *De pietate* 2, col. 76, p. 106.

134 Cf. Pindar, Olympian II, 58; Aeschylus, *Supplices* 230ff.; *Eumenides* 273ff.; Lysias, *Contra Diogiton* 13; Ps.–Demosthenes, *Timocrates* 104.

135 *Republic* II, 364 e.

136 *Republic* X, 613 e – 621; *Phaedo* 107 a – 114 d; *Gorgias* 523 a – 527 d.

137 Cf. Ps.–Demosthenes, *Aristogiton* 1. 53 – οἱ ζωγράφοι τους ἀσεβεῖς ἐν Ἅιδου γράφουσιν, and Plautus, *Captivi* 988 (based upon a Hellenistic original) – *vidi ego multa saepe Picta, quae Acherunti fierent/cruciamenta*. For the evidence of Apulian ware, see K. Schauenburg, 'Die Totengötter in der unteritalischen Vasenmalerei' *Jahrbuch des deutschen Archäologischen Instituts* 73 (1958) 48–78; M. Pensa, *Rappresentazioni dell'oltretomba nella ceramica apula* (Rome, 1977); A. Winkler, *Die Darstellungen der Unterwelt auf unteritalischen Vasen* (Breslau, 1888).

138 *Principal Doctrines* 2.

139 DL 10. 63.

140 Lucretius, *DRN* II. 233; Plutarch, *Adv. Col.* 1118 (US 314); Aëtius 4. 3. 11 (US 315).

141 Scholion to DL 10. 67; Lucretius, *DRN* III. 94–135; Plutarch, *Adv. Col.* 20 (US 314); Aëtius 4. 3. 11 (US 312).

142 DL 10. 67. That Epicurus argued his position more fully elsewhere may be assumed from Lucretius' treatment of the rival theory of Aristotle's pupils Dicaearchus and Aristoxenus, namely, that the soul is not an independently existing substance but a 'harmony' or accidental condition of the body (III. 95–135).

143 *DRN* III. 177–322.

144 Cf. Plutarch, *Adv. Col.* 1118 (US 314); Aëtius 4. 3. 11 (US 315). Bailey, *Atomists*, Appendix V, pp. 580–7, following C. Giussani (*Studi Lucreziani* (Turin, 1896) pp.183–217), has argued convincingly that Lucretius' *quarta natura* is not to be identified with the *animus*.

145 III. 138–9: sed caput esse quasi et dominari in corpore toto/consilium quod nos animum mentemque vocamus. Cf. III. 279–81: sic tibi nominis haec expers vis facta minutis/ corporibus latet atque animae quasi totius ipsa/proporrost anima et dominatur corpore toto.

146 Cf. DL 10. 32; Aëtius 4. 8. 2 (US 249).
147 Cf. Lucretius, *DRN* IV. 722–31. For a comprehensive treatment of the sources bearing upon the meaning of ἐπιβολὴ τῆς διανοίας, see Bailey, *Atomists*, Appendix II, pp. 557–76.
148 Cf. Lucretius, *DRN* IV. 722–31.
149 Cf. Lucretius, *DRN* IV. 732–43.
150 Cf. Lucretius, *DRN* IV. 757–76.
151 See above, p. 54 and notes 128 and 129.
152 Lucretius, *DRN* IV. 877–906.
153 Lucretius, *DRN* II. 251–93.
154 D. J. Furley, 'Aristotle and Epicurus on voluntary action' in *Two Studies*, p. 232. Rist (op. cit., p. 94) agrees that 'It is our mind in general that must be freed by the swerve, not each separate decision', but would allow for an 'indeterminate and small number'. Long (op. cit., pp. 59–61) argues that 'the swerve of a single atom is a relatively frequent event'.
155 Cf. Lucretius, *DRN* III. 307–13; Plutarch, *Adv. Col.* 20, 1118d (US 314); Aëtius 4. 3. 11 (US 315).
156 Cf. Lucretius, *DRN* II. 284–93.
157 DL 10. 63–5 (Herodotus). Cf. Lucretius, *DRN* III. 323–49; III. 119–23. For the full array of Epicurean arguments for the mortality of the soul, see the long section in *DRN* III (417–829) where Lucretius, basing himself probably upon Epicurus' Περὶ Φύσεως and Μεγάλη Ἐπιτομή, arranges his arguments in the form of twenty-nine 'proofs'.
158 DL 10. 124–5; cf. Lucretius, *DRN* III. 830–1094.

CHAPTER 3   THE INVASION OF ITALY

1 Cf. D.N. Sedley, 'Epicurus and the mathematicians of Cyzicus', Cronache Ercolanesi 6 (1976) 23–54; 'Epicurus and his professional rivals' in J. Bollack and A. Laks, *Études sur l'epicurisme antique* (Lille, 1976) pp. 119–60; H. Steckel, *Realencyclopädie der classischen Altertumswissenschaft* Supplementband XI (Stuttgart, 1968), sv. Epikuros, col. 584.
2 Cf. Sedley, 'Epicurus and his professional rivals', pp. 127–32; R. Philippson, *Realencyclopädie der classischen Altertumswissenschaft* VI A (Stuttgart, 1937), sv. Timokrates, cols 1266ff.; E. Bignone, *L'Aristotele perduto e la formazione filosofica di Epicuro* (Florence, 1936), vol. 2, pp. 223ff.
3 For a catalogue of Epicurean portraits extant and once extant, see G. M. A. Richter, *The Portraits of the Greeks* (London, 1965), vol. 2, pp. 194–207 and figs 1149–1339 – Epicurus (29), Metrodorus (16), Hermarchus (21), Colotes (?8). In addition we have the evidence of Pliny that Epicureans kept likenesses of Epicurus in their bedrooms and also carried them around with them (*Hist. nat.* xxxv, 5 – *Epicuri vultus per cubicula gestunt et circumferunt secum*), and the evidence of Cicero that Epicurus' likeness was carried on drinking cups and rings (*De finibus* V. 1. 3 – *nec tamen Epicuri licet oblivisci, si cupiam, cuius imaginem non modo in tabulis nostri familiares sed etiam in poculis et in anulis*

habent). For a catalogue of rings see G. M. A. Richter, *The Engraved Gems of the Romans* (London, 1971), nos. 438–43, and F. H. Marshall, *Catalogue of the Finger Rings, Greek and Etruscan, in the Department of Antiquities, British Museum* (London, 1907), no. 1638.

4 Bernard Frischer, *The Sculpted Word: Epicureanism and Philosophical Recruitment in Ancient Greece* (Berkeley, 1982).

5 DL 10. 25–6. On Epicureans in Syria, see W. Crönert, "Die Epikureer in Syrien", *Jahreshefte des Arch. Institut in Wien* X (1907) 146ff.

6 Plutarch, *Lat. viv.* 3. 1.; Cicero, *De finibus* II. 44. 49; Pliny, ep. 10. 96; Lucian, *Alexander* 25; *CIG* 4149.

7 Cf. H. I. Marrou, *A History of Education in Antiquity*, trans. George Lamb (London, 1956), part III ch. 2, pp. 242–54.

8 Athenaeus XII. 547ᵃ; Aelian, *Varia Historia* 9, 12. There is some uncertainty as to whether the expulsion of Alkios and Philiskos occurred in 173 or 154, but the earlier seems the preferred date; for opinions see Pierre Boyancé, *Lucrèce et l'Épicurisme* (Paris, 1963), p. 7 and n. 3.

9 Norman W. De Witt, 'Notes on the history of Epicureanism', *Transactions of the American Philological Association*, 63 (1932) 172.

10 *De fin.* II. 119; *Acad.* II. 106; *Ad fam.* VI. 11. 2.

11 Tenney Frank, *Vergil: a Biography* (New York, 1922), p. 56. John H. D'Arms notes that the area around the bay of Naples, as well as being a lively centre of Greek culture, seems to have been particularly favoured by Epicureans; M. Pompilius Andronicus, a Syrian Epicurean who abandoned a career as a teacher of grammar in Rome, settled at Cumae (Suetonius, Gram. 8), and the villa of L. Manlius Torquatus, the Epicurean spokesman in Cicero's *De finibus*, was probably also situated there (*Romans on the Bay of Naples* (Cambridge, Mass., 1970), pp. 55–61 and Catalogue I.27).

12 *De fin.* II. 119: 'familiares nostros, credo, Sironem dicis et Philodemum, cum optimos viros, tum homines doctissimos'.

13 *Tusc. Disp.* IV. 6; II. 7; V. 116.

14 We may note Cicero's commendation of Philodemus as an Epicurean of wide interests: 'est autem hic de quo loquor non philosophia solum, sed etiam ceteris studiis, quae fere ceteros Epicureos neglegere dicunt perpolitus' (*In Pisonem* 70).

15 For an evaluation of Philodemus' influence as a poet, see J. I. M. Tait, *Philodemus' Influence on the Latin Poets* (Bryn Mawr, 1941).

16 For an account of the excavations and a description of the villa and library, see the following: D. Comparetti and G. de Petra, *La Villa Ercolanese dei Pisoni* (Turin, 1883); D. Comparetti, 'La bibliothèque de Philodème', in *Mélanges Chatelain* (Paris, 1910) pp.120ff.; D. Mustilli, 'La villa pseudourbana ercolanese', *Rendiconti del' Accademia di Archeologia, Lettere e Belle Arti di Napoli*, n.s. 31 (1956) 77–97; D'Arms, op. cit., 173–4; H. Bloch, 'L. Calpurnius Piso Caesoninus in Samothrace and Herculaneum', *American Journal of Archeology* 44 (1940) 485–93.

17 Cf. A. Korte, 'Augusteer bei Philodem', *Rheinisches Museum* 45 (1890) 172–7.

18 Pap. Herc. 312, ἐδόκει δ᾽ ἐπανελθεῖν μεθ᾽ ἡμῶν εἰς τὴν Νεάπολιν πρὸς τὸν ἡμέτερον Σίρωνα καὶ τὴν περὶ αὐτὸν ἐκεῖ διαίτησιν καὶ φιλοσόφους ἐνεργῆσαι συλλαλίας Ἡρκλανέῳ τε συχνότερον παρενδιατρῖψαι.

19 Writing to Gaius Cassius in 45 BC Cicero mentions that Catius Insuber has recently died (Ad fam. XV. 16. 1); a letter from Cassius to Cicero in the same year links Catius and Amafinius (Ad. fam. XV. 19. 2); Rabirius and Amafinius are mentioned together at Academica I. 5. For arguments concerning the date of Amafinius, see G. Della Valle, Tito Lucrezio Caro e l'epicureismo campano (Naples, 1933), pp. 169–81; Herbert M. Howe, 'Amafinius, Lucretius, and Cicero', American Journal of Philology 77 (1951) 57–62.

20 Academica I. 5.

21 Tusculan Disputations IV. 7.

22 Ad fam. XV. 19. 2: 'mali verborum [Epicuri] interpretes'.

23 Tusculan Disputations IV. 7: 'C. Amafinius exstitit dicens, cuius libris editis commota multitudo tulit se ad eam potissimum disciplinam, sive quod erat cognitu perfacilis, sive quod invitabantur illecebris blandae voluptatis, sive etiam, quia nihil prolatum erat melius, illud, quod erat, tenebant'.

24 Academica I. 5.

25 Cf. Tusculan Disputations V. 116, where Cicero remarks that the Epicureans of the period generally knew no Greek (Epicurei nostri Graece fere nesciunt).

26 For a review of the testimony of Jerome, Donatus, the Codex Monacensis, and the 'Vita Borgiana', see C. Bailey (ed.), Lucretius, De Rerum Natura: Text, Translation, and Commentary (Oxford, 1947) vol. 1, pp. 1–5.

27 Ad quintum fratrem II. ix. 2: Lucreti poemata, ut scribis, ita sunt, multi luminibus ingeni, multae tamen artis. That Cicero 'edited' Lucretius' poem, as Jerome states (aliquot libros . . . quos postea Cicero emandavit), is not generally accepted.

28 Benjamin Farrington, Science and Politics in the Ancient World (London, 1939), p. 217. See also Farrington, 'The gods of Epicurus and the Roman state', The Modern Quarterly I(3) (1938) 214–32. Cf. Constantin Vicol: 'In tal modo la dottrina di Epicuro appariva a questi rivoluzionari non come una dottrina che prediciva la molle teoria del piacere, ma come uno stimulante di energia, di azione, in lotta di emancipazione contro l'oligarchia aristocratica' ('Cicerone expositore critico dell'epicurismo', Ephemeris Dacoromana 10 (1945) 172–3.)

29 Farrington, Science and Politics in the Ancient World, pp. 191–3.

30 Farrington, 'The Gods of Epicurus . . .', pp. 223ff.

31 Cf. Cyril Bailey, Phases in the Religion of Ancient Rome (Oxford 1932), pp. 218–21.

32 De natura deorum I. 71; De divinatione 2. 24. 51.

33 Tusculan Disputations I. 5: 'Philosophia iacuit usque ad hunc aetatem nec ullum habuit lumen litterarum Latinarum'. Cf. IV. 6.

34 De rerum natura V. 335–7: denique natura haec rerum ratioque

repertast/nuper, et hanc primus cum primis ipse repertus/nunc ego sum in patrias qui possim vertere voces. Cf. I. 922–50.

35 I. 942ff.

36 Howe, op. cit., p. 59.

37 *Journal of Roman Studies* XXXI (1941) 149–57; see also C. J. Castner, *Prosopography of Roman Epicureans*, Studien zur klassischen Philologie 34 (Frankfurt-am-Main, 1988).

38 *Ad Att.* XII. 52. 3: ἀπόγραφα sunt: minore labore fiunt; verba tantum adfero, quibus abundo.

39 Cf. *Tusculan Disputations* II. 26; II. 61; III. 61; V. 113.

40 *De natura deorum* I. 10.

41 Cf. *Academica* II. 7.

42 *Academica*, ed. J. S. Reid (London, 1885), p. 22.

43 On Sextius, see Seneca, *Ep.* lix. 7; lxiv. 2–3; on Arius Didymus and Athenodorus of Tarsus, see p. 79.

44 For the careers of Thrasea and Barea Soranus under Nero, and Helvidius Priscus under Vespasian, see Tacitus, *Annals* XIV. 57, XVI. 22 and *Histories* IV. 5–6.

45 See *Inscriptiones Latinae Selectae* (H. Dessau) no. 7784 (= *Inscriptiones Graecae* 2/3² 1099); *Sylloge Inscriptionum Graecarum* (W. Dittenberger) no. 834; E. M. Smallwood, *Documents of Nerva, Trajan and Hadrian*, no. 442 (Cambridge, 1966).

46 Cf. Lucian, *Eunuchus* 3, and Philostratus, *Lives of the Sophists* 566.

47 Diogenes Laertius 10. 9.

48 On St Paul and Epicureanism, see with caution Norman De Witt, *St Paul and Epicurus* (Minneapolis, MN, 1954). On relations between the Christian and Epicurean communities, see Wayne A. Meeks, *The First Urban Christians* (New Haven, CT, 1983), pp. 83–84, and A. J. Malherbe, 'Self-definition among Epicureans and Cynics', in *Jewish and Christian Self-Definition*, ed. Ben E. Meyer and E. P. Sanders (London, 1982), vol. 3 pp. 46–59.

49 For the text of the inscription, see J. William (ed.), *Diogenis Oenoandensis fragmenta* (Leipzig, 1907); A. Grilli (ed.), *Diogenis Oenoandensis fragmenta* (Milano, 1960); C. W. Chilton, *Diogenis Oenoandensis fragmenta* (Leipzig, 1967); M. F. Smith in *American Journal of Archeology* 74 (1970) 51–62, 75 (1971) 357–389, *Journal of Hellenic Studies* 92 (1972) 147–155, *Denkschriften der österreichische Akademie der Wissenschaften* 117 (Wien, 1974), *Hermathena* 118 (1974) 110–129, *Études sur l'Épicurisme antique*, eds Bollack, J. and Laks, A. (Lille, 1976), 279–318, *Anatolian Studies* 28 (1978) 39–92, 29 (1979) 69–89, *Prometheus* 8 (1982) 193–212, *Anatolian Studies* 34 (1984) 43–57; Diskin Clay, *American Journal of Philology* 97 (1976) 306–309. For a full list of studies of Diogenes, see Smith, M. F., 'A Bibliography of Work on Diogenes of Oenoanda, 1892–1981' in *Syzetesis: studi sull'epicureismo greco e romano offerti a Marcello Gigante* (Napoli, 1983) 683–695. For a brief history of the excavations at Oenoanda, see C. W. Chilton, *Diogenes of Oenoanda, the Fragments: a Translation and Commentary* (Oxford, 1971).

50 Chilton (*Diogenes of Oenoanda, the Fragments*, pp. xliv–xlv) estimates

120 or more columns stretching some 45.51 metres in three courses. the topmost course being perhaps shorter than the two below; Smith (*Thirteen New Fragments*, pp. 48–9) regards Chilton's estimate as conservative.

51 Cf. Bignone, *L'Aristotele perduto*, vol. 2, pp. 216ff.; Festugière, *Epicurus and His Gods* (trans. C. W. Chilton), p. 44, n. 31.

52 For a review of opinions, see Chilton, *Diogenes of Oenoanda, the Fragments*, pp. 107–8; Chilton himself regards the letter as genuine.

53 On this last instance, see Smith, *Thirteen New Fragments*, pp. 21ff.

54 On the probable date of Cleomedes' work, see Richard Goulet, *Cléomede: théorie élémentaire* (Paris, 1980), pp. 5–8, and W. Schumacher, *Untersuchungen zur Datierung des Astronomen Kleomedes*, Diss. (Köln, 1975).

55 Book II, Ch. 1, or pp. 120–68 in the modern edition by H. Ziegler, *Cleomedis de motu circulari corporum caelestium* (Leipzig, 1891).

56 *Lettres de Peiresc*, ed. Philippe Tamizey de Larroque (Paris, 1888–98), iv. no. 11, pp. 179–80: 'je vous puis asseurer que de tant d'autheurs qui mastinent ce pauvre homme à peine en ay-je veu aucun qui le traitte plus mal que cestuy ci'.

57 Ziegler, 168.

58 Cf. *Demosthenes* 2. 2.

59 For the text and history of the Lamprias Catalogue, see the Loeb edition of the *Moralia*, vol. XV, translated by F. H. Sandbach; also R. H. Barrow, *Plutarch and His Times* (Bloomington, Ind., 1967), pp. 193–4. The anti-Stoic items in the Catalogue are nos. 59, 78, 152, 154, 149, 76, 77, and 79, of which the last three are extant; the anti-Epicurean items are nos. 81, 82, 178, 80, 129, 133, 143, 155, and 159, of which the first three are extant; no. 148 (*Selections and Refutations of the Stoics and Epicureans*) is directed against both Schools.

60 *Principal Doctrines* 7; cf. *Vatican Sayings* 81; Philodemus, *Rhetorica* ii, p. 154, fr. 13 (Sudhaus); Cicero, *Ad Atticum* XIV. 20. 5, *De legibus* I. 13. 39, *Ad familiares* VII. 12; Diogenes of Oenoanda fr. 2 (Chilton). For the 'unnoticed life' as a commonplace in Augustan literature, see Horace, *Epistles* I. 17. 10 (*nec vixit male qui natus moriensque fefellit*), I. 18. 102 (*secretum iter et fallentis semita vitae*), and Ovid, *Tristia* III. 4. 25 (*crede mihi; bene qui latuit, bene vixit*).

61 *De rerum natura* II. 1–6. Cf. III. 59–64; V. 1120–35.

62 See W. Crönert, *Kolotes und Menedemos* (Studien zur Palaeographie und Papyruskunde, VI), (Leipzig, 1906), and Proclus, *Commentaria in Platonis Rem Publicam*, vol. ii, p. 105, 23–106. 14, ed. Kroll.

63 C. P. Jones, *Culture and Society in Lucian* (Cambridge, Mass., 1986), pp. 147–8 notes that a generation after Lucian the Sophist Aelian recommended the burning of Epicurean books as a punishment for Epicureans who profaned the Eleusinian mysteries (Aelian, ed. Hercher, fr. 39).

64 The closest commentary on the *Alexander*, and the most helpful in this regard, is M. Caster, *Études sur Alexandre ou le faux prophète de Lucien* (Paris, 1938); see also Jennifer Hall, *Lucian's Satire* (New York, 1981), pp. 26–7, 207–11, C. P. Jones, op. cit., pp. 133–48, and A. D. Nock,

'Alexander of Abonuteichos', *Classical Quarterly* 22 (1928) 160–2.

65 For a balanced assessment of Lucian's religious satire in the context of the literary tradition and the contemporary religious scene, as well as a useful discussion of his attitude towards 'sincere religious convictions', see Hall, op. cit., pp 94–207. For other opinions, see M. Caster, *Lucien et la pensée religieuse de son temps* (Paris, 1937), and J. Bompaire, *Lucien écrivain, imitation et creation* (Bibliothèque des Écoles françaises d'Athènes et de Rome 190) (Paris, 1958).

66 For a more positive assessment of Lucian's Epicurean 'sympathies', see C. P. Jones, op. cit., pp. 26–8 and 39–41.

67 Cf. Hall, op. cit., p. 172.

CHAPTER 4   THE CHRISTIAN REACTION

1 *Ep.* 118. 12. Cf. C. W. Chilton (*Diogenes of Oenoanda*, Oxford, 1971, p. xxvii): 'By the middle of the fourth century [Epicureanism] was dying or dead . . . the school itself was quite finished by the end of the fourth century'; F. Cumont (*Lux Perpetua*, Paris, 1949, p. 127): 'Lorsque le mysticisme et la théologie triomphèrent dans le monde romain, l'épicurisme cessa d'exister. Il avait disparu au milieu du ive siècle'; Emile Brehier (*The Philosophy of Plotinus*, trans. Joseph Thomas, Chicago, 1958, p. 14): '[the third century] witnesses the final and irreparable overthrow of the dogmatic philosophies, Stoicism and Epicureanism'.

2 I adopt the estimate of 5 million out of a total population of 60 million given by Ramsey MacMullen, *Christianizing the Roman Empire* (New Haven, 1984), p. 32 and p. 135, n. 26. Cf. R. M. Grant, *Early Christianity and Society: Seven Studies* (New York, 1977), pp. 5–9, and Adolph Harnack, *Mission und Ausbreitung des Christentums*, 4th edn (Leipzig, 1924), pp. 946–58; for a somewhat lower estimate see E. Molland, 'Besass die alte Kirche ein Missionsprogramm?', *Die alte Kirche*, ed. H. Frohnes und U. W. Knorr (Munich, 1974), p. 54, and H. Von Soden, 'Die christliche Mission in Altertum und Gegenwart', ibid., p. 35. For a considerably higher estimate see L. von Hertling, 'Die Zahl der Christen zu Beginn des vierten Jahrhunderts', *Zeitschrift für Katholische Theologie* 58 (1934) 243–53.

3 See MacMullen, op. cit., p. 83.

4 M. L. W. Laistner, *Christianity and Pagan Culture in the Later Roman Empire* (Ithaca, 1951), p. 5: 'From AD 312 their [the Christians'] progress was indeed triumphant, but paganism and its cults showed remarkable tenacity, so that it would be a grave error to suppose that these rapidly disappeared under the Christian emperors.' See also R. MacMullen, *Paganism in the Roman Empire* (New Haven, 1981); A. Alfoldi, *The Conversion of Constantine and Pagan Rome* (Oxford, 1948), pp. 118ff.; J. Geffken, *The Last Days of Greco-Roman Paganism*, trans. Sabine MacCormack (Amsterdam, 1978), pp. 25ff.; and Robin Lane Fox, *Pagans and Christians* (New York, 1987).

5 For the nature and widespread impact of the Second Sophistic, see G. Bowersock, *Greek Sophists in the Roman Empire* (Oxford, 1969).

6 We should acknowledge, however, P. Merlan's comment, with particular reference to the philosophy of Plotinus, that 'the *cummunis opinio* that Epicureanism is not included in late Greek syncretism needs some qualification' (in *The Cambridge History of Later Greek and Early Mediaeval Philosophy*, ed. A. H. Armstrong, Cambridge, 1967, p. 63, n. 1).

7 We may note the following comment by the second-century AD Platonist Numenius of Apamea:

> And the Epicureans . . . were never seen on any point to have opposed the doctrines of Epicurus in any way; but by acknowledging that they held the same opinions with a learned sage they naturally for this reason gained the title themselves; and with the later Epicureans it was for the most part a fixed rule never to express any opposition either to one another or to Epicurus on any point worth mentioning: but innovation is with them a transgression or rather an impiety, and is condemned. And for this reason no one even dares to differ, but from their constant agreement among themselves their doctrines are quietly held in perfect peace. Thus the School of Epicurus is like some true republic, perfectly free from sedition, with one mind in common and one consent; from which cause they were and are, and seemingly will be zealous disciples
>
> ap. Eusebius, *Praeparatio Evangelii*, XIV. 5 (trans. E. H. Gifford, Oxford, 1903).

8 Many of the references in the following pages, as well as certain lines of interpretation, are owed to the researches of R. P. Jungkuntz in his *Epicureanism and the Church Fathers*, Ph.D. thesis (unpublished) (University of Wisconsin, 1961), and W. Schmid, 'Epikur', in *Reallexicon für Antike und Christentum*, ed. T. Klauser, vol. 5 (Stuttgart, 1962), cols 774–816. See also H. Hagendahl, *Latin Fathers and the Classics* (Göteborg, 1958); J. Philippe, 'Lucrèce dans la théologie chrétienne', *Revue de l'histoire des religions* 32 (1895) 284–302; E. Rapisarda, 'L'epicureismo nei primi scrittori latini cristiani', *Antiquitas* I (1946) 49–54, and 'L'epicureismo nei primi scrittori latini cristiani: la polemica di Lattanzio contro l'epicureismo', *Antiquitas* II–V (3–4) (1947–50) 45–54; Adelaide D. Simpson, 'Epicureans, Christians, atheists in the second century', *Transactions of the American Philological Association* 62 (1941) 372–81.

9 Aristides, *Apologia* i. 1. 5; Origen, *De oratione* 31. 3; Augustine, *Epistolae* 118. 25.

10 Theophilus, *Ad Autolycum* i. 3; Lactantius, *De ira* 4; Tertullian, *Adversus Marcionem* ii. 16. We may note that Arnobius, Lactantius' teacher, took the Epicurean side (*Adversus nationes* i. 18).

11 Tertullian, *Adversus Valentinianos* vii. 4, *Apologeticus* 47. 6, *Ad Nationes* ii. 2. 8; Eusebius, *Theophania* ii. 19; Basil, *Hexaemeron* ii. 2.

12 *Adversus Colotem* 27, 30; *Non posse* 20–23.

13 For an example of the closeness of early Christian and Stoic phraseology with respect to providence, see Clement of Rome's *Epistle to the Corinthians*, XX, in *Ancient Christian Writers*, ed. J. Quasten and J. C. Plumpe (Westminster, Md., 1946), and G. Bardy, 'Expressions stoïciennes dans la Prima Clementis', *Recherches de*

Science Religieuse 12 (1922) 73–85. On the relation between early
Christian and Stoic thought in general, see Marcia L. Colish, *The
Stoic Tradition from Antiquity to the Middle Ages*, vol. 2: *Stoicism in
Christian Latin Thought through the Sixth Century* (Studies in the History
of Christian Thought, 35) (Leiden, 1985); M. Spennent, *Le Stoicisme
des Pères de l'Église* (Paris, 1957); H. Chadwick, *Early Christian Thought
and the Classical Tradition* (Oxford, 1966).

14 Athenagoras, *Legatio* 25. 3; Lactantius, *Divinae institutiones* iii. 17, vii 3;
Clement, *Stromateis* v. 14; Minucius Felix, *Octavius* 17–19; Athanasius,
De incarnatione verbi 2; Hilary, *Tractatus* (in Ps. 1. 7); Basil, *Hexaemeron* i.
2; Gregory of Nyssa, *De anima et resurrectione* 21 A, 24 B; Augustine,
Epistolae 118. 31; and especially Dionysius of Alexandria in *On Nature*,
a treatise aimed specifically against the Epicureans and preserved in
extract in Eusebius, *Praeparatio Evangelii* XIV. 23–7; cf. XV. 5.

15 See Basil, *Hexaemeron* v. 5, ix. 5; Titus of Bostra, *Adversus Manichaeos*
ii. 20, 22, 24; Origen, *Contra Celsum*, iv. 78ff., vi. 56; Ambrose, *De
officiis ministrorum* i. 3, ii. 3; Gregory of Nyssa, *De hominis opificio* 7. 1;
Lactantius, *De opificio Dei* 2. 10, 3. 1; *Divinae institutiones* vii. 4;
Eusebius, *Theophania* i. 47; Jerome, *In Iesaiam* vii. 18. 1; Nemesius, *De
natura hominis* 44. 64.

16 *De anima* 5; cf. *De resurrectione carnis* 17 and 35. For other references to
the corporeal nature of the Epicurean soul, see Nemesius, *De natura
hominis* 2. 11, Claudianus Mamertus, *De statu animae* ii. 9.

17 *De anima* 14.

18 *De testimonio animae* 1.

19 Cf. Lactantius, *Divinae institutiones*, vii. 9:

> Can any one, when he has considered the nature of other animals, which the
> providence of the Supreme God has made abject, with bodies bending down
> and prostrated to the earth, so that it may be understood from this that they
> have no intercourse with heaven, fail to understand that men alone of all the
> animals is heavenly and divine, whose body raised from the ground, and
> elevated countenance, and upright position, goes in quest of its origin . . .?
> Since therefore wisdom, which is given to man alone, is nothing else but the
> knowledge of God, it is evident that the soul does not perish, nor undergo
> dissolution, but that it remains for ever, because it seeks after and loves God,
> who is everlasting, by the impulse of its very nature perceiving either from
> what source it has sprung, or to what it is about to return.
>
> (*The Ante-Nicene Fathers*, Amer. edn (Buffalo/New York, 1884–6), vol. 7,
> p. 206.)

20 Lucretius, *De rerum natura* III. 526–47; Tertullian, *De anima* 53.

21 *De rerum natura* IV. 907ff.; *De anima* 43.

22 *De rerum natura* III. 425–669; *Divinae institutiones* vii. 12.

23 *De resurrectione mortuorum* 19 (*Ante-Nicene Fathers*, vol. 2, p. 159). Cf.
Legatio 12.

24 *Adversus nationes* ii. 30 (*Ante-Nicene Fathers*, vol. 6, pp. 445–6). Cf.
Origen, *Contra Celsum* iii. 80.

25 *Epistolae* 104. 3 (*A Select Library of Nicene and Post-Nicene Fathers*, ed. P.
Schaff (Buffalo/New York, 1886–1900), vol. 1, p. 428). Cf.
Confessiones vi. 6.

26 Justin, *Second Apology*, vii, xv.

27 *Contra Jovinianum* i. 4.

28 Theophilus, *Ad Autolycum* iii. 6; Clement, *Stromateis* ii. 23;
Pseudo-Clement, *Homiliae* v. 18; Ambrose, *De officiis ministrorum* i. 13;
Epiphanius, *Panarion* 3. 29; Peter Chrysologus, *Sermones* 5; Filastrius,
De haeresibus 106; Augustine, *Epistolae* 118. 14, *Contra Academicos* iii.
18. 41; *Sermones* 150. 5, 8.

29 See R. M. Ogilvie, *The Library of Lactantius* (Oxford, 1978), pp. 84–7.
While Ogilvie's study is confined to the reading of Lactantius it is
clear enough that as far as Epicurus is concerned Lactantius is not
untypical.

30 See Ogilvie, op. cit., pp. 66–71.

31 See H. Hagendahl, *Augustine and the Latin Classics* (Göteborg, 1967),
vol. 2, p. 524 and vol. 1, pp. 76–9.

32 *Stromateis*, ii. 21. On the similarities between Clement's objections to
Epicureanism and those of Middle Platonism, see Salvatore R. C.
Lilla, *Clement of Alexandria* (Oxford, 1971), p. 46.

33 *Contra Julianum* iii. 21. 48, iv. 15. 76; *Epistolae* 118. 14, 17; *Confessiones*
vi. 16. 26; *De civitate Dei* XIV. 2.

34 *Epistolae* 63. Cf. G. Madec, *Saint Ambroise et la philosophie* (Paris,
1974), pp. 87–8.

35 *De officiis ministrorum* ii. 2; cf. Cicero, *De finibus* II. 6. 19.

36 *De natura hominis* 18. 38.

37 See Diogenes Laertius 10. 127, 149; *Principal Doctrines* 29; *Vatican
Sayings* 20. At *De finibus* I. 13. 45 Cicero puts an accurate statement
of the classification in the mouth of the Epicurean spokesman
Torquatus, but goes on to criticize it himself as illogical and
misleading (II. 9. 26).

38 *De anima* 38. 3.

39 *Stromateis* iii. 1.

40 *De natura hominis* 18. 37.

41 *Refutatio omnium haeresium* I. proem. 8–9.

42 *Panarion* 64. 72. 9. Cf. Chadwick, op. cit., pp. 100ff.; Chadwick also
notes (p. 159, n. 1) that Epiphanius was anticipated by Marcellus of
Ancyra, who charged that Origen had begun to preach too soon
after studying Greek philosophy (Eusebius, *Contra Marcellum* i. 4).

43 *Panarion*, prooem. 1. 3. 2; 1. 5. 2.

44 *Apologia* i. 10. 1, ii. 13. 3, ii. 8. 4. On the derivation of Greek
philosophy from Moses, see also Tatian, *Oratio* 40; for references to
the same theme in Philo, see Lilla, op. cit., p. 28. We may note that
Justin's contemporary, the Platonist and anti-Christian propagandist
Celsus, rejects the alleged dependence of Plato upon Moses, insisting
that the dependence was the other way around (Celsus, ed. Bader,
vi. 6 and 12).

45 W. R. Schoedel (ed. and trans.), *Athenagoras: Legatio and De
Resurrectione* (Oxford, 1972), p. xxiii.

46 Chadwick, op. cit., p. 33.

47 *Stromateis*, vi. 8. For other positive references to Greek philosophy in the *Stromateis*, see Lilla, op. cit., p. 10, and for a listing of the literature on Clement's attitude, see p. 10, n. 1. For useful studies of the attitudes of Justin, Clement, and Origen, see Chadwick, op. cit., W. Jaeger, *Early Christianity and Greek Paideia* (Cambridge, Mass., 1961), pp. 26ff., and Lilla, op. cit., pp. 9–59.

48 'Sed Marcion principalem suae fidei terminum de Epicuri schola agnoscat, dominum inferens hebetem', *Adversus Marcionem* v. 19. 7.; cf. ii. 16. 2–3; iv. 15. 2–3; see also Epicurus, *Principal Doctrines* 1; Seneca, *De beneficiis* vii. 31. 3.

49 Tertullian, *Adversus Valentinianos* iv. 7; Irenaeus, *Adversus haereses* iii. 24. 2.

50 *Adversus haereses* ii. 14. 3; *Adversus Valentinianos* iv. 14. The fourth-century Christian poet Prudentius employs vocabulary which suggests that in his mind it is from Epicurus that the Manichaeans have borrowed their notion of Christ as an empty phantom made up of tiny atoms loosely held together:

> Est operae pretium nebulosi dogmatis umbram
> Prodere, quam tenues atomi compage minuta
> Instituunt: sed cassa cadit, ventoque liquescit
> Assimilis, fluxu nec se sustentat inani.
> Aerium, Manichaeus ait, sine corpore vero
> Pervolitasse Deum mendax phantasma, cavamque
> Corporis effigiem, nil contrectabile habentem.
>
> *Apotheosis* 953–9

51 *De resurrectione carnis* 2. 1.

52 *De haeresibus* 5.

53 *Contra Jovinianum* 1. 48.

54 ibid., ii. 11.

55 ibid., i. 1; ii. 36. Cf. ii. 21.

56 *Contra Julianum* iii. 21. 48; iv. 3. 21.

57 Jerome, *Ep.* 33. 5; Ambrose, *Ep.* 63; Salvian, *De gubernatione Dei* 1.5.

58 Jungkuntz, op. cit., p. 67. Even though it takes us outside the apologist–heretic context we should note also the case of Origen and the anti-Christian propagandist Celsus, since it confirms the stigma which had become attached to the name 'Epicurean'. The identity of Celsus, the author of the *True Doctrine*, to which Origen's *Contra Celsum*, written around the middle of the third century, is a reply, is not known, and was not known to Origen himself. That he was not the Epicurean friend of the satirist Lucian, nor even an adherent of the Epicurean school, has been convincingly argued by Henry Chadwick (*Origen: Contra Celsum*, Cambridge, 1953, pp. xxiv–xxix). Whether Origen himself believed that Celsus was an Epicurean we cannot be sure, but, as Chadwick points out (p. xxvi), the Platonic colouring of Celsus' arguments should have convinced Origen of Celsus' allegiance to the Platonic school, and Chadwick is probably right in suggesting that Origen presents Celsus as an Epicurean in order to discredit him. Even if Origen is speaking from conviction

when he claims that Celsus is masking his Epicureanism behind a feigned Platonism (*Contra Celsum* iii. 22, 35, 80), the point remains. We may note also that the word 'Epicurean' came to have a similar derogatory force in later Rabbinic writings; cf *Sanhedrin* 10. 1:

> And these are they that have no share in the world to come: he that says there is no resurrection of the dead prescribed in the law; and [he that says] that the law is not from Heaven; and an Epicurean [Apikoros].
>
> trans. H. Danby, *The Mishnah* (Oxford, 1933), p. 397.

Danby has the following note on 'Epicurean': 'It is in no way associated with teachings supposed by the Jews to emanate from the philosopher Epicurus; to Jewish ears it conveys the sense of the root *pakar*, and so licentious and sceptical' (n. 4). Cf. *Tos Sanhedrin* 13. 5 and *Ros ha-Shunah* 17a, where 'Epicureans' are grouped with heretics, informers, apostates, and those who deny the truth of the Torah as doomed to eternal punishment in hell (G. F. Moore, *Judaism*, Cambridge, Mass., 1927, vol. 2, p. 387).

59 *De anima* 5; Lucretius, *De rerum natura* I. 305: *Tangere enim et tangi nisi corpus nulla potest res.*

60 *Contra Jovinianum* i. 48, ii. 11. We may note that Clement is convinced that Epicurus' condemnation of marriage is no more than a justification of licentious living (*Stromateis* ii. 23).

61 *De anima* 17. Cf. Lucretius, *De rerum natura* IV. 438–42. IV. 353ff. Tertullian stops short of endorsing the more general Epicurean position that whenever we arrive at false knowledge it is the mind which is at fault for making a wrong inference (see Lucretius, *De rerum natura* IV. 379–86; IV. 462–6).

62 *Stromateis* ii. 4. Cf. Theodoret, *Therapeutica* 1. 813 D.

63 See chapter 2, pp. 26–7, and Diogenes Laertius 10. 33.

64 See Jungkuntz, op. cit., pp. 117–35.

65 *Divinae institutiones* vii. 1. 7.

66 ibid., vii. 3. 13; Lucretius, *De rerum natura* V. 156ff.

67 *Contra academicos* iii. 11. 26.

68 *Adversus Colotem* 27 (1123 A).

69 *Alexander* 17.

70 *Alexander* 38.

71 Cf. W. Schmid, op. cit., cols 808–9. Schmid concurs with R. Philippson ('Philodem über die Frömmigkeit', *Hermes* 55 (1920) 231ff.) that 'Im Grunde beruht . . . die gesamte Götterkritik der Alten seit dem Ende des 2 Jh. v.C auf epikureischer Grundlage' (col. 809).

72 *Contra Celsum* vii. 3; viii. 46. We may note that at iii. 25 Origen may be relying upon Epicurean arguments; see Chadwick, *Origen*, p. 143, n. 2.

73 *Divinae institutiones* i. 16. 3; i. 21. 45; ii. 3. 10–11; the Lucretian passages are *De rerum natura* I. 931, II. 14, V. 5, and VI. 1197ff.

74 *Praeparatio evangelii* iv. 2. 13 (trans. Gifford); cf. iv. 3. 14.

75 'patronus voluptatis' (Ambrose, *De officiis ministrorum* i. 13. 50); 'adsertor voluptatis' (Lactantius, *Divinae institutiones* iii. 17. 35); 'auctor voluptatis' (Peter Chrysologus, *Sermones* 5).

76 Cf. Seneca, *De vita beata* 12.4.
77 *Ep.* 63. 19 (*Select Library of Nicene and Post-Nicene Fathers*, vol. 10, p. 459).
78 *Contra Jovinianum* ii. 11.
79 *Poemata Moralia* X. 787ff.
80 'Nor do we say that men act or experience what they do according to fate, but rather that each man does right or wrong according to the choices he makes' (Justin, *Second Apology* vii 3; cf. *First Apology* xliii; *Dialogue with Trypho* 141; Tatian, *Oratio* 9.
81 Cf. *Principal Doctrines* 14; *Vatican Sayings* 58; Lucretius, vv. 1120–8.
82 Cf. Basil, *Epistolae* 9; Theodoret, *Epistolae* 62; Gregory Nazianzen, *Orationes* ii. 6. 7;
83 *De Pallio*, 5 (trans. C. N. Cochrane, *Christianity and Classical Culture*, New York, 1957, p. 213).
84 *Contra Celsum* viii. 75 (trans. Chadwick).
85 Cf. *Epistle to Diognotus* 5: '[Christians] Ἐπὶ γῆς διατρίβουσιν, ἀλλ' ἐν οὐρανῷ πολιτεύονται·'
86 Lucretius, V. 1–8; Arnobius, *Adversus nationes* i. 38; Lactantius, *Divinae institutiones* iii. 14. 1.

CHAPTER 5   MEDIEVAL INTERLUDE

1 Cf. Augustine, *De doctrina Christiana* II. 40.
2 See Pierre Riché, *Education and Culture in the Barbarian West*, trans. John J. Contreni (Columbia, S. Carolina, 1976), pp. 21–38, and R. R. Bolgar, *The Classical Heritage and its Beneficiaries* (Cambridge, 1954), p. 405, n. 97.
3 Cf. Riché, op. cit., p. 40 and n. 161.
4 See L. D. Reynolds and N. G. Wilson, *Scribes and Scholars*, 2nd edn (Oxford, 1975), p. 72.
5 Cf. Riché, op. cit., p. 45: 'Having forgotten Greek, the lettered of the sixth century had no contact with the culture which previously came to them from the East, that is, philosophical culture.' For a more positive judgment, see Pierre Courcelle, *Les Lettres grecques en Occident de Macrobe à Cassiodore*, 2nd edn (Paris, 1948), pp. 257ff.
6 Cf. Riché, op. cit., pp. 60ff.
7 Caesarius of Arles, for example, attacks classical poetry and philosophy as the breeding-ground for immorality and heresy (*Sermo* XCIV, in *Sancti Caesarii opera omnia*, ed. Germain Morin (Maredsous, 1937–42), I. 589) in much the same terms as Tertullian (*De anima* 3. 1).
8 Riché, op. cit., pp. 89–95.
9 We may note St Gregory's stern criticism of Bishop Desiderius of Vienne for introducing his students to secular literature (*Registrum epistolarum*, ed. P. Ewald and M. Hartmann, in *Monumenta Germaniae historica: Epistolae* I–II (Berlin, 1891–9), IX. 34. 303). Riché (op. cit., p. 97 and n. 115) draws attention to the *Statuta ecclesiae antiqua* issued from Provence during the second half of the fifth century which

contain (Canon 5) an explicit injunction against the reading of
pagan texts (in *Sancti Caesarii opera omnia*, II. 91); A. H. M. Jones
(*The Later Roman Empire* (Oxford, 1973), vol. 2, p. 1005) notes that
similar injunctions are contained in the *Canons of the Apostles*, which
commanded wide authority in the eastern churches; see especially
1. 6 (F. X. Funk, *Didascalia et constitutiones Apostolorum*, Paderborn,
1905).

10 Cf. Cassiodorus, *Institutiones*, preface.

11 See Justinian's specific instruction in 554 that regular salaries be
paid to teachers of grammar, rhetoric, medicine, and law at Rome in
order to ensure a steady pool of students suitably trained in the
liberal arts (*Novella pro petitione vigilii, Corpus iuris civilis: Novellae*,
App. VII (ed. Schöll), p. 802).

12 Cf. Riché, op. cit., pp. 184–206 and 246–65.

13 On the production of manuscripts of Christian authors in
Merovingian Gaul between 500 and 750, see R. McKitterick, 'The
scriptoria of Merovingian Gaul: a survey of the evidence', in
Columbanus and Merovingian Monasticism, ed. H. B. Clarke and M.
Brennan (British Archeological Reports, International Series 113),
(Oxford, 1981) pp. 173–207. We may note that of the 264 books
which survive from the period between *c.* 550 and *c.* 750, as listed in
Codici Latini antiquiores (ed. E. A. Lowe, 11 vols and supplement,
Oxford, 1934–71) only twenty-six are pagan works, and only one of
these (a fragment of Lucan) is of a non-technical nature. Cf. L. D.
Reynolds, *Texts and Transmission* (Oxford, 1983), p. xvi.

14 Cf. Bolgar, op. cit., pp. 93–4.

15 Cf. Bede, *Ecclesiastical History*, ed. Bertram Colgrave and R. A. B.
Mynors (Oxford, 1969), iii. 27:

> At this time [664] there were many in England, both nobles and commons,
> who, in the days of Bishops Finan and Colman, had left their own country and
> retired to Ireland either for the sake of religious studies or to live a more ascetic
> life. In the course of time some of these devoted themselves faithfully to the
> monastic life, while others preferred to travel round the cells of various teachers
> and apply themselves to study. The Irish welcomed them all gladly, gave them
> their daily food, and also provided them with books to read and with
> instruction, without asking for any payment.
>
> (trans. Colgrave)

16 Cf. Bede, *Ecclesiastical History*, iv. 2:

> And because both of them were extremely learned in sacred and secular
> literature, they attracted a crowd of students into whose minds they daily
> poured the streams of wholesome learning. They gave their hearers instruction
> not only in the books of holy scripture but also in the art of metre, astronomy,
> and ecclesiastical computation. As evidence of this, some of their students still
> survive who know Latin and Greek just as well as their native tongue.
>
> (trans. Colgrave)

17 Bede, *Ecclesiastical History*, iii, 18.

18 In general, see Wilhelm Levison, *England and the Continent in the
Eighth Century* (Oxford, 1946), ch. VI, 'Learning and scholarship';

M. L. W. Laistner, *Thought and Letters in Western Europe, AD 500–900*, 2nd rev. edn. (London and Ithaca, 1957), pp. 136–166; on the availability of texts, see M. L. W. Laistner, 'The Library of the Venerable Bede', in *Bede: His Life, Times and Writings*, ed. A. Hamilton Thompson (Oxford, 1935; New York, 1966); J. D. A. Ogilvy, *Books Known to Anglo-Latin Writers from Aldhelm to Alcuin* (The Mediaeval Academy of America, Studies and Documents, no. 2) (Cambridge, Mass., 1936); T.J. Brown, 'An historical introduction to the use of classical Latin authors in the British Isles from the fifth to the eleventh century', *Settimane* 22 (1) (1975) 237–299; H. Gneuss, 'A preliminary list of manuscripts written or owned in England up to 1100', *Anglo-Saxon England 9 (1981) 1–60)*, and in *The Survival of Ancient Literature*, ed. R. W. Hunt (Exhibition Catalogue, Bodleian Library) (Oxford, 1975), pp. 46–48.

19 Cf. *Versus de Patribus Regibus et Sanctis Euboricensis Ecclesiae*, ed. Peter Godman (Oxford, 1982), 11. 1426–53.

20 *Epistola Bedae ad Ecgbertum episcopum*, in *Councils and Ecclesiastical Documents relating to Great Britain and Ireland*, eds. W. A. Haddon and W. Stubbs [Haddon–Stubbs], 4 vols (Oxford, 1869–78), III. 314–25; *Explanatio Apocalypsis* (Migne, PL, XCII. 134).

21 *Monumenta Germaniae historica: Epistolae* (Hannover and Leipzig, 1862–), III. 350ff.

22 For the text of the Canons, see Haddon–Stubbs, III. 360–75.

23 Haddon–Stubbs, III. 444–61.

24 Preface to Gregory's *Pastoral Care* (trans. C. Oman, *England before the Norman Conquest*, 3rd edn, London, 1913, p. 476).

25 See S. J. Crawford, *Anglo-Saxon Influence on Western Christendom, 600–800* (Oxford, 1933), pp. 32–71; Levison, op. cit., pp. 45–93.

26 For the text of the *Epistola de litteris colendis*, see *Monumenta Germaniae historica: Leges*, ed. G. H. Pertz (Hannover, 1835) I. pp. 52–3; P. Lehmann, 'Fuldaer Studien, neue Folge', in *Sitzungsberichte der Bayerischen Akademie der Wissenschaften*, no. 2 (Munich, 1927) pp. 4–13.

27 For information on the school curriculum and the school texts used in the Carolingian period, see D. Illmer, *Formen der Erziehung und Wissensvermittlung im frühen Mittelalter* (Munich, 1971); G. Glauche, *Schullektüre im Mittelalter* (Munich, 1970).

28 The standard editions of Carolingian Latin poetry are *Monumenta Germaniae historica [MGH]: Poetae* i (ed. E. Dümmler) (Berlin, 1881); ii (ed. Dümmler) (Berlin, 1884); iii (ed. L. Traube) (Berlin, 1906); iv. 1 (ed. P. von Winterfeld) (Berlin 1909); vi 1 (ed. Strecker) (Berlin, 1953). For useful surveys, see F. J. E. Raby, *A History of Secular Latin Poetry in the Middle Ages*, (Oxford, 1962), vol. 1, pp. 178–209; M. L. W. Laistner, *Thought and Letters*, pp. 330–61; and especially Peter Godman, *Poetry of the Carolingian Renaissance* (London, 1985), Introduction, pp. 1–80, and *Poets and Emperors: Frankish Politics and Carolingian Poetry* (Oxford, 1987).

29 Cf. F. J. E. Raby, *A History of Christian Latin Poetry from the Beginnings to the Close of the Middle Ages* (Oxford, 1953) pp. 154–77.

30 Cf. Einhard (?), *Karolus Magnus et Leo Papa* (*MGH: Poetae* i. 366ff):

> Rex Karolus, caput orbis, amor populique decusque,
> Europae venerandus apex, pater optimus, heros,
> Augustus, sed et urbe potens, ubi Roma secunda
> Flore novo, ingenti magna consurgit ad alta
> Mole tholis muro praecelsis sidera tangens

(ll. 92–6).

31 Cf. Moduin, *Ecloga* (*MGH: Poetae* i. 385–6):

> Prospicit alta novae Romae meus arce Palemon
> Cuncta suo imperio consistere regna triumpho,
> Rursus in antiquos mutataque secula mores.
> Aurea Roma iterum renovata renascitur orbi!

(ll. 24–7).

32 Walafrid Strabo in the preface to Einhard's *Life of Charlemagne*; Lupus of Ferrières, epist. 31, 45, and 120 in L. Levillain (ed.) *Loup de Ferrières. Correspondence* (Paris, 1964).

33 F. von Bezold, 'Kaiserin Judith und ihre Dichter Walafrid Strabo', *Historische Zeitschrift* 130 (1924) 375–439.

34 On Charles the Bald's so-called 'palace school', see R. McKitterick, 'The palace school of Charles the Bald', in *Charles the Bald: Court and Kingdom*, ed. M. Gibson and J. Wilson, British Archaeological Reports 101 (London, 1981), pp. 385–400, and 'Charles the Bald and his library: the patronage of learning', *English Historical Review* 95 (1980) 28–47. For a more reserved view concerning the existence of a 'palace school', see Godman, *Poetry of the Carolingian Renaissance*, pp. 56–8.

35 See B. Bischoff, 'Das Benediktinische Mönchtum und die Uberlieferung der Klassischen Literatur', *Studien und Mitteilungen zur Geschichte des Benediktiner-Ordens und seiner Zweige* 92 (1981) 165–90.

36 On the palace library and scriptorium under Charlemagne, see B. Bischoff, 'Die Hofbibliothek Karls des Grossen', in *Karl der Grosse, Lebenswerk und Nachleben*, ed. W. Braufels (Düsseldorf, 1965), vol. 2, pp. 42–62.

37 For a list of classical Latin texts for which ninth-century manuscripts are extant, see Reynolds, op. cit., p. xxviii. For an account of the role played by particular monasteries, see R. McKitterick, *The Frankish Kingdoms under the Carolingians, 751–987* (London and New York, 1983), pp. 200–27.

38 On the cathedral schools, see J. Fleckenstein, 'Königshof und Bischofschule unter Otto den Grossen', *Archiv für Kulturgeschichte* 38 (1956) 38–62.

39 See Raby, *A History of Secular Latin Poetry*, pp. 307–48; Bolgar, op. cit., pp. 185–9.

40 See Reynolds, *Texts and Transmission*, pp. xxxi–xxxiv; for the classical authors copied at Montecassino during the tenth century, see E. A. Lowe, *The Beneventan Script: a History of the South Italian Minuscule* (Oxford, 1914), pp. 8ff.; on the translations of Greek and Arabic

medical sources produced at Montecassino during the last half of the eleventh century by Constantine the African and Alfanus of Salerno, see Marie-Thérèse d'Alverny, 'Translations and translators', in *Renaissance and Revival in the Twelfth Century*, ed. R. L. Benson and G. Constable (Cambridge, Mass., 1982), pp. 421–6.

41 Cf. Laistner, *Thought and Letters*, pp. 210–13.

42 *Hrosvithae opera*, ed. H. Homeyer (Paderborn, 1979), pp. 233–4; for an interesting treatment of Hrosvitha's 'Christianizing' of Terentian comedy and the importance of her plays for the development of medieval drama, see J. R. Bean, 'Terence chastened: two character types from the plays of Hrosvitha of Gandersheim', *Papers of the Michigan Academy of Science, Arts, and Letters*, 16(3) (1984) 383–90.

43 See G. R. Coffman, 'A new approach to medieval Latin drama'. *Modern Philology* 22(3) (1925) 264ff.

44 Petrus Damianus, *Dominus vobiscum* (Migne, PL, CXLV. 231). Cf. Manegold of Lautenbach, *Contra Wolfelmum*, c. 9 (Migne, PL, CLV. 158 B), quoted by Bolgar, op. cit., p. 415.

45 See B. L. Ullman, 'Classical authors in medieval florilegia', *Classical Philology* 27 (1932) 1–42; R. H. Rouse, 'Florilegia and Latin classical authors in twelfth- and thirteenth-century France', *Viator* 10 (1979) 131–60; R. J. Burton, *Classical Authors in the Florilegium Gallicum*, Dissertation, Toronto, 1981.

46 See William H. Stahl, *Roman Science: Origins, Development and Influence to the Later Middle Ages* (Madison, WI, 1962), pp. 193ff.

47 The following provide a useful starting-point for the study of medieval Latin translations, commentaries, and editions of Greek and Arabic texts: *Catalogus translationum et commentariorum: Mediaeval and Renaissance Translations and Commentaries* (Washington, DC, 1960–), vol. 1, ed. Paul O. Kristeller (1960); vol. 2, ed. Paul O. Kristeller and F. Edward Cranz (1971); vols 3 and 4, ed. F. Edward Cranz and Paul O. Kristeller (1976, 1980); C. H. Haskins, *Studies in the History of Medieval Science* (Cambridge, Mass., 1924; 2nd rev. edn, 1927; repr. 1960), and *The Renaissance of the Twelfth Century* (New York, 1927), chs IX–X; J. T. Muckle, 'Greek works translated directly into Latin before 1350', *Mediaeval Studies* 4 (1942) 33–42; 5 (1943) 102–14; G. Sarton, *Introduction to the History of Science*, (Baltimore, 1927–48), vol. 2, parts 1–2; Marie-Thérèse d'Alverny, op. cit., pp. 421–62.

48 See Marie-Thérèse Alverny, op. cit., pp. 457ff.

49 nec libri Aristotelis de naturali philosophia nec commenta legantur Parisiis publice vel secreto (H. Denifle, *Chartularium Universitatis Paris* (Paris, 1889), vol. 1, p. 70.

50 non legantur libri Aristotelis *de methafisica* et *de naturali philosophica* nec summe de eisdem (Denifle, op. cit., vol. 1, pp. 78–9).

51 ref. Deuteronomy 21: 11–13.

52 For a fuller treatment of what has been sketched in this and the preceding paragraphs, see Bolgar, op. cit., ch. V.

53 *De monarchia*, i, i, 4, quoted by R. W. Southern, *Mediaeval Humanism* (Oxford, 1970), p. 45.

54 Reynolds (*Texts and Transmission*, p. xxxvii) notes that other than the Latin translations from Greek or Arabic the only Latin text to surface for the first time in the thirteenth century was the *Gynaecia* of Caelius Aurelianus.

55 Cf. St Augustine, *De doctrina Christiana* II. 40.

56 See preface to Aristippus' translation of the *Meno*, ed. Victor Kordenter and Carlotta Labowsky, *Plato latinus* I (London, 1940), p. 6. There is no extant copy of a translation of Diogenes and we cannot be certain that Aristippus began or completed the task.

57 The following is indebted to the account and references in Reynolds, *Texts and Transmission*, pp. 218ff.

58 See B. Bischoff, in *Karl der Grosse, Werk und Wirkung* (Aachen, 1965), pp. 202–3.

59 See R. W. Hunt, in *Classical Influences on European Culture* AD 500–1550, ed. R. R. Bolgar, (Cambridge, 1971), p. 51.

60 See F. Dolbeau, 'Un nouveau catalogue des manuscrits de Lobbes au XIᵉ et XIIᵉ siècles', *Recherches Augustiniennes* 13 (1978) 3–36; 14 (1979) 191–248; and G. Becker, *Catalogi bibliothecarum antiqui* (Bonn, 1885), 79. 289.

61 Becker, op. cit., 32. 375.

62 See Reynolds, *Texts and Transmission*, pp. 112–15 and 124–8. For a listing of Lucretian passages cited by Isidore, see *Isidori Hispalensis Episcopi etymologiarum sive originum: Libri XX*, ed. W. M. Lindsay (Oxford, 1911) under 'loci citati', and Index in *Isidorus: De Natura Rerum*, ed. G. Becker (Berlin, 1859; repr. Amsterdam, 1967). See also I. Philippe's useful study in *Revue de l'histoire des Religions* 33 (1896) 27–34. On Isidore in general, see Jacques Fontaine, *Isidore de Seville et la culture classique dans l'Espagne visigothique* (Paris, 1959), and on the *Etymologies*, see Ernest Brehaut, *An Encyclopedist of the Dark Ages: Isidore of Seville* (New York, 1912, repr. 1967).

64 *De nuptiis philologiae et Mercurii et de septem artibus liberalibus*, ed. G. Willis (Leipzig, 1983), II. 213: 'Epicurus vero mixtas violis rosas et totas apportabat illecebras voluptatum.'

65 'Habes igitur ante oculos propositam fere formam felicitatis humanae, opes, honores, potentiam, gloriam, voluptatem. Quae quidem sola considerans Epicurus consequenter sibi summum bonum voluptatem esse constituit; quod cetera omnia iucunditatem animo videantur afferre.' *De Consolatione Philosophiae*, III. Prosa 2, ed. A. Fortescue (London, 1925), p. 63.

66 Jacob Burckhardt, *The Civilization of the Renaissance in Italy*, trans. G. G. Middlemore (New York, 1954), p. 374.

67 M. Manitius and R. Ulich (eds), *Vagantenlieder* (Jena, 1927), p. 98. See also *Carmina Burana*, no. 92 and no. 8 (Walther of Châtillon), in Edwin H. Zeydel, *Vagabond Verse* (Detroit, 1906), pp. 186–8 and 270. For further references to Epicurus, see *Carmina medii aevi posterioris Latina* 11/6, ed. Hans Walther (Göttingen, 1969) – *Register der Namen*, p. 63.

68 *Canterbury Tales*, Prologue, 331–8.

69 *The Complete Works of John Gower*, ed. G. C. Macaulay (Oxford, 1901), I. III (ll. 9529–40).

70 Frontispiece to *De vita et honestate civili* in the *Novella in libros Decretalium* of Giovanni Andrea, illuminated by Nicolo da Bologna in 1353 (Bibliotheca Ambrosiana, Milan, B 42 inf.), and the *Cantica* (1355) of Bartolomeo di Bartoli (Chantilly, Muse Conde, ms. lat. et ital. 1426, fol 6). See Philippe Verdier, 'L'Iconographie des arts libéraux' in *Arts libéraux et philosophie an moyen age* (Actes du quatrième Congrès international de philosophie, Montreal, 1967) (Montreal and Paris, 1969), p. 312 and n. 22. Verdier also notes (p. 330, n. 65 bis) that the same scene was depicted in a fresco painted in 1367 by Giusto de' Manabuoi in the Capella Cortellieri at Padua.

71 *Policraticus* VIII, xxiv, trans. Joseph B. Pike, *Frivolities of Courtiers and Footprints of Philosophers* (Minneapolis, 1938), pp. 399–400.

72 *Policraticus* VIII, xvi (Pike, op. cit., pp. 346–7).

CHAPTER 6   THE HUMANIST DEBATE

1 *La Divina Commedia, Inferno*, Canto X, 13–15.

2 For an indication of the great excitement which these excursions aroused in Poggio and his friends, and an account of the sorry neglect of manuscripts in such monasteries as St Gall, see Poggio's 1416 letter to Guarino Veronese (Phyllis W. G. Gordon, *Two Renaissance Book Hunters: the Letters of Poggius Bracciolini to Nicolaus de Niccolis* [P. W. G. Gordon] (New York and London, 1974), Appendix, Letter III, pp. 193–6), and the letter of one of Poggio's companions, Cencio da Rusticci, to his teacher Francesco da Fiano (P. W. G. Gordon, Appendix, Letter I, pp. 186–90).

3 See Poggio's letter to Francisco Barbaro (P. W. G. Gordon, Appendix, Letter VIII, p. 213. Cf. A. C. Clark, 'The literary discoveries of Poggio', *Classical Review* 13 (1899) 119–30; Remigio Sabbadini (*Le scoperte dei codici latini e greci ne' secoli XIV e XV*, (Florence, 1905 and 1914; repr. 1967), vol. 1, p. 192) argues for Fulda as the most likely place.

4 See the following letters in P. W. G. Gordon: XXXI (p. 89), XXXIV (p. 92), XLVII (p. 110), LXXIX (p. 154), LXXXII (p. 160).

5 See P. W. G. Gordon, Letter XLIX (p. 114).

6 For an account of the Italian manuscripts of the *De rerum natura*, see M. D. Reeve, 'The Italian tradition of Lucretius', *Italia Mediaevale e Umanistica* 23 (1980) 27–48.

7 P. W. G. Gordon, Letter XXXV (p. 92).

8 P. W. G. Gordon, Appendix, Letter VII (pp. 207–8).

9 For a general account of the work, see B. L. Ullman, *The Humanism of Coluccio Salutati* (Padova, 1963), pp. 21–6.

10 'Diximus ergo poetas in Orpheo delectabilia sequentes Epycurios figurasse. Nam qui non solummodo disputant sed arbitrantur,

241

docent, et tenent voluptatem esse summum bonum delectabilia sine dubio prosequuntur' (IV. 6. 2).

11 IV. 7. 3.

12 IV. 7. 10.

13 IV. 7. 32.

14 Manuscript copies of the *De felicitate* are housed in Padua (Biblioteca del Seminario, Codex 196, and Biblioteca Museo Civico, Fondo B. P. Codex 2042); copies of the only printed edition are housed in Biblioteca Museo Civico (Padua), 1, 3710 and Biblioteca San Mario (Venice), 11. Lat. 13, cod. 41. For an examination of the *De felicitate* in relation to Bartolomeo Platina's *De falso et vero bono* and Bartolomeo Fazio's *De vitae felicitate*, see Umberto Caregaro-Negrin, 'Il "De felicitate" di Francesco Zabarella e due trattati sul bene e la felicita del secolo XV', *Classici e neo-Latini* 2 (1906) 281–93. See also Thomas Edward Morrissey, *Franciscus De Zabarellis (1360–1417) and the Conciliarist Traditions*, Ph.D. Diss. (Cornell, 1973), p. 19, n. 3.

15 Cf. Riccardo Fabbini in *Poggio Bracciolini 1380–1980*, Instituto Nationale di Studi sul Rinascimento, Studi e Testi VII (Firenze, 1982), p. 27, n. 62.

16 On the composition of the *De voluptate (De vero bono)*, see M. de Panizza, 'Le tre redazzioni del "De voluptate" del Valla', *Giornale Storico della Litteratura Italiana* 121 (1943) 1–22; 'Le tre versioni del "De vero bono" del Valla', *Rinascimento* 6 (1955) 349–64. The treatise (Version II, 1433), has been edited as 'De vero falsoque bono' by M. de Panizza Lorch (Bari, 1970) and translated into English most recently by A. Kent Hieath (*Lorenzo Valla on Pleasure*, New York, 1977). All references will be to Lorch's text as printed in Hieath/Lorch.

17 See the following: G. Mancini, *Vita di Lorenzo Valla* (Florence, 1891), pp. 61-2; F. Gabotto, 'L'Epicureismo di Lorenzo Valla', *Rivista di filosofia scientifica* 8 (1889) 655-72; B. J. H. M. Timmermans, 'Valla et Erasme défenseurs d'Epicure', *Neophilologus* 23 (1938) 414–19; Don Cameron Allen, 'The rehabilitation of Epicurus and his theory of pleasure in the early Renaissance', *North Carolina University Studies in Philology* 41 (1944) 6–7; Charles Trinkaus, *In Our Image and Likeness* (Chicago, 1970), vol. 1, pp. 103–70; F. Gaeta, *Lorenzo Valla: filologia e storia nell'umanesimo italiano* (Naples, 1955), pp. 35–51; G. Radetti, 'La religione di Lorenzo Valla', *Mediaevo e Rinascimento, Studi in Onore di Bruno Nardi* (Florence, 1955), vol. 2, pp. 595–620, and commentary in his 'L'Epicureismo nel pensiero umanistico del quattrocento', *Grande Antologia Filosofica*, 6 (1964) 854–61; M. de Panizza Lorch, 'Voluptas, molle quoddam et non invidiosum nomen: Lorenzo Valla's defence of *voluptas* in the preface to his *De voluptate*', in *Renaissance Essays in Honour of Paul Oskar Kristeller*, ed. Edward P. Mahoney (New York, 1976), pp. 214–28; Giovanni di Napoli, *Lorenzo Valla: filosofia e religione nell'umanesimo Italiano* (Rome, 1971), ch. V 'Etica e Christianesimo', pp. 177ff.; J. E. Seigel, *Rhetoric and Philosophy in Renaissance Humanism* (Princeton, 1968) ch. V, 'Lorenzo Valla and the subordination of philosophy to rhetoric', pp. 137ff.

18.

> Et sicut horum quos modo nominavi alter [sc. David] gladio hostis arrepto in illius necem usus est, alter [sc. Jonathan] adversarios ferrum inter se stringere compulit, ita nos bene speremus putemusque fore ut allophilos, id est philosophos, partim suo mucrone iugulemus, partim in domesticum bellum et mutuam perniciem concitemus; hec omnia fide nostra, si qua nobis fides adest, efficiente et Dei verbo.
>
> (Preface [6]).

19.

> Tum Laurentius: 'Preclare, inquit, promittis, Vegi, et non modo attentiorem nos exigis sed ad quendam etiam aurorem. Nam ita me dii ament ut tacitus in te meus inclinat animus et opto (pace Catonis dixerim) ut istud probes quod promisisti, rem profecto mihi iocunditati futurum, quod item ceteris spero contingere.'
>
> (I. XVI. 4)

20 For a useful study of this aspect of humanist dialogue, see D. Marsh, *The Quattrocento Dialogue: Classical Tradition and Humanist Innovation* (Cambridge, Mass., 1980).

21 Cf. Marsh, *op. cit.*, p. 74ff.

22 Cf.

> Caput autem ad beatitudinem optinendam est procul dubio honestas, Christiana inquam honestas non philosophorum. Nec inficias eo multa apud illos esse fructuosa ac salutifera, sed hec ipsa tum demum valuerunt et fructum afferre ceperunt post Christus, vivorum pariter et mortuorum salus, a patre missus hanc mundi aream spinis obsitam fruticibusque purgarit aptamque ad ferendos fructus reddidit.
>
> (III. XI. 1)

23 Cf. Trinkaus, op. cit., p. 149:

> The Stoic, the Aristotelian, the Platonist all sought in differing ways to regulate this natural condition of human existence with rules of reason variously justified philosophically, but unless these rules contained gratification of some kind of human pleasure – sensual, emotional, psychological, intellectual – they had no chance of acceptance since all of them demanded self-denial in place of some other act of self-gratification.

My own treatment of the *De voluptate* owes much to Trinkaus's much fuller examination.

24

> Nam ea [voluptas] duplex est: altera nunc in terris, altera postea in celis . . . . Verum nostra hec incertior et fallacior, illa vero explorata et stabilis. Neque vero deest in hac vita probabilis quedam voluptas et ea maxima que venit ex spe future felicitatis, cum mens sibi conscia recti et animus considerandis divinis assiduus quasi candidatum se quendam putat et promissos honores sibi depingit et quodammodo presentes facit.
>
> (III. X. 1–2)

> 'Ille [Deus] enim est fons boni, sed quia hoc bonum gaudii multiplex est, dicamus etiam fons bonorum. Ipsum igitur a quo tanta bona accepimus si amaverimus, nimirum omnem virtutem atque ipsam germanam honestatem adepti sumus' (III. XIII. 7).

25 *De morali disciplina libri quinque* (Venice: G. Scottum, 1552), pp. 1–2.
26 Voluptatem duplicem esse scimus: alteram animi, alteram corporis, Cyrenai-
cus Aristippus voluptate corporis summum bonum constare existimavit, qua
ipsa in re utramque voluptatem secutus est Epicurus, qui quamvis improbe-
tur a multis, video tamen ab illo eam voluptatem maxime omnium laudari
quae sit animi, quae sapientiam virtutemque consequatur.

Epistolae familiares (Venice, 1502), VIII. 53.

We may note that Gassendi will quote this testimony in his *De vita et
moribus Epicuri* (Lyon 1647), p. 191.

27 In *Dante con l'expositioni di Cristoforo Landino, e d'Alessandro Vellutello*
(Venice, 1578), p. 61.
28 'Clamat ipse Epicurus: non posse cum voluptate vivi, nisi iuste,
temperate, prudenterque vivatur, neque iuste, temperate, prudenter,
nisi cum voluptate' (*Isagogicon moralis disciplinae*, in *Leonardo Bruni
Aretino: humanistisch-philosophische Schriften*, ed. H. Baron (Leipzig and
Berlin, 1928), p. 28).
29 In Baron, op. cit., p. 25.
30 From *Canzone morale*, in Baron, op. cit., p. 151.
31 Cf. V. Rossi, in *Il quattrocento*, ed. A. Vallone (Milan, 1956), pp. 44ff.
32 Codex Ambrosianus B 124 sup., f. 108ᵛ.
33 Cf. Mario E. Cosenza, *Biographical and Bibliographical Dictionary of the
Italian Humanists*, 2nd rev. edn (Boston, 1962), vol. 2, pp. 1128–9;
G. Santini, 'Cosma Raimondi umanista ed epicureo', *Studi Storici* 8
(1899) 153–6; G. Radetti, 'L'Epicureismo nel pensiero umanistico del
quattrocento', pp. 846–7; R. Sabbadini, *Storia e critica di testi latini*
(Catania, 1914), pp. 113–21; S. F. Di Zenzo, *Un Umanista Epicureo
del sec. xv e il ritrovamento del suo epistolario* (Napoli, 1979).
34 The tract (*Defensio Epicuri contra Stoicos, Achademicos, et Peripateticos*) was
discovered in a manuscript owned by the bookseller Giuseppe Martini
by Guido Santini, and published as an Appendix to Santini's study
'Cosma Raimondi umanista ed epicureo' (*Studi Storici* 8 (1899) 159–68)
with the title 'Cosmae Raimondi cremonensis ad Ambrosium
Tignosium quod recte Epicurus summum bonum in voluptate
constituerit maleque de ea re Achademici, Stoici, Peripathetique
senserint'. The title 'Defensio Epicuri . . .' is preserved in Ashburnum
ms. 267 (Laurentian Library, Florence), identified by Eugenio Garin
(*Rinascimento* II (1951) 100–7). An Italian translation has been
published by E. Garin in *Filosofici italiani del quattrocento* (Florence,
1942), pp. 113–49, and the Latin text (Ashburnum ms. 267) in *La
cultura filosofica del Rinascimento italiano* (Florence, 1961), pp. 87–92.
References below will be to Garin's Latin text [Garin].
35 Ego vero nec Marcum illum quidem Regulum, quem suis omnibus libris
tantopere extollunt et praedicant, cum cruciaretur, nec si qui praestantissima
virtute, fide, innocentia in tauro uratur Phalaridis, aut patria exulet, vel
acerbiore fortuna aliqua indignissime vexetur, non modo non beatos
homines, sed miserrimos etiam habendos puto; eoque miseriores quod, cum
tanta tamque excellens eorum virtus exitum foeliciorem fortunatioremque
emerita esset, in has tantas calamitates inciderunt.

(Garin, 89)

36. Ut igitur eum irrideam, qui in sede regali sedens regem se appellet, nullis comitibus nullisque servis, aut eum venustum principem non existimen, qui servos incomptos inornatosque habeat, sic hi irridendi qui in constituenda hominis foelicitate corpus ab animo seiungunt, et cuius corpus crucietur lacereturque beatum tamen esse contendunt.

(Garin, 89)

37 Garin, 90.

38 'Postremo virtus, quae voluptatis effectrix est et gubernatrix, nosque admonet atque continet ut quando quasque oporteat prosequamur limitibus item aliis omnibus servatis, quibus circumscripta ipsa est virtus, cur expetitur, nisi ut fugiendis prosequendisque quas deceat voluptatibus iocundissime vivatur?' (Garin, 91).

39 Etenim, si quis est qui existimet, quod voluptatem supremum esse bonorum omnium dixerit, ita sensisse illum ut in commessationibus, potationibus, alea, ludisque et femineis amplexibus quotidie versaremur, ne valde quidem commendandus esset iste gloriosus Epicurus, et praeclara eius doctrina magnopere requirenda, si gulosos, si ebrios, ganeones histrionesque ac libidinosos nos esse voluisset. Sed vir sapientissimus hoc non dicit nec postulat, tantumque abest ut sine virtute esse nos velit, ut etiam servandis prosequendisque illius institutis maxime virtus sit necessaria, quae et sensus omnes de quibus supra disputatum est coerceat et his nisi cum opus sit uti nos non sinat.

(Garin, 91–2)

40 The letter (Laurentian, plut. 76. 55, fol. 28–46) was published by Ludwig Stein, 'Handschriftenfunde zur Philosophie der Renaissance. I. Die erst "Geschichte der antiken Philosophie in der Neuzeit"', *Archiv für Geschichte der Philosophie* 1 (1888) 534–53.

41 We may note that in this respect Buoninsegni is less perceptive, or less generous, than Ficino himself, who records the Epicurean concept of *voluptas* with precision:

Summum bonum esse voluptatem, non eam quidem que in motu corporis sensuumque suavitate consistit, cum dolori mixta sit eiusmodi voluptas neque ullam habeat stabilitatem, sed eam potius que et corporis optima affectione quam illi indolentiam nominant et animi tranquillitate percipitur. (P. O. Kristeller (ed.), *Supplementum Ficinianum* (Florence, 1937), vol. 2, pp. 9ff.)

42 'Eaque ipsa nondum mortua est, atque haud scio an serpat in dies latius', Buoninsegni, *Epistola* . . . (Stein, op. cit., p. 547); 'in hanc sententiam agminitim pedibus eunt docti pariter et indocti', Filippo Beroaldi, *De foelicitate*, in *Opuscula* (Basel, 1509), f.xxc^v.

43 The text of the dispatch is printed in L. Pastor, *Storia dei Papi* (Rome, 1925), vol. 2, pp.741–8. Agostino Patrici, in a letter which confirms the ambassadors' general account, also refers to the members of the group as 'Epicurei'; see Adolpho Cinquini, 'Anedotti per la storica politica e literaria del quattrocento' in *Miscellanea Ceriani* (Milan, 1910), pp. 457ff.

44 *The Unfortunate Traveller* (1594) in *The Works of Thomas Nashe*, ed. R. B. McKerrow (Oxford, 1904–10), vol. 2, p. 301. Cf. *Summers Last Will and Testament* (*Works*, vol. 3, p. 277):

> Nay, I will iustifie there is no vice,
> Which learning and vilde knowledge brought not in
> Or, in whose praise some learned men have not wrote.
> The arte of murther Machiavel hath pend:
> Whoredome hath Ovid to uphold her throne:
> . . .
> Gluttonie Epicurus doth defend.

45 *The Scholemaster* (1570), p. 28, verso (Folger copy).
46 For the most thorough listing and discussion of editions of Lucretius, see Cosmo A. Gordon, *A Bibliography of Lucretius* (London, 1962; repr. 1985). See also the foundation work of Munro, who owned a copy of all the early editions of the *De rerum natura* except the *editio princeps*, in *T. Lucreti Cari, De rerum natura*, 4th edn, ed. H. A. J. Munro (Cambridge, 1886), vol. 1 pp. 1ff.
47 C. A. Gordon, op. cit., p. 14.
48 ibid., pp. 194ff.
49 'Ut nullus de caetero ludi magister audeat in scholis suis exponere adolescentibus poemata aut quaecumque alia opera lasciva et impia, quale est Lucreti poema, ubi animae mortalitatem totis viribus ostendere nititur' (J. D. Mansi, *Sacrorum Conciliorum Nova . . . Collectio* 35, Florence, 1902, col. 270), cited by W. B. Fleischmann, *Catalogus Translationum et commentatiorum*, vol. 2 (Washington, DC, 1971), p. 352.
50 Cf. C. A. Gordon, op. cit., pp. 294–6.
51 In 1557 Epicurean doctrine does come in for quite extravagant praise from Arnould du Ferron, a Frenchman studying at Padua:

> At magnus ille voluptatis assertor clamat non posse iucunde vivi nisi sapienter, honeste, justeque vivatur. Clamat honestum propter se eligendum, voluptatem et indolentiam virtute, justitia, bono et honesto parari. Clamat ille, philosophiae servas oportet ut tibi contingat vera libertas . . .. Clamat ille sic nobis vivendum integre. (*Arnoldi Ferroni pro Aristotele adversus Bessarionem libellus*, Lyon, 1557, pp. 77–8, cited by Henri Busson, *Le Rationalisme dans la littérature française de la Renaissance* (Paris, 1957), p. 104, n. 4)

However, du Ferron is not speaking as a committed Epicurean (he was an ardent defender of Aristotle), but seeking to prove that dissension among philosophers does not discredit philosophy itself by demonstrating that there is something of value in the teachings of each and every school.

52 Evidence from library catalogues is admittedly inconclusive. Jean le Féron, advocate of the Parlement, owned a copy of Lucretius in 1547, as did Gaston Olivier, *aumônier* of Henry II, in 1552, while the poet Remi Belleau owned two copies, a Lambin edition and the first French printing of 1514. On the other hand, there is no record of a Lucretius in the library of Belleau's fellow poet Pontus de Tyard, in the large library of Antoine du Prat, Prefect of Paris, catalogued in 1557, nor in the catalogues of the Bibliothèque du Roi; see Simon Fraisse, *L'Influence de Lucrèce en France au seizième siècle* (Paris, 1962), pp. 38, 130, 139; Roger Doucet, *Les Bibliothèques parisiennes au 16ᵉ siècle* (Paris, 1956), p. 142; Françoise Lehoux, *Gaston Olivier, aumônier du roi*

Henri II, bibliothèque parisienne et mobilier du XVIe siècle (Paris, 1957); M. Connat, 'Mort et testament de Remi Belleau', *Bibliothèque d'Humanisme et Renaissance*, (1945); S. Baridon, *Inventaire de la bibliothèque de Pontus de Tyard* (Geneva, 1950); H. J. Martin, 'Ce qu'on lisait à Paris au XVIe siècle', *Bibliothèque d'Humanisme et Renaissance* 21 (1) (1959) 222–30.

53 Cf. Preface to 1570 quarto edition (Paris: Jean Bienné).
54 'At Lucretius animorum immortalitatem oppugnat, Deorum providentiam negat, religiones omneis tollit, summum bonum in voluptate ponit. Sed haec Epicuri, non Lucretii culpa est' (Paris: G. Roville, 1563–4, a 2 – e 3, Dionysius Lambinus Karolo Valesio nono regi christianissimo).
55 *P. Gallandii . . . Pro schola Parisiensi contra Novam Academiam P. Rami oratio* (Paris, 1551), p. 44.
56

> Je ne vois pourtant qu'on doive estimer une langue plus excellente que l'autre seulement pour être plus difficile, si on ne voulait dire que Lycophron fut plus excellent qu'Homère pour être plus obscur, et Lucrèce que Virgile pour cette même raison.
>
> *Defense et Illustration de la langue française*, Ch. XI

57.

> mais parce qu'il a escrit ses frenesies, lesquelles il pensoit estre vrayes selon sa secte, et qu'il n'a pas basti son oeuvre sur la vraysemblance et sur le possible, je luy oste du tout le nom de Poete, encore que quelques vers soient non seulement excellents mais divins.
>
> Preface to *La Françiade (Oeuvres Complètes*, ed. Paul Laumonier, Paris, 1914–60, vol. 16, p. 338)

58 For a detailed study of these and other Lucretian passages in the poetry of Ronsard, Du Bellay, Étienne Jodelle, Jean-Antoine de Baïf, and Amadis Jamyn, see Fraisse, op. cit., pp. 75–101. In general, see also E. Belowski, *Lukrez in der französischen Literatur der Rennaissance* (Berlin, 1934), and G. R. Hocke, *Lukrez in Frankreich von der Renaissance bis zur Reformation* (Cologne, 1935). Du Bellay's 1558 translation of the 'Invocation to Venus' is printed by C. A. Gordon op. cit., pp. 153–4.
59 See Fraisse, op. cit., pp. 127–46, and Albert-Marie Schmidt, *La Poésie scientifique en France au seizième siècle* (Paris, 1938). We may note that the scientific poets were not alone in using Lucretius as a source of information on natural phenomena. In his *Commentarii in quatuor libros Aristotelis meteorologicorum* of 1556 Francesco Vicomercato, Professor of Philosophy at the Collège de France, not only makes extensive use of the *De rerum natura* in matters of detail, but also applauds Lucretius for his rationalist approach to the secrets of nature; cf. Busson, op. cit., pp. 209–10.
60 Cf. Pontus de Tyard: 'En quel labyrinthe d'opinion entre-t-il [Epicurus], resvant ses atomes, son Vuide ou Rien, sa monstreuse infinité? . . . Les Epicurées, bien qu'ils ayent confessé la divinité, l'ont descrit tant impiement qu'ils sont indignes d'entrer en rang de l'autre compagnie' (*The Universe of Pontus de Tyard*, ed. J. C. Lapp (Ithaca, 1950) pp. 56 and 169), cited by Fraisse, op. cit., p. 31; and Ronsard:

> Vous qui sans foi errés á l'aventure,
> Vous qui tenés la secte d'Epicure,
> Amandés vous, pour Dieu ne croyés pas
> Que l'ame meure avecques le trespas.

in *Le Bocage* (1554), *Oeuvres Complètes*, ed. P. Laumonier, VI. 40 and 'Crains Dieu sur toute chose, et le fard d'Epicure,/Ne te face jamais errer à l'aventure' in *Les Oeuvres, Poemes*, Bk. V, ed. Laumonier, X. 368.

61 *Les Oeuvres de Guillaume de Salluste, Sieur du Bartas* (Paris, 1611), p. 149 A, cited by Fraisse, op. cit., p. 158.

62 Cf. C.-A. Fusil, 'La Renaissance de Lucrèce en France au XVIe siècle', *Revue du Seizième Siècle* 15 (1928) 147–9. We may note in this regard that in his *Adages*, whose publication commenced in 1500, Erasmus includes not a single Lucretian citation.

63 Cf. Busson, op. cit., pp. 119–20.

64 'Baptistum Egnatium quem *Officia* Ciceronis et Lucretium interpretantem Venetiis iuvenis audivi', *Commentarium linguae latinae*, I, p. 1156. On the intellectual atmosphere at Padua during the first part of the sixteenth century, see J. Roger Charbonnel, *La Pensée italienne au XVIe siècle et le courant libertin* (Paris, 1919; repr. Geneva, 1969), pp. 220ff.

65 C.-A. Fusil, 'Rabelais et Lucrèce', *Revue du Seizième Siècle* 12 (1925) 159.

66 Cf. Abel Lefranc, 'La Pensée secrète de Rabelais', *La Revue de France*, 2 pt 3 (1922) 326–58.

67 Cf. Pierre Villey, *Les Sources et l'évolution des éssais de Montaigne*, 2nd edn (Paris, 1933), pp. 187–90. Examination of the text of the citations confirms that Montaigne used the 1563 Lambin edition.

68 We may note that Montaigne's relative lack of interest in the technical portions of the *De rerum natura* accords with his stated aversion to science in general; see *Essais* I. 26 (p. 146) in *Les Essais de Michel de Montaigne*, ed. Pierre Villey, re-edited by V.-L. Saulnier, (Paris, 1965; 3rd edn 1978). All references to the *Essais* will be in this form: volume (I), chapter (26), page (p. 146).

69 *Essais* II, 10, pp. 410–11; cf. III, 5, pp. 872–3.

70 II, 12, p. 545.

71 II, 12, p. 587.

72 II, 12, p. 592.

73 II, 12, pp. 549–50.

74 II, 12, p. 554:

> c'estoit vrayment bien raison que nous fussions tenus à Dieu seul, et au benefice de sa grace, de la verité d'une si noble créance, puis que de sa seule liberalité nous recevons le fruit de l'immortalité, lequel consiste en la jouyssance de la beatitude eternelle.

75 For a useful study of Montaigne's Pyrrhonism, and particularly the influence in this context of the newly published Latin edition of Sextus Empiricus' *Pyrrhoniarum hypotyposes*, see Richard H. Popkin, *The History of Scepticism from Erasmus to Descartes* (Assen, 1964), pp. 44–66.

76 Cf. II, 12, p. 524 (on the plurality of worlds) II, 12, p. 521 (on the enormities of superstition), and II, 12, p. 555 (against the transmigration of souls).

77 II, 12, p. 563: 'posteriora res illa reperta/Perdit, et immutat sensus ad pristina quaeque' (*De rerum natura* V. 1413–14).

78 II, 12, p. 502: 'Nil sciri quisquis putat, id quoque nescit/An sciri possit quo se nil scire fatetur' (*De rerum natura* IV. 468–9).

79 For a penetrating analysis of Lucretian citations in the *Apologie*, see P. Hendrick, 'Lucretius in the *Apologie de Raimond Sebond*', *Bibliothèque d'Humanisme et Renaissance* 38 (1976) 457–66; see also C.-A. Fusil, 'Montaigne et Lucrèce', *Revue du Seizième Siècle* 13 (1926) 265–81; G. Ferreyrolles, 'Les citations de Lucrèce dans *L'Apologie* de Raymond Sebond', *Bulletin de la Société des Amis de Montaigne*, 5th ser. (1976) 49–63; W. G. Moore, 'Lucretius and Montaigne', *Yale French Studies* 38 (1967) 109–14.

80 *De rerum natura* I. 926–30:

> avia Pieridum peragro loca nullius ante
> trita solo. iuvat integros accedere fontis
> atque haurire, iuvatque novos decerpere flores
> insignemque meo capiti petere inde coronam
> unde prius nulli velarint tempora musae.

81 See P. Peterson, *Geschichte der Aristotelischen Philosophie im protestantischen Deutschland* (Leipzig, 1922).

82 'Est igitur explodenda opinio Epicuri, praesertim a Christianis, cum Christus tam multa de cruce concionetur, et tamen scimus interim bona corporis suo loco recte expeti, modo ut praeferatur virtus', *Opera*, ed. C. G. Bretschneider and H. Bindsell (Halle, 1850), vol. XVI, col. 37.

83

> Epicurei vident ista, nec assentiuntur esse transitum a turbulento genere vitae ad quietem, ideo iactant Epicureas istas voces: Post mortem nulla voluptas. Pereat, qui crastina curat. Summum nec metuas diem, nec optes. Ita confortant se ad contemptum mortis, et tollunt simpliciter timorem, id est, spem immortalitatis.
> Martin Luther, *Werke*, 58 vols (Weimar: H. Böhlau; Graz: Akademische Druck- u. Verlagsanstalt, 1964–), 43, p. 373, ll. 35–39

Cf. 43, p. 374, ll. 9–11; 44, p. 717, ll. 30–1; 44, p. 385, ll. 25–6.

84 'Illi [Epicurei] enim moti infinita rerum inaequalitate et confusione in hac vita, qua vident improbos foeliciores esse bonis et piis, eo delabuntur: ut negent hanc custodiam et ministerium angelorum: quin ipsam Dei providentiam', 44, p. 66, ll. 19–21; cf. 43, p. 567, ll. 21–3.

85 Cf. 44, p. 549, ll. 20–2; 19, p. 206, ll. 1–2.

86 54, p. 226, ll. 26–7. Cf. 'Papa dat concilium in Germania':

> *Der Papst auf einer Sau reitend*
> Sau du must dich lassen reiten:
> Und wol spoern zu beiden Seiten.
> Du Wilt han ein Concilium
> Ja dafür hab dir mein merdrum.

in *Ubbildung des Bapsttums* (1545) (54, pp. 367–8). The woodcut illustration is included at the end of vol. 54.

87 'Necesse est louanienses esse crassissimos porcos Epicuri et prorsus
Atheos, qui sine timore tanta impudentia mentiuntur et blasphemant in
conspectu Dei et hominum', *Contra XXXII articulos Lovanensium
theologistarum* (54, p. 428, ll. 23–5).

88 'Epicurus sentit hominem tantum procreatum ad edendum et
bibendum. Hoc autem est hominem non separare ab aliis bestiis, quae
etiam suas voluptates habent et sequuntur', 42, p. 42, ll. 74–7;
'Epicuraei comessantur, ludunt, saltant', 43, p. 180, l. 39; 'hominum
carnalium, qui delectantur carnalibus voluptatibus, et eis indulgent,
sicut Epicurei', 42, p. 372, ll. 25–7; cf. 43, p. 334, l. 37; 20, p. 704,
ll. 26–7.

89 'So ist es denn uns mit Deutsch land und wird *Fuit* heissen', 51, p. 236,
l. 20.

90 'Insurgit enim nunc saeculum pestilentissimum, et multiplicantur
Epicurei, quod est argumentum certissimum confusionis omnium rerum
et appropinquantis iudicii', 43, p. 363, ll. 16–8; cf. 51, p. 236, ll. 20–6;
letter to Wenceslas Linc in *Briefwechsel*, 10, p. 335.

91 'inhalas mihi grandem Epicuri crapulam', 18, p. 609, ll. 21–2.

92 'significas te in corde Lucianum aut alium quendam de grege Epicuri
porcum alere', 18, p. 605, ll. 28–9.

93 'quasi cum Epicuro fabulas esse putes verbum Dei et futuram vitam', 18,
p. 626, l. 2.

94 *Desiderii Erasmi opera omnia*, ed. Joannes Clericus (Jean Leclerc), Leiden,
1703–6 (rep. Olms: Hildesheim, 1962), X, 1260 C; 1260 E; 1260 F; 1261
A; 1266 B; 1273 F; 1295 E; 1299 A; 1309 A; 1334 E–F; 1336 B. This
edition is hereafter referred to as LB (*Lugduni Batavorum*/Leiden).

95 *Erasmi epistolae*, ed. P. S. Allen, H. M. Allen and H. W. Garrod, 12 vols
(Oxford, 1906–58), VI, p. 309 (ep. 1690: Faber); VI, p. 269 (ep. 1670:
John Elector of Saxony); VI, p. 306 (ep. 1688: Luther).

96 *Briefwechsel*, 5, p. 28 (ep. 1388), ll. 11–12.

97 *Tischreden*, 1, no. 280 (1530), p. 398, ll. 11–12; no. 1193 (1530), p. 592,
ll. 4–5; no. 352 (1532), p. 146, ll. 7–8; no. 432 (1532), p. 186, l. 34,
p. 187, l. 4; no. 466 (1533), p. 202, l. 27.

98 Cf. *Enchiridion militis Christiani*, LB, V, 42 C; *Antibarbari*, LB, X, 1699
C–D; 1720 E; 1727 B. On Erasmus' elaboration of the detached
'Epicureanism' of the monastic life in chapter XI of *De contemptu mundi*
(LB, V, 1257 A – 1259 A), see R. Bultot, 'Erasme, Epicure et le
"Contemptu mundi" ', in *Scrinium Erasmianum* II, ed. J. Coppens
(Leiden, 1969), pp. 205–38.

99 In placing the 'Epicureus' in the context of the ongoing debate between
Erasmus and Luther, I follow Marjorie O'Rourke Boyle (*Christening
Pagan Mysteries: Erasmus in Pursuit of Wisdom* (Toronto, 1981), pp. 63–95),
to whose analysis of the whole episode I am much indebted.

100 'Imo clamitant omnes hanc esse vocem pecudis, non hominis', LB, I,
882 D.

101 'amor impudicus, libido illicita, comesatio ac temulentia . . . febris,
capitis dolor, alvi tormina, ingenii stupor, famae macula, memoriae

detrimentum, vomitus, et ruina stomachi, tremor corporis', 884 F – 885 A.
102 'nulli magis sunt Epicurei quam christiani pie viventes', 882 D.
103 We should note that the publication of the 'Epicureus' was to have its own sequel. In a letter to Nicolas von Amsdorf (*Briefwechsel*, VII, p. 32 (ep. 2093)), Luther attacked Erasmus on a number of theological points, again associating certain of Erasmus' doctrinal positions with the philosophy of Epicurus, and Erasmus replied with his *Purgatio adversus calumniossissimam epistolam Martini Lutheri* of 1534 (LB, X, 1537–58). Yet, even this was not the end. In 1538, two years after Erasmus's death, Luther composed for him a suitably 'Epicurean' epitaph (*Tischreden*, 4, no. 3963, p. 37, ll. 22–3':

> vixit et mortuus est ut Epicurus,
> sine minestero et consolatione.
> Ist gefaren in bus correptam.

CHAPTER 7   FRENCH REVIVAL

1 *Petri Gassendi opera omnia*, 6 vols (Lyon: Anison/Devenet, 1658; reprinted Stuttgart, 1964), VI. 341 A. All references to the text of Gassendi will be to this edition, cited by volume, page, and (where appropriate) column.
2 Much of the material for this chapter will be derived from my *Pierre Gassendi 1592–1655: an Intellectual Biography* (Nieuwkoop, 1981) and the Introduction in my *Pierre Gassendi's Institutio Logica* (Assen, 1981). A listing of books and articles relating to Gassendi will be found in the bibliography to the former (pp. 303–16), to which should be added R. Tack, *Untersuchungen zum Philosophie- und Wissenschaftsbegriff bei Pierre Gassendi (1592–1655)* (Meisenheim am Glan, 1974); W. Detel, *'Scientia rerum natura occultarum', Methodologische Studien zur Physik Pierre Gassendis* (Berlin, 1978); B. Brundell, *Pierre Gassendi: From Aristotelianism to a New Natural Philosophy* (Dordrecht, 1987); M. Messeri, *Causa e spiegazione: la fisica di Pierre Gassendi* (Milan, 1985); Lynn S. Joy, *Gassendi the Atomist: Advocate of History in an Age of Science* (Cambridge, 1988).
3 III. 106 A: 'Quid ad veram enim Philosophiam, germanumque studium veritatis farrago illa immensa disputationum inutilium?'
4 III. 106 A: 'At vero tamen sic congredi, ut disputationes fiant publica quaedam spectacula, ut populus spectator accedat . . . haeccine potest vera veritatis inquisitio?'
5 III. 108 A: 'Hinc ipsimet ubi ad hanc veram rerum naturam ventum est, caligant prorsus, et obstupescunt.'
6 III. 111 A: 'malle se errare cum Aristotele, quam bene sentire cum aliis'.
7 III. 112 A: 'Seu Scotistas enim, seu Thomistas claviger Aristoteles detinet semper sub ferula: et, ut aves cavea inclusas, saltitare quidem per virgulas patitur: at libero tamen caelo explicare alas non concedit.'

8 Cf. III. 99 and VI. 1–2 (letter to du Faur).

9 III. 99: 'illud tamen ingenue fateor, nihil umquam mihi perinde arrisisse ex omnibus, ac laudatam illam Academicorum, Pyrrhoneorumque, ἀκαταληψίαν.

10 III. 100: 'Hinc etsi bene noverim multorum in me invidiam concitam iri'; cf. ibid. 'Isti enim ratum habentes quicquid Aristoteles in quacumque materia sancivit, illud mordicus arreptum tuentur, piaculoque egere putant, si tueantur oppositum, et quaestionem propositam in utramque edisserant partem.'

11 VI. 35 B: 'Parum abfuit quid prodromus ille, quod solita approbatione non prodiisset praemunitus, excitaret Tragoediam.'

12 The note is added at the end of Book II of the *Exercitationes* in the 1658 edition of the *Opera omnia* (III. 210).

13 The degree to which the Aristotelians felt threatened by criticism may be gauged from the affair of Jean Bitaud, Etienne de Clave, and Antoine Villaud, who were condemned in the early part of 1624 for defending theses contrary to the teachings of Aristotle. It is difficult to determine whether this incident was a factor in Gassendi's decision to publish only Book I of the *Exercitationes* (he would have been made aware of the affair upon his arrival in Paris from Grenoble later in the year), but the episode does indicate that the Aristotelians were in a repressive mood and were not prepared to allow Aristotle to go undefended.

14 VI. 11 B: 'Scilicet ego tanto viro paravi Apologiam, destinato ipsius doctrinae volumine integro, quod Paradoxicarum Exercitationum adversus Aristoteleos volumini, cuius ideam, primumque librum feci iam iuris publici, attexatur.'

15 VI. 15 B (8 March 1629).

16 *Correspondence de Mersenne*, ed. P. Tannery and Cornelis de Waard, 10 vols to date (Paris, 1933–), II, 465:

> Quocirca, ubi D. Gassendum salutavero, finem scribendi faciam. Multa de ipsius Epicuro, imo plura quam ipse apud me pollicitus est, promittis; tu enim totam illam philosophiam, ille vero dumtaxat partem quam 'practicam' vocant, mihi pollicebatur, quod, si tu verum dicis, doleo illum sua modestia me fefellisse meque illum non diutius invitum in meis aedibus retinuisse.

17 For a full account of the discussions between Gassendi and Beeckmann, see B. Rochot, *Les Travaux de Gassendi sur Epicure et sur l'atomisme 1619–1658* (Paris, 1944), pp. 34–40.

18 See *Lettres de Peiresc*, ed. Ph. Tamizey de Larroque, in *Collections de documents inédits sur l'histoire de France*, 2ᵉ ser. (Paris, 1893), II, 129 (12 July 1629); II, 131 and 133 (21 July 1629).

19 *Lettres de Peiresc*, IV, no. XI, p. 203.

20 See the following: VI. 24 B – 25 A: 'spero proxima occasione mittere ad te Elenchum praecipuorum Capitum Philosophiae Epicuri' (letter to Vossius); VI. 25 A – 25 B: 'Tu vero, qui nullum insignem Authorem intactum relinquis, iuvare potes, vel nullus alius' (letter to Heinsius); VI. 25 B – 26 A: 'Siquidem Viri Philosophiam habebo

prae manibus brevi' (letter to Golius); VI. 26 A: 'Habebo brevi prae manibus meum Epicurum' (letter to Beeckmann).

21 *Lettres de Peiresc*, IV, 233 (6 November 1629).

22 VI. 27 A – 27 B (16 December 1629).

23 VI. 31 B – 33 B; cf. *Lettres de Peiresc*, IV, 218 (Gassendi to Peiresc, 11 September 1629).

24 VI. 396 A – 399 B (30 October 1630).

25 *Lettres de Peiresc*, IV, 249–52.

26 VI. 44 B – 45 A (20 August 1631).

27 VI. 46 A – B (2 March 1632).

28 VI. 48 A – 50 B.

29 *Lettres familières à François Luillier pendant l'hiver 1632–1633*, ed. Bernard Rochot (Paris, 1944), no. XVI, p. 79 (16 February 1633): 'j'ai commencé à donner quelques traits de plume de ce qui reste de la Physique'.

30 Cf. *Correspondence de Mersenne*, III, no. 240 (Peiresc to Gassendi, 23 February 1633).

31 *Lettres familières à François Luillier*, no. XXI, pp. 100–1 (Gassendi to Luillier, 2 April 1633).

32 *Lettres de Peiresc*, IV, 402 (Gassendi to Peiresc, 28 December 1633).

33 *Lettres de Peiresc* IV, 414–15, 428, and 444.

34 Letter of Peiresc to Schickard, 25 August 1634 (Bibliothèque Inguimbertine, Carpentras, ms. 1774, fol. 140).

35 VI. 92 A (Gassendi to Galileo, 18 November 1636).

36 *Lettres de Peiresc*, IV, no. XLV, pp. 172–3.

37 VI. 111 B – 160 B.

38 VI. 407 B (7 May 1632); VI. 408 A–B (4 July 1632).

39 VI. 54 A–B (2 November 1632). We may note that in 1614 Campanella had written in similar vein to Galileo, warning him that his attachment to atomism gave grounds to his enemies for calling into question the validity of his discoveries in astronomy – see Campanella to Galileo, 8 March 1614, in *Galileo Galilei, opere*, ed. A. Favaro (Florence, 1890–1899), XII, p. 32. Whether or not one accepts the thesis advanced by Redondi that the crucial hidden factor involved in Galileo's condemnation in 1633 was the 'atomism' of *The Assayer* (1623), Redondi's discovery in the Archives of the Vatican Holy Office of an unsigned 'denunciation' of *The Assayer*, on the grounds that Galileo's presentation of a corpuscular theory of sensible qualities posed a serious threat to Christian dogma concerning the Eucharist, is proof enough that atomism did not go unnoticed by guardians of Christian teaching; see Pietro Redondi, *Galileo: Heretic*, trans. Raymond Rosenthal (Princeton, 1987); the text of the document (ms., Archive of the Sacred Congregation for the Doctrine of the Faith, Rome, Series AD EE, fols 292 v, 293 r, and 293 v) is given on pp. 333–40.

40 VI. 155 B (26 September 1642).

41 VI. 157 B (17 October 1642).

42 VI. 158 A (24 October 1642); cf. de Valois's reply, VI. 345 B (4 November 1642).

43 VI. 159 B (14 November 1642).
44 VI. 447 A (Sorbière to Gassendi, 8 June 1642); VI. 447 B (Sorbière to Gassendi, 25 August 1642).
45 VI. 155 B (Gassendi to Sorbière, 26 September 1642).
46 VI. 453 A–B (Sorbière to Gassendi, 9 May 1643).
47 The *De vita et moribus Epicuri* is printed in the *Opera omnia*, vol. V, 167–236.
48 See H. Jones, *Pierre Gassendi: an Intellectual Biography*, pp. 228–42.
49 V. 201 B.
50 *Lettres de Peiresc*, IV, no. XIII (Gassendi to Peiresc, 11 September 1629).
51 VI. 295 A–296 B.
52 See VI. 552 A (Hobbes); 522 B – 523 A (Claude-Bartholemy Morisot); 523 A–B (Joannes Michael Ougevigny); 524 A–B, 530 B – 533 A, 536 A – 537 A (Jean Louis Castagny); 533 A–B (François du Prat); 539 A – 540 A (Marcus Meibomius).
53 V. 1–166.
54 The *Syntagma philosophicum*, an imposing structure filling the first two volumes of the *Opera omnia*, was put together by the editors using revisions which Gassendi himself had completed (Tours. ms. 706), and those portions of the manuscript versions of the *Animadversiones in decimum librum Diogenes Laertii* which he had not had time to rework (Tours. mss. 707, 708). See further René Pintard's invaluable analysis of the Gassendi manuscripts in *Le M. Le Vayer, Gassendi, G. Patin: étude bibliographique* (Paris, 1943), ch. III, pp. 41–4.
55

> Ce à quoy je m'occupe maintenant, c'est traduire le Xe livre de Laërce qui est tout d'Epicure rempli de tant de [fautes] qu'[il n'] est pas presque recognoissable en tous les lieux les plus importants. J'ay devant moy diverses traductions, notes et manuscrits et conferant le tout avec la petite cognoissance que j'ay de la philosophie de cet homme, je tasche d'en faire une traduction à ma mode, et que je puisse quand j'employeray l'authorité de Laërce.
> *Lettres de Peiresc* IV, no. XIII (Gassendi to Peiresc, 11 September 1629)

56

> Ea mihi mens est, ut quoties non modo ad graviora illa capita pervenero, sed etiam quoties quidpiam occurret quod videri possit vel quam minimum fidei sacrae dissentaneum in Epicurum nervos contendam ac eius sententiam quam maximo semper rationis vigore potero convellam.
> V. 171

Cf. VI. 155.
57 Cf. I. 279 B–280 B.
58 I. 5 A.
59 For a useful review of the specific points on which Gassendi compared and contrasted Epicurean and Aristotelian doctrine, see Brundell, op. cit., pp. 54ff.
60 'Atque hic praecipue est, ubi cognitio, scientiaque humana arguitur infirmitatis ac incertudinis: Hic est, ubi praecipua iaciuntur Pyrrhonismi fundamenta, stabiliturque maxime illud *Nihil Sciri*' (III. 102).

61 'Quid superest nisi conludamus sciri non posse cuiusmodi res aliqua sit secundum se, vel suapte natura; sed dumtaxat cuiusmodi his aut illis appareat' (III. 203 A).

62 'Si quidem et nos ex iis sumus quibus veritas in profundo est, at multum lucri existimamus si ex nostris studiis ac laboribus verismilitudinem reportemus' (Carpentras ms. 1832, f. 236ʳ).

63 'Revera enim, si ut antiqui animum applicaremus, eveheremur longe altius; illorumque adiuti subsidiis in giganteam quandam molem excresceremus tandem aliquando' (III. 115 B).

64 'frustra esset adpetitus ingenitus . . . irrita omnia instrumenta, vani libri, vani praeceptores, vani quotcumque vel incumbunt vel incubuerunt hactenus ad cognoscendum intimius, perfectius et uberius res quam a rudibus vulgo cognoscantur' (Carpentras ms. 1832, f. 237ʳ).

65 Cf. Carpentras ms. 1832, f. 236ᵛ – f. 237ʳ:

> Attamen imprimis neque Epicurus neque ullus omnino sapiens profitetur se rerum omnium naturas perspectas habere. Imo neque ullius rei omnes recessus intimos. Sed quam plurimis qualitatibus proprietatibusque explicata contineatur [sc. natura] hinc fieri dicit Epicurus ut qui aliquas alicuius rei proprietates noverit naturam illius novisse dicatur non tam perfecte ille quidem quam alius qui noverit plureis. Sed perfectius tamen quam alius qui vel paucas vel unicam, adeo proinde ut natura intima alicuius rei secundum gradus cognoscatur, sed semper tamen cognoscatur.

66 'Caeterum, ut videamus paucis quid in hac tanta opinionum [diversitate] circa veritatis Criteria dici probabiliter possit: media quaedam via inter Scepticos (quo nomine omneis Criteria tollenteis complector) et Dogmaticos videtur tenenda' (I. 79 B).

67 Cf. François Bernier, *Favilla ridiculi muris, hoc est, dissertatiunculae ridicule defensae a Joan. Baptist. Morino astrologo adversus expositam a Petro Gassendo . . .*, Paris, 1653; *Abregé de la philosophie de Gassendi*, 8 vols; Lyon 1678; Jean François Sarasin, *Discours de morale sur Épicure* (1646), reprinted in 1651 as *Apologie pour Épicure*, and again in 1674 as *Discours de morale* (see *Oeuvres de Jean François Sarasin*, ed. Paul Festugière, Paris, 1926).

CHAPTER 8   EPICURUS BRITANNICUS

1 *Memoirs of John Evelyn*, ed. William Bray (London, 1818), pp. 247–8.

2 See Thomas Franklin Mayo, *Epicurus in England (1650–1725)* (Dallas, 1934), p. xxvi.

3 George Joye, *The exposicion of Daniel the prophete*, xii, p. 222; Thomas Cooper, *An admonition to the people of England*, 118; Henry Smith, *An Arrow against Atheists* (1622 edn), p. 49; Hugh Latimer, *Sermon before Edward VI*, p. 54.

4 Sir John Davies, *Immortality of the Soul* (1876 edn), I, p. 26.

5 *A Theatre for Worldlings. A Theatre wherein be represented as wel the miseries and calamaties that follow the Voluptuous Worldlings, also the greate ioyes and*

pleasures which the faithful do enjoy. An Argument both profitable and delectable . . ., Devised by S. John Vander Noodt, Imprinted at London by Henrie Bynneman, dwelling in Knight rider street, at the signe of the Marmaid, anno 1599, p. 105 (Huntington Library copy 62764).

6 Richard Brathwaite, *The English Gentleman* (1630), p. 88; Sir John Ferne, *The Blazon of Gentrie* (1586), p. 20.

7 Shakespeare, *King Lear* I.iv.265. Cf. *Antony and Cleopatra* II. i.24, 'Tie up the libertine in a field of feasts,/Keep his brain fuming; epicurean cooks/Sharpen with cloyless sauce his appetite.'

8 John Bale, *Choice or Chance, & C* (1606), p. 56. Cf. William Whately, 'Such an Epicure was Pothar . . . to please his tooth and pamper his flesh with delicacies', *Prototypes or the primarie precedent* (1639), p. 165; Thomas Nashe, 'His horses . . . are provendered epicurely', *Nashes Lenten Stuffe* (1599), p. 109.

9 Grant McColley, 'Nicholas Hill and the "Philosophia Epicurea"', *Annals of Science* 4 (1939) 390–405 (pp. 390–1); cf. Charles T. Harrison, 'The ancient atomists and English literature of the seventeenth century', *Harvard Studies in Classical Philology* XLV (1934) 1–79 (p. 4).

10 Robert H. Kargon, *Atomism in England from Hariot to Newton* (Oxford, 1966), chs II–IV.

11 Henry Percy, *Advice to his Son*, ed. G. B. Harrison (London, 1920), p. 70, cited by Kargon, op. cit., p. 14.

12 See 'Thomas Harriot and the first telescopic observations of sunspots', in J. O. North, *The Universal Frame: Historical Essays in Astronomy, Natural Philosophy and Scientific Method* (Ronceverte, 1987).

13 Johann Kepler, *Gesammelte Werke*, ed. Max Caspar, W. Von Dyck, and F. Hammer, 19 vols (Munich, 1938–63), vol. XV, no. 403, pp. 365–8. The relevant portions of the letter are quoted in Kargon, op. cit., pp. 24 and 26.

14 For a summary of Hariot's atomistic world-view based upon an examination of the manuscript evidence (B.M. Add. mss. 6782/6785/6788 and B.M. Birch mss. 4458), see Kargon, op. cit., pp. 24–6.

15 The relevant item in Hariot's will is quoted by John W. Shirley in *Thomas Harriot* (Oxford, 1983), p. 2.

16 For the subsequent history of the Hariot manuscripts, see Shirley, op. cit., pp. 6–33.

17 Cf. Shirley, op. cit., p. 5; Henry Stevens, *Thomas Hariot, the mathematician, the philosopher, and the scholar* (London, 1900), pp. 172 and 174.

18 The relevant passage is quoted in G. B. Harrison, *Willobie His Avisa* (London, 1926), p. 208. For a general study of Raleigh's 'atheism', see George T. Buckley, *Atheism in the English Renaissance* (New York, 1965), pp. 137–52.

19 Cf. Shirley, op. cit., p. 180. Shirley notes (p. 180, n. 11) that by including the *Advertisement* in a list of works which made reference to him Hariot identified himself as the 'coniurer'; see also John W. Shirley and David P. Quinn, 'A contemporary list of Hariot

references', *Renaissance Quarterley* 22 (1) (spring 1969), 9–26; in general, see Ernest A. Strathmann, *Sir Walter Raleigh: a Study in Elizabethan Skepticism* (New York, 1951), pp. 25ff.

20 For the full text of Baines's report, see Shirley, op. cit., pp. 181–3.

21 The documents of the Cerne Abbas proceedings are preserved in B. L. Harleian ms. 6849, fol. 183–190, and are reproduced in Harrison, op. cit., pp. 255–71.

22 Cited in Shirley, op. cit., p. 316.

23 John Aubrey, *Brief Lives*, ed. Andrew Clark, 2 vols (Oxford, 1898), vol. I, p. 286.

24 We should note that much the same kind of thing occurred with respect to Hariot's association with the Earl of Northumberland. At the time that the Earl was arrested in connection with the Gunpowder Plot of 1605, Hariot, at the instigation of James I, was investigated on suspicion of having been involved in casting the King's nativity. His rooms and study at Sion House were searched, and although no material evidence was uncovered he was confined to the Gatehouse of the Tower for an undetermined period.

25 For a detailed examination of the question of Hariot's reputation for unorthodoxy, see Jean Jacquot, 'Thomas Harriot's reputation for impiety', *Notes and Records of the Royal Society of London* 9 (1952) 164–87.

26 Francis Bacon, *Works*, ed. J. Spedding, R. Ellis, and D. Heath, 14 vols (London, 1857–74; repr. Stuttgart–Bad Constatt, 1963), V. 419 (Latin text in III. 15).

27 ibid., V. 466 (Latin text, III. 84).

28 ibid., VI. 559.

29 *Novum organum*, Book I, Aphorism LI (IV. 58).

30 ibid., Book I, Aphorism LXVI (IV. 68).

31 ibid., Aphorisms XIX–XX and LXVI (IV. 50 and 67).

32 *Novum organum*, Book II, Aphorism VIII (IV. 126).

33 ibid., Aphorism VII (IV. 124–6).

34 Mrs Hutchinson's dedicatory letter to the Earl of Anglesey, from which the quotations in this section are taken, is preserved in B.M. Add. mss. 19333 and printed in *Memoirs of the Life of Colonel Hutchinson by his widow Lucy*, ed. C. H. Firth (London, 1885), vol. II, Appendix XV, pp. 399–405. The period when Mrs Hutchinson was working on her version of the *De rerum natura* is not precisely known. In 1658 Sir Aston Cokayn wrote to his friend Alexander Brome, who was toying with the idea of translating Lucretius the following:

> I know a Lady that hath been about
> The same designe, but she must needes give out:
> Your poet strikes too boldly home sometimes,
> In geniall things, t'appear in womens rhimes.
> The task is masculine, and he that can
> Translate *Lucretius*, is an able man . . .
>> 'To my ingenious Friend Mr. Alexander Brome on his Essay to
>> translate Lucretius', *Small Poems of Divers Sorts* (London, 1658),
>> p. 204).

If the 'Lady' to whom he alludes is indeed Mrs Hutchinson, the poem suggests that Mrs Hutchinson was busy with Lucretius during the early 1650s; however, she says in her dedicatory letter that she 'turned it into English in a roome where my children practicd the severall quallities they were taught with their Tutors'. Since she was married in 1638 and bore children soon thereafter, the mid- or late-1640s would seem a more plausible date. Cf. Samuel A. Weiss, 'Dating Mrs. Hutchinson's translation of Lucretius', *Notes and Queries* CC (1955) 109. For quotations from Mrs Hutchinson's English version and a somewhat flattering appraisal of the accuracy and quality of her translation, see H. A. J. Munro, 'Mrs. Lucie Hutchinson's translation of Lucretius', *Journal of Classical and Sacred Philology* 4 (1857–8) 121–39.

35 For a useful review of the scientific career of Charles Cavendish and his relations with the French intellectuals, see Jean Jacquot, 'Sir Charles Cavendish and his learned friends', *Annals of Science* 8 (1952) 13–27.

36 For a more extended treatment of Hobbes, Petty, and Digby, see Kargon, op. cit., pp. 54–60 and 69–72.

37 For Margaret Cavendish's 'atomism', see the first group of poems (pp. 7–46) in *Poems and Fancies* (London, 1653). For the most recent study of Margaret Cavendish, see Sara Heller Mendelson, *The Mental World of Stuart Women* (Brighton, 1987).

38 *Mans Mortalitie or a Treatise wherein 'tis proved, both Theologically and Philosophically, that the whole man (as a rationall creature) is a compound wholly mortall, contrary to that common distinction of Soule and Body: and that the present going of the Soule into Heaven or Hell is a meer Fiction, etc.*, Amsterdam, printed by John Canne AD 1644. For a modern edition, see Harold Fisch (ed.), *Mans Mortalitie* (Liverpool, 1968).

39 Cf. Mayo, op. cit., pp. 28–9; Mayo refers also to two anonymous pamphlets – *The Prerogative of Man: Or, The Immortality of Humane Soules Asserted Against the vain Cavils of a late Worthlesse Pamphlet, Entitled, Mans Mortality* (1645), and *The Immortality of Mans Soule, Proved both by Scripture and Reason, Contrary to the Fancie of R.O.* (1645).

40 For a study of contemporary reaction to Hobbes, see Samuel Mintz, *The Hunting of Leviathan* (Cambridge, 1962); for a check-list of anti-Hobbes literature published between 1650 and 1700, see Appendix, pp. 157–60.

41 *Poems and Fancies* (London, 1653), p. 5.

42 For the most detailed account of Charleton's early life and career, see Lindsay Sharp, 'Walter Charleton's early life 1620–1659, and his relationship to natural philosophy in mid-seventeenth century England', *Annals of Science* 30 (1973) 311–40.

43 On Charleton's interest in Helmontianism, see R. M. Rattansi, 'Paracelsus and the Puritan revolution', *Ambix* 11 (1963) 24–32, and N. R. Gelbert, 'The intellectual development of Walter Charleton', *Ambix* 18 (1971) 149–68.

44 Cf. Sharp, op. cit., pp. 325–6.
45 *An Elegant and Learned Discourse of the Light of Nature*, ed. Robert A. Greene and Hugh MacCallum (Toronto, 1971), p. 150.
46 *The Darkness of Atheism dispelled by the Light of Nature: A Physico-theologicall treatise*, 'Advertisement to the Reader'.
47 ibid., p. 44.
48 ibid., p. 61.
49 The *Physiologia* has been reprinted by Johnson Reprint Co., New York and London, in the series *The Sources of Science* 31 (1966) with an introduction by R. H. Kargon.
50 Kargon, *Atomism*, p. 89.
51 See William E. Simeone, 'A letter from Sir Richard Fanshawe to John Evelyn', *Notes and Queries* CXCVI (1951) 315–16.
52 Jeremy Taylor to John Evelyn, 16 April 1656 in *Diary and Correspondence of John Evelyn*, ed. William Bray, 4 vols (London, 1850–2), III. 72.
53 John Evelyn to Jeremy Taylor, 27 April 1656, ibid., III. 73ff.
54 John Evelyn to Meric Casaubon, ibid., III. 246ff. We should note that Evelyn did receive requests to translate the remaining books of Lucretius' poem, the most touching perhaps from his old schoolmaster, the Rev. Edward Snutt, who assured his former pupil that 'the five younger brethren will grieve if you not clothe them in as rich garments as their elder brother, and the elder will rejoice to see them as richly clothed as himself'.
55 *Sermons on Several Occasions by the most Reverend Dr. John Tillotson, Late Lord Archbishop of Canterbury*, 12 vols (London, 1742–4), viii, 3369; cf. viii, 3527; viii, 3430; viii, 2278; we may compare the following from a perhaps unexpected source:

> But put the case there were such Atomes, out of which all things are made; yet no man that has his sense and reason regular, can believe, they did move by chance, or at least without sense or reason, in the framing of the world, and all natural bodies, if he do but consider the wonderful order and harmony that is in Nature, and all her parts.
> Lady Margaret, Princess of Newcastle, *Observations upon experimental Philosophy, to which is added the Description of a New Blazing World* (London, 1606), pp. 24–5.

56 Tillotson, *Sermons*, viii, 3321.
57 'A Conclusion defending the Soul's Immortality against the Somatists or Epicureans and other Pseudophilosophers', in *Reasons of the Christian Religion* (London, 1667), p. 498.
58 *Of Credulity and Incredulity*, Part I (London, 1668), pp. 167, 226, and 203.
59 *History of the Royal Society*, 2nd edn (London, 1702), part III, sec. XIV, p. 345.
60 Cf. *The Vanity of Dogmatising* (London, 1661), p. 248:

> It is a vulgar conceit, that *philosophy* holds a confederation with *Atheism* it self; but most *injurious*: for nothing can better antidote us against it; and they may

as well say, that *physitians* are the only *murtherers*. A *Philosophick Atheist*, is as good sense as a *Divine one*.

61 *The Usefulness of Natural Philosophy*, Part I (London, 1663), p. 62.
62 *A Letter to Peter du Moulin* (London, 1689), p. 30. For the text of the letter and a valuable study of the range of attacks launched against the Royal Society, see Michael R. G. Spiller, '*Concerning Natural Experimental Philosophie': Meric Casaubon and the Royal Society*, International Archives of the History of Ideas 90 (The Hague, 1980).
63 *Letter to Sir J. B.* in *The Genuine Remains of . . . Dr. Thomas Barlow* (London, 1693), cited by Spiller, op. cit., pp. 30–1.
64 *The Works of the Honourable Robert Boyle*, ed. Thomas Birch (new edn, 6 vols., London, 1772), iv, pp. 68–9.
65 'Some Specimins of an attempt to make Chymical Experiments useful to illustrate the notions of the Corpuscular Philosophy', Preface, in *Certain Physiological Essays* (London, 1661), *Works*, I, 356. Cf.:

> That you may not mistake what is driven at in many of the experiments and reasonings delivered or proposed in the ensuing notes about particular qualities, I must desire you to take note with me, what it is, that I intend to offer you some proofs of. For if I took upon me to demonstrate, that the qualities of bodies cannot proceed from (what the schools call) substantial forms, or from any other causes but mechanical, it might be reasonably enough expected, that my argument should directly exclude them all. But since, in my explication of qualities, I pretend only, that they may be explicated by mechanical principles, without enquiring, whether they are explicable by any other; that, which I need to prove, is not that mechanical principles are the necessary and only things, whereby qualities may be explained, but that probably they will be found sufficient for their explication.
>
> (*Experiments, Notes, etc . . .*, Advertisement, *Works*, IV, 232)

For more detailed treatments of Boyle's corpuscularianism, see Kargon, *Atomism*, pp. 93–105; Marie Boas, 'The establishment of the mechanical philosophy', *Osiris* 10 (1952) 412–541; Marie Boas Hall, *Robert Boyle on Natural Philosophy* (Bloomington, 1966), pp. 57–80.
66 Bernard Nieuwentijdt, *The Religious Philosopher . . .*, translated from the original [*Het regt gebruik der werelt beschowingen, 1715*] by John Chamberlayne (London, 1719), p. 844. John Ray, the botanist, may be taken as representative of general opinion:

> I attribute the various species of inanimate bodies to the divers figures of the minute particles of which they are made up. And the reason why there is a set and constant number of them in the world, none destroyed nor any new ones produced, I take to be because the sum of the figures of those minute bodies into which matter was at first divided is determinate and fixed. Because those minute parts are indivisible, not absolutely, but by any natural force; so that there neither is nor can be more or fewer of them. For

were they divisible into small and diversely figured parts by fire or any other
natural agent, the species of Nature must be confounded.
(The Wisdom of God Manifested in the Works of Creation (London, 1690), p. 60)
On Newton's relation to atomism, see S. I. Vavilov, 'Newton and
the atomic theory', in *Royal Society Newton Tercentenary Celebrations*
(Cambridge, 1947), pp. 43–55; Henry Guerlac, *Newton et Epicure*
(Paris, 1963); Kargon, *Atomism*, pp. 118–32.

67 Boyle, *Works*, III, 1–2.
68 Ralph Cudworth, *The True Intellectual System of the Universe* (London,
1678), p. 12; see Joel M. Rodney, 'A godly atomist in seventeenth
century England: Ralph Cudworth', *History* 32 (1970) 243–9;
Danton Sailor, 'Moses and atomism', *Journal of the History of Ideas*
XXV (1964) 3–16.
69 'To the unknown DAPHNIS on his Excellent Translation of
Lucretius', sig. (C) r – (C4) r.
70 Theophilus Cibber, *The Lives of the Poets of Great Britain and Ireland*,
5 vols (London, 1753), III, p. 186. The best study of Creech's life and
his translation of the *De rerum natura* is Herman Josef Real,
Untersuchungen zur Lukrez-Übersetzung von Thomas Creech (Bad Homburg,
1970). For excellent studies of Lucretian influences in late
seventeenth-century literature, see Harrison, op. cit., John Henry
Wagenblass, *Lucretius and the Epicurean Tradition in English Poetry*, Ph.D.
Diss. (Harvard University, 1946), Ch. III, pp. 107–87, and W. B.
Fleischmann, *Lucretius and English Literature 1680–1740* (Paris, 1964).
71 Nathan Drake, *Literary Hours or Sketches Critical and Narrative* (London,
1798), p. 11, cited by Real (op. cit., p. 149), who gives a useful
review of the varying opinions of Creech's work (pp. 141–53).
72 For an analysis of Dryden's translation, see Mary Gallagher,
'Dryden's translation of Lucretius', *Huntington Library Quarterly*
XXVIII (1964) 19–29, and Paul Hammond, 'The integrity of
Dryden's Lucretius', *Modern Language Review* 78 (1983) 1–23.

SELECTED BIBLIOGRAPHY

Alfoldi, A. (1948) *The Conversion of Constantine and Pagan Rome*, Oxford.

Allen, D. C. (1944) 'The rehabilitation of Epicurus and his theory of pleasure in the early Renaissance', *North Carolina University Studies in Philology* 41: 6–7.

Bailey, C. (1928) *The Greek Atomists and Epicurus*, Oxford.

Baron, H. (ed.) (1928) *Leonardo Bruni Aretino: humanistisch-philosophische Schriften*, Leipzig and Berlin.

Barrow, R. H. (1967) *Plutarch and His Times*, Bloomington, Ind.

Bayet, J. (1954) 'Lucrèce devant la pensée grecque', *Museum Helveticum* 11: 89–100.

Belowski, E. (1934) *Lukrez in der französischen Literatur der Renaissance*, Berlin.

Beye, C. R. (1963) 'Lucretius and progress', *Classical Journal* 58: 160–9.

Bignone, E. (1920) *Epicuro*, Bari.

——(1936) *L'Aristotele perduto e le formazione filosofica di Epicuro*, Florence.

Boas, M. (1952) 'The establishment of the mechanical philosophy', *Osiris* 10: 412–541.

Bolgar, R. R. (1954) *The Classical Heritage and its Beneficiaries*, Cambridge.

Bollack, J. (1975) *La Pensée du plaisir – Epicure: textes moraux, commentaires*, Paris.

Bollack, J. and Laks, A. (1976) *Études sur l'épicurisme antique*, Lille.

Bompaire, J. (1958) *Lucien Écrivain, imitation et creation* (Bibliothèque des Écoles françaises d'Athènes et de Rome 190), Paris.

Borle, J. P. (1962) 'Progrès ou déclin de l'humanité? La conception de Lucrèce', *Museum Helveticum* 19: 162–76.

Bowersock, G. (1969) *Greek Sophists in the Roman Empire*, Oxford.

Boyancé, P. (1963) *Lucrèce et l'Épicurisme*, Paris.

Boyle, M. O'Rourke (1981) *Christening Pagan Mysteries: Erasmus in Pursuit of Wisdom*, Toronto.

Brehaut, E. (1912) *An Encyclopedist of the Dark Ages: Isidore of Seville*, New York (repr. 1967).

Brundell, B. (1987) *Pierre Gassendi: From Aristotelianism to a New Natural Philosophy*, Dordrecht.

Buckley, G. T. (1965) *Atheism in the English Renaissance*, New York.

Bultot, R. (1969) 'Erasme, Epicure et le "Contemptu mundi"' in J. Coppens (ed.) *Scrinium Erasmianum*, vol. II, Leiden, pp. 205–38.

Bury, J. B. (1920) *The Idea of Progress*, London.

Busson, H. (1957) *Le Rationalisme dans la littérature française de la Renaissance*, Paris.

Caregaro-Negrin, U. (1906) 'Il "De felicitate" di Francesco Zabarella e due trattati sul bene e la felicita del secolo XV', *Classici e neo-Latini* 2: 281–93.

Caster, M. (1937) *Lucien et la pensée religieuse de son temps*, Paris.

——(1938) *Études sur Alexandre ou le faux prophète de Lucien*, Paris.

Castner, C. J. (1988) *Prosopography of Roman Epicureans*, Studien zur klassischen Philologie 34, Frankfurt-am-Main.

Chadwick, H. (ed.) (1953) *Origen: Contra Celsum*, Cambridge.

——(1966) *Early Christian Thought and the Classical Tradition*, Oxford.

Charbonel, J. R. (1919) *La Pensée italienne au XVIᵉ siècle et le courant libertin*, Paris.

Chilton, C. W. (1971) *Diogenes of Oenoanda, the Fragments: a Translation and Commentary*, Oxford.

Cochrane, C. N. (1957) *Christianity and Classical Culture*, New York.

Comparetti, D. (1910) 'La bibliothèque de Philodème', in P. Champion (ed.) *Mélanges Chatelain*, Paris, pp. 120ff.

Cosenza, M. E. (1962) *Biographical and Bibliographical Dictionary of the Italian Humanists*, 2nd rev. edn, Boston.

Courcelle, P. (1948) *Les Lettres grecques en Occident de Macrobe à Cassiodore*, 2nd edn, Paris.

Crawford, S. J. (1933) *Anglo-Saxon Influence on Western Christendom, 600–800*, Oxford.

D'Arms, J. H. (1970) *Romans on the Bay of Naples*, Cambridge, Mass.

De Lacy, P. (1948) 'Lucretius and Epicureanism', *Transactions of the American Philological Association* 79: 11–23.

——(1969) 'Limit and variation in the Epicurean philosophy', *Phoenix* 23: 104–13.

Della Valle, G. (1933) *Tito Lucrezio Caro e l'epicureismo campano*, Naples.

Detel, W. (1978) *'Scientia rerum natura occultarum'. Methodologische Studien zur Physik Pierre Gassendis*, Berlin.

De Witt, N. W. (1932) 'Notes on the history of Epicureanism', *Transactions of the American Philological Association* 63: 166–76.

——(1936) 'Organisation and procedure in Epicurean groups', *Classical Philology* 31: 205–11.

——(1954) *Epicurus and His Philosophy*, Minneapolis.

——(1954) *St Paul and Epicurus*, Minneapolis.

Diano, C. (1935) 'Note epicuree', *Studi Italiani di Filologia Classica* 12: 61–86.

——(1936) 'Quaestioni epicuree', *Reddiconti dell'Academia dei Lincei* 12: 819–95.

——(1974) *Scritti Epicurei*, Florence.

Diogenes Laertius (1922) *Epicuri epistolae tres et ratae sententiae*, ed. P. von der Muehll, Leipzig.

——(1964) *Diogenis Laertii vitae philosophorum*, ed. H. S. Long, Oxford.

Epicurus (1887) *Epicurea*, ed. H. Usener, Leipzig (repr. Stuttgart, 1966).
——(1926) *Epicurus: the Extant Remains*, ed. C. Bailey, Oxford (repr. Hildesheim, 1970).
——(1946) *Epicuri Ethica*, ed. C. Diano, Florence.
——(1960) *Epicuro: Opere*, ed. G. Arrighetti, Turin (2nd edn 1973).
——(1965) *Epicuro, Etica. Opere e frammenti*, ed. R. Sammartino, Bologna.
——(1974) *Opere di Epicuro*, ed. M. I. Parente, Turin.
Farrington, B. (1939) *Science and Politics in the Ancient World*, London.
——(1938) 'The Gods of Epicurus and the Roman state', *The Modern Quarterly* I(3): 214–32.
——(1967) *The Faith of Epicurus*, London.
Ferreyrolles, G. (1976) 'Les citations de Lucrèce dans *L'Apologie de Raymond Sebond*', *Bulletin de la Société des Amis de Montaigne*, 5th ser.: 49–63.
Festugière, A. J. (1955) *Epicurus and His Gods*, trans. C. W. Chilton, Oxford.
Fleischmann, W. B. (1964) *Lucretius and English Literature 1680–1740*, Paris.
Fontaine, J. (1959) *Isidore de Seville et la culture classique dans l'Espagne visigothique*, Paris.
Fox, R. L. (1987) *Pagans and Christians*, New York.
Fraisse, S. (1962) *L'Influence de Lucrèce en France au seizième siècle*, Paris.
Frank, T. (1922) *Vergil: a Biography*, New York.
Fredonille, J.-C. (1972) 'Lucrèce et le "double progrès contrastant"', *Pallas* 19: 11–27.
Frischer, B. (1982) *The Sculpted Word: Epicureanism and Philosophical Recruitment in Ancient Greece*, Berkeley.
Furley, D. J. (1950) 'The purpose of Theophrastus' characters', *Symbolae Osloenses* 30: 56–60.
——(1967) *Two Studies in the Greek Atomists*, Princeton.
——(1971) 'Knowledge of atoms and void' in J. P. Anton and G. L. Kustas (eds) *Essays in Ancient Greek Philosophy*, New York pp. 607–19.
——(1978) 'Lucretius the Epicurean on the history of man', in *Entretiens sur l'antiquité classique 24: Lucrèce*, Geneva, 1–27.
——(1987) *The Greek Cosmogonists. Vol. I The Formation of the Atomic Theory and its Earliest Critics*, Cambridge.
Fusil, C.-A. (1925) 'Rabelais et Lucrèce', *Revue du Seizième Siècle* XII:159.
——(1926) 'Montaigne et Lucrèce', *Revue du Seizième Siècle* XIII: 265–81.
——(1928) 'La renaissance de Lucrèce en France au XVIᵉ siècle', *Revue du Seizième Siècle* XV: 134–50.
Gabotto, F. (1889) 'L'Epicureismo di Lorenzo Valla', *Rivista di Filosofia Scientifica* 8: 655–72.
Gallagher, M. (1964) 'Dryden's translation of Lucretius' *Huntington Library Quarterly* XXVIII: 19–29.
Garin, E. (1961) *La cultura filosofica del Rinascimento italiano*, Florence.
Geffken, J. (1978) *The Last Days of Greco-Roman Paganism*, trans. Sabine MacCormack, Amsterdam.

Gelbert, N. R. (1971) 'The intellectual development of Walter Charleton', *Ambix* 18: 149–68.

Godman, P. (1985) *Poetry of the Carolingian Renaissance*, London.

——(1987) *Poets and Emperors: Frankish Politics and Carolingian Poetry*, Oxford.

Gordon, C. A. (1962) *A Bibliography of Lucretius*, London.

Gordon, P. W. G. (1974) *Two Renaissance Book Hunters: the Letters of Poggius Bracciolini to Nicolaus de Niccolis*, New York and London.

Goulet, R. (1980) *Cléomede: théorie élémentaire*, Paris.

Grant, R. M. (1977) *Early Christianity and Society: Seven Studies*, New York.

Green, W. M. (1942) 'The dying world of Lucretius', *American Journal of Philology* 63: 51–60.

Grilli, A. (ed.) (1960) *Diogenis Oenoandensis fragmenta*, Milano.

Guerlac, H. (1963) *Newton et Epicure*, Paris.

Hadzits, G. D. (1908) 'The significance of worship and prayer among the Epicureans', *Transactions of the American Philological Association* 39: 73–88.

Hagendahl, H. (1958) *Latin Fathers and the Classics*, Göteborg.

——(1967) *Augustine and the Latin Classics*, Göteborg.

Hall, J. (1981) *Lucian's Satire*, New York.

Hall, M. Boas (1966) *Robert Boyle on Natural Philosophy*, Bloomington.

Hammond, P. (1983) 'The integrity of Dryden's Lucretius', *Modern Language Review* 78: 1–23.

Hardie, W. F. R. (1968) *Aristotle's Ethical Theory*, Oxford.

Harnack, A. (1924) *Mission und Ausbreitung des Christentums*, 4th edn, Leipzig.

Harrison, C. T. (1934) 'The ancient atomists and English literature of the seventeenth century', *Harvard Studies in Classical Philology* XLV: 1–79.

Haskins, C. H. (1924) *Studies in the History of Medieval Science*, Cambridge, Mass. (2nd rev. edn 1927).

——(1927) *The Renaissance of the Twelfth Century*, New York.

Hendrick, P. (1976) 'Lucretius in the *Apologie de Raimond Sebond*', *Bibliothèque d'Humanisme et Renaissance* 38: 457–66.

Hertling, L. von (1934) 'Die Zahl der Christen zu Beginn des vierten Jahrhunderts', *Zeitschrift für Katholische Theologie* 58: 243–53.

Hicks, R. D. (1910) *Stoics and Epicureans*, London.

Hocke, G. R. (1935) *Lukrez in Frankreich von der Renaissance bis zur Reformation*, Cologne.

Howe, H. M. (1951) 'Amafinius, Lucretius, and Cicero', *American Journal of Philology* 77: 57–62.

Jacquot, J. (1952) 'Sir Charles Cavendish and his learned friends', *Annals of Science* 8: 13–27.

——(1952) 'Thomas Harriot's reputation for impiety', *Notes and Records of the Royal Society of London* 9: 164–87.

Jaeger, W. (1961) *Early Christianity and Greek Paideia*, Cambridge, Mass.

Jones, A. H. M. (1973) *The Later Roman Empire*, Oxford.

Jones, C. P. (1986) *Culture and Society in Lucian*, Cambridge, Mass.

Jones, H. (1981) *Pierre Gassendi 1592–1655: an Intellectual Biography*, Nieuwkoop.

——(1981) *Pierre Gassendi's Institutio Logica*, Assen.

Joy, L. S. (1988) *Gassendi the Atomist: Advocate of History in an Age of Science*, Cambridge.

Jungkuntz, R. P. (1961) *Epicureanism and the Church Fathers*, Ph.D. Thesis, University of Wisconsin.

Kargon, R. H. (1966) *Atomism in England from Hariot to Newton*, Oxford.

Keller, A. C. (1951) 'Lucretius and the idea of progress', *Classical Journal* 46: 185–8.

Laistner, M. L. W. (1951) *Christianity and Pagan Culture in the Later Roman Empire*, Ithaca.

——(1957) *Thought and Letters in Western Europe, AD 500–900*, 2nd rev. edn, London and Ithaca.

Levison, W. (1946) *England and the Continent in the Eighth Century*, Oxford.

Lilla, S. R. C. (1971) *Clement of Alexandria*, Oxford.

Long, A. A. (1971) 'Aisthesis, prolepsis, and linguistic theory in Epicurus', *Bulletin of the Institute of Classical Studies* 18: 114–33.

——(1974) *Hellenistic Philosophy*, London.

Long, A. A. and Sedley, D. N. (1987) *The Hellenistic Philosophers*, Cambridge.

Lorch, M. de Panizza (1976) 'Voluptas, molle quoddam et non invidiosum nomen: Lorenzo Valla's defence of *voluptas* in the preface to his *De Voluptate*' in Edward P. Mahoney (ed.) *Renaissance Essays in Honour of Paul Oskar Kristeller*, New York, pp. 214–28.

Lovejoy, A. O. and Boas, G. (1935) *Primitivism and Related Ideas in Antiquity*, Baltimore.

Lucretius (1947) *De rerum natura*, ed. C. Bailey, Oxford.

McColley, G. (1939) 'Nicholas Hill and the "Philosophia Epicurea"', *Annals of Science* 4: 390–405.

McKitterick, R. (1981) 'The scriptoria of Merovingian Gaul: a survey of the evidence', in H. B. Clark and M. Brennan (eds) *Columbanus and Merovingian Monasticism*, Oxford, pp. 173–207.

McKitterick, R. (1983) *The Frankish Kingdoms under the Carolingians, 751–987*, London and New York.

MacMullen, R., (1981) *Paganism in the Roman Empire*, New Haven.

——(1984) *Christianizing the Roman Empire*, New Haven.

Madec, G. (1974) *Saint Ambroise et la philosophie*, Paris.

Malherbe, A. J. (1982) 'Self-definition among Epicureans and Cynics', in Ben E. Meyer and E. P. Sanders (eds) *Jewish and Christian Self-definition*, London, vol. III, pp. 46–59.

Manitius, M. and Ulich, R. (eds) (1927) *Vagantenlieder*, Jena.

Marrou, H. I. (1956) *A History of Education in Antiquity*, trans. G. Lamb, London.

Marsh, D. (1980) *The Quattrocento Dialogue: Classical Tradition and Humanist Innovation*, Cambridge, Mass.

Martin, H. J. (1959) 'Ce qu'on lisait à Paris au XVIᵉ siècle', *Bibliothèque d'Humanisme et Renaissance* XXI (1): 222–30.

Mayo, T. F. (1934) *Epicurus in England (1650–1725)*, Dallas.

Meeks, W. A. (1983) *The First Urban Christians*, New Haven.

Mendelson, S. H. (1987) *The Mental World of Stuart Women*, Brighton.
Merlan, P. (1950) 'Lucretius – primitivist or progressivist?', *Journal of the History of Ideas* 11: 364–8.
Merlan, P. (1960) *Studies in Epicurus and Aristotle*, Wiesbaden.
Messeri, M. (1985) *Causa e Spiegazione: la fisica di Pierre Gassendi*, Milan.
Mette, H. J. (1978) 'Epikuros 1963–1978', *Lustrum*: 45–114.
Mintz, S. (1962) *The Hunting of Leviathan*, Cambridge.
Moore, W. G. (1967) 'Lucretius and Montaigne', *Yale French Studies* 38: 109–14.
Morrissey, T. E. (1973) *Franciscus De Zabarellis (1360–1417) and the Conciliarist Traditions*, Ph.D. Diss., Cornell.
Munro, H. A. J. (1857–8) 'Mrs. Lucie Hutchinson's translation of Lucretius', *Journal of Classical and Sacred Philology* 4: 121–39.
Nock, A. D. (1928) 'Alexander of Abonuteichos', *Classical Quarterly* 22: 160–2.
Novara, A. (1982) *Les Idées romaines sur le progrès* Paris.
Ogilvie, R. M. (1978) *The Library of Lactantius*, Oxford.
Ogilvy, J. D. A. (1936) *Books Known to Anglo-Latin writers from Aldhelm to Alcuin*, Cambridge, Mass.
Panizza, M. de (1955) 'Le tre versioni del "De vero bono" del Valla', *Rinascimento* 6: 349–64.
Philippe, J. (1895) 'Lucrèce dans la théologie chrétienne', *Revue de l'Histoire des Religions* 32: 284–302.
Pintard, R. (1943) *Le M. Le Vayer, Gassendi, G. Patin: étude bibliographie* (Paris)
Pollitt, J. J. (1972) *Art and Experience in Classical Greece*, Cambridge.
Popkin, R. H. (1964) *The History of Scepticism from Erasmus to Descartes*, Assen.
Raby, F. J. E. (1953) *A History of Christian Latin Poetry from the Beginnings to the Close of the Middle Ages*, Oxford.
——(1962) *A History of Secular Latin Poetry in the Middle Ages* Oxford.
Radetti, G. (1964) 'L'epicureismo nel pensiero umanistico del quattrocento', *Grande Antologia filosofica*, VI: 846–61.
Rapisarda, E. (1946) 'L'epicureismo nei primi scrittori latini cristiani' *Antiquitas* I: 49–54.
——(1947–50) 'L'epicureismo nei primi scrittori latini cristiani: la polemica di Lattanzio contro l'epicureismo', *Antiquitas* II–V (3–4): 45–54.
Real, H. J. (1970) *Untersuchungen zur Lukrez–Übersetzung von Thomas Creech*, Bad Homburg.
Redondi, P. (1987) *Galileo: Heretic*, trans. Raymond Rosenthal, Princeton.
Reeve, M. D. (1980) 'The Italian tradition of Lucretius', *Italia Mediaevale e Umanistica* 23: 27–48.
Reynolds, L. D. (1983) *Texts and Transmission* Oxford.
Reynolds, L. D. and Wilson, N. G. (1975) *Scribes and Scholars*, 2nd edn, Oxford.
Riché, P. (1976) *Education and Culture in the Barbarian West*, trans. John P. Contreni, Columbia, S. Carolina.

Rist, J. M. (1972) *Epicurus: an Introduction*, Cambridge.
Robin, L. (1916) 'Sur la conception Épicurienne au progrès', *Revue de Métaphysique et de Morale* 23: 697–719.
Rochot, B. (1944) *Les Travaux de Gassendi sur Epicure et sur l'atomisme 1619–1658*, Paris.
Rodney, J. M. (1970) 'A godly atomist in seventeenth century England: Ralph Cudworth', *History* 32: 243–9.
Rose, H. J. (1957) 'The religion of a Greek household', *Euphrosyne* 1: 95–116.
Rouse, R. H. (1979) 'Florilegia and Latin classical authors in twelfth- and thirteenth-century France', *Viator* 10: 131–60.
Ruch, M. (1969) 'Lucrèce et le problème de la civilisation. *De rerum natura*, chant V', *Les Études Classiques* 37: 272–84.
Sabbadini, R. (1905, 1914) *Le scoperte dei codici latini e greci ne' secoli XIV e XV*, Florence (repr. 1967).
Sailor, D. (1964) 'Moses and atomism', *Journal of the History of Ideas* XXV: 3–16.
Santini, G. (1899) 'Cosma Raimondi umanista ed epicureo', *Studi Storici* 8: 153–68.
Schmid, W. (1951) 'Götter und Menschen in der Theologie Epikurs', *Rheinisches Museum* 94: 97–156.
——(1962) 'Epikur' in T. Klauser (ed.) *Reallexicon für Antike und Christentum*, (Stuttgart) vol 5, cols 774–819.
Schmidt, A.-M. (1938) *La Poésie scientifique en France au seizième siècle*, Paris.
Sedley, D. N. (1976) 'Epicurus and his professional rivals' in Bollack, J. and Laks, A., *Études sur l'epicurisme antique*, Lille, pp. 119–60.
——(1976) 'Epicurus and the mathematicians of Cyzicus', *Cronache Ercolanesi* 6: 23–54.
Seigel, J. E. (1968) *Rhetoric and Philosophy in Renaissance Humanism*, Princeton.
Sharp, L. (1973) 'Walter Charleton's early life 1620–1659, and his relationship to natural philosophy in mid-seventeenth century England', *Annals of Science* 30: 311–40.
Shirley, J. W. (1983) *Thomas Harriot*, Oxford.
Simpson, A. D. (1941) 'Epicureans, Christians, atheists in the second century', *Transactions of the American Philological Association* 62: 372–81.
Solmsen, F. (1953) 'Epicurus on the growth and decline of the cosmos', *American Journal of Philology* 74: 34–51.
Spiller, M. R. G. (1980) *'Concerning natural experimental philosophie': Meric Casaubon and the Royal Society* (International Archives of the History of Ideas 90), The Hague.
Stahl W. H. (1962) *Roman Science: Origins, Development and Influence to the Later Middle Ages*, Madison, WI.
Stevens, H. (1900) *Thomas Hariot, the Mathematician, the Philosopher, and the Scholar*, London.
Strathmann, E. A. (1951) *Sir Walter Raleigh: a study in Elizabethan Skepticism*, New York.
Tack, R. (1974) *Untersuchungen zum Philosophie- und Wissenschaftsbegriff bei Pierre Gassendi (1592–1655)*, Meisenheim am Glan.

Tait, J. I. M. (1941) *Philodemus' Influence on the Latin Poets*, Bryn Mawr.

Taylor, M. (1947) 'Progress and primitivism in Lucretius', *American Journal of Philology* 68: 180–94.

Timmermans, B. J. H. M. (1938) 'Valla et Erasme défenseurs d'Epicure', *Neophilologus* XXIII: 414–19.

Trinkaus, C. (1970) *In Our Image and Likeness*, Chicago.

Ullman, B. (1932) 'Classical authors in medieval florilegia', *Classical Philology* 27: 1–42.

Ullman B. L. (1963) *The Humanism of Coluccio Salutati*, Padova.

Urmson, J. O. (1968) 'Aristotle on pleasure', in J. M. E. Moravcsik (ed.) *Aristotle: a Collection of Critical Essays*, London, pp. 323–33.

Usher, R. G. (1977) 'Old Comedy and character', *Greece and Rome* XXIV: 71–9.

Vavilov, S. I. (1947) 'Newton and the atomic theory', in *Royal Society Newton Tercentenary Celebrations*, Cambridge, pp. 43–55.

Villey, P. (1933) *Les Sources et L'Évolution des essais de Montaigne*, 2nd edn, Paris.

Von Soden, H. (1974) 'Die christliche Mission in Altertum und Gegenwart', in H. Frohnes and U. W. Knorr (eds) *Die alte Kirche*, Munich, I 18–31.

Wagenblass, J. H. (1946) *Lucretius and the Epicurean Tradition in English Poetry*, Ph.D. Diss., Harvard University.

William, J. (ed.) (1907) *Diogenis Oenoandensis fragmenta*, Leipzig.

Zeydel, E. H. (1906) *Vagabond Verse*, Detroit.

INDEX

Adalbero of Laon 129
Aelian 228 n63
Aemilius Macer 67
Aeschines 18
Aeschylus 55
Alammani, Andrea 149
Albert of York 124
Albertus Magnus 134
Alcuin 122, 123, 124, 125
Aldhelm 122, 123
Alexander of Abonouteichos 72, 92–3, 112
Alexander of Aphrodisias 132
Alexander of Hales 133
Alexander the Great 5, 6, 9
Alfarnus of Salerno 238 n40
Alfred the Great 124
Alkios 65
Allen, Thomas 188
Amafinius 62, 65, 67, 69, 70, 72, 73, 74, 75, 76, 226 n19
Ambrose 102, 104, 109, 113
Ambrosius Traversarius 136, 145
Amphiareus 143
Anaxagoras 40
Anaximander 40
Angilbert 125
Anselm 133
Antimachus 9
Antiochus 77
Antipater of Tyre 79
Apelles 108
Apollodorus of Tyre 64
Apollonides 79
Apollonius Rhodius 8
Apsley, Sir Allen 195
Aquinas, St Thomas 134

Arator 119, 126
Aratus of Soli 9
Arcesilaus 90
Archimedes 132
Aristides 97
Aristippus 49, 149, 153
Aristophanes 3, 4, 7, 12
Aristotle 15, 17, 50, 96, 98, 109, 111, 130, 132, 133, 135, 139, 147, 148, 149, 158, 162, 167, 168, 169, 179, 193, 205, 221 n108
Arostoxenus 223 n142
Arius Didymus 79
Arnobius 101
Ascham, Roger 154
Asclepiades 9
Asclepius, 13
Athenagoras 97, 100, 106, 107
Athenodorus of Tarsus (1) 79
Athenodorus of Tarsus (2) 79
Aubrey, John 192, 199
Augustine, St 95, 97, 101, 102, 103, 104, 109, 111, 122, 133, 135
Augustus Caesar Octavianus 81, 82, 83, 84
Avicenna 132
Avitus of Vienne 119, 126

Bachiler, John 198
Bacon, Francis 193, 194, 195, 197, 200
Baif, Jean-Antoine de 157
Baines, Richard 191
Bale, John 256 n8
Barancy, François 175, 176
Barbaro, Francisco 241 n3
Barlow, Thomas, bishop 208

Bartas, Guillaume Salluste, Sieur du 157, 158
Bartholemew the Englishman 132
Barzizza, Gasparino 150
Basil, St 97
Basilides 64, 105, 108
Baudry of Bourgeuil 129
Baugulf of Fulda, abbot 124
Baxter, Richard 206, 207
Bayle, Pierre 182
Beccadelli, Antonio (Panormita) 145
Bede, the Venerable 122, 123, 132, 138, 236 n16
Beeckmann, Isaac 169
Behn, Aphra 212
Bellay, Joachim du 157
Belleau, Rémi 157
Bembo, Pietro 159
Benedict Biscop 122
Bérault, Nicolas 156, 159
Bernard of Chartres 133
Bernard Sylvestris 133
Bernier, François 184
Beroaldi, Filippo 153
Bitaud, Jean 252 n13
Blanco, Giovanni 153
Boccacchio 134
Boethius 119, 132, 138, 139
Bonaventura, St 133
Boniface 123, 124
Boswell, William 197
Bouchard, Jean-Jacques 171
Boyle, Robert 207, 208, 209, 210
Brahe, Tycho 176
Brathwaite, Richard 187
Bruni, Leonardo 145, 147, 149, 150
Bruno, Giordano 188, 190
Buoninsegni, Giovan Battista 153
Burley, Walter 136

Caesarius of Arles 118, 119, 235 n7
Calcidius 127
Callimachus 9
Calpurnius Siculus 126
Campanella, Tommaso 173, 253 n39
Candido, Pietro 154
Capece, Scipione 155
Carneades 78
Casaubon, Meric 205, 206, 207, 208
Cassiodorus 119, 122, 132
Catiline 80
Catius Insuber 69, 73, 226 n19

Cato the Censor 65
Cato the Younger 79
Catullus 68
Cavendish, Sir Charles 196
Cavendish, William 196
Celsus 93, 112, 116, 233 n58
Charlemagne 124, 125, 126, 127, 128
Charles IX 156
Charles the Bald 126, 127
Charleton, Dr. Walter 186, 199–203, 205, 206
Charron, Pierre 168, 183
Chaucer 134, 140
Cherbury, Lord Herbert of 171
Chrysippus 63, 80, 109
Cibber, Theophilus 212
Cicero 20, 39, 51, 52, 54, 62, 64, 66, 67, 69, 70, 71, 72, 73, 74, 76, 77, 78, 79, 89, 97, 101, 102, 103, 104, 115, 118, 135, 137, 138, 147, 150, 152, 163, 164, 167, 168, 186, 202, 232 n37
Clement of Alexandria 102, 103, 104, 105, 107, 108, 111, 112
Clement of Rome 230 n13
Cleomedes 87, 88, 92
Cokayn, Sir Aston 257 n34
Colotes 16, 90, 91
Constantine 94
Constantine the African 238 n40
Cooper, Thomas 187
Copernicus, Nicolas 176, 188
Creech, Thomas 211, 212, 213
Critias 12
Critolaus 78
Cudworth, Ralph 210, 211
Culverwell, Nathaniel 200
Cuthbert, archbishop 123
Cybele 13, 85
Cyrenaics 49, 50, 90, 104

Daniel, bishop 122
Dante 134, 135, 142, 149, 166
Dardanus 78
Davies, Sir John 187
De Clave, Etienne 252 n13
Deacon Gunzo 128
Demetrius of Magnesia 15
Demetrius of Phalerum 16
Demetrius Poliorcetes 16
Democritus 17, 18, 23, 29, 31, 32, 33, 36, 37, 40, 90, 158, 188, 193, 198, 210
Demonax (the Cynic) 93

Demosthenes 5, 10, 18
Descartes, René 172, 183, 184, 197, 208
Desiderius of Vienne, bishop 235 n9
Deusdedit, archbishop 121
Dicaearchus 223 n142
Digby, Sir Kenelm 196, 197, 199
Diodati, Elie 171
Diodotus 77, 79
Diogenes Flavianus (Oenoanda) 86, 87, 92
Diogenes Laertius 14, 20, 24, 26, 27, 28, 50, 64, 85, 136, 137, 145, 148, 152, 156, 175, 177, 188, 202, 205, 215 n19
Diogenes of Babylon 78, 79
Diogenes of Tarsus 64
Dionysius 64
Dionysius of Alexandria 231 n14
Diotimus the Stoic 19
Dolet, Etienne 159
Donatus 130
Drake, Nathan 212
Dryden, John 212, 213
Duccio 134
Dungal 125, 137

Egbert of York 122, 123
Egnazio, J.-B. 159
Einhard 126, 238 n30
Elbert of York 122
Elizabeth I 191
Empedocles 41, 90
Ennodius of Pavia 119
Epictetus 84
Epiphanius 102, 106
Erasmus, Desiderius 163–5, 248 n62
Ermenrich of Ellwangen 137
Esperiente, Callimacho 153
Estienne, Robert 158
Euclid 127, 130, 132
Euripides 7
Eurydice 82, 143, 144
Eusebius 97, 112
Eustathius 136
Evelyn, John 186, 199, 203, 204, 205, 206

Faber, Joannes 164
Fanshawe, Richard 204
al Farabi 132
Farinata 142
Fazio, Bartolomeo 242 n14
Ferne, Sir John 187

Ferrandus, Thomas 154
Ferron, Arnould du 246 n51
Fiano, Francesco da 241 n2
Ficino, Marsilio 153, 245 n41
Filastrius 102, 108
Filelfo, Francesco 148, 149, 150
Fludd, Robert 171
Frederick II 142
Fridenperger, Paulus 154
Fulgentius 119

Gaffarel, Jacques 169
Gaius Cassius 69, 74, 76
Gaius Marius 80
Gaius Memmius 70, 71
Galen 132
Galileo, Galilei 170, 171, 172, 253 n39
Galland, Pierre 157
Gassendi, Pierre 166–85, 196, 197, 201, 202, 203, 205, 206, 208
Gerbert of Rheims 128
Gifanius 155, 177, 211
Giotto 134
Glanvill, Joseph 207, 208
Godfrey of Rheims 129
Golius, J. 169
Gottschalk 127
Goulart, Simon 158
Gower, John 140
Gregory IX, Pope 134
Gregory of Nazianzus 113
Gregory of Nyssa 100
Gruter, Isaac 197
Gryph, Sebastien 159

Hadrian, bishop 121, 122
Hadrian, emperor 85
Hariot, Thomas 188, 189, 190, 191, 192
Hedeia of Cyzicus 19
Heinsius, Daniel 169
Heiric 127
Henricus Aristippus 136
Hercules 88, 143
Hermarchus 15, 17, 19, 63, 64
Hermes Trismegistus 188
Hero of Alexandria 132
Herodotus (Epicurean) 23, 29
Hesychius of Miletus 136
Hilderbert of Lavardin 129
Hill, Nicholas 188
Hippocrates 12, 132
Hippolytus 92, 106
Hobbes, Thomas 196, 198, 199

Homer 126, 186
Horace 68, 155, 157, 158, 161, 186
Hraban Maur 127, 134, 138
Hrosvitha of Gandersheim 129, 130, 239 n42
Hues, Robert 188
Hugh of St Victor 134
Hutchinson, John, colonel 195
Hutchinson, Lucy 195, 196

Iamblichus 95, 211
Idomeneus 63
Irenaeus 108
Isidore of Seville 120, 122, 132, 138
Isis 13, 85

James, I 257 n24
Jamyn, Amadis 247 n58
Jerome, Saint 45, 102, 109, 110, 111, 113, 134
Jodelle, Etienne 247 n58
John Elector of Saxony 164
John Philagathos 128
John of Salisbury 140
Jovinian 109, 113
Joye, George 186
Julian, bishop 109
Julius Caesar 65, 75, 76, 118
Justin Martyr 102, 106, 107
Justinian 120, 131
Justinus 127
Juvenal 129, 156
Juvencus 126

Kepler, Johannes 170, 171, 189
al-Khwarizmi 132

La Poterie, Antoine de 168
Lactantius 97, 99, 100, 103, 111, 112, 153
Laeto, Pomponio 153
Lambert of St Omer 132
Lambinus (Denys Lambin) 155, 156, 157, 162, 177, 211
Landino, Cristoforo 149, 150
Landriani, Gerardo, bishop 150
Latimer, Hugh, bishop 187
Le Féron, Jean 246 n52
Le Fevre, Tanneguy 211
Le Fevre de la Boderie 157
Leofwin 124
Leontion 17, 19, 88

Leontius 63
Lepidus of Amastris 93
Leucippus 23, 29, 37, 188, 193, 198, 210
Lilburne, General John 198
Linc, Wenceslas 164
Liutprand of Pavia 128
Lothar 127
Louis the German 127
Louis the Pious 126, 127
Lucan 118, 126, 130
Lucas, Lady Margaret (Marchioness of Newcastle) 196, 197, 198, 199
Lucian 71, 72, 92, 93, 111, 112, 164
Lucius Calpurnius Piso Caesoninus 65, 67, 68, 75
Lucretius 33, 36, 37, 38, 39, 40, 41, 42, 43, 44, 45, 46, 47, 48, 54, 56, 57, 58, 59, 60, 66, 69, 70, 71, 72, 73, 74, 75, 76, 77, 78, 82, 84, 89, 99, 100, 103, 220, 111, 112, 116, 127, 136, 137, 138, 142, 143, 144, 148, 152, 154, 155, 156, 157, 158, 159, 160, 161, 162, 168, 177, 186, 188, 195, 196, 203, 204, 211, 212, 213, 231 n20, 234 n59, 234 n61
Luillier, François 169, 171, 172, 178
Lupus of Ferrieres 126
Luther, Martin 163–65
Lycophron 246 n56

Ma 85
Mans, Jacques Pelletier du 157
Marbod of Rennes 129
Marchetti, Alessandro 155
Marcion 108
Marcus Antonius 76, 82
Marcus Aurelius 84, 85, 202
Marcus Terentius Varro 69, 70
Marlowe, Christopher 191
Martial 68, 126, 129
Martianus Capella 119, 122, 132, 139
Marullus 155
Melancthon, Philip 162, 163
Meleager 9
Melissus 90
Menander 8
Menoecius 23
Mersenne, Père Marin 169, 170, 171
Metrodorus 15, 19, 63
Mithras 85
Mnesarchus 78
Moduin of Autun 126, 238 n31

Montaigne, Michel de 159, 160, 161,
162, 168, 183, 248 n68, 248 n75
Montepulciano, Bartolomeo da 142,
143
Montmor, Henri-Louis Herbert de 176
Moses 106, 191, 210, 211, 232 n44
Musonius Rufus 84

Nashe, Thomas 153, 245 n44, 256 n8
Naudé, Gabriel 170
Nausiphanes of Teos 14, 15, 17, 23,
216 n23
Navagero, Andrea 154
Nemesian 126
Nemesius 104, 105
Newton, Sir Isaac 260 n66
Nicander of Colophon 9
Nicholas of Cusa 188
Nicolo Niccoli 142, 143, 144, 145
Nieuwentijt, Bernard 210
Nigrinus 93
Nonius Marcellus 138
Notker 127
Numenius of Apamea 230 n7

Octavius Musa 67
Oenomaus 92
Olivier, Gaston 246 n52
Origen 97, 106, 112, 116, 233 n58
Orpheus 82, 143, 144, 148
Othlo of St Emmeram 130
Otto I 128, 129
Otto III 128
Overton, Richard 198
Ovid 118, 119, 126, 129, 157, 158, 161,
186

Paleario Aonio 155
Pamphilus 14, 17, 23
Panaetius 70
Parmenides 90
Parsons, Robert 91
Paschasius Radbertus 127, 129
Patin, Guy 177
Patrici, Agostino 245 n43
Paul the Deacon 125
Paul, St 85, 109, 227 n48
Paulinus of Aquileia 119, 125
Paulus Albarus 129
Payne, Robert 196
Peiresc, Nicolas-Claude Fabri de 169,
170, 171, 172, 174, 177
Pell, John 196

Percy, Henry 188, 189
Perdiccas 15
Pericles 5
Persius 129
Peter Chrysologus 102
Peter Damian 130
Peter Lombard 133
Peter of Pisa 125
Petrarch 134
Petrus Olivi 133
Petty, William 196, 197
Phaedrus 68, 77, 112
Phidias 6
Philip II of Macedon 1
Philiskos 65
Philo 77, 232 n14
Philodemus of Gadara 65, 66, 67, 68,
69, 70, 73, 74, 75, 84, 112, 225 n14,
225 n15
Philostephanus of Cyrene 9
Philostratus 95
Photius 136
Pythocles 23
Pico della Mirandola, Gian Francesco
168
Pindar 55
Pius, Joannes Baptista 156
Platina, Bartolomeo 153, 242 n14
Plato 4, 17, 32, 52, 55, 90, 91, 96, 98,
111, 130, 132, 136, 158, 167, 186,
193, 205
Plautus 158
Pliny the Elder 127, 158
Plotinus 95, 230 n6
Plotius Tucca 67, 69
Plutarch 49, 88, 89, 90, 91, 92, 97, 109,
111, 115, 160, 202
Poggio Bracciolini 142, 143, 144, 155
Politianus 155
Polyaenus 16, 19
Polybius 71, 72
Polyeuktos 10
Polystratus 64
Pompey the Great 79
Pontanus 155
Popillius Theotimus 85
Porphyry 95
Posidippus 9
Posidonius 77, 78, 79, 211
Prat, Antoine du 246 n52
Praxitiles 11
Priscian 130, 138
Proclus 132

Prodicus 12
Propertius 68
Protagoras 4, 12, 210
Prudentius 119, 126, 233 n50
Ptolemy 132
Ptolemy the Black 64
Ptolemy the White 64
Publius Cornelius Sulla 80
Puerbach 176
Puteanus, Erycius (Van de Putte) 168, 169
Pythagoras 130
Pythocles 16, 17

Quintilius Varus 67, 69

Rabelais, François 159
Rabirius 69, 73, 226 n19
Ragazzonibus, Theodorus de 154
Raimondi, Cosma 150–2
Raleigh, Sir Walter 191, 192
Ramus, Petrus 157
Rathier 128
Ray, John 260 n66
Regiomontanus (Johann Müller) 176
Reneri, Henri 169
Rho, Antonio da 145
Robert Grosseteste 134
Ronsard, Pierre de 157, 247 n60
Ross, Alexander 198
Rossi, Agostino de' 153
Rusticci, Cencioi da 241 n2

Sacco, Catone 145, 146
Sadducees 108
Sallust 118
Salutati, Coluccio 143, 148
Salvian 108, 109
Sarapis 13
Sarasin, Jean François 184, 202, 203
Sceptics 111, 180, 182
Sceve, Maurice 157
Scheiner, Christopher 170
Schickard, Wilhelm 168, 170
Scipio Aemilianus 79
Sedulius, Caelius 119, 126
Sedulius, Scottus 127
Seguier, Pierre 175
Seneca the Elder 127
Seneca the Younger 84, 109, 113, 152, 160, 167, 202
Servatus Lupus 127

Sextus Empiricus 28, 168
Sforza, Galeazzo Maria 153
Shakespeare, William 186
Sidonius of Clermont 119
Silanion 10
Silius Italicus 118
Siro 65, 66, 67, 68, 69, 70, 73, 74, 81
Smith, Henry 187
Smith, John 198
Snutt, Rev. Edward 259 n54
Socrates 3, 4, 12, 90
Sophists 3, 4, 12
Sophocles 4
Sorbière, Samuel 174, 184
Spartacus 80
Sprat, Thomas 207
Stanley, Thomas 205, 206
Statius 118, 126
Stephanus of Byzantium 136
Stephen of Novara 128
Stilpon 90
Stoics 36, 39, 40, 77, 78, 88, 96, 97, 98, 99, 111, 146, 150, 152, 162
Strabo 211
Stubbe, Henry 208
Suidbert 124

Tatwine, bishop 122
Taylor, Jeremy 204
Tennyson, Alfred Lord 226 n126
Terence 118, 129
Tertullian 96, 97, 98, 99, 100, 105, 108, 110, 111, 116
Themista 19
Theocritus 9
Theodore of Tarsus, bishop 121, 122
Theodulph 125
Theophanu 128
Theophilus 97
Theophrastus 8, 15, 17, 19, 52
Theseus 143
Thierry of Chartres 133, 134
Throckmorton, Elizabeth 191
Thucydides 2, 3, 6, 12, 214 n3, 214 n4
Tibullus 68, 118
Tignosi, Ambrogio 151, 152
Tillotson, John 206
Timocrates 16, 63
Timocrates of Heraclea 93
Torporley, Nathaniel 188, 190, 191
Tyard, Pontus de 157, 246 n52, 247 n60
Tzetzes 136

Valentinus 108
Valerius Maximus 118
Valerius Probus 138
Valla, Lorenzo 144, 145, 146, 147, 148, 150, 162
Valois, Louis-Emmanuel de 166, 172, 173, 177, 178
Vander Noodt, John 187
Van Helmont, Johannes Baptista 169, 199
Varius Rufus 67, 69
Vegio, Maffeo 145, 146, 147, 150
Venantius Fortunatus 126
Verdier, Antoine du 158
Vergerio, Pier Paolo 144
Vicomercato, Francesco 247 n59
Vieta, François 190
Villani, Giovanni 139
Villaud, Antoine 252 n13
Villiers, Elizabeth 201, 202
Vincent of Beauvais 134
Virgil 65, 66, 67, 69, 74, 81, 82, 83, 84, 118, 119, 126, 144, 155, 157, 160, 161, 186
Vitalian, Pope 121
Vitruvius 127

Vives, L. 168, 183
Vossius, Gerhard-Johannes 169

Walafrid Strabo 126, 127
Ward, Seth 192
Warner, Walter 188, 190, 191, 196
Whately, William 255 n8
Wilfrid of York 124
Wilkins, John 199
William of Conches 133
Willibrord 124
Willihad 124
Winifred, bishop 122
Wordsworth, William 220 n92

Xenocrates 15, 17

Zabarella, Francesco 144
Zabarella, Giacomo 144
Zacharias, Pope 123
Zeno (Epicurean) 68, 69, 77
Zeno of Sidon 64
Zeno (Stoic) 78
Zeno of Tarsus 78